"This is the most practical and grounded treatment of AI in consular work I've seen... It should be required reading for anyone responsible for modernizing border, identity, and citizen services."

James W. Herman, *Retired U.S. diplomat with senior consular leadership experience*

"This is an AI guide done right: deeply rooted in consular practice, clear and enthusiastic about the technology's potential, yet grounded in the conviction that human judgment and values are what will make AI both effective and legitimate."

Bruce A. Bassett, *Distinguished Professor of Computer Science and Applied Mathematics, with expertise in artificial intelligence*

"This is essential reading for anyone working in the field of border security or immigration. Regardless of your current role in this field, this book will expand your thinking about not only what is possible, but help you prepare for the evolution of this field."

Sarah Wardwell, *Public-service professional with experience in international and consular operations*

"Balanced and persuasive — this book charts a logical path forward for harnessing AI as a tool to assist, not replace, human judgement in consular affairs."

Anthony Pagliai, *Government professional with global consular and management experience*

I0875921

AI Use Cases for Consular Affairs

AI Use Cases for Consular Affairs explores applications for artificial intelligence (AI) across issues such as visas, passports, border security, disaster evacuation, and identity verification. It shows how AI can improve fairness, expand access, and return precious time to public servants, while confronting the risks and ethical dilemmas head-on.

Drawing on more than sixty years of combined diplomatic experience—including the adjudication of tens of thousands of visas and leadership through crises, evacuations, and fraud investigations—retired U.S. Foreign Service Officers Dr. Don Kilburg and Virginia Blaser reveal how AI is reshaping global mobility—from biometric identity verification and fraud detection to crisis alerts, multilingual access, and workflow optimization. Every year, millions of people apply for visas, renew passports, flee disasters, or struggle to prove their identity across national lines. Behind each of these moments lies a hidden world of high-stakes consular decisions—made under immense pressure, with limited time and imperfect information. AI has the power to transform that world.

This book is essential reading for public servants, policymakers, diplomats, state officials, and anyone working in consular affairs. But its lessons reach much further, to any institution now turning to AI. Used well, AI scales not by replacing human judgment but by protecting it. In the end, what earns AI a place in the systems we rely on is not raw power. It is fairness, accountability, and trust. *AI Use Cases for Consular Affairs* offers that guide on a global scale.

AI Use Cases for Consular Affairs

Smarter Passports, Visas, and Border Security

Don Kilburg and Virginia Blaser

CRC Press
Taylor & Francis Group
Boca Raton London New York

CRC Press is an imprint of the
Taylor & Francis Group, an **informa** business
A CHAPMAN & HALL BOOK

Designed cover image: Shutterstock

First edition published 2027
by CRC Press
2385 NW Executive Center Drive, Suite 320, Boca Raton FL 33431

and by CRC Press
4 Park Square, Milton Park, Abingdon, Oxon, OX14 4RN

CRC Press is an imprint of Taylor & Francis Group, LLC

© 2027 Don Kilburg and Virginia Blaser

Reasonable efforts have been made to publish reliable data and information, but the author and publisher cannot assume responsibility for the validity of all materials or the consequences of their use. The authors and publishers have attempted to trace the copyright holders of all material reproduced in this publication and apologize to copyright holders if permission to publish in this form has not been obtained. If any copyright material has not been acknowledged please write and let us know so we may rectify in any future reprint.

Except as permitted under U.S. Copyright Law, no part of this book may be reprinted, reproduced, transmitted, or utilized in any form by any electronic, mechanical, or other means, now known or hereafter invented, including photocopying, microfilming, and recording, or in any information storage or retrieval system, without written permission from the publishers.

For permission to photocopy or use material electronically from this work, access www.copyright.com or contact the Copyright Clearance Center, Inc. (CCC), 222 Rosewood Drive, Danvers, MA 01923, 978-750-8400. For works that are not available on CCC please contact mpkbookspermissions@tandf.co.uk

For Product Safety Concerns and Information please contact our EU representative GPSR@taylorandfrancis.com. Taylor & Francis Verlag GmbH, Kaufingerstraße 24, 80331 München, Germany.

Trademark notice: Product or corporate names may be trademarks or registered trademarks and are used only for identification and explanation without intent to infringe.

ISBN: 978-1-041-06302-5 (hbk)
ISBN: 978-1-041-06301-8 (pbk)
ISBN: 978-1-003-63477-5 (ebk)

DOI: 10.1201/9781003634775

Typeset in Times
by Newgen Publishing UK

Dedication

To Keely, Sonora, Vier, and Kesten.
To Mitch, Rebecca, Benjamin, Abigail, and Isabella.
For your unwavering support across every post, relocation, and crisis.
And to consular professionals everywhere:
You are all that stands between a person and the systems that would reduce them to mere data. You carry the judgment that cannot be automated and the humanity that must never be surrendered.

Contents

PART V People First

Imagine

We are one species on one planet, but we have spent much of our history sorting ourselves into groups and keeping others out. Every passport, visa, and border is proof of this. Yet we have also outlawed slavery, eradicated many diseases through cooperation between rival powers, dismantled much formal colonial rule, set aside a continent for peace in Antarctica, and built a shared home in orbit with the International Space Station. The virtue of common humanity is as real as the instinct toward tribe.

Now we are building AI that will carry our values forward far beyond our own lifetimes to future generations not yet born. What we encode is what will endure.

If we encode only the logic of division, we will have built ourselves a permanent cage, one we taught a potentially superior intelligence to perfect on our behalf. But if we encode a vision of one human family, even as just a shared aspiration, then the most powerful tools ever created can become partners in that journey.

This is the choice of our generation: not whether to build AI systems, but what to teach them about who we are and who we intend to become.

Foreword

Every nation's credibility rests, in part, on the integrity of its borders and the trustworthiness of its identity systems. A passport or visa is more than a travel document. It is a government's guarantee that the person presenting it is who they claim to be, that their movement will not compromise security, and that their identity can be trusted by other nations. For most citizens, these documents are symbols of mobility and freedom. For governments, they are instruments of protection, legitimacy, and service. At the intersection of those imperatives lies consular work, which is one of the most human and yet increasingly technical responsibilities of public service.

AI has entered this domain not as a distant promise but as a daily reality. Consular sections around the world face extraordinary demand: long lines, high caseloads, and a growing expectation for speed, accuracy, and fairness. Officers must make hundreds of decisions a day, often in minutes, with profound implications for people's lives. AI offers a way to manage this scale by handling volume without sacrificing vigilance, and to direct human attention where it is most needed.

We sometimes talk about AI as though it were something apart from governance, a new world that officials must somehow adapt to. In truth, it is simply the next evolution of what government has always been asked to do: make sense of vast amounts of information, apply judgment consistently, and deliver equitable outcomes at scale. The question is not whether to adopt AI, but how to do so in ways that strengthen trust and reflect the democratic values we serve.

This book—*AI Use Cases for Consular Affairs: Smarter Passports, Visas, and Border Security*—arrives at exactly the right moment. It translates the abstract conversation about AI into the tangible realities of consular work, including identity verification, fraud detection, visa adjudication, and crisis response. The authors understand that consular affairs is more than an administrative function; it is a frontline expression of diplomacy, national security, and citizen services. They show that the responsible application of AI is not about replacing human decision-making but about restoring the time and focus needed for it.

That distinction matters. Technology succeeds in government not only on performance metrics, such as speed and accuracy, but on legitimacy. Citizens must believe that the systems evaluating their applications or verifying their identities operate in ways that are transparent, consistent, and fair. AI will fail, no matter how efficient, if it erodes public trust. That is why governance, oversight, and accountability must remain at the core of every deployment.

Those principles are not theoretical. They are learned the hard way through experience in digital transformation across large, complex institutions. I have seen how powerful AI can be when used responsibly, and how quickly adversaries and fraudsters exploit the same tools to sow confusion or erode trust. We are reminded that innovation is never neutral. The same algorithms that help detect forged identities can also be used to create them. The difference lies in governance, essentially how systems are built, audited, and explained to the people they serve.

These lessons are not abstract. The threats are already here. Deepfake passports, synthetic identities, and AI-generated forgeries are emerging in real visa and border systems, testing the integrity of the very processes designed to protect them. Fraudsters no longer need to break a system outright. They only need to erode confidence in it. That is why responsible AI governance is not a technical preference; it is a matter of national credibility and national security.

In the hands of consular professionals, AI has already begun to reshape the rhythm of work. When algorithms prescreen low-risk renewals or summarize complex case histories, they return something invaluable: time. Time to listen carefully during an interview. Time to focus on high-risk cases. Time to think, to deliberate, to exercise judgment. In this sense, AI's greatest contribution may not be computational, but human. It restores capacity for empathy and discernment within systems designed for speed.

If that sounds idealistic, it is also profoundly practical. Consular sections face rising demand every year. Even modest efficiency gains of minutes per case, for example, can mean hours returned to officers each day. Those hours can reduce burnout, improve decision quality, and enhance the applicant experience. These are measurable, operational outcomes that build public trust in government.

That is where AI becomes more than a tool of administration. It becomes a measure of effective governance. How we use technology in our public institutions signals what kind of government we aspire to be. Democracies must lead by example, showing that technology can strengthen both security and freedom. When AI enables a family to reunite more quickly, prevents a fraudulent passport from being issued, or helps citizens abroad during a crisis, it demonstrates that democratic innovation is not only possible but effective.

This is, in its own way, a form of digital diplomacy. The systems we build to serve our citizens become symbols of national competence and values. Around the world, governments are experimenting with AI. Some use it to empower; others, to surveil and control. The difference between these paths will define the credibility of democratic governance in the digital century.

The authors of this book understand that reality deeply. They do not romanticize technology or shy away from its risks. Instead, they offer a framework for adoption rooted in transparency and human accountability. They make clear that AI in consular affairs is not a futuristic abstraction but a living system. A system that must evolve with both technical precision and moral purpose.

The lesson is simple. The digital world is changing rapidly, and standing still is not an option. Inaction carries as much risk as innovation, and sometimes more. But the answer is not to automate blindly. It is to design carefully, test rigorously, and deploy wisely, guided always by the principles that define public trust.

As you read these chapters, you will see that the real story here is not about technology alone. It is about the renewal of government capacity in an era of complexity. It is about how we translate the speed and creativity of our private sector into public systems worthy of the people they serve. It is about ensuring that our government's digital future reflects the same innovative spirit that defines our nation.

The contest over identity, mobility, and trust will shape the coming century. Consular services, standing as they do at the intersection of diplomacy, security, and human connection, can lead by example. If applied thoughtfully, AI can help governments manage volume without losing humanity, improve outcomes without sacrificing fairness, and strengthen legitimacy in a world where trust is under strain.

That is the vision this book invites us to imagine and, more importantly, to build.

Jennifer Ewbank

Strategic Advisor and Board Director on AI, Cybersecurity, and National Security; and Former Deputy Director for Digital Innovation, CIA

Preface

We spent our careers overseas in consular work and diplomacy, standing with people where borders, identity, vulnerability, and aspiration intersect. Whether during a natural disaster, at a crowded visa window, or in an interview room where a single decision could alter a life, we witnessed how profoundly citizens and travelers depend on consular services, and how demands on those services grew far beyond what earlier generations imagined. Volumes surged. Public expectations intensified. Fraud evolved. Crises accelerated. The gap between what consular sections needed to deliver and the tools available to deliver it widened year after year.

Through it all, one truth remained constant: the human core of consular work was irreplaceable. Fair decisions under pressure, empathy in moments of fear, clarity amid uncertainty. These qualities defined the profession. Yet, much of the daily work required precision rather than judgment: reviewing hundreds of identical documents, transcribing data, reconciling records, answering routine inquiries. Hours consumed by these tasks were hours taken from work that only humans can do.

These tensions shaped our careers in different but complementary ways.

Don entered the Foreign Service after years as an experimental psychologist, studying how people perceive risk, make decisions, and interpret subtle cues under cognitive load. That grounding followed him through 22 years as a U.S. diplomat across Asia, Europe, and Latin America. In major visa environments, including fraud prevention work at U.S. Embassy Mexico City, he saw the immense cognitive demands on officers: interviewing at pace, processing biometrics at scale, detecting fraud that adapted faster than workflows could manage. He helped bring the late Paul Ekman's micro-expression research into consular training, giving officers structured ways to interpret emotional cues across cultures, not to replace judgment but to refine it and strengthen rapport. This work anticipated today's AI debates: how structured signals can support, but never a substitute for, human discernment. During Hurricane Wilma in 2005, he helped evacuate over 25,000 American citizens across the Yucatán Peninsula. The experience exposed the fragility of information systems during crisis and demonstrated how indispensable calm, trained judgment becomes when fear travels faster than verified information.

Virginia's 34-year diplomatic career included a sustained focus on consular operations at their most demanding. She led the U.S. government's largest overseas passport operation in London, oversaw hundreds of consular officers and locally employed staff across her career, and personally adjudicated tens of thousands of visa and passport cases. As a senior Foreign Service Officer, she held leadership positions across three continents—including a decade of service as Deputy Chief of Mission and five full years as Chargé d'Affaires—coordinating crisis responses from natural disasters to evacuations to public health emergencies. In each, she saw the same pattern: officers making life-altering decisions under extreme pressure while outdated tools forced manual workarounds that consumed hours needed for judgment, empathy, and human connection.

Together, these experiences led us to write this book at a pivotal moment. Though our examples draw primarily from U.S. practice, the operational pressures are universal. Every nation handling visas, passports, identity verification, or citizen services faces rising demand, increasing fraud sophistication, accelerating crises, and intensifying expectations for fairness, speed, and transparency. The daily realities of consular work mirror challenges facing emergency response, public health, transportation security, humanitarian logistics, and border management. The tools and frameworks here are designed to be adaptable across borders, systems, and sectors.

This book has a companion. In 2025, one of us published *AI Use Cases for Diplomats: Applying Artificial Intelligence to Diplomacy* (Kilburg 2025), a broad survey of AI across all seven functions of embassy work—from executive leadership and political affairs to economic and management operations. Chapter 6 of that volume examined AI in consular affairs at an introductory level, establishing that visa processing, fraud detection, crisis response, and citizen services are ripe for AI-assisted transformation. The response to that chapter—from practitioners, students, and policymakers alike—made clear that the subject deserved its own dedicated treatment. This book is that treatment. Where the prior volume offered breadth across diplomatic functions, this one offers depth within a single domain. Readers familiar with *AI Use Cases for Diplomats* will find the foundational framing familiar; readers coming to this subject for the first time will find everything they need here. The two volumes are companions, not prerequisites.

AI is already reshaping this landscape: summarizing waiver files, clustering suspicious documents, enhancing biometric verification, deflecting routine inquiries, detecting fraud patterns, optimizing appointments, and supporting crisis communication. Yet it brings real risks: algorithmic bias, demographic disparities in accuracy, opaque logic, data sprawl, digital exclusion, and the temptation to over-automate decisions that demand human judgment. This book's purpose is neither to celebrate AI nor to resist it, but to help consular professionals, and those in similarly demanding environments, use it responsibly, ethically, and effectively.

Those entering consular operations today will shape how emerging technologies influence mobility, identity integrity, and public trust for decades. We offer this book with deep respect for consular professionals worldwide, and with the conviction that the age of AI, when guided by wisdom and principled design, can strengthen the qualities that have always made consular service indispensable: judgment, empathy, and trust.

But we also believe the tools, frameworks, and hard-won lessons gathered here travel well beyond the consular window. Anywhere humans deploy artificial intelligence under conditions of urgency, volume, vulnerability, and trust, the same disciplines apply. They apply in emergency rooms and courtrooms, in humanitarian operations and immigration tribunals, in social services offices and public agencies of every kind. The pressure to decide quickly without deciding carelessly, the obligation to honor the individual standing before the system, the need to keep human authority meaningful as machines grow more capable: these are not consular problems. They are the defining problems of any institution asked to act on behalf of the public in the AI era.

The consular context is specific; the principles are universal. We offer this book in that spirit.

Acknowledgments

We are grateful to the following individuals for reviewing early drafts of this book: Bruce A. Bassett; Maura Harty; James W. Herman; Anthony Pagliai; Taylor Susong; and Sarah Wardwell. Their expertise, candor, and generosity with their time made the book immeasurably better.

Any errors that remain are our own.

About the Authors

Don Kilburg is a global strategist, former U.S. diplomat, and psychologist. As Founder and CEO of Mind Leap Institute, LLC, he helps individuals, leaders, and organizations build the human capabilities needed to flourish in the age of AI. He holds a Ph.D. in experimental psychology (social cognition) from DePaul University and was a Japanese Government Monbusho Research Fellow. For over 30 years, he has applied behavioral science and emerging technology to complex challenges in international governance and public engagement.

Dr. Kilburg served in the U.S. Foreign Service from 2003 to 2025, most recently as Public Affairs Officer in the Bureau of Global Public Affairs at the U.S. Department of State. His diplomatic career included assignments in Latin America, Asia, Europe, and the former Soviet Union, plus headquarters service in Washington, DC, and work in four languages. Assignments included Spokesperson for the Bureau of Energy Resources and Press Attaché at the U.S. Embassy in Beijing. He contributed intelligence reports to the President's Daily Brief, briefed secretaries of state and ambassadors, and in 2024 pioneered the "ChatGPT Diplomacy" project, helping thousands of U.S. diplomats adopt AI. His innovations earned him multiple Superior and Meritorious Honor Awards.

Before entering the U.S. Foreign Service, Dr. Kilburg served as a U.S. Army infantry soldier and taught psychology at Eastern Washington University. He is the author of *AI Use Cases for Diplomats* (Routledge, 2025), with further books from Routledge, including *AI Use Cases for Public Diplomacy* and *Mind Leap: How to Think, Feel, and Flourish in the Age of AI.*

Today, Dr. Kilburg leads Mind Leap Institute full-time, delivering keynotes, workshops, and advisory engagements for organizations that want to build real human capacity, not simply deploy AI tools. He has carried his central thesis—that the decisive factor in AI adoption is not the technology but the human judgment behind it—into new territory, founding the interdisciplinary field of *Cognitive Civic Studies* in 2026. His aim holds constant: to help people and institutions meet the age of AI with their judgment, values, and humanity intact.

Virginia Blaser is a retired senior U.S. Foreign Service Officer, AI executive and practitioner, and author whose 34-year diplomatic career combined extensive consular leadership with hands-on implementation of emerging technologies. A member of the Senior Foreign Service, she served five full years as Chargé d'Affaires across five countries—including a two-year assignment in Tanzania—and held leadership positions in some of the most complex consular environments in the U.S. diplomatic network.

Blaser oversaw the U.S. government's largest overseas passport operation in London, adjudicated tens of thousands of visa and passport cases, led crisis responses for American citizens abroad, and negotiated with foreign governments on visa reciprocity, fraud prevention, law enforcement cooperation, and deportation policy. She received the Presidential Rank Award and numerous Superior and Meritorious Honor Awards from the U.S. Department of State.

Throughout her career, Blaser worked closely with consular teams to evaluate and implement new technologies as they entered operational service—including the first generation of biometric fingerprint readers—and as the senior officer leading the consular section in El Salvador, helped assess and deploy modernization initiatives during a period of significant change in consular technology. That combination of senior operational leadership and direct technology implementation over decades forms the foundation of her perspective in this book.

After leaving government, Blaser served as chief executive of an open-source intelligence company and founded and led a tech-enabled business operations company. She delivered AI training and presentations for the United Nations and private and multilateral diplomatic education institutions, spoke at AI and technology forums including the Women in Tech Global Summit, published multiple articles on AI and diplomacy in the Foreign Service Journal, and co-authored scholarly work on AI and transnationalism. She is co-inventor of a patent-pending AI-enabled technology platform.

Blaser now works as an independent consultant, advising international organizations, private companies, and nonprofits on governance, leadership, diplomacy, and the responsible use of emerging technologies. She serves on multiple boards and lectures internationally on diplomacy, leadership, and artificial intelligence.

Statement on AI Use in Writing This Book

In writing this book about AI use cases for consular affairs, we made a deliberate choice to "practice what we preach" and thereby embrace various AI tools throughout our writing process, including ChatGPT (version 5.2), Claude (versions Sonnet 4.6 and Opus 4.5), Gemini (version 3), and Perplexity. Using AI helped us to expand our thinking about the subject matter and to write the book quickly, in hopes of forging new knowledge at a pace that could keep up with AI advancement. We recognize that there is currently lively debate over the extent to which writers should use AI in their writing process, including for diplomacy.

We would therefore like to be specific about how AI assisted in creating this book, as we believe transparency about AI use in writing can help advance an important discussion in our field. We used AI tools as our thought partners and editorial assistants. The tools helped us to brainstorm ideas, organize research, create structured outlines, improve clarity, and ensure consistent formatting. Throughout our AI-assisted writing process, we found ourselves reflecting on how such collaborative approaches might benefit diplomatic work. Our experience came with careful consideration about where to draw the lines, particularly in balancing innovation with tradition, efficiency with deliberation, and technological capability with our own human judgment. Did we always succeed? Probably not.

Nevertheless, we have come to see AI-assisted writing on a spectrum, with different tools and approaches being appropriate for different tasks and contexts, rather than a simple yes/no choice for authors. Some aspects of writing and diplomacy (or any field) may benefit greatly from a degree of AI assistance, while others may require more traditional human-centered approaches. As AI tools continue to evolve, we believe authors, diplomats, and professionals should share their experiences openly and engage in constructive dialogue about best practices. We feel no guilt about openly using AI as a writing assistant—if anything, avoiding AI while writing a book on conscientious AI adoption would be disingenuous.

While we are confident in the value this human–AI collaboration has brought to the project, we also recognize that we are all walking unique paths as these technologies evolve. We invite you to engage critically with the ideas presented here, drawing on your own experiences and perspectives. Our hope is that by being transparent about our own approach, while remaining open to diverse viewpoints, we can collectively develop thoughtful frameworks for integrating AI tools into diplomatic practice. The future of diplomacy will likely be neither purely human nor predominantly automated, but rather a careful synthesis of human wisdom and technological capability. We look forward to exploring this path forward together!

Introduction

Somewhere in the world right now, a consular officer at an embassy or consulate abroad is facing a morning that looks much like thousands of others. The waiting room is full. The appointment calendar shows no breaks until late afternoon. The inbox has grown overnight with inquiries in half a dozen languages. A fraud case from last week still needs documentation. A citizen called in distress, and the officer promised to follow up before noon. There is too much to do, too little time, and the sinking feeling that something important will slip through the cracks.

This pressure is not new. Consular work has always demanded more than any single person can comfortably deliver. What has changed in recent years is the scale. Demand for visas and passports has surged beyond what consular missions can process with existing staff. Applicants expect faster service and clearer communication. Fraud has grown more sophisticated. Crises unfold at speeds that outpace manual workflows. And through it all, officers are expected to maintain the fairness, empathy, and discretion that define diplomatic service.

It is worth pausing to name what consular work actually is. Consular officers are diplomats, stationed in foreign countries, immersed in cultures and political realities they come to know deeply over the course of their careers. The judgments they make—whether to grant or refuse a visa based on an assessment of the applicant's credibility and intent, whether a passport applicant meets the legal requirements for citizenship that entitle them to that document, when to intervene on behalf of a citizen in crisis—draw on cultural fluency, interpretive skill, and an understanding of their own country's strategic interests that no algorithm can replicate. This is not administrative processing. It is one of the most consequential forms of human decision-making in government, carried out under conditions of complexity, ambiguity, and high stakes. Any serious discussion of AI in this field must begin from that recognition.

AI enters this landscape not as a savior but as a practical partner. The tools described in this book—machine-learning models that triage cases, chatbots that answer routine questions, biometric systems that verify identities, scheduling algorithms that predict no-shows—are not speculative. They are already deployed in and around consular operations worldwide, from Canada's immigration service, to Singapore's airports, to emergency response systems used by international organizations. The question for most missions is no longer whether AI has a role in consular affairs, but how to adopt it responsibly.

This book provides answers grounded in real-world practice. It is written for consular officers from any diplomatic service who need to understand what AI can and cannot do, for policymakers who must govern its use, and for students who will inherit a profession increasingly shaped by technology. But its lessons extend further. Anyone working at the intersection of AI and consequential human decisions—in emergency response, public health, humanitarian logistics, immigration, social services, or any high-stakes public institution—will find the frameworks, principles, and hard-won field experience here directly applicable. It is not a technical manual for engineers, nor is it advocacy for unchecked automation. Instead, it offers a practitioner's guide: balanced, evidence-based, and focused on the enduring challenge of keeping human judgment, fairness, and empathy at the center of systems built for speed and scale.

WHAT YOU WILL FIND IN THESE PAGES

Every chapter in this book opens with a scenario set in the Republic of Z, a fictional country. We chose a fictional setting deliberately—using a real country risked confusing readers with that country's actual circumstances, and we wanted the scenarios to belong to everyone. When you read about a flood response in Z, or a visa fraud ring uncovered by AI, or an officer reclaiming three hours in her day, imagine your own country's embassy or consulate operating there. A Canadian diplomat, a Brazilian consular officer, a British visa adjudicator—any reader from any diplomatic service should see their own work reflected in these fictional vignettes. The challenges and solutions have direct counterparts in consular practice across diverse national contexts and diplomatic traditions.

A note on terminology, because it matters and because it is genuinely complex. An embassy is a country's principal diplomatic facility in a host country, headed by an Ambassador who serves as Chief of Mission. A consulate general or consulate is a subordinate diplomatic facility operating under the embassy—it may be located in a major commercial city, a border region, or wherever demand justifies a permanent presence. Both embassies and consulates may house consular sections: the teams responsible for visa adjudication, passport services, citizen services, fraud prevention, notarials, and other consular functions. Importantly, the facility type does not determine the function. A consulate general or consulate may or may not perform consular functions; conversely, an embassy may not house the primary consular operation. In South Africa, for example, the main U.S. consular office and function is performed at the Consulate General in Johannesburg, with additional consular sections in the Consulate General in Cape Town and the Consulate in Durban, while the Embassy in Pretoria has no consular function embedded in it.

The consular section is the functional unit that performs this type of work and it can sit inside any type of diplomatic facility. A large consular section may be headed by a senior officer with the title of Consul General; that is a different role from a Consul General heading a consulate general, who may have no consular responsibilities at all.

"Post" in diplomatic vernacular simply means any location where a diplomat is assigned—it is not a precise term for a facility type. "Mission" refers to the embassy together with its constituent consulates and posts in the host country, all under the authority of the Chief of Mission. In this book, when we refer to consular work, we mean the function—performed by a consular section, wherever that section sits. When the type of facility matters to the point being made, we say so explicitly.

One more term deserves clarification. Throughout this book, we use "consular affairs" in the broad, generic sense to describe the functional area encompassing visas for foreign nationals, passports for citizens and potential citizens, services to nationals abroad, and related consular functions. The term parallels how diplomatic missions typically organize their work—alongside political affairs, public affairs, economic affairs, and management affairs. In the U.S., the Bureau of Consular Affairs is the formal name for the organization within the Department of State that provides leadership, management, and policy direction for all U.S. consular operations worldwide; every consular section at a U.S. embassy or consulate reports to this bureau in Washington, DC. Other countries structure these functions under their own organizational models, which this book does not attempt to catalog. When we write "consular affairs," we mean the work itself—wherever and by whomever it is performed. Similarly, every diplomatic service provides assistance to its own nationals when they are abroad. In the U.S., this function is now called U.S. Citizen Services, formerly American Citizen Services. Throughout this book, we refer to it generically as "overseas citizen services" or just "citizen services," meaning the support any country's diplomatic mission provides to its own nationals overseas.

One further dimension of consular staffing deserves mention here, because it shapes how AI will actually be experienced in the field. At virtually every diplomatic mission worldwide, the majority of consular personnel are locally employed staff—citizens of the host country, and in some cases third-country nationals or family members of posted officers, who provide language skills, cultural knowledge, and institutional continuity that no rotation of diplomats can replicate. They screen documents at intake, manage appointment systems, handle correspondence and cashiering, assist with fraud investigations, verify translations, and keep consular operations functioning through every officer turnover. They do not make adjudicatory decisions—that authority rests with commissioned officers—but they are essential to virtually every process that surrounds and supports those decisions. In some diplomatic services, locally employed staff fill senior consular management roles; in others, their responsibilities are more circumscribed. What is universal is their presence, their importance, and the fact that consular AI cannot succeed without them.

When AI enters a consular section, locally employed staff will often be the first to work with it daily—configuring chatbots, reviewing AI-generated translations, maintaining the knowledge bases that feed retrieval systems, and testing new tools against local realities that no headquarters developer could anticipate. They will also, understandably, be among the first to ask hard questions. Staff who have spent years, sometimes decades, building expertise in the rhythms of a consular section may reasonably wonder whether tools designed to automate routine tasks are ultimately designed to make their positions redundant. That concern deserves a direct answer: the AI described in this book depends on local knowledge, contextual judgment, and sustained human engagement to function at all. It is not a replacement for the people who sustain consular operations—it is a set of tools that makes their expertise more visible and more consequential. The chapters that follow address locally employed staff not as an afterthought but as participants in every phase of AI adoption, from pilot design through to governance.

Beyond the vignettes, each chapter follows a consistent structure. Applications are organized by role—what line officers can use, what fraud prevention units gain, what section chiefs need to know, and how headquarters staff can support the field. Practical tools and implementation frameworks appear throughout, ready to adapt for your own mission regardless of which diplomatic service you represent. Sidebars capture informal lessons—small hacks, warnings, and reminders that shape culture as much as systems. Cross-references connect themes across chapters, showing how triage in visa processing relates to scheduling optimization or how biometric verification intersects with fraud detection.

The book is divided into five parts. Part I lays conceptual foundations, explaining what AI actually means in consular context and drawing lessons from past technology transitions. Part II covers core consular services—visa adjudication, passport issuance, multilingual citizen communication, and crisis response. Part III addresses fraud, forgery, and identity integrity, where governance is most critical. Part IV turns to operations, showing how AI can reclaim time lost to no-shows and inbox overload, and providing frameworks for deploying AI at the mission level. Part V closes with a human-centered framework, asking what kind of consular future we want AI to create and providing leadership playbooks for achieving it.

HOW TO USE THIS BOOK

Not every reader needs to consume this book sequentially. If you are a line officer processing visas or issuing passports, you might begin with Chapter 1 for the conceptual grounding, then dive directly into Chapters 2 through 4, which address your daily work. Chapter 8, on appointments and workflows, offers immediate tools for reclaiming time. Chapter 9 provides comprehensive guidance for deploying AI at the mission level.

If you work in a fraud prevention unit, Chapters 6 and 7 should be your focus. These examine how AI can cluster suspicious documents, expose metadata anomalies, and verify biometric continuity across jurisdictions. Chapter 1 provides the governance frameworks that make these tools legitimate, while Chapter 10 addresses the ethics of deploying technology in domains where false positives can harm innocent applicants.

Section chiefs and mission leadership will benefit most from Chapters 1, 8, 9, and 10. These cover the management and deployment strategies needed to introduce AI without destabilizing morale or compromising trust. You will find guidance on forming teams, choosing vendors, budgeting for pilots, and measuring success in ways that go beyond raw efficiency.

For policy staff and headquarters-based officers, Chapters 1, 5, 6, 7, and 10 provide the oversight frameworks and risk assessments that ministries and central offices need. Part III, which addresses fraud, forgery, and identity, is especially relevant if you are shaping enterprise-wide standards or briefing senior leadership.

If you are a technology provider, contractor, or consultant seeking to understand the consular environment, Chapter 9 offers guidance on how AI tools are evaluated, procured, and deployed at diplomatic missions, and what responsible partnership looks like in this space. Chapters 1 and 10 provide the governance principles and trust frameworks that shape what consular sections will and will not accept from vendor partners.

Students and those new to consular affairs should read the book sequentially. It builds from foundations to implementation, and the vignettes provide a sense of how consular work actually feels—the pressures, the trade-offs, the responsibility of making decisions that shape lives. By the final chapter, you will have a clear picture not only of what AI can do but also of why governance, fairness, and human judgment remain central to diplomatic practice worldwide.

CORE CONCEPTS THAT RECUR THROUGHOUT

Certain ideas appear in every chapter because they define what responsible AI looks like in consular affairs. The first is the "Time Dividend." This concept reframes AI's value not as speed or cost savings but as hours returned to officers. When a chatbot deflects routine inquiries, when a scheduling tool predicts no-shows, when a summarizer condenses a 200-page waiver file, the benefit is not just efficiency—it is the reallocation of human effort toward the highest end of the value chain: credibility assessment, empathic engagement, cultural interpretation, and the exercise of discretionary authority under uncertainty. These are capabilities that AI cannot replicate, and they are precisely where consular work is most consequential. The Time Dividend is not simply about giving officers more free time. It is about freeing them up to provide more of what only humans can—the judgment, presence, and moral accountability that define the profession. That is how we measure whether AI serves its purpose.

The second recurring principle is human-in-the-loop, always. No system described in this book makes final decisions. AI may draft, flag, cluster, or predict, but officers decide. This is not a cautious hedge—it is the foundation of legitimacy. Visa adjudications, passport issuances, and crisis responses all involve trust, culture, and the exercise of discretion under uncertainty. These are domains where accountability must rest with people, not algorithms. Every chapter reinforces this boundary.

This principle extends beyond adjudication to every aspect of consular service. In citizen services and emergency contexts especially, human contact must always remain available. AI may extend a mission's reach—operating outside business hours, handling initial triage, providing information in multiple languages—but a human officer must be accessible whenever a citizen or applicant needs one. No chatbot, however capable, substitutes for the presence of a person in a moment of crisis.

The third concept is the four governance pillars: transparency, explainability, fairness, and privacy. Transparency means declaring when AI is used and how. Explainability means providing reason codes, not black boxes—outputs that officers can interrogate and applicants can—when appropriate—challenge. Fairness means auditing outcomes across demographic groups and ensuring that efficiency does not come at the expense of equity. Privacy means minimizing data collection, enforcing retention limits, and respecting consent. These pillars appear in every chapter because they are not optional add-ons but the conditions under which AI can be trusted.

You will also encounter the idea of "Goldilocks problems"—challenges that are important enough to matter but bounded enough to solve in a few months. The most successful pilots do not try to overhaul entire systems overnight. They start with a specific pain point: inbox triage, photo rejections, appointment no-shows. By delivering a quick win, they build confidence for the next stage. This principle of graduated implementation—start narrow, measure rigorously, scale cautiously—has proven effective across missions worldwide.

WHAT THIS BOOK COVERS (AND WHAT IT DOES NOT)

This book focuses on consular affairs: visa adjudication, passport issuance, services to nationals abroad, fraud detection, crisis management, and the internal workflows that consume officer time. It examines how AI can triage cases, summarize documents, verify identities, translate communications, and optimize schedules. It provides playbooks for deploying these tools at multiple levels—from individual missions to enterprise-wide operations—and frameworks for governing them responsibly.

What the book does not cover is embassy IT infrastructure broadly, diplomatic security operations, or classified intelligence analysis. These domains have their own considerations and governance requirements. Similarly, this is not a technical manual for engineers. It explains concepts like retrieval augmented generation or multimodal biometrics in plain language, but it does not teach you to code machine-learning models. The audience is practitioners—officers, managers, and policymakers from any diplomatic service—who need to understand what AI can do, how to evaluate vendors, and how to govern deployments responsibly.

The examples span a spectrum and draw from diverse national contexts. Some tools, like Canada's Immigration, Refugees, and Citizenship Canada analytics program or Singapore's passport-less biometric clearance, are fully operational. Others, such as Estonia's government-wide digital assistant Bürokratt or United Nations High Commissioner for Refugees's (UNHCR) WhatsApp-based refugee support systems, demonstrate how multilingual AI extends access to vulnerable populations. Still others are forward-looking scenarios, showing where the field is heading as technology matures. The book clearly labels each so you can distinguish proven practices from emerging possibilities.

A NOTE ON CURRENCY AND EVOLUTION

AI evolves quickly. By the time you finish reading this, new tools will have emerged and older ones will have been refined or retired. This book reflects the state of consular AI at time of writing, but its principles are designed to endure. Transparency, explainability, fairness, and privacy will remain relevant even as algorithms improve. The Time Dividend will still measure success better than raw processing numbers. Human-in-the-loop design will still be the foundation of legitimacy.

To stay current beyond this book, consult a few key sources. The U.S. National Institute of Standards and Technology publishes updates to its AI Risk Management Framework and conducts independent evaluations of biometric systems. The International Civil Aviation Organization maintains standards for machine-readable travel documents and e-passports. The European Union's Artificial Intelligence Act, adopted in 2024, sets binding standards for high-risk systems in migration and border control. Civil society organizations like Amnesty International and oversight bodies in various countries provide external accountability. Together, these sources offer a balanced view of what works, what fails, and why governance matters.

The citations throughout this book draw heavily on official sources—government reports, international standards, and peer-reviewed research—because consular professionals need evidence, not speculation. Real-world anchors from Canada, Singapore, Estonia, India, Kenya, and international organizations show what responsible deployment looks like across different administrative and legal contexts. Civil society critiques ensure that enthusiasm for efficiency does not blind us to risks of exclusion, bias, or overreach.

THE AUTHORS' PERSPECTIVE

We wrote this book because we believe AI has real potential to strengthen consular work, but only when deployed with transparency, fairness, and accountability. Our complementary expertise—Don's foundation in behavioral science and decades in diplomatic strategic communication, Virginia's 34 years of frontline consular leadership and post-government technology experience—allows us to bridge the gap between what AI promises and what it can responsibly deliver in diplomatic practice.

We consulted with current and former colleagues during the development of this book, but the views and recommendations are entirely our own. We chose to write as independent practitioners rather than as representatives of any government, because the challenges described here transcend any single diplomatic service. An independent perspective, informed by decades of experience but untethered to any institution's current policy posture, allows us to be candid about both the promise and the risks of AI in ways an official publication cannot. Importantly, we also aim to elevate the profession of diplomacy across the board.

We have both witnessed the pressures described in these pages as lived realities: the packed waiting rooms, the multilingual inquiries, the fraud rings, the crises that unfold faster than manual workflows can manage. While our direct experience is with U.S. consular operations, the challenges we describe are universal. Diplomatic professionals worldwide face similar throughput paradoxes, resource constraints, and the imperative to balance efficiency with fairness. We have drawn lessons from consular innovations in Canada, Singapore, Estonia, and elsewhere precisely because effective practices transcend national boundaries.

Our stance is one of cautious optimism. AI can protect officer time, expand access across languages, surface fraud patterns that no human could spot in isolation, and sustain resilience during crises. But these benefits materialize only when systems are designed to keep humans at the center. Officers must retain authority over decisions. Applicants must have pathways to challenge errors. Equity must be measured, not assumed. Privacy must be protected, not sacrificed for convenience.

This book does not advocate for unchecked enthusiasm, nor does it counsel paralyzing fear. It argues for responsible adoption: disciplined, evidence-based, and grounded in the principle that technology serves people, not the other way around.

That balance—between innovation and accountability—is the thread running through every chapter.

FINAL THOUGHTS BEFORE YOU BEGIN

This is not a book about technology taking over consular work. It is a book about making professionals more effective, more present, and more humane by offloading the repetitive tasks that drain time and morale. Every chapter reinforces that AI is a partner, not a replacement. Success is measured not by efficiency alone but by trust—from applicants who experience fairer processes, from citizens who receive timely assistance, and from individuals who feel their judgment is protected rather than undermined.

You do not need to understand everything before acting. Chapter 1 provides the vocabulary and conceptual framework. Later chapters let you dive deep into the domains most relevant to your work. The practical guidance makes theory actionable. And the vignettes from the Republic of Z remind you that the challenges you face are neither unique nor insurmountable.

Somewhere in the world right now, a consular officer is launching a pilot that will save her section three hours a week. Another is using AI to surface a fraud ring before it issues a single visa. A third is sending multilingual crisis alerts to thousands of citizens in minutes, then turning her attention to those who need the most help. These are not distant futures—they are present realities, happening in missions that chose to experiment responsibly.

The path forward is not about giant leaps but disciplined steps. Start where you are. Measure carefully. Scale cautiously. Keep humans at the center. And trust that when AI is governed well, it amplifies rather than diminishes the craft of consular work, wherever in the world that work is carried out.

Let us begin.

Part I

Foundations

Before you explore specific applications of AI in consular affairs, you must first establish common ground. What do we mean by AI in this context? What can these tools realistically accomplish, and what must remain firmly in human hands? This part addresses these foundational questions, setting the conceptual stage for everything that follows—for consular teams, and for anyone navigating the same pressures of volume, fairness, and high-stakes decisions about people.

AI is not a single technology but a collection of practical methods—machine learning, NLP, computer vision, and robotic process automation—each mapping to tasks you may already perform as a consular officer. Understanding this taxonomy matters because it replaces vague promises with specific capabilities. A machine learning model that triages visa applications operates very differently from a chatbot answering routine inquiries, and both differ from computer vision systems checking passport photos against international standards. Clarity about what each tool does, and does not do, is your first step toward responsible adoption.

This section also grounds AI in the historical arc of consular modernization. The shift from paper visa forms to the DS-160 (in the U.S.), the introduction of biometric collection, the adoption of crisis communication chatbots—each transition triggered skepticism, encountered setbacks, and ultimately expanded consular capacity. AI follows this lineage. The lesson is not that technology always succeeds, but that success depends on governance: human oversight, explainability, fairness, privacy protection, and security. That lesson is not unique to diplomacy. Healthcare systems, financial regulators, municipal agencies, and any organization managing

DOI: 10.1201/9781003634775-1

high volumes of consequential decisions about people face the same governance imperatives.

This part introduces concepts that recur throughout the book. The "Time Dividend" reframes AI's value not as automation for its own sake but as hours returned to you for judgment, empathy, and discretion. The distinction between tasks suited for delegation and those that must remain human provides a compass for evaluating every application in subsequent chapters. Five principles for responsible adoption—human-in-the-loop design, explainability over mystique, intentional fairness, nonnegotiable privacy, and verifiable security—establish the guardrails within which you can trust AI.

By the end of this opening section, you will have a shared vocabulary and evaluative framework. You will understand not only what AI can do but how to assess whether it should. Consular affairs is the lens; the principles are broadly portable. This foundation prepares you—and any reader navigating AI in high-stakes public service—to engage critically with the detailed use cases, implementation guidance, and governance frameworks that follow.

1 Reimagining Consular Work with AI

Artificial intelligence is not our friend … It can assist us in many ways if it is properly understood and contained. But we are racing headfirst into a new era of artificial intelligence that is going to have dramatic effects on how we live, how we think, how we relate to each other.

—Hillary Clinton, former U.S. Secretary of State, Senator, and First Lady (quoted in Bernard 2017)

We've committed to promoting safe, secure, trustworthy AI systems that respect human rights and further economic and social progress.

—Antony Blinken, former U.S. Secretary of State (2024)

How do you regulate a technology that is transnational, that knows no borders, and that we don't have a monopoly on?

—Marco Rubio, then Senator of Florida (quoted in U.S. Congress 2023)

Winning the AI Race is non-negotiable. America must continue to be the dominant force in artificial intelligence to promote prosperity and protect our economic and national security.

—Marco Rubio, U.S. Secretary of State (quoted in The White House 2025)

Opening Vignette: 120 Green Lights by 08:00

At dawn in the capital of the Republic of Z, a long line already stretches around the consular compound. Students clutch folders filled with transcripts, parents balance paperwork alongside restless children, and business travelers pace nervously as the day's first interviews approach. Inside, consular teams brace for another exhausting morning. In recent months, demand for visas and passport renewals in Z has surged well beyond what the consular section can comfortably

DOI: 10.1201/9781003634775-2

process. The staff know the pattern: endless queues, repetitive case reviews, and the sinking feeling that they will never get ahead.

But this morning, something is different. Overnight, an experimental AI triage system has quietly sifted through the caseload. When the first officer logs in, her dashboard shows that 120 routine cases have been preflagged as "low risk." The system has pulled relevant excerpts from prior waivers, assembled concise case briefs, and flagged only the details that require a closer look. Instead of combing through stacks of files, the officer now faces a clear, well-organized starting point. The AI has not made any final decisions—it has simply done the heavy lifting of preparation.

By mid-morning, the change is visible on both sides of the counter. Renewal cases flow more smoothly; officers have time to ask thoughtful questions instead of rushing through forms. Applicants notice the difference too. A student seeking to continue her studies abroad remarks that, for once, the process feels less like a battle with bureaucracy and more like a genuine conversation. In the break room, one officer admits his skepticism has softened: "It didn't change my standards," he says. "It gave me my time back."

This story is fictional, but it reflects the real pressures faced by consular sections worldwide, including those in the Republic of Z. The lesson is simple yet profound: when applied carefully, AI does not replace human judgment in consular work. Instead, it amplifies it—freeing officers and their teams from repetitive drudgery so they can invest more attention in the complex, human-centered cases where empathy, cultural sensitivity, and discretion are indispensable (U.S. Department of State 2024; GAO 2025; Kilburg 2025).

WHAT "APPLIED AI" MEANS IN CONSULAR WORK

AI is often spoken of in abstract terms, as though it were a single, mysterious technology arriving fully formed to replace human effort. In reality, AI in consular affairs is not one monolith but a collection of practical methods that align neatly with the tasks consular professionals already perform. To understand its potential, it helps to break the field into four families of tools: machine learning, NLP, computer vision, and robotic process automation (RPA). Each maps to a familiar aspect of consular work, and each requires safeguards to ensure fairness, transparency, and trust (Blaser and Kilburg 2025).

Machine learning is best understood as a way to identify patterns in data. In consular practice, this often means flagging visa cases that resemble known fraud profiles or predicting which appointments are most likely to result in no-shows. The key benefit is prioritization. Rather than replacing the officer's judgment, these models surface clusters of risk or opportunity that deserve closer review. It matters greatly what form these outputs take. A system that flags a case for additional scrutiny—surfacing an anomaly in travel patterns or a document that warrants a second look—is fundamentally different from one that recommends approval or denial. The former sharpens an officer's attention; the latter risks substituting for it, particularly when officers are inexperienced or under time pressure. Responsible design draws this line clearly: AI should direct the officer's gaze, never replace it. Canada's immigration service has already published details on how advanced analytics support triage, allowing low-risk renewal cases to move quickly while preserving officer discretion for complex or sensitive applications (IRCC 2025). Such examples show how machine learning can sharpen human focus while avoiding the trap of black-box decision-making.

Let's put this need for prioritization into the reality of the visa line. Having worked many combined years in visa sections, the authors know that consular work at many posts is inherently a high-volume process. The U.S. Department of State does not generally release global averages for adjudications per officer, but the operational tempo at high-demand posts has been documented in external reviews. The clearest example comes from a 2019 Office of Inspector General (OIG) inspection of Embassy Bogotá—the sixth-busiest nonimmigrant visa post in the world in FY 2018—which found that managers required adjudicators to average 30 in-person interviews per hour, a pace the OIG concluded was incompatible with adequate security review and sustainable working conditions (U.S. Department of State 2019). A full-time visa officer at a busy post may spend six or more hours on the line interviewing applicants, and the OIG's findings underscore that throughput at the upper end of that range comes at a real cost to adjudication quality.

At that pace, each case collapses into a two-minute window. Within it, the officer must perform not only the core judgment task—the interview itself—but also the rote, repetitive work attached to every file: reviewing the online application for completeness, checking security clearances, confirming documentation, and setting up the next case. This is the tyranny of the short interview, and it is precisely the dynamic the OIG identified when it warned that quota-driven adjudication risks rushed security reviews and inadequately justified decisions.

This is the point at which machine learning systems achieve their most profound impact. An AI triage system doesn't need to save the officer twenty minutes per case; saving even one minute transforms the operational environment. Across a representative hundred-case day, that single minute returns over an hour and a half of high-value time to the officer. This time dividend can be reinvested in the cases that warrant it—spending six minutes on a complex fraud case instead of two—or used to create the administrative breaks that prevent the rushed-decision dynamic the OIG identified.

By automating rote review and efficiently structuring the preinterview workload, AI directly addresses the necessity of speed, ensuring that the officer's limited time and energy are preserved for the complex, human-centered decisions that only they can make.

Natural language processing, and more recently large language models, have transformed how governments interact with text. Consular staff manage a constant flow of emails, waiver requests, and policy references. Tools like the U.S. State Department's "FAM Search" project use AI to retrieve relevant passages from vast regulatory manuals in seconds, a task that once consumed hours (Foreign Affairs Manual; U.S. Department of State 2024). In the same way, LLMs can draft plain-language explanations of refusal letters or assemble waiver summaries, provided they are constrained to verified sources and reviewed by humans. Here, the safeguard is clear: retrieval augmented generation is designed to ground AI-written text in official guidance, with citations officers can check before sending.

Computer vision applies similar principles to document images. Passport photos and supporting documents must conform to strict international standards, yet thousands of images arrive each day with minor flaws: incorrect backgrounds, glare, or digitally altered features. Vision algorithms can catch many of these issues at intake, guiding applicants to resubmit before an officer ever touches the file. More sophisticated tools can also detect forgeries or biometric anomalies.

The necessity of this automation underscores a critical point: humans are notoriously unreliable at accurate photo ID matching, a failing often worsened by the well-documented "Other-Race Effect" where recognition accuracy is lower for unfamiliar ethnic groups (Meissner and Brigham 2001). To circumvent this cognitive bias, experienced consular officers developed manual tricks, such as turning photos upside down during comparison. This technique forces the brain to process individual features analytically rather than holistically, which is a system prone to error. Moreover, officers can be misled by significant, nonfraudulent changes; for example, one case involved a client whose skin-lightening medical treatments made them appear so different that most adjudicators wrongly flagged the case as fraud. Only a highly experienced, local fraud expert was able to confirm the true identity after extensive and time-consuming reviews and interviews. This is precisely where consistent, benchmarked AI tools offer a critical safeguard: by reducing the human bias and fatigue that cause such errors, they can efficiently and accurately filter both subtle fraud and complex, legitimate changes, thus preventing unnecessary officer intervention and misjudgments.

The International Civil Aviation Organization (ICAO) maintains detailed specifications for e-passports and the chips embedded within them (ICAO 2015–2024). Compliance with those standards ensures that AI systems for photo checks or biometric verification operate consistently across borders. The safeguard here lies in international benchmarking: governments should procure only systems tested against agreed standards such as ICAO Doc 9303 or the U.S. National Institute of Standards and Technology (NIST) Face Recognition Vendor Tests (Grother, Ngan, and Hanaoka 2019).

RPA is the simplest of the four families. RPA bots do not "think"—they follow instructions, executing repetitive digital tasks the same way every time. In a consular section, that means transferring case data between systems, generating appointment reminders, or assembling document packets for officer review.

Much of this work is currently done by hand. Thousands of locally employed staff at missions worldwide spend their days on data entry and file preparation—tasks that are essential but that do not require the security clearances or adjudicative authority of commissioned officers (U.S. Department of State n.d.-j). The process is expensive to manage, labor-intensive to oversee, and vulnerable to the kind of human error that repetition breeds. An RPA bot can reduce that error. It does not get tired at 3 p.m., skip a field, or transpose a number. Federal guidance already exists in the U.S. for agencies implementing RPA responsibly, including methods for measuring return on investment and ensuring accountability (CIO Council 2020). By automating the clerical, consular sections free both officers and locally employed staff to focus on the work that requires human judgment, local expertise, and direct engagement with applicants—the work that automation cannot and should not touch.

Together, these four families of AI illustrate a simple truth: applied AI in consular work is less about futuristic disruption than about matching proven tools to urgent operational needs. The risk lies not in the technology but in how it is governed. Human-in-the-loop review, explainability, and transparent error handling are not optional extras—they are the conditions under which these systems earn trust. Far from replacing the consular officer, applied AI becomes a partner: one that extends human capacity while preserving the fairness and integrity at the heart of international mobility.

Foreign ministries worldwide are actively exploring AI in consular operations, though the pace and scope of adoption vary significantly across governments. Some have launched formal pilot programs; others are watching from the sidelines. No single government has yet published a comprehensive doctrine for AI in consular affairs, and institutional positions are evolving rapidly. This book aims to inform that evolution—offering frameworks, use cases, and governance principles that practitioners can adapt regardless of where their own ministry currently stands.

LESSONS FROM PAST DIGITAL TRANSITIONS

For many consular staff, the prospect of adopting AI feels both urgent and unsettling. The pace of change is fast, the terminology can be opaque, and the stakes—people's identities, travel, and security—are unusually high. Yet history suggests that consular affairs has repeatedly absorbed disruptive technologies, often after initial resistance, and emerged stronger for it. The transition to AI, if handled responsibly, follows in this lineage.

One of the clearest precedents is the shift from paper-based visa forms to the DS-160, the online nonimmigrant visa (NIV) application introduced by the U.S. in 2008. When first deployed, consular professionals worried that digital intake would increase errors, frustrate applicants, or strip away the context provided by paper files. For a time, those fears seemed justified: applicants struggled with internet access, systems crashed under heavy loads, and officers and their teams had to learn new workflows. Over time, however, the benefits became undeniable. Structured digital data allowed for faster searches, automated flagging of incomplete entries and answers of concern, and better integration with other systems. What once seemed like an unwelcome disruption became an indispensable foundation for modern visa processing (U.S. Department of State 2021).

Biometrics offer another instructive case. When fingerprint and facial data collection was first proposed, it triggered skepticism from consular professionals and concerns about public resistance. Would travelers balk at surrendering fingerprints? Would the technology prove reliable enough in everyday conditions? Two decades later, biometric verification is a cornerstone of border security and identity integrity worldwide. The key to overcoming this initial skepticism was the establishment of rigorous, independent standards. International specifications, such as the ICAO's Doc 9303 for machine-readable travel documents, and large-scale, public evaluations by NIST in its Face Recognition Vendor Tests (FRVT), provided the technical rigor needed to build confidence (Grother, Ngan, and Hanaoka 2019). Today, biometric checks are so normalized that many travelers pass through them without a second thought, and consular staff rely on them to protect both applicants and national borders.

Not all lessons from the biometric era were about ergonomics, however. The post–September 11 reforms deserve particular attention because they illustrate a principle central to this book. When several of the September 11 attackers obtained U.S. visas through the regular adjudication process, the institutional response was not to remove humans from the system or automate decisions. Instead, the focus turned to strengthening the broader security architecture around visa adjudication. Intelligence sharing improved, watchlisting systems expanded, training was intensified, and review procedures were tightened. The lesson was not that officers had failed in their judgment, but that critical information had not reached the adjudication process in time. When the stakes are this high, the answer is not less human judgment but better information supporting it. AI adoption should honor that same principle. The tools described in this book are designed to make officers better informed, more efficient, and more alert to risk—but never less accountable for the decisions they make.

The adoption of chatbots in crisis communication further illustrates this pattern. Early pilots were sometimes dismissed as gimmicks, offering canned responses of limited use. Yet during natural disasters, political unrest, and public health emergencies, automated systems have proven their worth by delivering fast, multilingual updates to citizens abroad. Tools like the UNHCR's WhatsApp-based assistants show how conversational AI can reach vulnerable populations with clarity and speed (UNHCR 2022). What began as a novelty is now considered an essential component of crisis communication infrastructure.

The lesson across these examples is that skepticism is natural, even healthy, but it need not be paralyzing. Each past digital transition involved growing pains, yet each ultimately expanded the capacity of consular services. The same pattern is likely with AI. Early tools may frustrate or fall short of expectations, but with careful design, strong governance, and persistent iteration, they can evolve into invisible infrastructure—quietly handling the repetitive tasks so consular staff can devote themselves to the human work that technology cannot replicate.

During an early beta test of biometric capture equipment at one large U.S. consular section, consular staff noticed a puzzling problem: applicants kept hesitating to place their hands on the fingerprint scanning plate. The equipment was working fine. The issue was the indicator light—it was red. Across dozens of cultures, red means "danger," "stop," or "hot—do not touch." Applicants were flinching from the scanner before the process even began. Consular staff flagged the problem, and the light was changed to green—a universally understood signal for "go" or "safe" (Sanders and McCormick 1993, ch. 11). The slowdown vanished.

The episode illustrates a point that technical literature on biometric systems consistently makes: effective design requires attention not just to algorithms but to human interaction and the cultural, social, and legal context in which technology is used (National Research Council 2010). AI can manage enormous complexity, but it cannot notice that a red light is scaring people. That kind of observation—practical, cross-cultural, immediate—is what humans bring to every system they touch.

There is a deeper institutional reason why AI must be designed to reinforce rather than diminish the consular staff's role, particularly the commissioned consular officer's role. In many countries, consular functions have periodically been the subject of bureaucratic competition—domestic agencies, immigration authorities, or private contractors arguing that they could handle the work more efficiently. In the U.S., the Department of State has consistently defended the position that consular services belong with the diplomatic corps, resisting efforts to transfer these functions elsewhere. The argument rests on the principle that runs through this book: consular adjudication requires cultural knowledge, in-country presence, and strategic perspective that only diplomatic professionals stationed abroad can provide. If AI were to reduce consular work to something that looked like routine processing, it would weaken the very case for keeping it in diplomatic hands. Deployed responsibly, however, AI does the opposite—it clears away the administrative burden so that the irreplaceable human dimensions of the work become more visible, not less.

None of this means that consular professionals work in isolation. On the contrary, consular officers and staff routinely coordinate with colleagues from adjacent agencies—law enforcement, border authorities, intelligence services, and international organizations—particularly in complex cases involving cross-border crime, trafficking, extradition, or national security. Effective consular work depends on these partnerships. The distinction that matters is between coordination and cession. Consular teams share information, align efforts, and contribute to joint investigations, but the authority to make consular decisions—who receives a visa, who is issued a passport, how a citizen in distress is assisted—remains with the diplomatic service. AI tools that facilitate interagency coordination, such as shared watchlist queries or cross-system biometric checks, should be designed to respect that boundary: enhancing collaboration without blurring the lines of responsibility.

PRINCIPLES FOR RESPONSIBLE ADOPTION

The defining question for AI in consular affairs is not whether it can work, but how it should work. The systems under discussion are not trivial conveniences; they touch the lives, rights, and identities of tens of millions of people. For that reason, the principles that shape adoption are as important as the technologies themselves.

The first principle is human-in-the-loop by design. Consular adjudication has always rested on human judgment—credibility assessments, contextual understanding, and the ability to weigh exceptional circumstances. In the U.S., since the codification of the consular function in the Immigration and Nationality Act of 1952 (INA), the officer's authority to decide has been the legal bedrock of the process. AI tools can structure and accelerate information, but they must never replace the officer's authority to decide. This principle is embedded in emerging regulatory frameworks. The EU Artificial Intelligence Act explicitly categorizes migration and border control applications of AI as "high risk," requiring human oversight for consequential decisions (European Union 2024a, 2024b). Similarly, U.S. federal guidance stresses that AI systems with safety or rights implications must include clear escalation pathways to human review (Office of Management and Budget 2024).

Digital Frontlines: EES Goes Live, Europe's AI Border Revolution Begins

October 12, 2025 marked the launch of the EU's Entry/Exit System (EES)—a continental-scale AI infrastructure that replaced passport stamps with digital biometric registration for the 400+ million non-EU travelers who cross Schengen borders annually (European Commission 2025). At crossing points like the Eurotunnel terminal in Calais, 224 new biometric kiosks equipped with computer vision algorithms began processing facial scans and fingerprints in the largest deployment of automated border control in human history.

The process is straightforward: first-time visitors scan their passports, place four fingers on biometric readers (children under 12 are exempt), and look into cameras that capture live facial images—a process Eurotunnel estimates takes about two minutes (Financial Times 2025). Return visitors proceed faster with just a passport scan and facial check, provided they're traveling within the three-year data retention window.

To prevent gridlock, authorities implemented a deliberate six-month phase-in, prioritizing coaches and freight while major crossing points balanced automation with accessibility (O'Carroll 2025). Eurostar maintained manual processing lanes alongside biometric channels, while Dover continued fine-tuning checkpoint placement as passenger volumes tested the systems.

The system's inclusivity provisions reflect careful implementation: religious head coverings are permitted if faces remain visible for capture, wheelchair-accessible kiosks accommodate disabled travelers, and manual processing remains available for those unable to use the technology (European Commission 2025b; Royal Netherlands Marechaussee 2025).

Behind the scenes, EES records every entry, exit, and refusal, retaining compliant travelers' data for three years—or five years if overstays or missing exit records trigger extended monitoring. Designated law enforcement authorities and Europol can access this information under strict legal conditions, while travelers can exercise EU data protection rights through published contact points with national authorities (European Union 2017; European Commission 2025b).

What makes EES historically significant is the data foundation it creates. Every facial scan and entry–exit pattern becomes a structured data point in a continental database. Early indicators suggest success: facial recognition caught identity mismatches that human officers and their teams might miss, while digital records provided authorities cleaner data for managing migration flows.

Yet questions remain about whether authorities will resist layering on predictive analytics that could transform border crossing from identity verification into behavioral assessment. EES represents Europe's bet that AI-enhanced borders can be both more secure and more humane than their analog predecessors—a test case other regions are watching closely.

Second, explainability matters more than mystique. Black-box outputs, however statistically powerful, cannot build trust if officers cannot understand or articulate the basis of a flag or recommendation. This is not only a technical requirement but a cultural one: applicants deserve clarity, and officers need defensible reasons for their decisions. Independent evaluations such as NIST's FRVTs demonstrate the importance of transparent benchmarks, enabling agencies to choose systems with documented performance across demographics (Grother, Ngan, and Hanaoka 2019). The catastrophic failure of systems like the U.K. Post Office's Horizon software, which led to hundreds of wrongful convictions based on unauditable outputs, serves as a stark warning against opaque automation (Halper 2025).

Third, fairness and access must be intentional, not incidental. AI can widen equity gaps if it is not designed with multilingual, disability-accessible, and culturally sensitive paths in mind. Civil society critiques, such as Amnesty International's *The Digital Border*, warn of the risks of exclusion and discrimination when automation is deployed without safeguards (Amnesty International 2024). Consular services, often the public's first and most tangible encounter with a state, must err on the side of inclusion. That means not only testing systems for demographic bias but also ensuring that applicants with limited literacy or digital access can still receive fair treatment.

Fourth, privacy and minimization are nonnegotiable. Consular databases contain some of the most sensitive information governments hold—biometrics, travel histories, and personal narratives. The Consular Consolidated Database (CCD), for example, manages over 120 million nonimmigrant and immigrant visa records, including sensitive medical and financial disclosures (U.S. Department of State 2023b). AI systems must adhere to strict purpose limitations, collecting only what is necessary and retaining it only as long as needed. U.S. Department of State privacy impact assessments for the CCD emphasize these safeguards, underscoring that innovation cannot come at the expense of data protection (U.S. Department of State 2023b).

Security and provenance are essential to public trust. As forgeries, morphing techniques, and synthetic media become more sophisticated, governments must ensure that both inputs and outputs are verifiable. For example, deepfake documents and videos used in identity fraud increased roughly four-fold globally between 2022 and 2023, demonstrating the speed at which this threat is evolving (Sumsub 2024). Standards such as the Coalition for Content Provenance and Authenticity's specifications for content credentials provide one way to ensure that scanned documents and digital images carry a traceable chain of authenticity (Coalition for Content Provenance and Authenticity 2025). In parallel, consular AI tools must maintain audit trails—clear records of what the system flagged, how an officer responded, and how outcomes were reached.

Together, these principles form a simple but powerful charter for responsible adoption: AI should save time without eroding judgment, illuminate decisions without obscuring them, expand access rather than limit it, and protect privacy while enhancing security. In this light, AI is not a foreign imposition on consular practice but a continuation of its core ethic: serving the public with fairness, clarity, and integrity under changing conditions.

PRACTITIONER'S MAP OF EARLY-WIN USE CASES

If principles set the guardrails, use cases provide the on-ramps. One of the clearest lessons from recent deployments is that AI delivers the most value when applied to specific, bounded tasks that consume disproportionate amounts of officer time. Rather than trying to "automate diplomacy," successful pilots start with the practical burdens that every post recognizes—visa renewals, photo rejections, routine email replies—and design systems that return hours to officers without altering their authority.

Visa processing is an obvious starting point. Large language models can summarize request packets for waivers of ineligibility that often stretch to hundreds of pages, distilling them into structured briefs officers can scan quickly. Machine learning models can triage cases into lanes—renewals with a clean compliance history, complex first-time applications, or cases with potential fraud indicators. Canada's Immigration, Refugees and Citizenship Canada (IRCC) has already shown that advanced analytics can help streamline such workflows while keeping officers in control of final decisions (Immigration, Refugees and Citizenship Canada 2024). However, its deployment drew criticism for the lack of algorithmic transparency and concerns that the system's triage recommendations subtly erode officer discretion and accountability for decision outcomes (Nalbandian 2021; Luck n.d.).

Passport services also benefit from early applications. Computer vision tools can verify whether photos meet ICAO Doc 9303 standards for head size, lighting, and background, reducing the high rejection rates that frustrate applicants (ICAO 2015–2024). More advanced systems can perform age-progressed facial matching, verifying continuity of identity even when decades separate a new application from the old document. When paired with liveness detection standards such as ISO/IEC 30107, these tools make it harder for impostors or forged images to slip through (ISO/IEC 2023).

Overseas citizen services—ranging from lost passport emergencies to crisis alerts—are equally fertile ground. Multilingual chatbots, already in use by UNHCR to support refugee populations, demonstrate how conversational AI can bridge language and literacy gaps at scale (UNHCR 2022). For consular posts, this means 24/7 responses to routine questions in dozens of languages, with escalation to a human officer for complex or sensitive matters. In crises, AI-assisted translation and alerting can deliver timely, accessible updates that would overwhelm manual workflows.

Internal workflows may offer the fastest returns. Natural language processing tools can sort and classify incoming emails, draft replies grounded in policy references and generate summaries of lengthy threads for officer review. RPA, already mainstream in other federal agencies (CIO Council 2020), can handle routine case status updates, reconcile fee records, or compile document packets. These are the digital equivalents of moving boxes in a back office—tasks that add little judgment but consume enormous time.

Global Risk and Threat Monitoring presents a far more critical early win. Consular teams are tasked with assessing threats ranging from large-scale civil unrest and security risks to emergent fraud networks, a task that currently relies on manually synthesizing data from internal cables, news wires, and open-source intelligence. AI tools, specifically those using NLP, can conduct continuous, real-time scans of foreign language media, public health data, and global security advisories. This capacity allows AI to instantly synthesize thousands of data points into concise, policy-relevant alerts, providing officers with a level of situational awareness necessary to make proactive, risk-informed decisions, a capability that vastly exceeds the limits of manual research (Council on Foreign Relations 2024).

What unites these early-win use cases is not their technical sophistication but their fitness for purpose. They address the most repetitive elements of consular work, yield measurable time savings, and can be piloted in weeks rather than years. Crucially, they also lend themselves to clear metrics: processing time reduced, photo and document rejection rates lowered, satisfaction scores improved, critical security alerts generated, officer hours regained. These metrics create an evidence base that not only justifies continued investment but also builds staff confidence that AI serves their needs rather than the other way around.

DRILLING DOWN INTO AI USE CASES

The duties of a consular officers and staff are as varied as they are demanding: adjudicating visas, issuing passports, assisting citizens abroad in moments of crisis, managing staff, and serving as the front line against fraud. Each of these responsibilities requires quick thinking under pressure, careful adherence to law and policy, and a capacity for empathy in difficult situations. AI does not change the essence of these tasks, but it offers new tools that can make them more sustainable. Rather than standing in for human judgment, AI operates as an amplifier—handling the repetitive, data-heavy work so that officers and consular staff can devote their time to decisions that only people can make.

Visa adjudication offers one of the clearest illustrations of this partnership. Every year, consular teams process millions of visa applications worldwide, and much of their day is consumed not by the interview itself but by the background work: reviewing case files, checking documents for completeness, and ensuring that required waivers are properly summarized. AI-driven triage systems can presort cases into broad categories—routine renewals, complex first-time applications, or those with potential red flags—before an officer ever opens the file. Canada's immigration service has shown how this can be done transparently, publishing guidance on how advanced analytics support visa triage without removing human oversight (Immigration, Refugees and Citizenship Canada 2024). For the officer at the window, the result is more time to conduct meaningful interviews rather than scanning forms for missing entries. However, the Canadian case also highlights a core challenge: a lack of transparency in automated triage tools like the "Chinook" system has led to allegations from immigration lawyers that officers are issuing vague, templated refusal letters without adequately reviewing applicant files (Luck n.d.). This raises the critical issue of *algorithmic bias*, where systems trained on historical data may perpetuate or even amplify existing systemic biases against applicants from certain countries, undermining the promise of a fairer, more efficient process (Nalbandian 2021). For the officer at the visa window, the result is more time to conduct meaningful interviews rather than scanning forms for missing entries, but only if and when procedural fairness and accountability are maintained.

Passport adjudication provides another use case where AI can ease burdens without displacing responsibility. One of the most common frustrations for both applicants and staff is the rejection of photos that fail to meet technical standards. AI-enabled capture tools, whether integrated into mobile apps or available at kiosks, can guide applicants in real time to adjust lighting, framing, or expression. These systems enforce the standards set by the International Civil Aviation Organization's specifications for machine-readable travel documents, ensuring global consistency (ICAO 2015–2024). When paired with liveness detection standards developed by ISO, they also make it more difficult for fraudulent images or synthetic forgeries to slip through (ISO/IEC 2023). The result is faster processing, fewer time-consuming arguments with applicants about photo suitability, and greater confidence that submitted images meet international requirements. Critically, this instantaneous policy enforcement mitigates the cascade effect of past human errors. In high-volume environments, documents accepted through a lapse in judgment—such as those noncompliant with head covering or specific lighting rules—can be used as precedent for years. The AI system's capacity for uniform, real-time compliance prevents this systemic breakdown, eliminating the need for officers or staff to dedicate significant, nonstandard processing time to correcting issues that should have been caught at the point of intake. For consular officers, this means fewer preventable rejections and a smoother intake process that allows them to focus on adjudication rather than technical defects.

A case we observed from one of the largest U.S. consular sections overseas illustrates how a single lapse in enforcing photo standards can generate significant operational burdens years later. A Muslim applicant arrived to renew a U.S. passport, presenting her prior passport as proof of identity. That earlier document, issued years before, contained a noncompliant photograph in which only the applicant's eyes were visible—an image that did not meet established requirements at the time of issuance.

This one error immediately forced the renewal into a nonstandard workflow. Staff had to review older policy guidance, consult supervisors, and arrange for a female officer to privately verify the applicant's identity against childhood records. The applicant—who had traveled for hours—experienced avoidable stress and delays, while consular personnel expended substantial time resolving an issue that stemmed not from the current application but from the failure to enforce clear standards at the original intake point.

The case illustrates a core theme of this chapter: AI's greatest value in passport operations lies not only in accelerating routine tasks but in its consistent, automatic enforcement of policy, preventing small intake errors from evolving into time-consuming, sensitive, and emotionally taxing interventions years later.

Overseas citizen services, often the most human-facing side of consular work, also benefits from AI augmentation. Routine inquiries—how to replace a lost passport, what to do after an arrest abroad, how to notarize a document—arrive in overwhelming numbers by email and phone. Chatbots and multilingual assistants, anchored in retrieval augmented generation and verified knowledge bases, can provide 24/7 answers in multiple languages. The U.S. State Department's own experiments with tools like StateChat demonstrate that natural language systems can deflect repetitive inquiries, returning significant amounts of officer time each week (Doubleday 2024; Silson 2025).

Critically, this automated triage offers an immediate mitigation for a key operational challenge: the current three-tiered human handoff for afterhours emergencies. Outside of business hours, a distressed citizen's initial point of contact is usually the Marine Security Guard (MSG) answering after duty calls, who filters the call before escalating it to the Embassy Duty Officer (EDO)—a rotating role held by various direct-hire Americans (often non-consular specialists) with limited consular expertise (U.S. Department of State n.d.-j). Only if the EDO deems the issue a genuine, immediate crisis is the call finally passed to the highly trained Consular Duty Officer (CDO) (U.S. Department of State n.d.-g).

While this layered system ensures 24/7 in-country diplomatic presence (unlike the centralized call center models used by services like Australia's Department of Foreign Affairs and Trade [DFAT] and the U.K.'s Foreign, Commonwealth & Development Office [FCDO], which use global contact centers to provide remote first response regardless of time of day [Watts n.d.; U.K. Government n.d.-b]), it introduces a potential friction point where a crucial five-minute query must pass through a human judgment–heavy series of referrals before reaching the appropriate expertise. AI-driven front-line systems are not meant to console families in crisis or manage complex emergencies, but they can reduce the background noise, remove unnecessary stress from EDOs, instantly address nonemergency queries, and minimize mistriage risk, ensuring that initial, accurate guidance is delivered instantly so that specialized officers can give their full attention to the people who need them most.

Fraud prevention units are another area where AI can shift the balance of time and accuracy. Document mills, coached narratives, and fabricated financial records have become more sophisticated, especially as generative tools make forgeries easier to produce. AI systems that cluster documents, detect metadata anomalies, or flag recurring sponsor names can surface suspicious patterns across cases that no individual officer would have the bandwidth to detect. Benchmark datasets such as DocXPand-25k, created for ID document analysis, provide realistic ways to test these systems before field use (DocXPand Team 2024). Here again, the officer's role remains central: deciding whether a flagged pattern constitutes real fraud, whether to escalate to host country authorities, or whether to clear the applicant after review.

AI also has a role in internal management and leadership, tasks that grow in importance as officers progress in their careers. Supervisors managing consular sections often juggle resource allocation, training, and staff morale alongside adjudications. Predictive analytics can help forecast appointment demand, guiding shift assignments to reduce burnout. NLP tools can classify and summarize inbox traffic, giving section chiefs a clearer view of bottlenecks and staff workload. For headquarters-based officers supporting the field, AI-driven dashboards can surface global trends in visa demand or fraud patterns, helping to target training and resources where they are most needed (Office of Management and Budget 2024; U.S. Government Accountability Office 2025).

Taken together, these use cases show how AI can weave itself into the daily life of consular affairs without displacing the human element. The officer remains the decisive expert: the trusted adjudicator, the empathetic counselor, and the strategic manager. AI plays a quieter role—sorting, summarizing, detecting patterns, and forecasting demand. The effect, however, is far from quiet. It is a return of time, attention, and presence to the officer, ensuring that the most human parts of consular work—judgment, empathy, and reassurance—remain at the center of diplomacy.

CHANGE MANAGEMENT THAT WORKS

Even the most promising technology falters if people do not trust it. In the U.S. State Department's Consular Affairs Bureau, where officers carry the burden of legal responsibility for each adjudication, skepticism toward automation is not only natural but prudent. Effective adoption of AI therefore depends as much on change management as on algorithms. Leaders must cultivate both buy-in and engagement among staff before tools are deployed, drawing on established change-management practice that emphasizes early awareness-building and active participation over top-down rollout (Prosci n.d.; Kotter n.d.). Officers and consular staff must see that these tools protect their time, not their jobs, and that human judgment remains firmly in charge.

Narratives matter. In pilot programs at the U.S. State Department, leaders who framed AI as a way to return time to officers—"let the machine read, so you can decide"—found far greater buy-in than those who emphasized efficiency or cost savings (U.S. Department of State 2024a). The language used to introduce a tool shapes whether staff view it as a partner or a threat. Messages that highlight empathy, fairness, and officer empowerment resonate more than technical jargon, effectively creating a shared vision for AI as a tool of professional excellence (Prosci n.d.).

Roles also matter. Successful pilots in the U.S. government context typically designate a consular champion: an officer who experiences the day-to-day bottlenecks and can credibly advocate for change. Alongside them, a technical lead—often a locally employed staff member with IT skills—handles configuration and troubleshooting. A data steward ensures that inputs are accurate, labeled, and privacy-compliant, while a communications liaison keeps both staff and applicants informed about what is changing. This team-based approach distributes responsibility, reduces anxiety, and allows pilots to adapt quickly to feedback (Office of Management and Budget 2024).

Training is essential, but it must quickly build both the knowledge officers need to use a tool and the practical ability to apply it on the job (Prosci n.d.). Short "office hours" sessions, where staff can ask questions and see demonstrations, build confidence far more effectively than long manuals. A proven tactic is to deliver visible early wins first—automating a universally disliked task such as retyping data between systems or chasing down missing photo specifications. When officers and consular staff see an immediate reduction in drudgery, they are more willing to trust the tool on more complex tasks.

Feedback loops ensure that change sticks through continuous reinforcement. Systems should be piloted in "assist" mode, where AI makes recommendations, but officers retain full control, before expanding to broader use. Weekly reviews of outputs, error rates, and user satisfaction keep the deployment grounded in evidence rather than assumption. By embedding iteration into the culture, missions can turn skepticism into ownership, showing that AI evolves in response to officer experience rather than imposing itself from above.

Change management in consular affairs is ultimately about protecting dignity—both of officers and of the applicants they serve. When staff feel respected, heard, and empowered, they are far more likely to extend that same respect to the public. AI, introduced thoughtfully, can reinforce this ethic by giving officers back the time and energy to engage applicants as people rather than as files. This alignment of technology with core values ensures the change is institutionalized and sustains a focus on the service mission rather than mere efficiency. (Hicks 2015)

METRICS AND EVIDENCE

The promise of AI in consular work cannot rest on anecdotes or optimistic projections alone. For adoption to be sustainable, diplomatic offices and consular posts must measure outcomes rigorously and communicate them transparently. This is especially important in a domain where public trust and officer accountability are at stake. Clear metrics not only justify investments but also reassure staff and applicants that AI is serving its intended purpose.

Operational metrics are often the most visible. They include indicators such as average processing time, time to first review, and the percentage of cases correctly routed on first pass. In early U.S. State Department pilots, AI-driven triage reduced the time to retrieve and summarize relevant policy guidance, allowing officers to touch more cases earlier in the day (U.S. Department of State 2024a). For applicants, the effect was felt in shorter wait times and fewer repeat visits.

Quality metrics are equally important. If AI saves time but increases rework or error rates, it fundamentally undermines the very efficiency it promises. Prior to the capability to run real-time, deep analytics, a manual integrity check was a necessary standard: As one of the authors observed while serving as a consular manager, this often involved pulling a statistically relevant percentage of all visa cases (both issuances and refusals) for a senior-level review to judge if the decision was appropriately backed by notes in the system. This practice ensured the manager was actively "in the loop," brought integrity to the process, and allowed for follow-up with customers or additional training for officers whose cases were not firmly supported.

AI-driven quality metrics are the evolution of this rigorous, human-centered review. Instead of manual sampling, AI acts as a perpetual "human-in-the-loop" early warning system by tracking reversal rates on officer reviews, the clarity of applicant communications, and the consistency of adjudications. Independent audits, such as those carried out by the U.S. Government Accountability Office on passport processing backlogs, demonstrate how rigorous outside evaluation can expose systemic weaknesses and guide reforms (GAO 2025).

Equity metrics bring fairness into the frame. These may include satisfaction scores disaggregated by language, demographic parity in processing times, or the rate of false positives and false negatives across different applicant groups. Studies by NIST have shown that face recognition systems can exhibit demographic differentials if left unchecked (Grother, Ngan, and Hanaoka 2019). Building such audits into regular reporting helps ensure that AI systems do not reproduce or exacerbate inequities.

Trust metrics reflect how officers, consular staff, and applicants feel about the systems. These are more qualitative but no less significant. Surveys must go beyond simple satisfaction to capture officer sentiments, such as "Percentage of officers who feel AI allows for a more thorough interview," which acts as a proxy for the higher-value work on the Time Dividend Ladder. Tracking burnout proxies and applicant perceptions of fairness provide early signals of whether AI is reinforcing or eroding confidence. Transparency and public accountability are paramount for legitimacy, as reports from the Privacy and Civil Liberties Oversight Board (PCLOB 2025) on agency data usage and face recognition have repeatedly highlighted. When combined, these layers of evidence—operational, quality, equity, and trust—form what might be called a "time dividend ladder." Hours saved at the baseline should not disappear into the void but should climb into higher-value activities: more thorough interviews, clearer explanations, and greater capacity for crisis response. By measuring not just speed but also fairness, clarity, and satisfaction, consular operations can demonstrate that AI is not a shortcut around responsibility but a scaffold that supports it.

RISKS, FAILURE MODES, AND FIXES

No technology introduced into consular operations is without its pitfalls. Paperless visa forms once crashed under peak loads, biometric systems raised privacy alarms, and early chatbots sometimes misled more than they helped. AI is no different. Its value depends not only on what it can do well but also on how consular operations anticipate and manage what it can do poorly. Understanding the failure modes of AI is essential to protecting applicants, officers, local staff, and institutions alike.

One of the most common risks is over-automation. When AI systems are allowed to operate unchecked, they can turn into silent decision-makers rather than advisory tools. This risks unfair outcomes and undermines officer authority. The remedy is simple but vital: maintain human checkpoints. Pilots should begin in "assist" mode, where the system suggests but does not decide, and adverse outcomes should always trigger mandatory human review. This approach aligns with regulatory expectations in both the EU and the U.S., which classify migration-related AI systems as high-risk precisely because of their potential to affect fundamental rights (European Union 2024a, 2024b; Office of Management and Budget 2024).

Another challenge is hallucination—the tendency of large language models to generate plausible-sounding but inaccurate information. In consular contexts, even a minor error in a visa waiver summary or policy citation could have serious consequences. The fix lies in retrieval augmented generation, which constrains systems to verified sources and attaches citations that officers can check before acting. Coupling this with service-level agreements that specify acceptable error thresholds ensures that vendors remain accountable for accuracy.

Localization failures present a subtler but equally significant problem. Models trained on data from one linguistic or cultural context may misinterpret input from another, leading to misclassification or inappropriate responses. This risk is present not only between languages (e.g., English vs. Arabic) but also in regional variations and dialects (e.g., the difference between Castilian and Latin American Spanish). A chatbot that works well with U.K. English terminology may stumble on U.S. English slang, or worse, cause an error by misinterpreting a specific dialect. This failure causes not only an error but also a failure to grant an applicant due respect and clarity. The safeguard here is rigorous, dialect-aware testing, readability checks, and continuous feedback from locally employed staff who understand how applicants phrase their questions. This testing must include satisfaction proxies for non-English interactions to ensure the dignity of the communication is maintained.

Data sprawl and shadow IT are risks that emerge when eager staff experiment with unapproved tools outside official channels. While often well-intentioned, such practices create vulnerabilities in privacy and security. The fix is not to ban experimentation but to channel it into approved marketplaces with clear logging, oversight, and exit clauses. Agencies such as the U.S. Department of State have emphasized the need to balance innovation with governance, encouraging staff to pilot tools while maintaining visibility into what data they touch (U.S. Department of State 2023a).

Taken together, these risks illustrate that failure is not an anomaly but an expected part of technology adoption. The difference between responsible and irresponsible use of AI is not whether mistakes occur but whether organizations have designed ways to detect, mitigate, and learn from them. Crucially, the introduction of AI to handle repetitive tasks—which are often subject to fatigue and data entry errors—should result in a net reduction of overall systemic mistakes in consular operations. By normalizing safeguards such as human review, source-grounding, bilingual testing, and logged experimentation, consular operations can turn potential liabilities into opportunities for resilience and sustain the integrity of their mission.

CLOSING REFLECTION

At dawn in the Republic of Z, the line still stretches around the building. The applicants are no fewer, the stakes no lower, and the officer's responsibility no lighter. What has changed is the space in which that responsibility is exercised. When AI handles the repetitive—triaging cases, flagging anomalies, translating inquiries, reconciling data—it returns something that no staffing increase alone can provide: time for the officer to look up from the screen, listen to the person across the counter, and apply the judgment that no algorithm can replicate. That is the Time Dividend, and it is the measure by which every tool in the chapters that follow should be judged. Technology changes; the mission does not. AI succeeds in consular affairs only when it protects the human presence at the heart of the work.

CROSS-WALK TO LATER CHAPTERS

This first chapter has introduced AI not as an abstract concept but as a practical amplifier of consular work. By showing how AI can triage, summarize, translate, and automate, the present chapter has set the stage for deeper exploration of the ways technology intersects with passports, visas, crisis response, and identity integrity. Each of these domains carries its own challenges, safeguards, and opportunities, and the chapters that follow build on the foundation established here.

In visa processing, for example, machine learning can separate low-risk renewals from high-risk anomalies, while large language models help condense complex waiver files. Chapter 2 examines how these tools operate in practice, the governance frameworks that guide them, and the pitfalls to avoid. Passports, as the highest form of state-backed identity, pose different challenges: biometric verification across decades, detecting morphing attacks, and ensuring equity for applicants whose identities do not fit neatly into traditional templates. These themes take center stage in Chapter 3.

Chapter 4 expands the conversation to chatbots, language models, and multilingual access. The same retrieval augmented generation techniques introduced here reappear in public-facing tools that can answer routine questions in dozens of languages while escalating complex cases to officers. Chapter 5 shifts to crisis management, where AI's ability to sense and communicate rapidly can make the difference between timely evacuation and dangerous delay.

Fraud and forgery detection, the focus of Chapter 6, builds directly on the risks described in this chapter. There, the emphasis turns to how AI can uncover patterns invisible to human reviewers—cloned documents, recycled metadata, or financial anomalies—while still requiring human-in-the-loop safeguards. Chapter 7 revisits biometrics in greater depth, situating them within global identity architectures and showing how AI can both strengthen and complicate the integrity of identity systems.

The operational dimension, explored in Chapters 8 and 9, connects back to this chapter's attention to time savings. Appointment optimization, email triage, and local pilots are practical ways to reclaim hours in the consular day, with deployment models that can be scaled across missions. Finally, Chapter 10 closes the book by returning to the central theme: AI must serve the human mission of diplomacy, giving officers the time and clarity to act with dignity, fairness, and empathy.

By situating today's early pilots within the longer trajectory of digital transitions, and by identifying both opportunities and risks, this chapter lays the groundwork for the detailed case studies and playbooks to follow. Each subsequent chapter builds on this foundation, showing not only how AI can improve efficiency but also how it must be governed to preserve the trust at the heart of consular affairs.

FIELD CHECKLIST: IS YOUR OPERATION AI-READY?

Before a consular operation, office, or section experiments with AI, it must first take stock of its own readiness. The question is not only about technology but about people, culture, and process. AI succeeds where the groundwork has been carefully laid; it falters where missions rush to deploy tools without aligning them to their own realities. A field readiness scan offers a way to surface those conditions in plain terms.

The first element is leadership and culture. Consular operations that succeed with AI typically designate a champion—an officer or locally employed staff member who not only understands the pain points of consular work but is willing to shepherd change. This individual anchors the narrative that AI protects time rather than threatens jobs. Without such a voice, skepticism and the inertia of current processes can spread unchecked, and pilots may stall before they begin. Next is problem framing. The most effective pilots start with what might be called a "Goldilocks problem"—a challenge that is important enough to matter but bounded enough to be solved within a few months. This could be reducing rejected passport photos, triaging visa renewals, or cutting response times for routine email inquiries. When pilots are scoped too broadly, they drown in complexity; when scoped too narrowly, they fail to demonstrate value.

Data and content readiness are also critical. AI systems need current, structured, and reliable inputs to perform well. A knowledge base of up-to-date frequently asked questions, clear policies translated into multiple languages, and defined rules for handling personally identifiable information provide the foundation for safe and accurate automation. Without this preparation, even sophisticated tools will produce inconsistent results.

Equally important are tools and guardrails. Consular operations must ensure that pilots use approved platforms, that human-in-the-loop roles are clearly defined, and that data access follows role-based permissions. Privacy reviews and incident response plans should be in place before systems go live, not after. These controls are not bureaucratic hurdles but trust-building measures that allow officers to experiment with confidence.

Readiness requires a plan for measurement and learning. Missions that succeed with AI track their pilots through simple dashboards and scheduled reviews, treating early deployments as opportunities to learn rather than as permanent solutions. By reviewing metrics such as time saved, error rates, and satisfaction levels each month, consular operations create a cycle of continuous improvement. This approach not only strengthens the pilot itself but also prepares the mission to scale responsibly when tools prove their worth.

In short, an AI-ready post is one where people, problems, data, tools, and measurement align. It is a mission that knows why it is experimenting, who is responsible, what data it is working with, how it will safeguard privacy, and how success will be judged. Such readiness does not require perfection—it requires intention. With that foundation in place, even modest pilots can deliver meaningful dividends, showing officers and applicants alike that AI can enhance, rather than erode, the human heart of consular affairs.

GLOSSARY AND FURTHER READING

For many officers, consular staff, and students encountering AI in a consular context, the terminology itself can feel like a barrier. A handful of field-ready definitions can cut through the jargon. When colleagues speak of retrieval augmented generation, for example, they mean a safeguard for large language models: instead of inventing answers, the system pulls from approved sources and cites them. A confidence score is simply a numerical expression of how certain an algorithm is in its result, reminding users that outputs come with probabilities, not certainties. Red-teaming refers to stress-testing a system with deliberately difficult or adversarial inputs, a practice that helps uncover weaknesses before real applicants do. Prompt hygiene is the discipline of writing clear, neutral instructions for AI tools to reduce error and bias. And provenance is the chain of evidence showing where a digital object—whether a scanned passport photo or an AI-generated summary—came from and whether it can be trusted.

Readers who want to explore these issues in greater depth have no shortage of reliable resources. The U.S. Department of State's Enterprise AI Strategy and its AI inventories provide a candid look at how consular affairs is already experimenting with these technologies (U.S. Department of State 2023a, 2024b, n.d.-c). The U.S. Government Accountability Office has issued reports on both systemic passport processing backlogs and the costs of biometric identity systems, giving a sober view of the institutional challenges that drive interest in automation (U.S. Government Accountability Office 2023, 2025). On the standards front, the National Institute of Standards and Technology's AI Risk Management Framework offers a practical vocabulary for mapping, measuring, managing, and governing AI risks (National Institute of Standards and Technology 2023). The EU Artificial Intelligence Act, adopted in 2024, lays out binding obligations for "high risk" systems such as those in migration and border control, highlighting how governance is tightening at the global level (European Union 2024a, 2024b).

Taken together, these sources confirm the central lesson of this opening chapter: AI in consular affairs is neither speculative science fiction nor an unchecked force. It is a set of tools, governed by principles and standards, that can be applied responsibly to improve service, protect identity, and strengthen trust. The chapters ahead build on this foundation, examining in detail how AI intersects with visas, passports, crisis management, fraud detection, biometrics, and the daily rhythms of work at missions worldwide.

For those who wish to situate consular AI within the broader landscape of diplomatic technology, *AI Use Cases for Diplomats* surveys AI across all seven functions of embassy work—from executive leadership and political affairs to management and public diplomacy—and provides a useful introduction to the wider field from which consular applications draw their foundational concepts (Kilburg 2025).

Part II

Visas, Passports, and Citizen Services

Visa adjudication, passport issuance, citizen communication, and crisis response form the daily heartbeat of consular work. These are the services that bring you face to face with applicants and citizens—the encounters where efficiency, fairness, and human presence matter most. This part examines how AI is already transforming these core consular services, not by replacing staff but by reshaping the conditions under which you work.

The chapters in this section share a common structure. Each begins with the operational reality: surging demand, complex documentation, and the throughput paradox where more safeguards mean less time for the nuanced judgments that require human expertise. Each then maps AI capabilities to specific pain points—triage systems that separate routine renewals from complex cases, summarization tools that condense sprawling files, biometric verification that confirms identity across decades, multilingual chatbots that extend service around the clock and across language barriers, and crisis platforms that deliver multilingual alerts to thousands of citizens before staff even reach the office.

What unites these applications is a consistent philosophy. AI handles volume and repetition; officers retain authority over discretion and judgment. A visa triage system may route cases into green, amber, and red lanes, but an officer decides every outcome. A passport photo compliance tool may guide applicants to submit acceptable images, but an officer adjudicates identity. A chatbot may answer routine questions in dozens of languages, but escalation to a human remains two clicks away. A crisis alert system may notify thousands simultaneously, but a staff member coordinates

DOI: 10.1201/9781003634775-3

the response. This division of labor is not a limitation—it is the design principle that makes AI trustworthy.

This section also confronts failures directly. The U.K.'s abandoned visa streaming algorithm, which was retired after documented discriminatory impacts, serves as a cautionary tale repeated across chapters. Governance frameworks—transparency, explainability, fairness audits, and redress pathways—are not afterthoughts but prerequisites for deployment. Global examples from Canada, Singapore, Estonia, and international organizations demonstrate that responsible AI in core consular services is not hypothetical but operational.

By the end of this section, you will understand how AI can make visa processing smarter, passport services more secure, citizen communication more accessible, and crisis response faster and more equitable—without sacrificing the human judgment that defines consular professionalism.

2 Smarter Visa Processing with AI

The unprecedented speed and potential of AI's development and adoption presents both enormous opportunities to advance our mission and risks we must mitigate.

—Alejandro Mayorkas, former Secretary of Homeland Security (quoted in U.S. Department of Homeland Security 2024)

These technologies are vulnerable to bias and errors, and may lead to the storage, collection, and use of information that threatens the right to privacy, non-discrimination, and other human rights.

—Eliza Aspen, Researcher on Technology and Inequality, Amnesty International (quoted in Madan 2024)

The model's outputs are integrated into existing systems, which assist personnel in making informed decisions regarding traveler screening. Importantly, human judgment remains central to the process, as personnel retain the final authority in all decision-making related to border security operations.

—U.S. Customs and Border Protection, describing the Traveler Entity Resolution Model (U.S. Department of Homeland Security 2024, DHS-80)

Opening Vignette: 48 Hours in Z City

At the height of student visa season in the Republic of Z, the waiting room of the consular section was overflowing. Young applicants, many clutching identical manila folders, rehearsed their stories in hushed tones while parents lingered outside, anxious for news. Officers and their teams worked at a relentless pace, sifting through application packets that blurred together in their sheer volume.

The year before, a fraud ring had slipped through unnoticed. A cluster of applicants presented sponsorship documents that appeared legitimate on the surface—bank statements, tuition receipts, affidavits of support. Each officer, buried in their own caseload, saw only fragments of the pattern. By the time

DOI: 10.1201/9781003634775-4

suspicions mounted, dozens of visas had already been issued. The discovery left the section shaken and determined to do better.

This year, the mission had deployed an experimental AI overlay. Within 48 hours of the first wave of applications, the system flagged a suspicious cluster. It highlighted unusual similarities: identical metadata embedded in PDF sponsorship letters, recurring anomalies in ledger formats, and repeated sponsor names across otherwise unrelated files. Instead of delivering a mysterious "risk score," the dashboard displayed the reasons for each flag—pointing officers to the specific details that warranted a closer look.

When the flagged cases were routed to the Fraud Prevention Unit, the ring's tactics became clear. Applicants had been coached to use a recycled set of documents, slightly altered for each submission. With AI surfacing the connections, officers could move quickly, halting the approvals and preserving the integrity of the process. Legitimate renewals, meanwhile, moved forward faster than before, since the triage system cleared them with minimal delay.

In the staff meeting that followed, the mood was markedly different from the year prior. Officers emphasized that the system had not made the decisions—it had shown them where to look. "It didn't take judgment out of our hands," one adjudicator observed. "It gave us a map of what mattered." For the Republic of Z, the experiment demonstrated a new possibility: a fraud pattern that no single officer could catch in their own stack of files became unmistakable the moment a system could compare them all at once.

This vignette is fictional, but it reflects pressures and innovations emerging across visa operations worldwide.

WHY NOW: THE THROUGHPUT PARADOX

Visa sections across the world are facing an unprecedented surge in demand. In 2023 alone, the U.S. Department of State processed over ten million nonimmigrant visas, a number that climbed further in 2024, with visitor visas making up the overwhelming share (U.S. Department of State 2024). The case for AI in visa operations does not stand alone: it is part of a broader transformation underway across all embassy functions, from political analysis to crisis management, as documented in the wider literature on AI in diplomacy (Kilburg 2025). Other governments report similar pressures: Canada's Immigration, Refugees and Citizenship Office has expanded its use of advanced analytics to handle rising application volumes (IRCC 2023), while European missions prepare for new regulatory requirements under the Entry/Exit System and ETIAS that will increase both data collection and adjudication steps (European Migration Network (EMN) and Organisation for Economic Co-operation and Development 2022).

This dramatic increase in volume has exposed what might be called the throughput paradox. The more documents applicants provide, and the more governments impose safeguards to ensure fairness and security, the more officers and their teams find themselves submerged in repetitive tasks. Hours are spent combing through affidavits of support, parsing financial statements, or reviewing similar case files for signs of fraud.

The result is paradoxical: officers devote less time to the nuanced interviews and discretionary judgments that truly require their expertise, even as public expectations for faster, more transparent service continue to rise.

The paradox is not merely operational but political. Delays in student or work visas can jeopardize international partnerships and economic opportunities. Backlogs in family reunification cases can strain bilateral relations. Media coverage of long wait times or perceived inequities fuels public frustration and, in some cases, litigation. In the U.K., for instance, a visa application streaming algorithm was abandoned in 2020 after civil society groups successfully argued that it perpetuated discriminatory impacts (The Guardian 2020). Such episodes underscore that inefficiency and opacity are not just management problems—they carry reputational and legal risks.

A frequently cited example in debates over intelligence sharing and visa policy is the September 11 attacks of 2001. Investigations later determined that 19 hijackers carried out the attacks, 15 of whom were Saudi nationals (9/11 Commission Staff Statement 1). In 2001, U.S. posts in Saudi Arabia introduced a visa-processing system known as Visa Express. The program allowed visa applicants to submit their applications through designated travel agencies rather than applying directly at a U.S. embassy or consulate, and it was intended to streamline visa processing (9/11 Commission Staff Statement 1).

Subsequent investigations found that at least three of the 9/11 hijackers obtained their visas through the Visa Express program and were never interviewed by an American consular officer (9/11 Commission Staff Statement 1; U.S. National Commission on Terrorist Attacks 2004). The Commission's research also identified the role of Khalid Sheikh Mohammed as the principal planner of the attacks. Records show that a visa application was submitted through Visa Express on his behalf using a fraudulent Saudi passport and a false identity; whether the visa was ultimately approved or denied remains a matter of some dispute in the official record, and there is no evidence that he ever traveled to the U.S. on it (9/11 Commission Staff Statement 1).

Post-attack investigations also examined the information environment in which visas were adjudicated. At the time, consular officers relied primarily on the watchlist and database systems available to them, which did not include all intelligence information held by other U.S. agencies, including the Central Intelligence Agency. Every one of the hijackers' names was run through the available watchlist systems without producing a match, because the relevant intelligence was never shared with consular officers (U.S. National Commission on Terrorist Attacks 2004; Ryan 2001).

Leadership of the visa system also came under scrutiny. At the time, Mary A. Ryan served as Assistant Secretary of State for Consular Affairs. She was subsequently asked by Secretary of State Colin Powell to resign under intense congressional pressure, despite having argued that the failure was one of intelligence sharing rather than consular procedure. Ryan later discussed the information constraints facing consular officers prior to the attacks in an oral history interview with the Association for Diplomatic Studies and Training (Ryan, 2003).

AI enters this landscape as a response to volume, complexity, and expectation. Tools that can rapidly triage applications, summarize lengthy files, and surface fraud patterns offer a way to rebalance staff time. The goal is not speed for its own sake, but a redistribution of effort: to automate the repeatable so that human discretion can be preserved for the exceptional. Early deployments, such as U.S. State Department pilots using chatbots to deflect routine inquiries or Canada's transparent use of analytics in visa triage, suggest that AI can help consular systems escape the throughput trap if designed with governance and accountability at the core (Doubleday 2024a, 2024b; IRCC 2024).

In this sense, the paradox of throughput is also an opportunity. By reimagining visa processing with AI, governments can demonstrate that efficiency and fairness are not opposing values but mutually reinforcing. The challenge is to build systems that deliver faster outcomes while preserving the procedural integrity on which consular legitimacy depends.

FOUR CORE USE CASES FOR AI IN VISA PROCESSING

AI is not a panacea for every bottleneck in visa processing, but a handful of applications stand out as both feasible and high-yield. These "core use cases" align directly with existing consular staff pain points and can be piloted without reengineering entire systems. They illustrate how AI can preserve, rather than displace, human authority by focusing on triage, summarization, fraud detection, and validation.

AI Triage and Routing

Visa officers and their teams already sort applications into categories—renewals with strong compliance histories, complex first-time applicants, incomplete submissions, or cases that raise fraud indicators. AI-assisted systems can analyze structured data from visa forms and supporting documents to group cases into lanes—routine, complex, or potentially fraudulent—before officers even open the files. Instead of deciding outcomes, the system creates lanes: expedited green lanes for routine renewals, amber lanes for more complex adjudications, and red lanes for suspected fraud requiring specialist review.

Canada's Immigration, Refugees and Citizenship Canada (IRCC) has been a pioneer in this approach, using advanced analytics to streamline processing while keeping final decisions firmly in human hands (IRCC 2024). For the line officer, this means spending less time shuffling paperwork and more time in the interview room where their judgment has the greatest value.

Waiver and Long-File Summarization

Certain visa categories, such as humanitarian waivers, inadmissibility applications, or the Treaty Investor (E-2) visa, require officers to review application packets that routinely stretch to hundreds of pages. These files, particularly E-visa business plans, are often technically dense, containing complex financial projections, legal documentation, and operational details. This volume and complexity pose a severe challenge to the traditional consular model, which relies on generalist officers who are rotated through sections and rarely gain long-term, specialized expertise in intricate areas like investor visas (GAO 2005).

To cope with this overwhelming demand and lack of specialization, some consular posts have resorted to artificially limiting the application package size, with certain embassies imposing strict single-attachment PDF limits of 70 pages (U.S. Embassy in Paraguay n.d.-h). Such limitations often force applicants to omit critical supporting evidence, increasing the risk of denial or prolonged administrative processing. The result is excessive processing times, with E-visa consular reviews typically ranging from many weeks to six months or more, often extended by subsequent Requests for Evidence (RFEs) due to initial information gaps (Pandev Law n.d.).

Instead of forcing arbitrary limits on evidence, AI provides a superior solution. Large Language Models, when constrained by retrieval from verified sources, can condense these materials into structured briefs that highlight key evidence, inconsistencies, and legal citations. The safeguard here is retrieval augmented generation, which grounds summaries in official documents and makes every output auditable (NIST 2024a). This functionality allows the officer to begin with a clear map of the entire file, eliminating the need for page limits. The AI's ability to efficiently process all supporting documents transforms the adjudication from a hurried, manual triage of incomplete data into a substantive review where the generalist officer's judgment is applied to all the facts, ensuring a fairer, faster, and more robust decision.

Fraud and Forgery Detection

Fraud prevention units traditionally rely on officer intuition, tip-offs, and manual comparisons to uncover document mills or coached narratives. Today, AI can surface patterns that no single officer could see. This includes clustering nearly identical files, identifying metadata anomalies, or flagging recurring sponsor names across supposedly independent applications. For example, clustering algorithms can reveal reused sponsorship letters, ledger anomalies in financial statements, or recurring metadata fingerprints in supposedly independent files. Benchmark datasets such as DocXPand-25k are helping governments evaluate the reliability of these tools before deployment (DocXPand Team 2024). Combined with officer review, this approach helps collapse fraud rings that no single adjudicator could have spotted in isolation, allowing officers to ask probing questions without unfairly prejudging the case. The benefits compound over time. When AI-flagged cases lead to more targeted fraud interviews, the resulting findings—patterns of deception, common cover stories, recurring document techniques—feed back into the system, sharpening both the algorithm's detection capability and the officer's own lines of inquiry. This creates a virtuous cycle in which each successful investigation strengthens the next.

Systematic Validation Studies at Scale

Traditionally, assessing the effectiveness of visa adjudication has relied on small samples and intuition. AI opens the door to systematic validation studies at scale, allowing agencies to refine their risk models with evidence rather than intuition.

Once a visa is issued, the story does not end. The real test of any risk model is whether its predictions hold up—did the applicants it flagged as high risk actually overstay? Did the ones it waved through comply? Machine learning can now answer these questions at scale, tracking post-issuance outcomes across millions of cases and correlating patterns of overstay or noncompliance with specific application features—types of sponsorship, employment categories, or document profiles. The UN's Project Jetson applied similar predictive analytics to model displacement patterns in the humanitarian field (UN Global Pulse 2018–2022). For consular affairs, the payoff is sharper risk indicators: validation studies can reveal which factors genuinely predict noncompliance and which are just inherited assumptions dressed up as policy. Crucially, these models require continuous monitoring. Fraud tactics evolve, compliance patterns shift, and a model that was accurate last year can quietly decay—a phenomenon known as model drift—unless it is regularly recalibrated with fresh data. Equally important is how findings are applied: validation results should inform policy and resource allocation broadly rather than feed directly into individual case scores, where population-level correlations can function as proxies for structural bias. At the individual level, the same human-in-the-loop safeguards that govern all AI-assisted adjudication apply without exception.

Before algorithms could do this work, managers had to do it by hand. A case from a U.S. Embassy in Central America around 2007 shows what that looked like. Officers had long assumed that elderly parents of U.S.-based residents were a high overstay risk, and denial rates for this group were steep. To test the assumption, local consular management launched a grueling year-long validation study—tracking every single visa through phone calls, in-person interviews, and manual record checks. The finding was dramatic: the actual overstay rate was minimal, far below what the institution had feared. For this demographic, the pull of home proved stronger than any economic draw to stay. Officers came to recognize the pattern in a particularly vivid way: many of these travelers went to the U.S. carrying boxes of Pollo Campero, the beloved local fried chicken chain, as gifts for relatives—a small ritual that embodied a powerful truth about ties to home (Simon n.d.). That human-led study demonstrated that correcting inherited bias with empirical evidence is a core function of effective consular management—a function that modern AI systems are now designed to perform at massive scale and in near real time.

EXTENDING THE IMPACT TO MANAGEMENT AND TRAINING

Beyond the core four operational use cases, AI has fundamental implications for management and training. Section chiefs supervising teams of officers and locally employed staff can use AI dashboards to monitor workloads, track the pace of adjudications, and identify bottlenecks. For locally employed staff who manage intake queues, document screening, and appointment logistics, these dashboards also surface where their effort is being consumed by tasks AI could absorb—freeing them to apply their language skills and institutional knowledge where it matters most. Managers based in the home capital (e.g., Washington, DC) can aggregate these insights across posts, spotting regional fraud patterns or seasonal surges. This not only supports resource allocation but also provides a stronger evidence base for engagement with attorneys, congressional offices, and host governments, who expect consular sections to justify their practices with data as well as law (GAO 2025).

Digital Frontlines: Canada Opens the AI Black Box— Inside Government's Most Transparent Algorithm

Since 2018, IRCC has deployed machine learning to sort through temporary resident visa applications, using algorithms trained to recognize patterns that predict processing complexity. Unlike typical black-box AI systems in government, Canada chose radical transparency, publishing impact assessments, peer reviews, and performance data.

IRCC reports that routine files flagged by their "advanced analytics" system can be assessed 87% faster than traditional processing, contributing to quicker decisions while helping staff focus expertise where most needed (IRCC 2022). By 2022, the system was assisting with more than one million temporary resident visa files annually.

The technical architecture reveals a deliberate design philosophy keeping humans in control. The system never recommends refusals, only identifies straightforward cases for expedited processing. All final decisions remain with immigration officers, who retain explicit authority to overturn any algorithmic suggestion. A built-in quality assurance loop deliberately redirects a sample of would-be expedited cases back to full human review, ensuring continuous monitoring for bias and performance drift (Immigration, Refugees and Citizenship Canada. 2022).

The program operates under the Treasury Board's Directive on Automated Decision-Making, with a published Algorithmic Impact Assessment classifying the system's impact level as "moderate" and requiring specific safeguards: legal review, privacy analysis, Gender-Based Analysis Plus, and documented rules that don't evolve through machine learning (Immigration, Refugees and Citizenship Canada. 2024a). The transparency extends to public-facing explainers and peer review summaries.

Lucia Nalbandian of Toronto Metropolitan University, who studied the system's development, emphasized how the "tiered triage" model expedites low-complexity files while routing higher-complexity cases to officers—but stressed the critical need for continuous monitoring to prevent algorithmic drift and proxy bias as applicant demographics change (Nalbandian 2021).

The governance architecture offers a template other governments are studying: impact assessments before deployment, peer review during operation, quality assurance sampling, override logging to track human intervention, and public reporting to enable external scrutiny.

Challenges remain. "Automation bias" could lead officers to over defer to algorithmic cues, hidden proxies in data could generate unequal treatment across applicant groups, and questions persist about explaining to applicants why similar cases ended up on different processing tracks. These issues underscore the importance of the transparency and oversight mechanisms that make Canada's approach distinctive.

For visa applicants, the immediate impact is tangible: shorter wait times for straightforward cases and more focused attention from officers handling complex situations. For digital government globally, Canada's experiment provides evidence that citizens can have both AI-assisted public services and the transparency needed to hold those systems accountable.

These use cases illustrate that the most powerful role of AI in visa processing is not to replace officer judgment but to extend it. By handling the volume, organizing information, and surfacing hidden connections, AI allows human decision-makers to focus on where they add the most value: applying context, exercising discretion, and ensuring that the process remains fair and humane.

DATA AND MODEL DESIGN: FROM INPUTS TO DECISIONS

Every visa decision is only as sound as the information on which it rests. AI tools are no exception. Their performance depends on how data is collected, processed, and transformed into outputs that officers can interpret and act upon. Understanding the architecture—what goes in, how it is processed, and what comes out—is essential to ensure that these systems reinforce rather than distort consular judgment.

The inputs to visa AI systems are varied but familiar. They include structured application data drawn from digital forms such as the DS-160 or DS-261 (U.S. forms), biometric metadata like facial or fingerprint templates, uploaded documents such as bank statements and invitation letters, and unstructured officer notes from prior interviews. Increasingly, external signals like booking channel patterns or historical compliance records are added to enrich the dataset. Each of these inputs carries its own governance requirements, from privacy safeguards to retention limits, and must be validated for quality. An incomplete or poorly structured data feed can generate misleading outputs, no matter how advanced the model.

Once ingested, data passes through a pipeline. Optical character recognition and computer vision can normalize scanned documents; natural language processing extracts entities from narrative statements; machine learning models then convert these into features that can be compared across applicants. A feature store—essentially a memory of patterns seen before—allows the system to spot recurring anomalies, such as the same sponsor name appearing in multiple unrelated cases. Crucially, before deployment, the model must be subject to rigorous fairness testing to identify and mitigate proxy variables for protected characteristics, preventing the system from replicating historical patterns of discriminatory outcomes. At each stage, explainability is critical. Officers must be able to see why a system flagged a case, whether due to a formatting anomaly, an unusual financial pattern, or a similarity to known fraud clusters.

The outputs are not final adjudications but structured aids: a risk score accompanied by reason codes, a summarized request packet highlighting key evidence, or a triage lane assignment. The design principle is transparency. Officers should never be confronted with an opaque red or green light; instead, they need context to exercise discretion. The U.S. National Institute of Standards and Technology's AI Risk Management Framework stresses that explainability and human oversight are fundamental to responsible AI deployment (NIST 2023). Similarly, the Office of Management and Budget requires agencies to ensure that AI systems provide traceable rationale for their recommendations (Office of Management and Budget 2024).

Finally, the user interface is where design either builds or erodes trust. Dashboards that display scores without explanation risk alienating officers. By contrast, interfaces that show the factors influencing a recommendation, highlight similar past cases, and provide clear override options foster confidence. The officer remains the final decision-maker, but now with a map of the data terrain at their fingertips.

In sum, effective visa AI design begins with clean, well-governed inputs, passes through transparent processing pipelines, and culminates in outputs that inform rather than dictate. The officer's role does not diminish—it is clarified. The system handles the volume and structure; the human applies context, judgment, and accountability.

TRIAGE PLAYBOOK: OPERATIONAL PATTERNS

One of the clearest ways to see AI in action is through triage—the sorting of visa cases into operational categories that align with officer expertise and risk levels. Properly designed, a triage system does not replace human review but organizes it, ensuring that scarce officer attention is directed where it is most needed.

A green lane captures low-risk renewals. Applicants with a history of compliance, clean biometric records, and straightforward documentation can be routed here for expedited processing. Machine learning models trained on past compliance data can highlight such cases with high accuracy, allowing officers to confirm and move quickly. The advantage is not just speed but consistency: renewals are treated uniformly rather than depending on which officer happens to receive the file.

An amber lane handles first-time or complex cases. These are the files where rules may be clear, but context matters—students with unusual funding arrangements, workers sponsored by new companies, or travelers from regions with rapidly changing political conditions. AI tools can surface the complexities but stop short of recommendation, preserving officer discretion. By clearly flagging that a case is "amber," the system signals that human judgment is the decisive factor.

A red lane identifies high-risk or potentially fraudulent cases. Here, clustering algorithms and anomaly detection can reveal reused sponsorship letters, suspiciously uniform bank statements, or shared contact details across multiple applicants. The system's role is to surface suspicion not to adjudicate. Red-lane cases are routed to Fraud Prevention Units or senior adjudicators, where deeper investigation and interagency coordination often follow.

Finally, an auto-cure lane manages incomplete or defective submissions. Natural language processing can detect missing documents or inconsistencies and automatically generate requests in the applicant's preferred language. This saves officers from drafting repetitive deficiency letters and reduces back-and-forth delays.

Each of these lanes has a parallel in traditional consular practice; AI simply accelerates and structures the sorting. By aligning digital triage with familiar categories, posts minimize the learning curve and build officer confidence. Crucially, officers retain override authority at every stage, with the system logging when and why an override occurs. This log should include a mandated narrative justification, tying the override to a specific policy or contextual factor the algorithm missed. These logs not only protect accountability but also provide valuable data for retraining models and refining thresholds. The override log effectively becomes the gold standard for continuous model improvement and is subject to mandatory, periodic audit.

When implemented carefully, triage is more than a workflow optimization—it is a redistribution of scarce human attention. Routine renewals move faster, incomplete applications are addressed automatically, fraud rings are surfaced earlier, and officers can devote their time to the amber cases where judgment, empathy, and discretion are indispensable.

ETHICS, GUARDRAILS, AND GOVERNANCE

The use of AI in visa processing raises not only operational questions but also ethical and legal ones. The stakes are unusually high: decisions can affect an individual's education, employment, or family life, and errors risk reputational harm to the consular system itself. For AI to be credible in this environment, it must be governed by clear guardrails that protect rights while enabling efficiency.

The first and most fundamental safeguard is human-in-the-loop oversight. AI may triage, summarize, or flag anomalies, but the authority to grant or refuse a visa must remain with an officer. This principle is enshrined in regulatory frameworks such as the EU Artificial Intelligence Act, which classifies migration and border control systems as "high risk" and therefore subject to strict requirements for human review (European Union 2024). The U.S. Office of Management and Budget similarly mandates that safety- or rights-impacting AI systems be subject to inventories, impact assessments, and human decision checkpoints (Office of Management and Budget 2024).

Explainability is the second guardrail. Officers cannot defend or explain decisions if the tools they rely on are opaque. AI outputs must be accompanied by clear reason codes, confidence scores, and links back to source documents. The U.S. National Institute of Standards and Technology's AI Risk Management Framework stresses that explainability is not a technical luxury but a prerequisite for trust and accountability (NIST 2023). Without it, officers risk becoming passive enforcers of algorithmic outputs, a scenario incompatible with the discretionary nature of consular work.

Third, systems must be designed for fairness and inclusion. Civil society critiques of digital border systems warn that poorly governed automation can entrench bias and deepen inequities (Amnesty International 2024). This risk is particularly acute in visa processing, where applicants from marginalized backgrounds may lack access to the kinds of documentation or financial records that models assume as "normal." Agencies must therefore conduct regular audits for disparate impacts across demographic groups and ensure that alternative pathways—such as interviews, affidavits, or humanitarian exceptions—remain robust.

To move beyond post-hoc auditing, agencies must define and commit to quantitative algorithmic fairness metrics during the design phase. For instance, achieving fairness may require ensuring equal false positive rates (false flags for fraud) or equal false negative rates (false denials) across defined demographic groups, a concept known as disparate mistreatment (NIST 2023). Successful mitigation often requires technical intervention, such as reweighting training data or modifying the model's learning objective, rather than relying solely on observational checks after deployment. The U.K.'s discontinuation of its visa streaming algorithm in 2020 after documented bias concerns serves as a cautionary case (The Guardian 2020).

In the past, consular managers may have tried to address this type of systemic bias manually—a process that required immense labor and time, as seen in the multi-month validation study on elderly overstay risk in Central America (U.S. Government Accountability Office 2008). The difference today is scale and speed: AI allows the system to continuously calculate these bias metrics across all demographics and posts in real time, making policy refinement an evidence-driven, ongoing process rather than a sporadic, resource-intensive audit.

Privacy and data minimization are equally nonnegotiable. Visa applications contain some of the most sensitive personal information governments handle. AI systems must limit data collection to what is strictly necessary, enforce retention schedules, and protect against unauthorized reuse. Privacy impact assessments, such as those published for the U.S. Consular Consolidated Database, demonstrate how agencies can document safeguards and reassure both applicants and oversight bodies (U.S. Department of State, Bureau of Consular Affairs 2023b).

Finally, transparency to the public matters. Applicants should be informed when AI is used in the processing of their cases and should have clear avenues to appeal or seek redress. Oversight reports such as the U.S. Privacy and Civil Liberties Oversight Board's examination of facial recognition at TSA provide a template for how agencies can balance security needs with accountability by publishing scope, safeguards, and outcomes (PCLOB 2025).

In sum, AI in visa processing can only succeed if it is bound by strong governance. Human oversight, explainability, fairness, privacy, and transparency are not optional—they are the conditions under which efficiency can coexist with rights. Without them, AI risks accelerating not just processing times but also mistrust. With them, it becomes a tool that strengthens both the legitimacy and the humanity of consular affairs.

There is a legal dimension to this governance imperative that deserves mention. In many countries, consular decisions—particularly visa refusals—enjoy a degree of protection from judicial review. Courts have traditionally deferred to consular officers on the grounds that visa adjudication involves the exercise of sovereign discretion by a trained professional. In the U.S., this principle is known as consular nonreviewability and has deep roots in immigration law. Similar doctrines, formal or informal, exist in other legal systems.

This protection matters for the AI discussion because it rests on an assumption: that a human officer genuinely exercised professional judgment. If an applicant could credibly argue that an algorithm made the effective decision and the officer merely ratified a machine-generated recommendation, the rationale for shielding that decision from review could weaken. Courts or oversight bodies might ask whether discretion was truly exercised or merely performed. This is one more reason why human-in-the-loop design must be genuine, not nominal. Officers must engage substantively with AI outputs—questioning, overriding, and documenting their reasoning—so that every decision remains defensibly human. The legal architecture that protects consular authority depends on it.

KPIS AND METRICS

No pilot can succeed without clear measures of progress. AI in visa processing is particularly sensitive because efficiency gains alone are not enough; posts must also demonstrate accuracy, fairness, and accountability. Key performance indicators (KPIs) therefore need to cover not just speed but also quality, equity, and trust.

Speed and throughput are the most visible metrics. Missions can track average decision times, the percentage of cases resolved without additional applicant follow-up, and the reduction in officer hours spent on repetitive tasks. In early deployments, even modest time savings—such as cutting an hour off the preparation of long waiver files—can translate into significant cumulative gains across thousands of cases.

Quality indicators measure whether automation improves or degrades adjudications. These include error rates, reversal rates on supervisory reviews, and the clarity of communications sent to applicants. If AI summaries or triage tools increase the rate of rework, the gains in speed are illusory. Beyond general error rates, a critical measure for any triage system is the Model Misclassification Rate (MMR). For instance, officers should track the rate at which the AI False Negatively classifies a case—a case that should have been routed to a fraud *red lane* but was instead sent to a routine *green lane*. Conversely, a high false positive rate (flagging too many legitimate cases as red) indicates algorithmic inefficiency that will severely strain officer time. Tracking this imbalance is essential to proving the automation is adding value, not simply shifting the officer's workload. Missions should track not only whether cases are processed faster but whether they are processed better.

Fairness metrics help ensure that efficiency does not come at the expense of equity. Agencies can monitor false positive and false negative rates across demographic groups, check for disparities in processing times by applicant type, and survey whether outcomes appear consistent across languages and nationalities. Independent studies such as NIST's demographic evaluations of face recognition demonstrate how systematic measurement can reveal performance gaps that would otherwise remain hidden (Grother, Ngan, and Hanaoka 2019).

Trust indicators provide a window into perception, which is as important as performance. Officer surveys can capture satisfaction with new tools, burnout proxies, or confidence in explainability features. Applicant surveys can gauge perceptions of fairness, transparency, and clarity of communication. Oversight reports such as those produced by the U.S. Government Accountability Office show how external evaluation can complement internal monitoring, reinforcing legitimacy (GAO 2025). Beyond surveys, a crucial behavioral indicator of applicant trust and perceived fairness is the Rate of Initial Appeals or Requests for Redress. A sudden spike in the volume of formal challenges, congressional inquiries, or legal actions following the introduction of an AI tool may signal that applicants perceive the system as opaque or unfair, eroding public faith in the consular process (GAO 2025). Monitoring this rate provides an objective, real-world proxy for systemic trust. Together, these KPIs form a balanced scorecard.

Efficiency is tracked, but only alongside fairness and trust. Missions that publish or at least share these metrics internally can build confidence among staff and stakeholders that AI is serving the mission's values as well as its workload. By measuring across these dimensions, consular sections can avoid the trap of chasing raw speed and instead demonstrate that AI is making the system both faster and fairer.

SIDEBARS AND GLOBAL POSTCARDS

The adoption of AI in visa processing is not confined to one country or region; it is a global phenomenon unfolding in diverse contexts. Looking outward offers practical lessons and cautionary tales that can inform how posts design and govern their own pilots.

In South Africa, the government is implementing a new AI-powered Electronic Travel Authorization (ETA) system with the explicit goal of revolutionizing security and scalability within its borders. Built to replace archaic, paper-based processes, the ETA leverages machine learning technology to fully automate the application review and adjudication process for short-term tourist visas, verifying up to 40 passport features and matching biometrics using facial recognition upon arrival (Home Affairs 2025). This digital transformation directly addresses systemic issues like high manual workload and susceptibility to corruption by reducing human interference and bias. By streamlining entry, the system serves as a model for scalable governance in the Global South, aiming to boost tourism numbers significantly while simultaneously strengthening national security against fraud and illicit entry.

In the Asia Pacific region, CGI Federal's Atlas360 initiative represents a vendor-driven model. Announced in 2023, the project integrates AI into U.S. visa-processing support, promising fraud detection and workflow optimization at scale (CGI 2023). While details remain limited, the move highlights how private sector systems are positioning themselves as overlays rather than replacements for existing consular infrastructure. The lesson here is that posts evaluating vendor offerings must insist on standards—explainability, auditability, and data sovereignty—before adoption.

VFS Global's ViVA chatbot, launched in 2025 across 141 countries, illustrates how service providers are using AI to manage front-end demand. By answering routine questions and guiding applicants through requirements, the system reduces pressure on consular inboxes (VFS Global 2025). While ViVA does not touch adjudication, its reach demonstrates how AI can reshape the applicant experience at scale. Missions can learn from this model by adopting similar 24/7 support tools, provided that escalation pathways to human officers remain clear.

Conversely, the U.K.'s decision to abandon its visa streaming algorithm in 2020 after civil society groups revealed discriminatory impacts serves as a stark reminder of what happens when transparency and fairness are neglected (The Guardian 2020). The episode damaged public trust and highlighted the need for continuous fairness audits and avenues for appeal.

These "postcards" show that there is no single path to AI adoption. Some governments lead with transparency, others with vendor partnerships, and still others with service provider tools. What unites the successful examples is not technology but governance: human-in-the-loop design, clear communication, and a willingness to correct course when tools fall short.

COMMON PITFALLS AND FIXES

Every innovation in consular affairs arrives with both promise and peril. AI is no exception. While the potential gains in speed, consistency, and fraud detection are real, early deployments have also revealed recurring missteps. Recognizing these pitfalls—and knowing how to fix them—can mean the difference between a successful pilot and a costly setback.

One of the most frequent problems is black-box fatigue. Officers quickly lose confidence when confronted with outputs that lack explanations. A red or green flag without context feels more like a command than a tool. The fix is straightforward but essential: require reason codes, confidence scores, and links to source documents for every AI output. This design choice transforms the system from a mysterious oracle into a transparent partner, one that officers can interrogate and override with confidence (NIST 2023).

A second pitfall is pilot sprawl. Enthusiasm for AI can lead missions to experiment with too many tools at once—triage dashboards, chatbots, waiver summarizers—without clear metrics for success. The result is confusion, uneven adoption, and wasted effort. The remedy is to start narrow: choose one "Goldilocks problem" that is important but tractable, define three measurable success indicators, and evaluate rigorously before expanding. Canada's approach to visa analytics illustrates this discipline, rolling out in phases and publishing clear scope statements (Immigration, Refugees and Citizenship Canada 2022).

Bias drift is a subtler but dangerous failure mode. Even well-calibrated models can begin to skew over time as fraud tactics evolve or as the applicant pool changes. Left unchecked, this drift can produce unfair outcomes across demographic groups. Regular fairness audits, modeled on the demographic evaluations conducted by the U.S. National Institute of Standards and Technology for facial recognition systems (Grother, Ngan, and Hanaoka 2019), provide a way to detect and correct drift before it erodes trust.

Finally, legacy system gridlock can stall even the best-designed pilots. Many consular IT platforms were not built to accommodate modern AI tools, making integration slow and cumbersome. Officers may respond by experimenting with unapproved "shadow IT" solutions, creating security and privacy risks. The fix here is to use overlays rather than replacements—tools that ingest data, analyze it, and return outputs without requiring wholesale reengineering of existing systems. Vendor contracts should also include exit clauses and data portability requirements to avoid lock-in (Office of Management and Budget 2024).

The common thread across these pitfalls is that none is insurmountable. Each has a corresponding fix grounded in transparency, discipline, and governance. By anticipating black-box fatigue, pilot sprawl, bias drift, and system gridlock, consular operations can approach AI adoption with realism rather than naïveté—ensuring that innovation strengthens, rather than undermines, the integrity of visa adjudication. However, achieving this disciplined adoption requires a corresponding shift in organizational culture and workforce expertise. Merely deploying robust AI models is insufficient if the human operators lack the skills to maintain model integrity, interpret complex confidence scores, or challenge algorithmic output when appropriate. Long-term success therefore hinges on moving AI from an experimental IT function to a core consular competency, necessitating substantial investments in data literacy, technical training, and new internal mechanisms for continuous algorithmic oversight.

FUTURE SIGNALS TO WATCH

Technology does not stand still, and neither can governance. Four emerging signals deserve attention from consular and immigration policymakers—not because they all require immediate action, but because the window for shaping their trajectory is closing.

The first and most urgent is synthetic fraud powered by generative AI. Tools that can produce convincing deepfakes, fabricated support letters, and polished personal statements are already in the hands of bad actors. A document mill that once needed skilled forgers can now generate realistic bank ledgers, sponsorship letters, and even identity photos using off-the-shelf software (ISO/IEC 2023). The challenge for fraud detection is fundamental: systems can no longer rely solely on spotting known forgery patterns. They must also verify where a document came from and whether it has been altered—a shift from pattern recognition to provenance verification. Standards for tracking the origin and integrity of digital content, such as those developed by the Coalition for Content Provenance and Authenticity (C2PA 2025), point the way forward, but they require policy mandates to take hold.

The second signal is the rise of verifiable digital credentials. Imagine an applicant who can prove she holds a university degree or a vaccination record without handing over a paper certificate—and without the consular section having to call the issuing institution. That is what verifiable digital credentials, built on standards from the World Wide Web Consortium (W3C 2025a), are designed to do. These credentials are cryptographically secured and privacy-preserving: they confirm a specific fact without exposing unnecessary personal data. The promise is faster verification with less data handling. The challenge is trust across borders. A consular officer in Nairobi needs to trust a credential issued by a university in São Paulo, and that trust requires internationally agreed standards and legal frameworks that do not yet exist at scale.

The third signal is coalition-based security screening. The EU's forthcoming ETIAS system (European Union 2018) represents a new model: multiple countries sharing a common pretravel screening platform rather than each running separate checks. This kind of cooperation distributes the burden of detection and allows intelligence to be pooled. But it also raises hard questions. When national AI systems are linked across sovereign borders, who is responsible when a shared algorithm produces biased results? Who governs the data? Policy must define transparent oversight mechanisms and clear rules for data sovereignty before these coalitions expand further.

The fourth signal is more speculative but worth watching: advanced anomaly detection. Today's AI models are good at spotting obvious red flags—a forged seal, a recycled template. They are less adept at catching contextual anomalies, cases where a data point is suspicious only in relation to its specific setting. A perfect score on an English proficiency exam from an applicant whose entire profile suggests limited English exposure, for example, is not a forgery—it is a puzzle that requires deeper analysis. Future computational advances will make this kind of multidimensional pattern detection faster and more powerful. The governance question is not about any single technology but about drawing boundaries now: how deep should automated profiling go, and at what point must a human review the flag before it influences a decision?

Taken together, these four signals—from the immediate threat of synthetic fraud to the longer-term questions of digital credentials, coalition screening, and deep anomaly detection—make one point clear: governance cannot afford to be reactive. The rules, standards, and ethical guardrails that will shape consular AI for the next decade need to be built now, while the technology is still taking form.

FIELD CHECKLIST: LAUNCHING A VISA AI PILOT

Before a visa section introduces AI into its adjudication workflow, it must ensure that scope, governance, data, and people are aligned before a single applicant file is processed by an algorithm. The following checklist, designed for both line officers and section chiefs, translates this chapter's core guidance into a prelaunch discipline. Each step is sequential: skipping ahead risks the failure modes this chapter identifies as most common—black-box fatigue, pilot sprawl, bias drift, and legacy gridlock.

Define a Single, Bounded Use Case

Choose one lane of the visa workflow: student renewals with clean compliance records, or document summarization for waiver-heavy applications. Apply the Goldilocks standard—important enough to matter if solved, small enough to test within 90 days, describable in one sentence. Confirm the scope in writing before proceeding. That written statement is your first defense against pilot sprawl.

Establish a Verified Baseline

Measure the status quo before any AI tool is introduced: average time per case review, rate of incomplete submissions, officer hours spent on document summarization weekly, and interview-to-approval ratios by case category. Without a baseline, post-launch efficiency claims are anecdotes rather than evidence. Responsible

AI governance requires missions to demonstrate what changed, and by how much, as a result of any deployment (NIST 2023).

Confirm Data Quality and Privacy Readiness

Review application inputs for completeness and consistency. Strip out any personally identifiable information not required for the pilot's function. Complete a short privacy impact assessment—modeled on those conducted for the Consular Consolidated Database—documenting what data the system accesses, how long it is retained, who can view outputs, and when records will be deleted. This documentation is the audit trail that protects both applicants and the mission if questions arise later.

Require Explainability Before Launch

Every risk score, flag, or triage recommendation must come with reason codes—plain-language explanations of why the system produced that result—and links to the source documents that drove the output. Write this requirement into vendor contracts or internal system specifications before deployment begins. Black-box fatigue—the loss of officer confidence that follows unexplained outputs—is among the most common causes of early pilot collapse (NIST 2023).

Embed Human-in-the-Loop Safeguards at Every Decision Point

Document in advance exactly where human judgment is required. In a triage system, no application is approved, denied, or advanced without officer review of the AI's recommendation. In a summarization tool, officers read source documents before relying on AI-generated summaries for consequential decisions. Escalation pathways—how a flagged case reaches a supervisor, how an affected applicant can seek review—must be operational before go-live. Migration-related AI carries the highest governance obligations of any public sector application, and human oversight is nonnegotiable.

Train Staff Before They Use the System

Staff who encounter an unfamiliar AI tool mid-caseload default to one of two failure modes: over-reliance, deferring to outputs without scrutiny, or avoidance, ignoring the tool entirely. Neither is acceptable. Prelaunch training should cover how the system works, what its known limitations and demographic performance gaps are, how to read and challenge outputs, and how to report anomalies. Automation bias—the documented tendency to overdefer to algorithmic cues even when they conflict with an officer's own judgment—is a known risk in AI-assisted visa adjudication and must be addressed explicitly in training, not assumed away (NIST 2023).

Name a Pilot Owner and Define a Stop-Loss Threshold

Every pilot needs a preagreed trigger for pause or shutdown: an error rate exceeding 5% of the baseline, or demographic performance gaps beyond defined tolerances.

Bias drift—the gradual skewing of model outputs as applicant pools or fraud tactics evolve—does not announce itself; it must be actively measured through regular fairness audits across demographic groups, running continuously for the life of the pilot, not just at launch. Document the stop-loss threshold and obtain section leadership sign-off before launch. Name a single pilot owner responsible for weekly metric reviews, staff feedback collection, and escalation if thresholds are approached. External oversight bodies have consistently found that pilots without named owners and defined exit criteria consume resources while delivering ambiguous results (GAO 2025).

When these seven conditions are met—bounded scope, verified baseline, privacy-ready data, explainable outputs, human oversight, trained officers, and a named owner with a stop-loss trigger—a visa section can move forward with confidence. The goal is not to make AI deployment easy. It is to make it auditable, reversible, and fair. A pilot built on this checklist is a disciplined experiment, not a gamble: one capable of proving, within weeks, that AI can return time to officers without displacing the judgment that visa adjudication demands.

CLOSING REFLECTION

The throughput paradox that opened this chapter—more applicants, more data, more scrutiny, less time—will not resolve itself. Staffing alone cannot close the gap, and speed without safeguards invites the failures that Visa Express and its aftermath made painfully clear. What AI offers is not a shortcut but a rebalancing: machines handling the volume so that officers can invest in the judgment. But that rebalancing will not happen on its own. Without explicit guidance from headquarters, the natural institutional response to any efficiency gain is to push higher volume—more interviews per hour, more cases per day. The Time Dividend must be protected by policy, not just principle. Headquarters guidance should direct that time reclaimed through AI be allocated to increased scrutiny of complex cases, more thorough interviews, and the kind of careful, human-centered adjudication that the technology was designed to protect. In the Republic of Z, that disciplined rebalancing gave a consular section 48 hours to catch a fraud ring it would otherwise have missed. The technology flagged the pattern; the officers made the call. Every visa AI pilot should preserve that sequence in the case record: what the system flagged, what evidence the officer reviewed, whether the alert was cleared or escalated, and why.

3 AI in Passport Services and Identity Verification

Modern e-passports can make passport fraud more difficult. However, the best tool to combat passport fraud is to utilize the digital photos contained in e-passports to biometrically verify that a person who presents a travel document is the true bearer of that document.

—U.S. Department of Homeland Security (U.S. Customs and Border Protection 2025)

Unregulated use of facial recognition technology poses significant risks to civil rights, especially for marginalized groups who have historically borne the brunt of discriminatory practices.

—Rochelle Garza, Chair of the U.S. Commission on Civil Rights (quoted in U.S. Commission on Civil Rights 2024)

A centralized database of biometric data belonging to refugees, without appropriate controls, could really lead to surveillance of those refugees as well as potentially coercive forms of scrutiny.

—Amos Toh, Senior Researcher, Artificial Intelligence and Human Rights, Human Rights Watch (quoted in Corrigan 2019)

Opening Vignette: 20 Years Later in the Republic of Z

At a passport office in the Republic of Z, a middle-aged traveler approaches the counter to renew a document first issued two decades earlier. The officer studies the old passport photo: a youthful face with different hair, smoother skin, and a gaze shaped by another stage of life. The applicant standing before her looks little like the image on record. Lines of age, a different hairstyle, and subtle shifts in facial structure complicate the comparison. The officer hesitates, aware of the stakes. A mismatch could mean weeks of delay, new interviews, or even denial.

DOI: 10.1201/9781003634775-5

But this morning, the officer has more than instinct to rely on. A biometric system enhanced with AI runs a one-to-one comparison between the decades-old photo and the live capture just taken. The algorithm accounts for age progression, adjusting for changes in skin texture, weight, and hair. At the same time, fingerprint verification provides a secondary match. Within seconds, the dashboard returns a high-confidence confirmation: despite the surface differences, the applicant is indeed the same person.

Relieved, the officer moves forward with the renewal. Processing that might once have dragged on for months—pending manual reviews and additional documentation—concludes in minutes. The applicant, who needs the new passport for a family emergency abroad, leaves the office reassured. The officer, too, feels a measure of confidence: her judgment has not been replaced, but reinforced by tools designed to bridge the gap between past and present identity.

The vignette is fictional, but the dilemma it portrays is real. Around the world, passport agencies confront millions of renewals where biometric continuity must be established across years or decades. The Republic of Z serves here as an illustration of what becomes possible when AI can hold a single identity steady across decades of change—reading past and present as the same person where the unaided eye can only hesitate.

WHY PASSPORT AI, WHY NOW?

Passports represent the highest form of state-backed identity. They serve not only as travel documents but also as gateways to mobility, security, and citizenship itself. Errors in their issuance or renewal carry consequences that are both personal and political. An applicant wrongly denied may face missed medical treatment, lost educational opportunities, or separation from family. A fraudulent passport granted to an impostor can compromise border integrity and national security. For these reasons, passport operations are among the most scrutinized in consular affairs, and the pressure to deliver speed without sacrificing integrity has never been greater.

Demand has surged in the years following the COVID-19 pandemic. In the U.S., for example, more than 24 million passports were issued in 2023, setting an all-time record and placing unprecedented strain on processing systems (GAO 2025). Similar trends have emerged worldwide, with governments struggling to meet public expectations for timely service even as applications grow more complex. Political leaders, confronted with public frustration over delays, have made passport backlogs a matter of national concern.

This pressure has accelerated interest in technology-assisted solutions not only in passport services but across consular and diplomatic operations more broadly—making passport modernization one front in a wider transformation already underway across embassy functions (Kilburg 2025). The challenge is compounded by the dual nature of the passport. Unlike visas, which vary by category and circumstance, passports are universal: every citizen is entitled to one. This universality makes volume management a permanent issue, not a seasonal one. It also magnifies the stakes. Each renewal or issuance must be accurate, equitable, and secure.

AI enters this space as a response to both volume and risk. AI-driven photo analysis can enforce compliance with International Civil Aviation Organization (ICAO) standards, reducing rejections for poor-quality submissions (ICAO 2015–2024). Biometric systems enhanced with machine learning can verify identity continuity even when decades separate the new applicant from the original passport. Antispoofing and morph detection tools, grounded in ISO/IEC presentation attack detection standards, provide defenses against increasingly sophisticated fraud attempts (ISO/IEC 2023).

Governance documents make clear that these capabilities are not optional luxuries. The U.S. Consular Consolidated Database's privacy impact assessments highlight how sensitive personal data must be handled with strict safeguards (U.S. Department of State 2023b). European regulations under the Entry/Exit System likewise emphasize biometric integrity as the cornerstone of trusted travel (European Union 2017). In short, the pressure to modernize is matched by an equally strong imperative to govern.

DRILLING DOWN INTO AI USE CASES

For consular staff, passport work is often the most direct expression of state authority over identity. Every application represents both a right and a responsibility: citizens are entitled to secure travel documents, and governments are obligated to ensure that those documents are authentic, accurate, and resistant to misuse. AI does not alter this responsibility, but strengthens the tools officers and their teams use to uphold it. By enhancing accuracy, reducing preventable delays, and detecting sophisticated forgeries, AI makes passport adjudication more efficient.

One of the most common frustrations in passport operations is the rejection of photographs. Applicants often submit images with poor lighting, incorrect head size, or distracting backgrounds, leading to repeat visits and long queues. AI-enabled capture systems can provide real-time feedback—"move closer," "neutral expression required," or "remove glare"—ensuring that images conform to the International Civil Aviation Organization's global standards for machine-readable travel documents (ICAO 2015–2024). When paired with liveness detection techniques, these tools also help prevent spoofing with altered or synthetic photos (ISO/IEC 2023). For staff, the result is fewer technical rejections and more time to focus on adjudication rather than resubmissions.

Beyond photos, AI supports biometric verification in renewals and identity continuity checks. Citizens renewing passports after decades may look very different from their original images, creating uncertainty at the counter. AI-assisted facial recognition models can account for age progression and natural changes, while fingerprint verification serves as a secondary anchor. Independent evaluations by the U.S. National Institute of Standards and Technology show how multimodal fusion—combining face and fingerprint data—reduces error rates compared to either system alone (Grother, Ngan, and Hanaoka 2019). For officers, this means confidence in approving routine renewals.

AI also enhances the fight against forgery and tampering, which remains central to consular fraud prevention. Breeder documents such as birth or marriage certificates are frequent targets for alteration, and the rise of generative tools has made forged files more convincing. AI-based forensic tools can analyze fonts, compression layers, and metadata inconsistencies to detect manipulations invisible to the human eye (Farid 2009). Standards for content provenance, such as those developed by the Coalition for Content Provenance and Authenticity, offer additional assurance by embedding digital credentials that prove whether a document has been altered (C2PA 2025). These technologies provide consular officers and their teams with clearer grounds to escalate suspicious cases, ensuring that legitimate applicants are served while impostors are intercepted.

For consular teams responding to crises, AI can streamline emergency passport issuance. In high-stakes scenarios like the 2021 Kabul evacuation, where citizens lacked physical documents or had expired credentials, officers and their teams must verify identity quickly with minimal information and maximum stress. AI tools accelerate this process by instantly comparing any available biometric data (e.g., stored fingerprints) against centralized repositories, allowing officers to approve travel letters and emergency passports with greater confidence and speed (U.S. Department of State n.d.-c). Singapore's Immigration and Checkpoints Authority has already demonstrated the feasibility of passport-less biometric clearance, showing how automated identity checks can operate at scale without slowing throughput (ICA 2024). While the stakes in ACS are higher because of the urgency, AI provides officers with faster and more reliable triage so they can focus on exceptional circumstances.

At the managerial level, section chiefs can use AI-driven dashboards to monitor processing times, rejection rates, and demographic parity in outcomes. This evidence base helps them justify staffing requests, communicate with headquarters, and engage with host governments about identity standards. At headquarters, policy officers and their teams can draw on validation studies that track how well biometric systems perform across populations, ensuring that equity and access are not sacrificed in the pursuit of speed (Valdivia, Corbera-Serrajòrdia, and Swianiewicz 2021). In this way, AI supports not only individual adjudications but also systemic improvements in fairness and transparency.

These use cases reaffirm a simple truth: passports are more than documents; they are symbols of trust between citizen and state. AI cannot—and should not—replace the officer who exercises judgment at the counter. But by enforcing technical standards, strengthening biometric verification, exposing forgeries, and streamlining crisis response, AI provides officers and their teams with the tools they need to protect both the integrity of the system and the dignity of the people they serve.

PHOTO COMPLIANCE AND LIVENESS: FIRST LINE OF DEFENSE

For most applicants, the passport photo seems like the simplest part of the renewal process. Yet in practice, it is one of the most frequent points of failure. Photographs are often rejected for poor lighting, incorrect backgrounds, improper head size, or outdated images that no longer reflect the applicant's appearance. Each rejection adds days or weeks to processing times and fuels public frustration. In high-volume environments, even small error rates translate into thousands of cases delayed.

AI can reduce these rejections by enforcing international standards at the point of capture. The International Civil Aviation Organization's Doc 9303 specifies requirements for machine-readable travel documents, including precise rules for photo composition—such as uniform background color, eye visibility, and proportion of head to frame (ICAO 2015–2024). AI-enabled photo capture systems, deployed via kiosks or mobile applications, can instantly check compliance and prompt applicants to adjust before submission. Simple cues like "move closer," "remove glare," or "neutral expression required" transform the photo stage from a recurring bottleneck into a streamlined entry point.

Equally important is liveness detection, the safeguard that ensures a photo represents a real, live individual rather than a manipulated or synthetic image. Standards under ISO/IEC 30107 define methods for presentation attack detection, ranging from blink and head movement cues to more advanced 3D analysis (ISO/IEC 2023). Such defenses are increasingly necessary as generative tools make it easier to create convincing forgeries or digitally altered images. By screening out spoofs at the earliest stage, liveness detection prevents fraudulent applications from advancing deeper into the system, where they would consume more officer time and pose higher risks.

These tools must also be accessible. Applicants should be able to complete the process across multiple platforms—mobile phones, kiosks, or local service centers—with guidance provided in multiple languages. Voice prompts, visual cues, and offline functionality can extend inclusivity, ensuring that people with limited literacy, poor connectivity, or disabilities are not excluded. The goal is not just to reduce errors but to make compliance achievable for everyone.

Field experience shows that even modest interventions can pay dividends. Posts that deployed QR-coded posters linking applicants to guided photo apps reported significant drops in rejection rates, saving hours of officer review time each week. These efficiencies compound at scale: fewer rejections mean fewer resubmissions, shorter queues, and more predictable workloads.

In sum, photo compliance and liveness detection form the first line of defense in AI-enabled passport services. By embedding international standards, antispoofing safeguards, and accessibility features into the intake process, missions can protect integrity while also improving the applicant experience. What was once a source of frustration becomes, with AI's support, a predictable and equitable gateway to the passport system.

Digital Frontlines: America's Digital Passport Revolution—When Government Goes AI-First

The U.S. State Department's online passport renewal system, fully launched nationwide in 2024, employs computer vision algorithms, automated fraud detection, and machine learning-assisted workflows to process applications. The platform represents a sophisticated AI deployment reshaping how America manages citizen identity in the digital age.

The eligibility requirements reveal careful design philosophy. Applicants must have been at least 16 years old when their most recent passport was issued, be renewing a ten-year book that's expiring within a year or expired less than five years ago, with no changes to core biographical information, and reside in the U.S. (U.S. Department of State 2025a). These restrictions channel straightforward renewals into AI-assisted processing while directing complex cases to human adjudication.

The system requires digital photos meeting precise specifications: JPEG format, at least 600×600 pixels, with ample margins for automated cropping. Common rejection messages reveal the AI at work—flagging backgrounds that aren't plain enough, images with poor exposure, heads positioned outside algorithmic tolerance, or compression artifacts that would later fail human review (U.S. Department of State 2024c). Human officers and their teams still conduct final photo reviews, while agencies increasingly pair quality checks with back-office tools that can flag suspected morphed photos or synthetic imagery before human adjudication (NIST 2025).

Passport records are retained for 100 years according to U.S. State Department schedules, while front-end web session data receives much shorter retention periods. Historical privacy assessments document the use of automated "Photo Quality Check" services while emphasizing human authority over final decisions (U.S. Department of State 2015, 2021).

The 2023 passport backlogs revealed important lessons about digital transformation limits. GAO analysis showed that specialists spent more time processing digital applications than paper ones during the pilot phase. The massive backlogs were ultimately resolved through mandatory overtime—over 250,000 additional staff hours—rather than technological improvements (GAO 2025). The lesson reinforced that AI-assisted processing must be carefully designed to complement rather than complicate human workflows during crisis periods.

Accessibility considerations demonstrate how thoughtfully designed AI systems can expand access to government services. The U.S. State Department maintains parallel channels for citizens who cannot use the online system, publishes dedicated guidance for people with disabilities, and provides Spanish-language resources (U.S. Department of State 2025b, 2025d).

Questions remain about algorithmic governance as photo submission becomes increasingly automated and AI-screened, including concerns about whether algorithmic assessments could inadvertently encode biases and how long human review will remain standard practice. The passport system's careful balance—automation for efficiency, humans for accountability, transparency about process—offers a template for responsible AI deployment across government functions.

MULTIMODAL BIOMETRICS IN THE REAL WORLD

The foundation of any passport system is identity integrity. Confirming that the person applying is who they claim to be—and not an impostor borrowing, altering, or fabricating credentials—has always been the central challenge of consular work. AI strengthens this foundation by enhancing biometric verification, particularly through multimodal approaches that combine face, fingerprint, and, in some cases, iris data.

Traditionally, passport renewals rely on one-to-one facial comparison: does the new photo match the old? Yet faces change with age, health, or cultural practices such as head coverings. AI-assisted systems can compensate for these variations by using models trained to recognize features that remain stable over time. Age progression algorithms, for instance, adjust comparisons for expected changes in skin texture or facial structure, reducing false negatives in renewals decades apart (NIST 2022).

Still, no single biometric modality is infallible. False matches and false nonmatches vary by demographic group, as documented in independent evaluations by the U.S. National Institute of Standards and Technology (Grother, Ngan, and Hanaoka 2019). To mitigate this, agencies increasingly use multimodal fusion, combining the strengths of face and fingerprint verification. Fingerprints, less subject to age-related drift, provide a stable anchor; facial recognition adds convenience and speed. When fused, the result is higher accuracy and lower error rates than either system alone. For a detailed analysis of multimodal fusion architecture and the metrics of accuracy and equity, see Chapter 7.

Operationally, multimodal systems are already in use. Singapore's Immigration and Checkpoints Authority has deployed biometric gates that combine face and iris recognition, allowing passport-free clearance for departing passengers (ICA 2024). In Europe, the now fully operational Entry/Exit System uses biometric data to digitally register non-EU short-stay travelers when they cross Schengen external borders, replacing passport stamps and strengthening identity verification and overstay detection (European Union 2017). These deployments demonstrate that multimodal approaches are not experimental—they are rapidly becoming the global standard.

For consular posts, the implications are significant. Multimodal biometrics can detect duplicate identities across databases, identify impostors attempting to assume another's record, and provide stronger assurance in complex cases such as twins, applicants with trauma-related changes, or transgender applicants undergoing transitions. Properly governed, these systems enhance both security and fairness: they protect against fraud while reducing the likelihood of legitimate applicants being unfairly flagged.

Yet safeguards remain essential. Thresholds must be calibrated carefully, and officers must retain the ability to override when results are ambiguous. Transparency is vital: applicants should know when biometrics are used and have access to redress channels if they believe errors have occurred. As Amnesty International and other watchdogs have noted, biometric systems carry risks of exclusion if governance lags behind technology (Amnesty International 2024).

THE IDENTITY GRAPH: CONNECTING THE RIGHT SYSTEMS

A passport is not simply a booklet with a chip—it is one thread in a web of identity records that stretches across agencies, countries, and decades. When an officer processes a renewal, the system behind the counter is quietly checking the applicant against prior passport records, visa histories, biometric databases, and sometimes law enforcement or international watchlists. AI can make those checks faster and more reliable, but only if the systems that hold the data are designed to talk to each other without compromising privacy.

Consular sections at U.S. embassies and consulates already sit at the center of large data networks. The Consular Consolidated Database (CCD) aggregates millions of visa, passport, and service records. It interfaces with the Department of Homeland Security's IDENT/HART biometric repositories, allowing officers and their teams to cross-check fingerprints and facial templates against immigration and enforcement records (DHS/OBIM 2024). In Europe, the Entry/Exit System (EES) and EURODAC serve a similar function, sharing biometric and travel data across member states (European Union 2018).

The question is how these systems should be connected. There are two basic approaches. In the first, a search request is sent out to multiple databases at once, and each one responds with its own results—but no data is copied from one system to another. Think of it as asking several libraries for a book without moving the book off the shelf. This is known as a federated query, and its advantage is privacy: each agency keeps control of its own records. In the second approach, data is copied into a single centralized repository so that searches run faster. The trade-off is risk: more copies of sensitive biometric and personal information mean more opportunities for misuse or breach.

AI can help navigate between these approaches. Machine learning models can determine which databases are most relevant to a given query, prioritize results, and flag conflicts. For example, if an applicant's biometric record appears in both the CCD and an INTERPOL database but with different identifiers—a different name spelling, a mismatched date of birth—AI can surface the discrepancy for officer review. The system should never resolve such conflicts on its own. That judgment belongs to a person.

Privacy safeguards must be built into the architecture from the start. Officers and their teams should see only the data they are authorized to view—a line officer processing a routine renewal does not need access to law enforcement files. Every search should be logged in records that cannot be altered after the fact, creating a clear trail of who looked at what and why. Data should not be kept indefinitely; retention schedules should trigger automated alerts when data reaches its retention limit, with deletion confirmed by an authorized officer. The U.S. State Department's privacy impact assessments for the CCD, and the EU's safeguards for EES and ETIAS, both show how technical integration must be matched by legal and procedural guardrails (U.S. Department of State 2023b; European Union 2018).

The best way to picture how all of this fits together is what technologists call an identity graph. Instead of thinking of an applicant as a single file, imagine a network of connected records: past passport applications, biometric templates, visa histories, and supporting documents, all linked to one person. AI tools can map those connections quickly, surfacing red flags—a duplicate identity filed under two names, a biometric match to a record in another country, an inconsistency between a current application and a decade-old file. The officer then decides what those connections mean: fraud, clerical error, or a legitimate explanation.

Done responsibly, the identity graph becomes a tool of clarity rather than surveillance. It allows officers and their teams to see applicants in context—continuity across decades, links across borders—while preserving rights through transparency, data minimization, and avenues for redress. In a world of increasing mobility and complexity, this connective layer is what makes passport systems both resilient and trustworthy.

FORGERY, TAMPERING, AND THE AI–AI ARMS RACE

Passports sit at the crossroads of trust and technology, and it is precisely this status that makes them attractive targets for fraud. For decades, impostors relied on crude alterations—erasures, glued photographs, or stolen blank booklets. Today, however, the threat landscape has shifted. High-resolution printers, editing software, and, increasingly, generative AI have given forgers new tools to mimic official documents with alarming fidelity. In response, governments are turning to AI not only to detect fraud but to anticipate how the next generation of forgeries will evolve.

The most common vulnerabilities begin with breeder documents: the birth certificates, marriage records, or custody decrees that serve as the foundation for passport applications. Fraudulent breeder documents are often created using cloned templates or manipulated metadata. Digital forensics can reveal subtle tells, such as inconsistent fonts, irregular kerning, or anomalies in compression layers. Classic methods of digital image analysis, detailed by scholars such as Hany Farid, remain highly relevant for training officers and their teams to spot these signs (Farid 2009). But increasingly, AI systems automate this process, flagging irregularities that human eyes might miss.

Generative adversarial networks (GANs) have introduced a new class of threats: synthetic documents. These can produce photographs or scanned pages that appear authentic yet are entirely fabricated. To counter this, AI models are being trained to detect the statistical fingerprints of generative forgeries. Just as spam filters learn to distinguish junk mail from legitimate correspondence, document forensics tools can learn to separate authentic scans from GAN-produced fakes.

One critical safeguard is provenance tagging. The Coalition for Content Provenance and Authenticity (C2PA) has developed specifications that allow images and documents to carry cryptographic credentials showing how and where they were created (C2PA 2025). Applied to passport photos and scanned supporting documents, these standards create a verifiable chain of custody, making tampering easier to detect. For consular officers and their teams, provenance data provides an extra layer of assurance: not only does the document look correct, but its metadata proves it has not been altered since capture.

The result is an AI–AI arms race. Fraudsters experiment with new ways to generate convincing forgeries; governments respond with algorithms designed to unmask them. The contest is uneven—fraudsters need only succeed occasionally, while agencies must maintain near-perfect defenses. Yet by grounding detection in international standards, benchmark datasets, and continuous retraining, consular systems can tilt the balance in their favor. Datasets like DocXPand-25k provide realistic testing grounds for evaluating document AI tools under adversarial conditions (DocXPand Team 2024).

Officers and their teams must retain the authority to question, override, and escalate when anomalies appear. AI may narrow the haystack by surfacing suspicious files, but it is human judgment—anchored in context, empathy, and accountability—that decides what those anomalies mean.

BEYOND THE PHYSICAL PASSPORT: AI AND THE DIGITAL IDENTITY CREDENTIAL

The consular identity mission is rapidly moving beyond the physical passport book. Digital identity credentials—stored on phones and chips rather than in booklets—are becoming the next frontier. This shift changes the role of AI from a one-time verification tool to something more like a continuous security system.

Consider the difference. With a physical passport, security is locked in at the moment of issuance. Once the booklet leaves the counter, there is no way to update it, monitor it, or disable it remotely. A digital credential works differently: it can be monitored, updated, and revoked in real time. AI makes this possible by watching for signs of compromise—unusual access patterns, attempted transfers, or misuse—and alerting authorities instantly. If a digital passport is stolen or cloned, the issuing government can disable it with a keystroke, something no paper document allows.

The privacy advantage is equally significant—and perhaps counterintuitive. Today, when an officer checks a physical passport, the document reveals everything: full name, date of birth, nationality, photo, and more. A digital credential can be designed to reveal only what is needed for a specific interaction and nothing else. Under international standards now being adopted (ISO/IEC 18013-5), an applicant could prove "I am a citizen" or "I am over 21" without disclosing their full name, birth date, or address. The underlying technique is called a Zero-Knowledge Proof—a way of confirming that a fact is true without revealing the data behind it. Think of it as showing a bouncer a card that says "yes, this person is old enough" without the bouncer ever seeing your name or birthday. In this model, AI is not a tool to extract more information from people; it is the engine that enforces minimum disclosure. For consular officers and their teams, this means future systems can be both more secure and more private than the paper-based processes they replace.

The challenge of these highly automated systems is not technical failure but algorithmic bias. Passport systems rely on biometric matching—face, fingerprint, iris—and their performance depends on the quality and diversity of their training data. Research has consistently shown that facial recognition algorithms exhibit higher error rates for certain demographic groups, notably people with darker skin tones and women, risking discriminatory denial or delay for legitimate applicants (Grother, Ngan, and Hanaoka 2019). Governing this technology requires mandatory auditing of disparate impact, not as an afterthought but as a condition of deployment.

EDGE CASES AND EQUITY

Even the most advanced systems struggle when faced with applicants whose identities do not conform neatly to expected biometric or documentary patterns. These "edge cases" reveal the limits of technology and underscore why equity must remain a guiding principle in passport services.

One especially difficult renewal arose at a U.S. consulate overseas. The applicant appeared for a passport renewal appointment wearing a full burka, with her face completely covered. Her new application included a photo in the same attire, showing no facial features at all. The most recent passport she presented as proof of citizenship and identity, issued roughly ten years earlier, and likewise carried a photo with only her eyes visible. To resolve the case, officers and their teams had to search deeper into older records and eventually located a child passport, issued prior to her conversion to Islam, that showed her full face. Even then, final confirmation required sensitive handling: a female officer escorted her to a private space where she briefly removed her covering so her identity could be verified against the older record. Only then could she be asked to return with a compliant photo showing her full face, as required under today's passport standards (U.S. Department of State 2024a, 2024b). The process took an enormous amount of time and was stressful for both the applicant and the staff, underscoring how legacy documents, evolving cultural practices, and rigid technical rules can collide at the passport counter.

Cases like this also highlight how AI-enabled prescreening could reduce unnecessary stress for both sides. If photo capture systems required applicants to upload their images before appearing in person, noncompliant photos—such as those with full face coverings—would be automatically rejected with clear guidance. The U.S. Department of State's rules already specify that while religious head coverings are permitted, the *entire face must remain visible from chin to forehead* (U.S. Department of State 2024b). An AI tool enforcing those standards at intake would have flagged the issue immediately, sparing the applicant a difficult in-person experience and allowing officers and their teams to focus on more complex identity challenges.

Children pose another challenge. Their faces change rapidly as they grow, making long-term biometric continuity harder to establish. Systems trained primarily on adult faces may struggle to verify identity across renewals, while strict thresholds risk high false rejections. Elderly applicants face the opposite problem: fingerprints degrade with age, and changes in facial texture can reduce accuracy. AI models must therefore be calibrated to apply differential match thresholds based on age data, reducing the likelihood of false negatives for faces known to be in rapid flux. Officers must remain alert to avoid unfair denials.

Transgender and nonbinary applicants face their own hurdles. Appearance may change significantly between issuances, and traditional gender markers in databases can complicate verification. Without thoughtful design, AI systems risk producing false negatives that erode dignity and trust. Human oversight and policies affirming continuity of identity even through transition are essential.

Stateless applicants and those displaced by conflict highlight another dimension of equity. Without consistent documentation, biometrics may be the only link to an official identity. AI matching can support continuity, but these applicants often face disproportionate scrutiny, raising concerns about fairness. UNHCR has emphasized the importance of biometrics for inclusion while warning against risks when governance lags behind technology (UNHCR 2022).

Civil society critiques remind us that fairness cannot be reduced to technical performance alone.

An AI system may achieve statistical parity across demographic groups while still disadvantaging those without access to digital infrastructure, literacy, or legal support (Valdivia, Corbera-Serrajòrdia, and Swianiewicz 2021). Edge cases therefore function as stress tests: they reveal whether systems are designed for flexibility and inclusion, or whether they optimize only for the majority. Addressing them requires more than technical fixes; it requires a culture of equity in consular services, one that treats outliers not as anomalies to be managed but as citizens equally entitled to identity and mobility.

The Governing Imperative: Privacy, Auditability, and the Human Backstop

Passport data is not like other government records. Biometrics and core identity files represent the highest form of state–citizen trust—the foundation of citizenship itself, not a provisional permission like a visa. That makes governance in this domain nonnegotiable. Privacy must be designed into every layer of the system, both technical and procedural, from the moment data is captured to the day it is deleted.

The first requirement is a complete and tamper-proof record of everything the system does. Every move the AI makes, every input an officer provides, and every output the model produces must be logged in a way that cannot be altered after the fact. The commissioned officer makes the adjudication decision, not the machine. If an auditor or privacy officer needs to investigate potential bias, system drift, or misuse six months later, the trail must be there—intact and readable. The NIST AI Risk Management Framework makes this kind of transparent logging a baseline expectation for any consequential AI system (NIST 2023).

The second requirement is that human authority over the system must be real, not nominal. The EU Artificial Intelligence Act explicitly classifies AI used in migration and border control as "high risk," imposing strict obligations for human oversight. In practice, this means two things. First, any consular officer must be able to override a system output at any time, for any reason, and that override must be recorded. The officer's judgment is the final word—always. Second, headquarters must define a clear trigger for pulling the system offline. If rejection rates spike beyond an established baseline, or if error patterns emerge that the model cannot explain, the response should be automatic: pause the feature, review the data, and recalibrate before resuming. This is sometimes called a "kill switch," and it exists to ensure that a malfunctioning tool is shut down before it harms applicants—not after.

Together, these safeguards—tamper-proof logging, absolute override authority, and a defined deactivation trigger—ensure that the push for speed never compromises the security or equity of the passport system (NIST 2023; European Union. 2024a; U.S. Department of State, Enterprise AI Strategy 2023).

GLOBAL SNAPSHOTS

Around the world, governments are experimenting with AI and biometrics in passport services, producing a range of lessons that consular posts can adapt. These global snapshots illustrate both the promise of innovation and the importance of governance.

In Singapore, the Immigration and Checkpoints Authority has fully rolled out passport-less clearance at Changi Airport. Travelers pass through automated lanes where face and iris recognition replace the need to present a physical document (ICA 2024). Behind the scenes, ICAO Doc 9303 standards and the ICAO Public Key Directory enable the system to verify chip data securely across borders. For passport-issuing authorities, this demonstrates how robust biometrics, anchored in international standards, can support seamless travel while maintaining trust. This level of integration in Singapore proves that high automation is possible, but it simultaneously forces a clear governance challenge: the system must be governed by a transparent consent framework that can coexist with speed—exactly the balance U.S. passport modernization must achieve.

India has adopted chip-based e-passports and AI-assisted photo capture to enforce compliance with ICAO requirements. By embedding digital security features into passports and supporting them with AI tools that screen out poor-quality photos, India has reduced rejections and made issuance more efficient. This shows how relatively low-cost interventions—standardized chips and guided photo apps—can deliver large improvements in integrity and throughput. The sheer scale of India's biometric system underscores the exponential risk of inequitable performance; if a biometric algorithm has a 1% failure rate, that represents millions of denied or delayed citizens, making the case for a Mandatory Disparate Impact Metric an international human rights imperative.

In Canada and the U.K., pilots have explored risk-based triage for remote renewals. Applicants who meet strict criteria—such as prior compliance and biometric continuity—can complete renewals by mail or online, with AI tools supporting the verification process. This approach reduces strain on in-person appointments while keeping higher-risk cases under officer review.

The EU is moving toward a comprehensive digital identity ecosystem. Regulations establishing the EES and ETIAS require biometric enrollment for travelers, and the AI-enabled infrastructures that support them will directly influence how member states handle passport issuance and renewal (European Union 2018). These large-scale systems illustrate how regional integration can drive adoption of interoperable standards and shared governance frameworks. The EU's binding classification of identity and migration systems as "high risk" validates the central argument of this chapter: the use of AI in passport services is not merely an IT project; it is a high-stakes governance decision requiring mandatory accountability.

These snapshots also highlight the need for balance. While Singapore's seamless gates showcase efficiency, they raise questions about privacy and consent. India's guided capture improves compliance but requires equitable access to technology for applicants in rural areas. EU-wide databases promise interoperability but demand strict oversight to prevent misuse. Each example reinforces the core lesson: technology can only be as trusted as the frameworks that govern it.

For consular posts, these cases provide not blueprints to copy wholesale but reference points to adapt. Local conditions—legal frameworks, cultural expectations, technical capacity—determine what will succeed. Yet the direction of travel is clear: AI-assisted biometrics and digital verification are becoming the norm in passport services, and missions that fail to prepare risk falling behind both operationally and politically.

FIELD CHECKLIST: PASSPORT AI IMPLEMENTATION

Introducing AI into passport services requires a deliberate approach. Unlike incremental adjustments to forms or staffing, AI touches data, privacy, and trust at the deepest levels of identity. For this reason, both headquarters and individual posts must proceed in a phased, transparent, and auditable manner. A clear implementation blueprint helps ensure that innovation strengthens rather than destabilizes the system.

The first step is decision design. Missions should map the renewal and issuance process into discrete stages—photo capture, liveness checks, biometric verification, duplicate detection, and document forensics. This decomposition makes it easier to identify which steps are amenable to automation and which must remain fully under officer control. Early pilots should focus on narrow, high-volume tasks such as photo compliance or one-to-one facial matching for renewals. These are low-risk entry points where AI can demonstrate immediate value without displacing officer judgment.

Next comes technical architecture. A layered model is preferable: data capture feeds into quality and liveness checks; verified inputs flow into biometric matchers; results are displayed to officers via dashboards that always allow override. Privacy by design must be embedded at every stage. Role-based access ensures that only authorized staff see sensitive data. Immutable audit logs record every system action, creating an accountability trail. Retention schedules should be enforced automatically, preventing mission creep by deleting data that is no longer needed.

At headquarters, governance frameworks are indispensable. Procurement guidelines should require vendors to provide explainability features, exportable logs, and compliance with international standards such as ICAO Doc 9303 and ISO/IEC 30107. Model cards—documents that describe a system's scope, data sources, limitations, and retraining schedules—should be mandated for any deployed tool. Oversight bodies, whether internal privacy officers or external auditors, need access to these materials to evaluate performance and fairness.

For consular sections, the emphasis is on pilots and feedback loops. A consular section might begin by piloting an AI-powered photo capture kiosk, running it in shadow mode alongside existing procedures. Consular staff compare outcomes, track error rates, and collect applicant feedback. Weekly reviews provide a chance to tune thresholds, adjust guidance, and document lessons. If performance meets agreed benchmarks, the pilot can expand gradually to other stages, such as duplicate detection or biometric fusion.

Team roles must be clear. A product owner oversees the pilot's scope and ensures alignment with mission needs. A fraud prevention lead validates the system against known adversarial tactics. A privacy counsel reviews data-handling practices. A technical administrator monitors performance and drift, retraining models as necessary. Distributing responsibilities across this small team—which in practice often includes locally employed staff serving as technical administrators or content reviewers—not only builds resilience but also prevents any single officer from carrying the entire burden.

By following this blueprint, consular operations foreign and domestic can move from curiosity to practice in measured steps. The result is a system that evolves responsibly, delivering efficiency and integrity gains without compromising fairness or public trust. AI in passport services does not require a leap into the unknown—it requires disciplined iteration, transparent governance, and unwavering commitment to the principle that human judgment remains central.

WHAT TO MEASURE (KPIS AND VALUE STORY)

The success of AI in passport services cannot be judged by anecdotes or vendor promises alone. It must be demonstrated through clear, measurable outcomes. Key performance indicators (KPIs) provide that evidence, showing whether AI tools are actually improving speed, integrity, and fairness. Just as importantly, they help build the value story—the narrative that explains why innovation is worth sustaining in the eyes of officers, applicants, and policymakers alike.

Quality metrics are the first pillar. These include false acceptance and rejection rates in biometric verification, the percentage of photos passing compliance checks on first submission, and liveness detection pass rates. If AI reduces error at intake, the benefits ripple throughout the system: fewer rejections, fewer resubmissions, and less officer time wasted on preventable delays. Benchmarking against independent standards, such as NIST's evaluations of biometric accuracy and fairness (Grother, Ngan, and Hanaoka 2019), ensures that reported improvements are not self-serving but verifiable.

Speed metrics matter as well, especially in the political context of passport backlogs. Consular sections should measure median processing times for renewals and new issuances, queue hours saved, and time to first officer review. When AI photo kiosks or biometric overlays cut days or weeks off average turnaround, these gains become visible not only to applicants but to legislators and the media. The U.S. Government Accountability Office has emphasized that systemic passport delays can erode public trust, making evidence of speed gains a critical part of the value story (GAO 2025).

Mandatory Disparate Impact Metric

For a high-risk system like identity verification, the most critical KPI is the quantifiable absence of bias. This requires moving beyond general "demographic parity" to measuring disparate impact across groups defined by race, gender, and age. The mandated metric must be the False Rejection Rate (FRR) differential. If the FRR for any protected demographic group exceeds a predefined variance (e.g., a 2% difference) from the lowest performing group, the system must be retrained or restricted until the disparity is eliminated. This metric establishes a nonnegotiable, evidence-based governing imperative for justice in automated identity services (Grother, Ngan, and Hanaoka 2019).

To see this in practice, consider the emerging pilots for the Digital Travel Credential (DTC) being developed under ICAO standards. The implementation phase of these projects is already generating the necessary data. For instance, a country running a pilot on a mobile renewal app can track two things in real time: First, the overall photo rejection rate (e.g., 5% of all applicants). Second, the rejection rate broken down by gender and ethnicity. If the system rejects photos from applicants with darker skin tones at a rate of 8%, while the rate for lighter skin tones is 3%, the system is showing a disparate impact greater than the 2% threshold. The mandatory metric is not just a number on a page—it's the automated flag that forces the agency to stop and retrain the algorithm before full deployment.

Equity and trust metrics bring fairness into view. Demographic parity in false match rates, the number of appeals or overrides granted, and applicant satisfaction surveys all help ensure that AI benefits are distributed fairly. Amnesty International's critiques of digital border systems underscore that efficiency without fairness can deepen inequities (Amnesty International 2024). Embedding equity metrics into reporting helps counter that risk and demonstrates commitment to inclusion.

The value story ties these numbers together. A consular chief presenting to headquarters or a foreign minister briefing parliament must be able to say not just "the system is faster," but "our error rates are down, applicant satisfaction is up, and officer time has been redirected from repetitive checks to complex adjudications." This story resonates with stakeholders because it frames AI not as abstract technology but as tangible improvement in service and security.

When measured in this way, AI adoption becomes evidence-based policy rather than speculation. Metrics reveal whether tools are delivering on their promise, while the value story explains why those results matter. Together, they turn innovation from an experiment into a durable part of the passport system.

RISKS, RED FLAGS, AND MITIGATIONS

Every technological advance in passport services carries its own set of vulnerabilities, and AI is no exception. Recognizing risks early—and designing mitigations into systems and workflows—is essential to maintaining both integrity and public trust.

One major risk is model drift. AI systems trained on past data may gradually become less accurate as fraud tactics evolve or applicant demographics shift. Left unchecked, drift can result in higher error rates and unfair outcomes. The mitigation is routine recalibration: quarterly retraining on updated datasets, complemented by "red-teaming" exercises in which adversarial cases are deliberately introduced to test resilience (NIST 2023).

A second red flag is over-automation. When consular staff defer too heavily to algorithmic outputs, they risk becoming passive executors rather than active adjudicators. This can erode discretion and accountability. Mitigation requires strict policy guardrails: human review for all adverse outcomes, mandatory override capacity, and dashboards that explain rather than dictate results. Independent oversight bodies, such as the U.S. Privacy and Civil Liberties Oversight Board, stress that meaningful human judgment must remain at the core of rights-affecting decisions (PCLOB 2025).

Privacy breaches represent another acute concern. Passport databases contain highly sensitive biometric and biographic information, making them attractive targets for malicious actors. Unauthorized access or leaks would not only harm individuals but also compromise the credibility of the issuing authority. Mitigation demands strong encryption, role-based access controls, immutable audit logs, and incident response playbooks rehearsed in advance. Privacy impact assessments, such as those conducted for the U.S. CCD, illustrate how transparency in data handling builds public trust (U.S. Department of State, Bureau of Consular Affairs 2023b).

Finally, there is the danger of equity gaps. AI systems may perform unevenly across demographic groups, leading to higher false rejection rates for certain populations. Studies by NIST have documented measurable demographic differentials in biometric accuracy, underscoring that fairness is not automatic but must be measured and enforced (Grother, Ngan, and Hanaoka 2019). Mandatory fairness audits that explicitly test for disparate impact across recognized demographic strata, paired with robust channels for appeal and redress when errors occur. In practice, these risks are not reasons to avoid AI altogether—they are reasons to design responsibly. Each red flag has a corresponding safeguard, and each safeguard reinforces the central principle that passports are more than documents: they are instruments of identity, dignity, and trust. By embedding mitigations into both technology and policy, missions can harness AI's benefits without compromising the values at the heart of consular affairs.

CROSS-REFERENCES

Passport services rarely operate in isolation. They sit at the center of a broader consular and border ecosystem, and the application of AI in this domain connects directly to themes explored throughout the rest of this book. Drawing these links makes it clear that passport AI is not a siloed experiment but part of a continuum of consular modernization.

The work of fraud detection, explored in Chapter 6, intersects closely with passport issuance. Techniques such as document clustering, metadata forensics, and provenance tagging are as relevant for spotting counterfeit breeder documents as they are for unmasking fraudulent visa sponsorship letters. Passport officers and their teams can benefit directly from the same AI-based tools used by Fraud Prevention Units, especially when dealing with doctored civil records.

Passport AI also depends on the integrity of biometric systems, the focus of Chapter 7. The multimodal fusion of fingerprints and faces described earlier in this chapter gains full effectiveness only when linked to robust biometric databases like DHS's HART or the EU's EURODAC. Shared lessons about fairness audits, demographic differentials, and transparency apply equally whether the biometric check is at a consular counter or a border kiosk.

In terms of workflow optimization, the insights of Chapter 8 on predictive scheduling and robotic process automation have immediate relevance. If AI reduces photo rejections or automates quality checks, those time savings feed directly into appointment capacity and officer bandwidth. Passport modernization therefore cannot be separated from broader consular efficiency gains.

Passport AI highlights the importance of human-centered governance, which anchors Chapter 10. The themes of explainability, equity, and trust are perhaps nowhere more sensitive than in the issuance of a state's highest identity document. The safeguards proposed for chatbots, crisis alerts, and mission-level deployments all converge here, reinforcing that technology succeeds only when it protects dignity as much as it improves throughput.

By tracing these cross-references, it becomes evident that passport services are both a beneficiary and a driver of AI adoption in consular affairs. Lessons learned here ripple outward into visas, fraud detection, crisis management, and beyond—making the passport chapter a keystone in the wider story of how AI is reshaping identity, mobility, and diplomacy.

CLOSING REFLECTION

Passports occupy a unique place in international life: they are at once personal and political, intimate and sovereign. For citizens, they are keys to opportunity, family connection, and safety. For governments, they are proof of identity and trust at the border. This dual significance explains why passport services are under intense pressure—facing heightened expectations for speed, and relentless attempts at fraud.

AI is emerging as both a shield and an amplifier in this environment. By enforcing photo standards at intake, screening for liveness, fusing multiple biometrics, and surfacing anomalies in supporting documents, AI strengthens the first line of defense against error and deception. By summarizing files, reducing rejections, and enabling faster renewals, it frees officers to focus on the cases that need closer review: a low-confidence match, a changed appearance, a missing breeder document, or an applicant whose explanation deserves a second look. Crucially, consular authority is sharpened only when the officer can see the reason for the flag, request alternate evidence, and document the final judgment.

Yet the risks are real. Over-automation, model drift, inequitable performance, and privacy breaches could erode the very trust that passports are meant to embody. That is why safeguards—human-in-the-loop review, fairness audits, provenance standards, and transparent communication—must be embedded at every stage. Technology cannot substitute for legitimacy; it can only support it.

The case of passports shows the broader truth that runs throughout this book: AI's promise in consular affairs lies not in novelty but in responsibility. When designed and governed carefully, these tools protect time, strengthen accuracy, and preserve dignity. When rushed or poorly supervised, they invite suspicion and undermine credibility.

As consular sections around the world begin to integrate AI into passport workflows, they are not just upgrading systems. They are making a statement about what kind of state–citizen relationship they want to uphold: one that is faster and smarter, yes, but also one that is fairer, more transparent, and more humane. The ultimate metric of success will not be the speed of a renewal, but whether the automated system can meet the highest human rights standard: equal error rates for every citizen, regardless of their demographic group. That balance—between efficiency and equity—is the measure by which AI in passport services will ultimately be judged.

4 Multilingual Access, Chatbots, and AI-Powered Communication

> What I think is really cool is we're seeing diplomats use StateChat to do their core job and allow them more time to do value-added work that only humans can do.
>
> —Kelly Fletcher, Chief Information Officer of the U.S. Department of State (quoted in Alder 2024b)

> AI is going to cause the next digital divide … I have no doubt about that.
>
> —Angela Siefer, Executive Director of the National Digital Inclusion Alliance (quoted in Quaintance 2024)

> What AI needs to be doing is collating and collecting this data that a human needs to make a decision and getting it to them in a way that makes sense, in a way that's quick, so they're able to make a decision with all the information they need as quickly as possible.
>
> —Gregory Barbaccia, Federal Chief Information Officer and Chief AI Officer (quoted in Alms 2025)

Opening Vignette: 2:07 a.m. at Consulate of the Republic of Z

Far from home, a citizen of the Republic of Z found herself in distress. While preparing to travel onward, she realized her passport was missing. Panicked, she sent a message to the nearest Z consulate in the country where she lived as a seasonal worker. It was two o'clock in the morning, and she wrote in her regional mother tongue—a language widely spoken in the northern provinces of Z but unfamiliar to most of the mission's staff.

Within seconds, an AI-powered assistant replied. Drawing from a verified library of official consular guidance, it explained how to request an emergency passport, what documents she would need, and when the consulate's duty window would open later that morning. The assistant delivered this information

DOI: 10.1201/9781003634775-6

in her own language, using respectful forms of address and avoiding technical jargon.

When the on-call officer logged in to review the system's transcript, the conversation was already annotated with an accurate translation into the official language of Z. Policy citations were attached to each instruction, making it easy for the officer to confirm the assistant's guidance. With this context in hand, the officer drafted a quick follow-up to reassure the applicant and prepare the file for her arrival.

By the time she came to the consulate at dawn, she carried the necessary paperwork and a clear understanding of the process. What might once have been a chaotic encounter instead unfolded smoothly: the applicant felt seen and supported, and the officer had the time and confidence to focus on the exceptional aspects of her case.

This vignette is fictional, but it reflects the real challenges faced by missions abroad. Citizens do not always communicate in a country's official language, emergencies rarely wait for office hours, and small gaps in clarity can cause major distress. In such moments, meeting a frightened citizen in her own language—at the hour she actually needs help, not when the office opens—turns what could be a night of panic into a process she can manage, with the officer's judgment waiting to meet her at dawn.

THE HUMAN SCALE OF MULTILINGUALISM AND THE INTEGRITY GAP

The need for multilingual service in consular work is not a matter of customer convenience; it is a governance requirement for process accuracy and equity.

The challenge is perhaps best captured by a scene that can unfold on any given day inside a high-volume mission. The experience of one of the authors while working a visa line in London offers a clear illustration: Vice Consuls sat shoulder to shoulder at tiny interview windows, each conducting interviews in a linguistic tower of Babel—Spanish, Mandarin, Arabic, Polish, French, English, Thai, and Portuguese. This level of linguistic talent is not simply a desirable asset; it is a diagnostic tool. Interviews conducted in an applicant's strongest language are demonstrably more accurate, enabling officers to better assess credibility, intent, and nuance (U.S. Department of State, Office of Inspector General 2013).

THE FISCAL AND INTEGRITY COST

Despite this necessity, the diplomatic mission's ability to staff for such diversity is structurally limited by cost and time. Achieving professional fluency in a high-priority language requires an officer to be taken out of service for nine months to two years of intensive training. This commitment carries a profound opportunity cost, as every year spent in training is a year not spent filling a critical position abroad.

The institutional price for this initial training, including the officer's salary, benefits, and the facility overhead for a full-time training seat, can easily cost hundreds of thousands of dollars a year (author's estimate, based on U.S. Federal Pay Scales and FSI training duration). This investment is essential, yet it is fundamentally unsustainable at the scale of global demand.

When native-level staff are unavailable—a common occurrence—the process integrity is immediately threatened. Consular sections are then forced to rely on ad-hoc translation: either internal volunteer lists (which are often poorly maintained or incomplete) or, most critically, the applicant's own accompanying interpreter. This last scenario introduces an unmanageable risk of bias, error, or even deception, jeopardizing the very accuracy that the officer strives to achieve. As one high-fraud post reported, officers sometimes adjudicate visas without fully understanding everything the applicants tell them during the interview (GAO-07-1154T).

The linguistic and fiscal constraints of human-only operations make one conclusion unavoidable: scalable multilingual access demands technological partnership.

AI provides that partnership. Properly governed, multilingual systems extend officers' linguistic reach while reinforcing the integrity of adjudications. They do not replace human judgment; they protect it.

WHY MULTILINGUAL AI BELONGS IN CONSULAR WORK

Consular affairs sit at the intersection of high demand, high stakes, and limited resources. Every year, millions of inquiries flow into consular offices worldwide: questions about visas and passports, appointment rescheduling, travel requirements, or emergency assistance. These queries arrive through emails, call centers, social media messages, and in-person visits, often in dozens of languages. Officers and other consular staff, already stretched by adjudications and crisis management, cannot keep pace with this torrent of routine requests.

The pressure is not just operational—it is also about equity. Applicants and citizens who cannot navigate consular information in the dominant language are at a structural disadvantage. Large language models have already demonstrated their value for public communications, visa guidance, and emergency templates across a range of diplomatic functions beyond consular affairs (Kilburg 2025), making the case for their application here both natural and well-grounded. They may misinterpret instructions, submit incomplete applications, or face longer waits because they require human translation support. Language barriers thus become access barriers, limiting who can engage effectively with their own government. Research on digital borders has highlighted this inequality: when automation and digitization proceed without multilingual capacity, they risk deepening rather than reducing exclusion (Amnesty International 2024; Beduschi and McAuliffe 2020).

AI offers a way to bridge these gaps. Chatbots, natural language processing, and LLMs can provide instant, round-the-clock answers to common questions in multiple languages. Machine translation, once error-prone and stilted, has reached a level where it can deliver understandable, context-sensitive responses in most major languages—and, increasingly, in regional and minority tongues as well. That progress rests on centuries of translation effort, though not always in ways we expect.

The Bible—translated into more than 3,600 languages—remains the single largest multilingual corpus in existence and a cornerstone of early AI translation research (Wycliffe Global Alliance 2024; Resnik and Smith 2003). It gave neural models access to aligned verses across thousands of linguistic pairs, but it also taught them formality and rhythm rather than slang or spontaneity. The result was accuracy without fluency: systems that spoke like scholars, not citizens. As AI translation matured, the same challenge facing consular officers reappeared—how to make language both correct and alive. When paired with official and verified policy libraries and human review for sensitive cases, these systems extend consular reach far beyond the limits of staffing or office hours.

In short, multilingual AI belongs in consular work because it addresses three overlapping imperatives: volume, equity, and trust. It reduces the burden on officers and consular staff writ large, ensures that language barriers do not block access to services, and builds credibility by delivering timely and consistent information. Far from being a luxury, it is rapidly becoming a necessity for missions operating in a multilingual, always-on world.

The promise of multilingual AI is clear—but to apply it safely, missions must first understand the building blocks behind it. The next section maps those tools in plain language, explaining how rule-based chatbots, natural language systems, and large language models each function—and where their limits lie.

TOOL TAXONOMY: A PLAIN-ENGLISH MAP

Not all chatbots and conversational AI systems are created equal. For consular affairs, where accuracy, clarity, and tone are as important as speed, it is essential to understand the spectrum of tools available. These categories are not mutually exclusive; in practice, most government-grade systems combine several layers. A simple taxonomy in plain language helps consular offices choose the right option for their needs, balancing ambition with risk.

At the most basic level are rules-based bots. These work like interactive FAQs: the system looks for a keyword in the user's message and responds with a prewritten answer. A question containing "passport renewal" triggers a standard reply outlining the required documents. Rules-based bots are inexpensive and reliable, but rigid. If an applicant phrases a question differently or asks something outside the script, the bot can only redirect them to a human.

More advanced are natural language processing (NLP) bots. These systems recognize intent rather than just keywords. Whether an applicant writes "I lost my passport," "my passport is missing," or "what if someone stole my passport," the bot understands that all three mean the same thing: a lost passport case. NLP bots can also collect structured pieces of information—dates, case numbers, nationalities—allowing them to guide applicants through simple forms step by step. These systems require more training and data but deliver more natural and helpful conversations.

The most powerful category is built on large language models (LLMs). These are the systems behind tools like ChatGPT and similar AI assistants—models that can generate fluent, context-sensitive responses, summarize long email threads, and explain policies in plain language. They shine in situations where questions are varied and unpredictable, which describes most consular inboxes.

But LLMs come with a serious risk. Because they generate language rather than retrieve it, they can produce answers that sound authoritative but are simply wrong—a phenomenon called hallucination. In a consular context, a hallucinated visa fee or an invented document requirement could mislead an applicant and trigger complaints or appeals. The safeguard is a design called retrieval augmented generation (RAG). Instead of letting the model answer from its general training, RAG forces it to pull facts only from an approved library of official sources—consular FAQs, policy guidance, verified instructions—before composing a response. Every answer comes with a citation that officers and their teams can check. If the library does not contain the answer, the system says so and refers the user to a human. This approach makes each response traceable and auditable, turning a powerful but unpredictable tool into one that can be governed.

Layered across these tiers are supporting technologies. Machine translation expands reach to more than 100 languages and counting. Voice AI enables speech-to-text and text-to-speech, a vital accessibility feature for applicants with disabilities or low literacy, and for those who rely on phone-based interaction. Omnichannel adapters let the same knowledge base flow across multiple platforms—websites, WhatsApp, SMS, Facebook Messenger, or even interactive voice response systems.

Understanding this taxonomy empowers missions to match tools with their capacity and risk tolerance. A small post might begin with a rules-based bot for passport FAQs, while a regional hub could pilot an NLP system integrated with appointment booking. LLM-based tools, while powerful, should be deployed only after governance maturity is proven—retrieval grounding in place, human-in-the-loop controls tested, and content libraries verified. The next section explores where such systems add the greatest value and the operational problems they can safely solve.

AI USE CASES FOR CONSULAR WORK: FROM ROUTINE TO HIGH-VALUE IMPACT

Once the tools are understood, the real question for missions is simple: where can conversational AI make the most difference without compromising accuracy or discretion? Across governments, humanitarian agencies, and vendor systems, a few high-value patterns have emerged—use cases that deliver measurable efficiency while preserving the human heart of consular work.

Routine Public Inquiries

Every mission faces the same avalanche of questions: how to renew a passport, what documents are required for a visa, whether an appointment is necessary, or how to report a lost travel document. These inquiries are predictable, repetitive, and language-intensive. A chatbot operating on the mission's website or messaging channels can answer them instantly—in multiple languages and at all hours. Governments from Australia to Estonia have already deployed multilingual AI assistants to handle such traffic, reporting faster response times and lower applicant error rates (European Commission 2023a; Australian Department of Home Affairs 2024). By deflecting routine inquiries, these systems allow officers to focus on complex cases while applicants receive clear, consistent guidance.

Applicant Assistance and Triage

Conversational AI can also support applicants *during* a process rather than before it. When completing an online form or preparing for an interview, users often make preventable mistakes that lead to refusals or delays. A well-designed chatbot can guide them step by step, alerting them if a required field is missing or generating a checklist tailored to their situation. If a traveler reports a lost passport, the bot can immediately provide the documents needed and direct them to the emergency appointment queue.

This kind of adaptive assistance improves fairness as much as efficiency—ensuring that applicants succeed or fail on the merits of their case, not on linguistic or procedural confusion.

Officer Copiloting and Communication Support

AI is increasingly valuable behind the counter as well. LLMs, when constrained by retrieval from official sources, can draft initial responses to complex emails, congressional or parliamentary inquiries, or public messaging. They can also summarize long correspondence threads and translate refusal or approval explanations into plain language.

Officers remain fully responsible for review, but the time saved allows them to focus their judgment where it matters most. Early pilots by several foreign ministries have shown measurable reductions in administrative workload without any decline in quality or accuracy (OECD 2024).

In this sense, AI functions as a *copilot* rather than a colleague: it prepares the ground so humans can act with greater precision and empathy.

Content Consistency and Crisis Communication

Perhaps the least visible but most transformative use of AI lies in maintaining a single, authoritative "source of truth." Consular sections often struggle to keep guidance aligned across web pages, handouts, call center scripts, and social media. AI systems can automatically cross-check these materials against the master library, flagging outdated language or inconsistencies.

During crises, the same infrastructure enables rapid multilingual alerts about curfews, evacuation points, or travel restrictions. Preapproved bilingual templates allow posts to push verified information immediately, while officers focus on exceptional cases requiring human judgment. Here, AI does what no team of humans

Digital Frontlines: The ETIAS Scam Wars—How Fake AI Sites Target Travelers During the Rollout

While European authorities prepare to launch the European Travel Information and Authorization System (ETIAS) in late 2026, fraudulent websites have proliferated to exploit traveler confusion—using automated ad buying, AI-generated content, and algorithmically optimized domain names to trap unwary visitors.

Frontex, the EU's border agency, has publicly warned that "unofficial ETIAS websites" have proliferated across the internet, with over 100 fraudulent sites identified charging inflated fees, harvesting passport data, and spreading misinformation about a system that doesn't yet exist (Frontex 2024). The European Commission has created an official "Report abuse" page cataloguing common scam tactics—misleading domain names, deceptive design elements, and price gouging that can exceed the legitimate €20 fee by several hundred percent (European Commission 2025b).

The scammer playbook follows a familiar pattern. Criminals purchase targeted search advertisements, register official-sounding domain names, and deploy automated content generation to create convincing replicas of government websites. They promise "instant approval" and "guaranteed processing"—claims that exploit confusion around ETIAS rules and timing—while harvesting credit card details and passport information.

ABTA, the U.K.'s leading travel association, has warned would-be visitors to Europe that the rollout has created considerable room for confusion, and that anyone who attempts to apply for ETIAS prematurely may be exposed to fraud (ABTA 2025). The warning has been echoed across mainstream travel media and government advisories, but scam sites continue proliferating faster than authorities can shut them down.

European officials envision AI-powered defensive strategies including multilingual AI assistants that provide trustworthy guidance, anchored to verified government sources. Such systems would need sophisticated governance mechanisms: incident registers tracking bad links, coordination protocols with national cyber agencies like the U.K.'s NCSC, and platform partnerships enabling rapid takedown of fraudulent content (NCSC 2025). The challenge is ensuring official AI assistants are more responsive and helpful than criminal alternatives while maintaining accuracy.

The ETIAS scam wars illuminate a broader tension about AI and authoritative information. Criminal organizations can deploy AI to generate convincing misinformation faster than human fact-checkers can debunk it. Search algorithms prioritize engagement over accuracy, often surfacing fraudulent sites above official sources.

Current scam patterns reveal how AI-powered deception operates. Fraudulent sites use automated translation to target multiple languages simultaneously, deploy sentiment analysis to optimize persuasive messaging, and leverage machine learning to identify and exploit gaps in official communications.

The defensive response requires matching sophistication with transparency. Effective anti-scam AI must cite authoritative sources, explain its limitations clearly, and escalate novel threats to human oversight while operating under governance frameworks that maintain public accountability.

can: preserve accuracy and consistency across every channel, even in moments of chaos.

In sum: AI currently excels where volume, repetition, and language barriers are greatest. It does not adjudicate, promise outcomes, or exercise discretion. Instead, it clears away the noise of routine tasks so officers can invest their energy where it matters—on fairness, empathy, and complex decisions. Governed by retrieval grounding, human oversight, and disciplined content control, conversational AI strengthens the integrity of consular judgment rather than replacing it.

GLOBAL EXEMPLARS

Building on these use cases, governments and international organizations are already demonstrating what responsible conversational AI looks like in practice. These examples show how multilingual systems can scale safely across diverse contexts—government, humanitarian, and private sector—while preserving trust and accountability.

Estonia: The Model of Interoperability

Estonia's Bürokratt remains one of the most ambitious examples of AI-enabled public service. Framed as a "virtual civil servant," it links dozens of government agencies through a single conversational interface that allows citizens to access services, submit requests, and receive updates in multiple languages. Built on open-source infrastructure and governed by interoperability standards, Bürokratt demonstrates how a unified knowledge base prevents the policy drift that occurs when agencies issue overlapping or inconsistent guidance (European Commission 2023a). For consular services, it offers a powerful model of accuracy, consistency, and citizen-centered design.

UNHCR: Inclusion Through Mobile-First Design

The UN Refugee Agency's La Chama project in Brazil shows how conversational AI can protect access and dignity in humanitarian settings. Operated through WhatsApp as part of UNHCR's global HELP platform, La Chama provides Venezuelan refugees with multilingual information on documentation, asylum procedures, and access to basic services. Since launch, it has handled more than 200,000 interactions, proving how widely used communication channels can deliver official information to vulnerable populations even when staffing and resources are strained (UNHCR 2022). For consular sections, La Chama illustrates how mobile-first tools can preserve accuracy and empathy in moments of crisis.

Australia: Scaling Accuracy Across Digital Channels

Australia's Department of Home Affairs has developed a multilingual digital assistant to answer visa and citizenship questions as part of its Digital Strategy 2030. The assistant triages inquiries and ensures consistent, policy-aligned responses across web and messaging platforms. By deflecting routine questions before they reach a mission, the system improves applicant experience while reducing administrative load (Australian Department of Home Affairs 2024). It illustrates how national-level governance and automation can coexist—producing reliability, not rigidity.

VFS Global: Multilingual Service at Vendor Scale

The private sector has also played a crucial role in proving scalability. VFS Global's ViVA chatbot, launched in 2024 across 141 countries in partnership with Microsoft Azure, provides visa applicants with multilingual voice and chat support 24/7. It guides users through requirements, deflects repetitive queries, and maintains compliance through built-in auditing and logging (VFS Global 2023). While vendor-operated systems require strong contractual safeguards to prevent data or governance risks, ViVA demonstrates how technical scale can align with service integrity when designed under strict oversight.

Together, these exemplars show that AI in government is no longer experimental—it is operational. From Estonia's interoperable governance to UNHCR's mobile-first inclusion and Australia's enterprise consistency, the lesson is clear: success depends less on technology than on disciplined governance. Missions that borrow these principles—single-source content, multilingual accessibility, privacy by design, and human oversight—can modernize consular operations without sacrificing empathy or trust.

ARCHITECTURE YOU CAN ACTUALLY RUN

The next question is how to make such systems work within a consulate's real technical and staffing constraints. For many diplomatic missions, the challenge of deploying conversational AI lies not in the concept but in the practicalities: what does such a system actually look like under the hood? A consular-ready chatbot need not be a mystery. Its architecture can be described in plain English as a series of layers, each with a clear job.

The first layer is what applicants see—the channels. This might be a chat window on the mission's website, a WhatsApp or SMS integration, a Facebook Messenger page, or even a phone-based voice system. A well-designed chatbot meets applicants where they already are rather than forcing them onto a single platform.

The second layer is the traffic controller—the part of the system that decides what happens to each incoming message. When a query arrives, this layer checks it against safety rules, determines whether it is routine or urgent, and routes it accordingly. An emergency message about a hospitalized citizen should never end up in the same queue as a question about photo requirements. If the system detects distress language, legal complexity, or repeated frustration, it hands the conversation to a human officer. Several commercial and open-source platforms can serve this routing function, and a mission's choice will depend on its hosting policies, budget, and technical capacity (Microsoft 2024; Google Cloud n.d.; Rasa n.d.). The specific product matters less than the principle: every message must reach the right destination, and urgent cases must always reach a person.

The third layer is where the answer is actually composed. This is the part that combines the tools described earlier in this chapter. A RAG component pulls relevant facts from the mission's approved library of policies and FAQs. A constrained language model drafts the response, but it must cite its sources so that officers and their teams can verify the text. For structured tasks—booking an appointment, collecting a case number, or walking an applicant through a checklist—a simpler, rules-based flow handles the interaction step by step. The result is a hybrid system: flexible enough to handle unpredictable questions but anchored firmly in approved content.

The fourth layer connects the chatbot to the consular systems that already run daily operations. These might include appointment scheduling platforms, case management databases, or crisis alert registries such as the U.S. State Department's Smart Traveler Enrollment Program (STEP), which allows citizens to receive security updates and enables embassies to contact them during emergencies (U.S. Department of State n.d.-r). With careful governance, the chatbot can check real-time appointment availability or push notifications into existing workflows, ensuring that automation is integrated into daily operations rather than siloed alongside them.

The fifth layer is what turns automation into accountability: logging and review. Every conversation should be recorded, with appropriate privacy safeguards in place. Dashboards should track key metrics—how many inquiries the bot resolved without human help, how quickly it responded, and how often it escalated. Periodic transcript reviews allow staff to spot errors, retrain the system, and ensure the tone stays right. Without this layer, the system is a black box. With it, AI becomes auditable, improvable, and trustworthy.

Together, these five layers make a chatbot both practical and governable. Missions can start small—a single channel, a modest FAQ library, and basic logging—and expand as confidence grows. What matters most is not which vendor or platform sits behind the curtain, but whether the design keeps human oversight, verified content, and multilingual access at the center. Get those right, and the architecture will serve the mission. Get them wrong, and no amount of technical sophistication will compensate.

BUILD VERSUS BUY: CHOOSING THE RIGHT PATH

Once a consular authority decides to adopt a chatbot or multilingual assistant, the next question is whether to build, buy, or combine approaches. Each path involves trade-offs in speed, cost, control, and risk. The goal is to select the model that best fits the mission's scale and governance capacity (NIST 2023; OECD 2024).

Buying an off-the-shelf service is usually the fastest to deploy. Cloud-based vendors provide configurable, multilingual bots that can be populated with consular content and launched quickly—an advantage for posts struggling with inquiry volume. The trade-off is dependence on external providers, which requires careful review of privacy, data sovereignty, and exit clause provisions.

Hybrid models strike a balance between speed and oversight. The mission or headquarters retains control of the knowledge base—policy documents, FAQs, emergency templates—while vendors supply infrastructure and multilingual delivery channels (web, WhatsApp, SMS). This keeps content authoritative and traceable while allowing technical scalability.

Building a chatbot from scratch offers maximum control but demands significant technical capacity. Governments pursuing this path gain full authority over data, customization, and integration with internal systems, yet few posts can sustain the staffing and maintenance such builds require. This option suits enterprise-level deployments where centralized IT or foreign affairs ministries can provide long-term support.

Whatever the choice, evaluation criteria—not hype—must guide decisions. Missions should ask:

- Are responses grounded in official sources?
- How well does the system handle multiple or minority languages?
- Is human hand-off seamless?
- Are privacy and logging standards enforced?
- What is the real cost per deflected inquiry?

For most consular leaders and offices, the prudent path may prove to be to start small with a narrowly scoped pilot—often hybrid or vendor-assisted—then scale once governance maturity and user trust are proven. Building may remain a long-term ambition, but starting lean and expanding responsibly delivers the quickest value while protecting officer authority and applicant trust (OECD 2024).

Emerging citizen-driven tools also may have a role to play. While most current deployments originate inside government or large vendors, the next frontier may come from citizen-facing innovation. Third-party apps already help travelers and applicants prepare compliant photos, complete visa checklists, or translate government forms. In these cases, it is the public—not the institution—driving accessibility. Consular ecosystems will need to adapt, ensuring such external tools can integrate safely with official systems while preserving data integrity and policy accuracy. Over time, this public–private collaboration layer may become a core part of how multilingual AI broadens equitable access without expanding government overhead.

CONTENT OPERATIONS: THE SECRET TO ACCURACY

The success of any consular chatbot depends less on the sophistication of its algorithms than on the quality of its content. A beautifully designed system with outdated or inconsistent information will frustrate applicants and erode trust faster than no chatbot at all. Conversely, a modest tool built on a well-maintained knowledge base can transform service delivery. Content operations—the discipline of curating, updating, and governing information—are therefore the true foundation of accuracy and trust (NIST 2023; OECD 2024).

At the heart of content operations lies the principle of a single source of truth. Every chatbot answer should originate from an authoritative, version-controlled repository of consular guidance. That repository may begin as a library of policy summaries, FAQs, and emergency templates, but it must be structured so translations can be maintained in sync. If one page changes, all dependent translations should update automatically. Without this discipline, missions risk a scenario where the website, chatbot, and call center each deliver slightly different instructions—a recipe for confusion and appeals (International Organization for Standardization and International Electrotechnical Commission 2023b).

Clear ownership is essential: headquarters may host the master repository, but posts must retain authority to flag local changes, correct translations, and push urgent updates during crises. A disciplined update workflow—who edits, who approves, and who verifies translation accuracy—prevents drift and keeps multilingual content synchronized worldwide.

Once the structure is established, governing change with precision becomes essential. Content should carry version numbers, effective dates, and rollback capacity. If a visa rule changes on January 1, the chatbot's answers must switch that same day—and staff should be able to verify that the new version is live. If an error appears, reverting to the previous version should be as simple as flipping a switch. This level of control—common in software and knowledge management—is now vital in consular communication (NIST 2023).

Tone and clarity are equally critical. Chatbots represent the voice of government, and that voice must be clear, plain, and empathetic. Plain-language standards such as those adopted under the U.S. Plain Writing Act (2010) and the U.K. Government Digital Service (2024) ensure messages are understandable without losing authority. In multilingual contexts, translations must be reviewed not only for accuracy but also for cultural appropriateness. An answer that reads well in English may need stylistic or tonal adjustments in Arabic, Spanish, or regional languages to convey the same respect and clarity.

Crisis response provides the ultimate stress test for content operations: in fast-moving emergencies, misinformation spreads quickly. Preapproved bilingual templates for evacuation alerts, curfews, or contact instructions allow missions to push accurate, timely information even before full staff mobilization. When paired with LLM-powered translation tools and human review, this approach preserves coherence and authority under pressure (OECD 2024).

Strong content operations transform a chatbot from a technical experiment into an institutional asset. They ensure that what the bot says is exactly what the mission means, and that applicants hear the same message regardless of channel. In consular affairs—where trust is fragile and consequences are high—content discipline is not optional. It is the backbone of retrieval grounding and the foundation of digital governance.

GUARDRAILS FOR SAFETY, ETHICS, AND COMPLIANCE

Multilingual chatbots can dramatically expand access to consular services, but without strong governance guardrails they risk creating more problems than they solve. Unlike websites, which present static information, conversational AI feels personal—its answers appear tailored to each user. That intimacy raises the stakes: if the system misleads an applicant, overpromises an outcome, or mishandles private data, the harm can be immediate and the reputational damage lasting. Guardrails ensure that these tools deliver value safely, ethically, and in compliance with law (NIST 2023; OECD 2024).

Hallucination control is the first line of defense. LLMs can produce answers that sound plausible but are factually wrong. In a consular context, even a minor fabrication—an invented document requirement or fee—can mislead applicants and generate appeals. The mitigation is RAG: every answer must be grounded in a curated knowledge base, with source citations displayed. When the AI does not know, it should say so clearly and refer the user to a human officer rather than speculate (NIST 2023).

Role limitation is equally critical. A chatbot must never adjudicate cases, guarantee outcomes, or offer legal interpretation. Its role is to explain process, not render judgment. Transparency notices should inform users that they are interacting with an AI assistant, not a consular officer, and that final authority rests with human staff. Clear escalation paths—ideally two clicks or fewer to reach a person—ensure applicants are not trapped in automated loops.

Privacy and data minimization form the third guardrail. Chatbots inevitably capture applicant data, whether through typed inquiries, uploaded documents, or metadata like phone numbers. Missions must limit collection to what is strictly necessary, mask identifying details in logs, and enforce deletion and retention schedules. Privacy Impact Assessments (PIAs)—modeled on those used for biometric systems and consular databases—should be mandatory for any deployment. Systems should comply with relevant frameworks such as the EU General Data Protection Regulation (GDPR) and U.S. Privacy Act of 1974 (OMB 2024).

The fourth guardrail concerns equity and accessibility. Systems must be usable by applicants with limited literacy, disabilities, or low bandwidth. Voice-to-text and text-to-voice options, simplified language modes, and offline-capable guides extend service to those who might otherwise be excluded. Regular fairness and translation-quality audits ensure that majority-language users are not advantaged at the expense of minority groups (OECD 2024).

Legal and oversight compliance provides the backbone. The EU Artificial Intelligence Act (2024) explicitly categorizes migration- and visa-related systems as *high risk*, requiring human oversight, transparency, and risk management. In the U.S., the Office of Management and Budget's Memorandum M-24-10 (2024) mandates that federal agencies log, assess, and publicly document AI systems that affect rights or safety. Aligning consular chatbots with these frameworks is not only best practice—it is a legal and political imperative (European Union 2024; OMB 2024).

When these guardrails are in place, AI assistants become what they should be: tools that expand access, reduce confusion, and protect officer time without displacing judgment or compromising rights. They remain instruments of service—not decision-makers. In consular affairs, where the smallest error can carry outsized consequences, that distinction is the foundation of trust through accountability.

METRICS AND KPIS

A chatbot that looks sleek but cannot be measured is worse than useless. In consular affairs, where accuracy and fairness carry high stakes, missions must define key performance indicators (KPIs) before launch, not after. These metrics make clear whether the system is improving service, protecting trust, and justifying continued investment. (NIST 2023; OECD 2024)

The most obvious measure is containment (or deflection) rate—the percentage of inquiries fully resolved by the chatbot without human help. In government pilots, containment rates between 60% and 80% are common, but efficiency cannot come at the expense of correctness. This is why first-contact resolution matters just as much: did the applicant receive a complete and accurate answer the first time, or did the bot generate confusion and repeat inquiries?

Accuracy remains the backbone. Responses must align with official policy. RAG makes this measurable: officers and their teams can verify whether every chatbot answer cites a valid source. Periodic transcript audits, ideally random and double-reviewed, help quantify the response integrity rate. Anything below a 95% benchmark should trigger retraining or tighter content control (International Organization for Standardization and International Electrotechnical Commission 2023b).

Humans, of course, make mistakes too—often more frequently than well-governed AI systems. In traditional consular operations, senior officers routinely reviewed random visa cases, monitoring issuance and refusal rates to identify anomalies. An officer whose approval rates spiked or dropped far beyond the section average would prompt mentoring, retraining, or managerial review. These patterns reflected a human learning curve: periods of over-approval, over-refusal, and eventual equilibrium.

The same principle applies to AI oversight. What matters is not the absence of error but the presence of structured accountability—a system that detects, explains, and corrects deviations quickly. Safety indicators measure how often the chatbot recognizes uncertainty and escalates rather than improvises. Monitoring the ratio of "I don't know" responses to unsupported answers provides a practical hallucination index. Over time, this metric can confirm whether governance mechanisms—like retrieval grounding and human oversight—are functioning as intended (NIST 2023).

Equity and accessibility demand their own metrics. Coverage across languages can be tracked by the proportion of interactions handled in minority or regional languages. Accessibility metrics, such as text-to-voice usage or screenreader compatibility, show whether applicants with disabilities are truly benefiting from the system. Regular fairness audits across languages ensure translation quality and response tone do not privilege majority groups (OECD 2024).

When viewed together, these measures create a balanced governance picture. Efficiency gains matter only if accuracy, safety, and equity are preserved. Sharing results internally—and when possible, publicly—builds officer confidence and stakeholder trust. In consular chatbot deployments, numbers are not mere performance indicators; they are the evidence base that makes innovation governable and credible.

RISKS AND MITIGATIONS

Chatbots can be powerful allies in consular work, but their very strengths—speed, scale, and linguistic reach—also create vulnerabilities. If left unmanaged, these risks can erode applicant trust and expose missions to reputational or even legal harm. The goal is not to eliminate risk, which is impossible, but to anticipate failure modes and build mitigations into the design from the start (NIST 2023; OECD 2024).

The most visible risk is hallucination, when LLMs fabricate answers that sound authoritative but have no factual basis. In a consular context, this might mean an invented visa requirement or a nonexistent fee—errors that can confuse applicants and damage confidence in the mission. The safeguard is RAG, ensuring that every response is drawn only from an approved and traceable policy library, with citations displayed. Red-team testing—where officers deliberately try to make the system fail—adds a vital layer of defense before public deployment (International Organization for Standardization and International Electrotechnical Commission 2023b).

A more subtle hazard is misinterpretation. Applicants often write informally, mixing languages or using regional slang. A model trained exclusively in formal policy language may fail to recognize intent or context. Preventing this requires bilingual and readability testing, paired with continuous feedback loops in which staff review transcripts and refine training data. Locally employed staff, with their fluency in community language and nuance, are especially valuable in this process.

The digital divide introduces another form of inequity. Not all applicants have smartphones, broadband, or high literacy levels. A chatbot that exists only on a website risks excluding those who rely on SMS, voice calls, or community intermediaries. Effective mitigation means multi-channel access—deploying the system across web, messaging apps, and interactive voice platforms—while also maintaining printable or broadcast materials for those who are offline.

Policy drift is quieter but equally dangerous. When content updates are not synchronized across the chatbot, website, and call center, applicants may receive conflicting instructions. Avoiding drift requires disciplined content operations—version control, effective date tagging, and rollback capacity—so that changes propagate immediately and outdated information can be corrected without delay (NIST 2023).

Finally, there is the risk of shadow knowledge. Officers and their teams often create their own macros, templates, or reference notes, which can gradually diverge from the official "single source of truth." When these private tools circulate outside the approved library, inconsistency becomes inevitable. Integrating officer-contributed materials into the central repository—subject to review and version control—ensures that institutional memory strengthens rather than fragments the system.

Each of these risks underscores a broader truth: the danger lies not in using AI, but in using it carelessly. With retrieval grounding, multilingual testing, inclusive channel design, disciplined content governance, and integrated knowledge management, missions can capture the benefits of speed and scale while preserving fairness, privacy, and trust—the enduring foundations of consular integrity.

These safeguards set the stage for the most important design principle of all: ensuring that technology amplifies human judgment rather than replaces it.

FIELD CHECKLIST: MULTILINGUAL CHATBOT DEPLOYMENT

Before launching a chatbot or multilingual AI assistant, consular teams should confirm that the following foundations are in place. These steps apply whether the tool is built in-house, adapted from open-source frameworks, or procured from a vendor.

1. Define scope and channel strategy. Specify which services the chatbot will cover—visa FAQs, appointment guidance, emergency alerts, or all three—and which channels it will operate on: web, SMS, WhatsApp, or voice. Maintaining parallel offline access ensures that applicants without smartphones or reliable connectivity are not excluded.
2. Build a verified content library. Every response must be grounded in an approved, version-controlled source—the consular section's own FAQs, official policy guidance, or headquarters-issued instructions. No free text generation without retrieval grounding. Assign a content steward responsible for updating the library when policies change.
3. Ensure multilingual quality. Translations must be reviewed by fluent speakers, not just machine-checked. Locally employed staff are essential partners in verifying tone, idiom, and cultural appropriateness. Test in every supported language before launch, and schedule periodic retesting as content evolves.
4. Design human escalation from the start. Every chatbot interaction must offer a clear path to a human officer—reachable within two steps. The system should automatically escalate when it detects distress language, legal complexity, or repeated user frustration. No applicant should feel trapped in a loop.
5. Embed privacy and data minimization. Define what data the chatbot collects, how long it is retained, and who can access transcripts. Personally identifiable information should be stripped from training data. A short privacy impact review, completed before launch, documents these decisions and supports accountability.
6. Log everything, review regularly. Every interaction should be logged. Weekly transcript reviews by staff catch errors, identify gaps in the content library, and surface questions the system cannot yet answer. These reviews also guard against hallucination and policy drift.
7. Set success metrics before launch. Define what success looks like: inquiry deflection rate, average response accuracy, escalation frequency, applicant satisfaction, and language coverage. Track these from day one so that the pilot can be evaluated honestly and improved iteratively.

With these foundations in place, a consular chatbot becomes a reliable extension of the mission's service—answering routine questions accurately across languages and time zones, while protecting the officer's time for the cases that demand human judgment.

CLOSING REFLECTION

Every consular mission—large or small—faces the same reality: more questions than staff hours. Multilingual AI earns its place when the handoff rules are clear: distress language, detention, hospitalization, child welfare, lost passports with imminent travel, repeated failed answers, low language confidence, or a direct request for a person should move the exchange out of automation and into human review. The value is not that the chatbot answers everything; it is that it knows when to stop.

The examples explored throughout this chapter—from Estonia's Bürokratt, to UNHCR's La Chama, to vendor-scale systems such as VFS Global's ViVA—prove that conversational AI is no longer experimental. It is already reshaping how people access public services across languages, platforms, and time zones. The question for consular operations is no longer *whether* these tools belong, but *how* to implement them responsibly, with transparency, fairness, and accountability at their core.

The true measure of success will never be how sophisticated the technology appears, but how effectively it strengthens access, equity, and trust. When consular teams can close their laptops at day's end knowing that applicants are still being served accurately, respectfully, and in their own languages, AI will have fulfilled its purpose—extending the mission's reach while preserving the human heart of diplomacy.

5 Crisis Management and Emergency AI

The ability to digest and provide near real-time insights at critical times is essential, and that's where AI systems can play a significant role.

—Ali Mostafavi, Professor of Civil and Environmental Engineering, Texas A&M University (quoted in Clark 2025)

AI presents a significant opportunity in modernizing our systems as well as better harnessing AI to advance our mission delivery … But the risk of adversarial use of AI is real as is the risk of disparate bias or unintended disparate impact from our use of AI.

—Eric Hysen, former DHS Chief Information Officer and Chief AI Officer (quoted in Johnson 2023)

I don't think the world will put up anymore with any of us (in the tech industry) coming up with something that has not thought through safety, trust, equity … These are big issues.

—Satya Nadella, Microsoft CEO (quoted in Letzing 2024)

Opening Vignette: 1,400 Alerts Before the Phones Rang

At dawn in the Republic of Z, torrential rains swelled rivers until they burst their banks, flooding homes and cutting off entire neighborhoods. In past years, the consular team's first hours of a crisis would have been chaotic: staff waking up duty rosters, calling numbers one by one, leaving voicemails that often went unheard, and drafting emergency emails while the situation worsened. The phones would ring endlessly, citizens and families desperate for guidance, but consular officers and other staff would still be struggling to establish the facts themselves.

This morning unfolded differently. By 6:10 a.m., before most staff even reached the chancery—the main administrative office—the diplomatic mission's crisis AI platform had already sprung into action. It ingested hazard data from regional meteorological feeds, cross-referenced it against the voluntary citizen registry, and identified who was likely to be in the flood zone. It then translated evacuation instructions into four languages, tailored them for

DOI: 10.1201/9781003634775-7

SMS, WhatsApp, and automated voice calls, and dispatched them across all channels simultaneously. When the duty officer logged in, a dashboard showed delivery rates climbing past 70%, with acknowledgments streaming in. Instead of being consumed by repetitive dialing and drafting, the officer could focus on exceptions: the families who had not responded, the elderly couple in need of rescue, and the hospital requesting coordination for patient transfers.

The story is fictional, but the operational contours are grounded in reality. Emergencies unfold at a tempo that human labor alone cannot match. Every minute saved in communication and triage can be redirected toward judgment calls that require empathy, local knowledge, and calm under pressure. In the Republic of Z, as in every consular post worldwide, the lesson is clear: when a crisis moves faster than people can dial a phone, AI buys back the minutes that let officers reach the few who cannot be reached by an automated message at all.

WHY CRISIS RESPONSE NEEDS AI NOW

Crisis management has always been part of consular work. From natural disasters to political unrest, officers and consular staff are called on to provide clarity, reassurance, and action when citizens abroad face their most vulnerable moments. The crises themselves have not changed—earthquakes still strike, governments still collapse, planes still go down. What has changed are the tools and tempo surrounding them. Information now moves faster than events, amplified by digital media and instantaneous communication. For consular missions, traditional methods—phone trees, inbox triage, paper rosters—struggle to keep pace with emergencies that unfold in real time. This pressure is felt across all diplomatic functions, not consular affairs alone, and has driven AI adoption across embassy operations worldwide (Kilburg 2025).

Before exploring what AI can do, it is worth recalling what crisis management looked like before data moved at digital speed. When U.S. airspace closed after the September 11 attacks, more than 4,500 flights were forced to land at alternate airports around the world, leaving tens of thousands of travelers stranded (National Archives 2021). London, one of the world's busiest transit hubs, became a temporary refuge for thousands of Americans suddenly caught in limbo. *The Guardian* reported that "more than 2,000 passengers were left stranded at Heathrow … camping out on the floor in the departure terminals," noting that the roughly 170 cancelled outbound flights to North America would normally have carried about 40,000 passengers (Wilson and Hopkins 2001).

Inside the U.S. Embassy in London, consular officers and embassy staff responded the moment the news broke. The embassy's phones rang without pause as staff fielded one anxious call after another. By Wednesday evening, several hundred Americans were stranded at Heathrow with no plan to find lodging, and two consular officers were sent to the airport to take stock and do what they could; many of the stranded had nowhere to stay, no medication, and no way onward. As the *Foreign Service Journal* recounted, the officers prevailed on an airline to lodge stranded Americans in hotels, secured discounted rates at other hotels, and saw that travelers who needed medication had their prescriptions filled—and when private American citizens arrived at the airport offering to open their homes, the officers helped match stranded travelers with these volunteer hosts ("FSOs and FSNs Recall" 2001).

Had the tools of today's AI existed then, passenger manifests could have been cross-referenced automatically with traveler registries, and multilingual chatbots could have delivered verified updates directly to phones. Instead, officers relied on phones, notebooks, and empathy—a reminder that compassion powered the system, even when technology did not.

The gap between expectation and capacity has widened. The digital environment has raised the required tempo of response. In a world where news and rumors spread instantly, a government's failure to provide validated, multilingual information across multiple channels in a crisis is not just an inconvenience—it is a strategic vulnerability that risks undermining public confidence and allowing misinformation to take hold. During the COVID-19 pandemic, for example, diplomatic missions worldwide faced crushing demand from citizens desperate for repatriation. Reports showed that call centers were overwhelmed, messages went unanswered for days, and citizens often turned to social media to plead for help when traditional channels failed them (GAO 2020). These failures were not the result of indifference but of systems designed for a slower world.

AI offers a set of tools matched to this new tempo—not a single magic solution, but a family of capabilities that each address a different piece of the crisis puzzle.

The first is speed of awareness. NLP can scan thousands of social media posts, local news reports, and government bulletins in minutes, surfacing early signs of unrest or misinformation that might otherwise take hours for a human team to notice.

The second is situational clarity. Geospatial analytics can combine satellite imagery, hazard models, and transportation data into a live map—showing officers not just where a crisis is unfolding but who is in the affected zone and which routes remain open.

The third is communication at scale. Large language models can draft and translate emergency instructions in seconds, giving officers and consular teams ready-to-review alerts that are plain, concise, and available in multiple languages simultaneously.

The fourth is anticipation. Predictive algorithms, already used in fields like supply chain management, can model cascade effects: a flood that will cut a power grid within hours, a protest likely to close an airport by morning, or a pandemic trajectory that will overwhelm local hospitals within weeks (Bjola 2022; Haseley et al. 2023).

Individually, each of these tools solves a specific problem. Their real power emerges when their outputs are combined—what federal disaster response researchers call data fusion, the integration of satellite feeds, social media signals, and logistical data into a single, actionable operating picture (Haseley et al. 2023). Instead of officers arriving at their desks during a crisis to face a dozen disconnected information streams, they find one coherent view of what is happening, who is at risk, and what resources are available.

The promise is not automation for its own sake but amplification of consular capacity. Instead of spending critical early hours collecting and formatting information, officers can begin their shifts with actionable insights already in hand. Instead of struggling to reach citizens one by one, they can focus on those who are unreachable or in greatest danger. AI earns its place when the triage record shows who is safe, who is unreachable, who needs a call back, and who requires immediate officer action; empathy, discretion, and duty of care remain the work the sorting is meant to prioritize.

DRILLING DOWN INTO AI USE CASES

For consular officers and staff, the real measure of any technology is whether it makes them more effective in the moments that matter. In crisis management, AI does this by not only accelerating existing tasks but by enabling fundamentally new, strategic forms of intervention. AI takes on the time-consuming tasks that demand speed, freeing consular teams to concentrate on judgment, empathy, and high-stakes leadership.

One high-value use case is predictive triage for the *unreachable citizen*. In a mass evacuation or security incident, the greatest concern is the traveler who fails to receive or acknowledge alerts. Instead of consular teams manually searching public records or waiting for family calls, AI can synthesize fragmented, consent-based data—voluntary registry entries, last known addresses, and recent geofenced mobile pings—to generate a Risk-of-Harm Score. This probabilistic model moves beyond the simple "responded/unresponsive" list, estimating the likelihood that a citizen is safe, missing, or in imminent danger. The approach mirrors methods used by the UN Refugee Agency (UNHCR) and the International Organization for Migration (IOM), which apply vulnerability scoring models to prioritize field interventions (Beduschi and McAuliffe 2020). For consular teams, the effect is profound: staff spend less time combing through lists and more time coordinating real-world rescues where they matter most.

A second, mission-critical use case is the rapid misinformation counteroperation. Crises create ideal conditions for falsehoods—fake evacuation routes, spoofed embassy messages, or manipulated videos—that spread faster than official corrections. AI-enabled monitoring systems can continuously scan local and regional digital spaces, including encrypted or niche platforms where security posture allows, to identify emerging narratives with high virality potential. LLMs trained for crisis communication can then draft verified, multilingual countermessages that officers review and approve before release. The World Health Organization (WHO) already deploys similar models to track rumor trajectories and craft culturally tailored rebuttals during public health emergencies (Purnat, Nguyen, and Briand 2023). For consular missions, this capability acts as an information firewall—allowing teams to push credible updates through trusted channels before panic or manipulation takes hold, preserving both accuracy and public trust.

A third strategic use case addresses a problem that emergencies reliably expose: the fairness gap. When a crisis hits, not everyone receives help at the same speed. People in remote areas, those without mobile phones, and minority-language speakers are often the last to get alerts—if they get them at all. Existing societal divides do not pause during disasters; they widen.

AI can help a diplomatic mission see this gap in real time. The principle is straightforward: as alerts go out and acknowledgments come back, the system tracks who is responding and who is not—broken down by location, language, and communication channel. If 90% of English-speaking citizens in the capital have confirmed receipt but only 20% of French-speaking citizens in a rural province have responded, the system flags the disparity immediately. The diplomatic mission does not have to wait for an after-action review to discover that an entire community was left in the dark.

That flag then drives action. Consular officers and their teams can shift strategy on the spot—switching from SMS to radio broadcasts, dispatching printed notices, or activating community intermediaries who can reach populations that digital channels cannot. The goal, consistent with UN OCHA's Data Responsibility Guidelines (UN OCHA 2025), is to ensure that assistance is allocated based on verifiable need and fairness, not just on who happened to have a smartphone and a strong signal.

A fourth advanced use case is Hyper-Personalized Triage and Resource Matching. Beyond simply triaging citizens based on safety risk, AI can analyze nuanced individual needs—such as pre-existing medical conditions, mobility issues, or family size—pulled from the voluntary registry. This allows the system to match the citizen directly to the optimal solution: a direct medical evacuation flight (MEDEVAC), specific accessibility accommodation on a bus, or a referral to a partner NGO specializing in infant care. This dynamic matching is a core principle in advanced logistics, drawing on machine learning algorithms developed to optimize the delivery of scarce, specialized resources during complex disaster relief operations (Rodríguez-Espíndola et al. 2023). This replaces the slow, general process of "register and wait" with dynamic resource allocation, ensuring limited assets (like seats on a flight or scarce supplies) are matched precisely to the highest-priority, complex human needs.

Fifth, an ambitious use case is Dynamic Interoperability Mapping. The critical failure point in large evacuations is often the lack of systems talking to each other. An advanced AI layer could function as a universal integration engine, synthesizing data from disparate systems: local police manifests, airline check-in lists, embassy inventory logs, and the citizen registry. The AI translates, normalizes, and maps these data streams in real time, creating a single, authoritative manifest. This capability is already being piloted in multinational security contexts to create a unified Common Operating Picture (COP) from siloed command systems, ensuring all partners—military, diplomatic, and host nation—are working from the same, verified data set (NATO 2024). This mapping capability would allow consular managers to visually confirm, without manual spreadsheet checks, which citizens are confirmed on a flight, who is still stuck at a checkpoint, and which assets are available—solving the core challenge of systemic information gaps during extreme urgency.

The most ambitious vision for crisis AI is full integration—combining all of the tools described above into a single system that not only reports what is happening but anticipates what is likely to happen next. This concept, which we call Cognitive Crisis Orchestration, remains theoretical, but it is worth describing because it shows where the technology is heading and what consular leaders should be preparing for.

The idea is that instead of officers or their teams switching between separate dashboards for alerts, citizen tracking, misinformation monitoring, and resource allocation, one integrated platform connects all of those streams and draws conclusions across them. Three capabilities would set such a system apart from today's tools.

The first is anticipation. By combining real-time data—equity gaps in alert responses, surging misinformation on social media, transportation disruptions—the system could forecast where the next problem is likely to emerge. If response rates are plummeting in one district while false evacuation rumors are spreading in another, the system might recommend that the consular chief reroute security teams or open an alternative evacuation corridor before the primary route is compromised. The officer or a team member still makes the call—but the call comes 12 hours earlier than it would have otherwise.

The second is adaptive resource matching. Crises are fluid, and plans break down. If a prebooked medical evacuation flight is delayed, the system could instantly identify which other assets are available, reroute lower-priority resources to protect the most vulnerable citizens waiting at the pickup point, and update all partner manifests so that every agency involved is working from the same information. Instead of a consular chief discovering the delay through a phone call and scrambling to improvise, the system presents options within minutes.

The third is real-time learning. During a crisis, the system would continuously check its own predictions against what actually happens. Did the team find the missing citizen where the model predicted? Did the rerouted convoy arrive on time? Each answer refines the system's confidence scores and improves its next recommendation. The system gets sharper as the crisis unfolds, not after it ends. When the emergency subsides, the platform generates a complete, time-stamped after-action report documenting every prediction, decision, and outcome—replacing weeks of manual reconstruction with an instant institutional record.

This level of integration does not yet exist in consular operations, and building it would require advances in both technology and governance. But the direction is clear. When crisis AI evolves from a set of separate tools into a connected system that anticipates, adapts, and learns, it transforms the mission's capacity—giving human leaders a degree of foresight, coordination, and accountability that manual processes alone cannot provide. The decisions remain human. The speed and scope of the information behind them do not.

For the consular staff in the middle of it all, these complex systems don't look like algorithms and dashboards—they look like time. Instead of sorting spreadsheets or fielding frantic calls, the officer now starts each shift with a clear list of who is safe, who is missing, and where the next problem may emerge. A data-driven system might highlight risk, but it is still the human consular officer or staff member who knocks on a hotel door, reassures a parent, or negotiates with local police. The technology becomes a quiet partner in judgment, not its replacement.

Each of these scenarios reinforces a single point: AI does not change what consular officers and their staff are responsible for in crises. They remain the decision-makers, the faces of reassurance, and the guardians of fairness. What AI changes is the rhythm. By compressing the time required for routine tasks, it gives officers and consular staff back the space to act as human diplomats in the moments that matter most.

Digital Frontlines: When the Digital Sky Falls—How One Cyberattack Paralyzed European Aviation

On Friday, September 19, 2025, Collins Aerospace, a subsidiary of RTX Corporation that provides digital backbone for passenger processing at hundreds of airports worldwide, was hit by ransomware. Their ARINC cMUSE platform—common-use passenger-processing software that handles everything from automated check-in to biometric boarding—was instantly crippled, paralyzing operations across Europe's busiest travel hubs.

The cascade effect was immediate. At Heathrow, airlines reverted to handwritten passenger lists as digital systems went dark. Berlin's Brandenburg Airport faced extended queues, forcing staff to improvise with iPads and laptops. Brussels suffered the most severe impact: 38 flights cancelled on Saturday (25 departures plus 13 arrivals), 75 total flights cancelled on Sunday (45 departures plus 30 arrivals), and approximately 140 departures cancelled out of roughly 280 scheduled on Monday (Reuters 2025b, 2025c).

The attack highlighted modern aviation's dependence on AI-enhanced systems: facial recognition algorithms that match passengers to boarding passes, machine learning models that optimize gate assignments, and predictive analytics that manage baggage flow—all reliant on digital infrastructure vulnerable to targeted attacks.

By Monday, September 22, the EU's cybersecurity agency ENISA had confirmed ransomware as the cause, dispelling early speculation about nation-state involvement (Reuters 2025a). The U.K.'s National Crime Agency arrested a suspect in West Sussex within a week on charges under the Computer Misuse Act, signaling criminal extortion rather than geopolitical warfare (The Verge 2025).

The incident revealed critical vulnerabilities. Manual backup procedures—designed for brief outages, not multi-day system failures—quickly overwhelmed staff. Multilingual communication systems failed under pressure. Most critically, a single vendor's software failure cascaded across multiple countries, stranding thousands of passengers even when air traffic control and airport infrastructure remained operational.

For cybersecurity experts, the attack represented a new threat category: supply chain ransomware targeting automated systems enabling modern mass transit. Unlike attacks on individual airlines or airports, hitting a common-use platform provider multiplied impact across entire regions.

The incident forced uncomfortable questions about resilience in an increasingly automated world. Who bears responsibility when automated systems fail: technology vendors who built them, airports that deployed them, or governments that certified them as safe? The attack occurred despite what industry sources described as standard cybersecurity practices, suggesting even well-protected systems remain vulnerable.

Recovery efforts revealed both fragility and resilience. While automated check-in and boarding remained disrupted for days, airlines and airports demonstrated adaptability, shifting to manual processes that kept essential services operating—though with dramatically reduced efficiency.

IMPLEMENTATION BLUEPRINT

The temptation in crises is to imagine that only the most advanced systems will suffice—satellite fusion, predictive analytics, and fully automated contact centers. While AI tools are inherently scalable, the implementation strategy must be tailored to the mission's resources, complexity, and budget. A clear blueprint, customized for consular section size, allows AI to be introduced in stages that build trust, manage risk, and deliver immediate value.

For a small consular section—typically staffed by a single officer and a handful of locally employed staff (LES)—the entry point is often lightweight and low-cost. The most valuable early tool is a basic communications hub. This integrates a simple citizen registry with a messaging API (like an SMS gateway), giving the mission the ability to push alerts to citizens with a single click and log acknowledgments. While social listening may be led by other embassy sections (i.e., by the Regional Security Office [RSO] for security surge issues), a consular-focused mission can utilize open-source tools to monitor chatter specifically for citizen distress signals, supply shortages, or access to service issues. The key is speed of deployment: consular sections can launch such a system in weeks rather than years, ensuring that the first pilot demonstrates value quickly.

Medium-sized posts can scale this approach with managed platforms. Software-as-a-service crisis tools now allow multilingual alerts across SMS, WhatsApp, email, and automated voice calls from a single interface. NLP modules can monitor local news feeds, while a consent-based registry enables clustering of citizens by exposure. These systems are more robust but still manageable by locally employed staff with light training. They give missions the flexibility to run drills, red-team tests, and after-action reviews without building an entire IT backbone.

Regional hubs and large missions may justify more advanced architectures. Here, data lakes and streaming analytics can combine hazard feeds, geospatial imagery, and citizen registries in real time. Consular staff monitor live dashboards that display delivery rates, distress signals, and resource allocations across multiple districts. Such systems are expensive and complex, but they make sense where thousands of citizens must be reached in hours, as in evacuations from major conflict zones.

No matter the scale, governance principles remain constant. Every deployment must begin with a clear scope—what data will be used, how long it will be retained, and who has access. Roles should be assigned in advance: a crisis AI lead to manage dashboards, a data steward to enforce privacy, channel captains among locally employed staff to test language accuracy, and a duty officer empowered to override or pause automated actions. Drills must be run before real crises, not during them, with red-team exercises designed to simulate misinformation, spoofed identities, or mass nonresponse.

This blueprint underscores a simple truth: technology can be scaled to context. A $1,000 pilot at a small mission and a multimillion-dollar platform at a regional hub both serve the same purpose—to extend officers' capacity in moments of extraordinary demand. What matters is not how advanced the system appears but how well it integrates into the rhythms of consular practice, preserving human discretion while expanding reach.

RISKS, ETHICS, AND EQUITY

Emergencies create enormous pressure to act fast, and in that pressure it is easy to forget that the very tools designed to save lives can also create risks if not governed carefully. AI accelerates communication and triage, but if left unchecked it can blur lines of consent, compromise privacy, or reproduce inequities in who receives help. For consular officers, the ethical obligation is not suspended during crises; if anything, it is heightened.

One risk is privacy erosion under urgency. Location data, social media monitoring, and citizen registries can be invaluable for targeting assistance, but their use must be bounded by consent and purpose. The U.S. Department of Homeland Security has emphasized in its privacy impact assessments that emergency data collection should be time-limited, with automatic deletion once the crisis ends (DHS/OBIM 2024). Without such controls, systems built for crisis response can drift into permanent surveillance infrastructures, a concern raised repeatedly by civil society groups (Amnesty International 2024).

Another concern is equity of access. Crises often expose divides between those who have smartphones and connectivity and those who do not. An SMS alert may never reach a citizen without a mobile subscription; an email may be useless in a blackout; a chatbot may exclude those with limited literacy. The Privacy and Civil Liberties Oversight Board, in its report on face recognition, highlighted how technologies deployed without attention to inclusivity risk entrenching disparities (PCLOB 2025). For crisis AI, this means that alerts must be redundant across multiple channels—including social media broadcasts (e.g., WhatsApp, X, TikTok), SMS, voice calls, printed posters, and radio—and available in multiple languages, including minority or indigenous ones.

A third risk lies in misinformation and over-automation. LLMs can generate alerts rapidly, but without human review, they may introduce errors in tone or substance. A mistranslated curfew order could cause panic or even harm, and bad information released by AI in a crisis is extremely difficult to claw back. Safeguards such as retrieval augmented generation, paired with officer verification before release, ensure that speed does not come at the expense of accuracy. Consular officers and their teams must also resist the temptation to allow automated systems to make eligibility decisions for evacuation or aid. These are fundamentally human judgments, shaped by law, policy, and compassion, and cannot be delegated to algorithms.

Beyond questions of privacy and fairness lies a quieter risk: the toll crises take on those who respond.

When the Indian Ocean tsunami struck on December 26, 2004, it killed more than 200,000 people and displaced nearly two million across the region. In the April 2005 *Foreign Service Journal* article "After the Tsunami: Assisting Americans in Distress," Steven Alan Honley documented the consular response across the Indian Ocean region, including the work of U.S. Embassy Bangkok. According to the article's Bangkok account, written by Ted Coley, chief of the American Citizen Services Section, embassy staff began working around the clock as soon as they learned of the disaster. The American Citizen Services Unit stayed open 24 hours a day, seven days a week, for almost three weeks and handled thousands of calls from people in the U.S. searching for loved ones in Thailand.

The work combined practical assistance with the emotional burden of helping families face devastating loss. In one case described in the article, a family of five had separated before the wave hit. The son was seriously injured, and one daughter was missing. A consular officer met the mother at Bangkok's airport and accompanied her to the hospital where her son was recovering; another officer helped the father return to the family's bungalow and retrace the wave's path, where they found belongings of the missing daughter. Her remains were later identified by the Thailand Tsunami Victim Identification teams.

The Bangkok operation also depended on improvised tracing work. As the number of Americans still listed as "not accounted for" fell below 100, staff used local American Citizen Services files, archived passport records, and, unusually, "bank, phone and immigration records in Thailand." They also "googled" names and followed unlikely leads, including one search that led from a golf handicap to a golf-club membership and finally to an email address. Of the more than 7,000 people Embassy Bangkok began looking for, nearly all were accounted for. The article does not discuss artificial intelligence or biometric matching. Read today, however, its lesson remains clear: technology can assist identification and tracing, but consoling families, bearing witness, and carrying the weight of grief remain irreducibly human work.

In March 2020, as COVID-19 cases rose, South Africa abruptly closed its borders and restricted international air travel (South African Government 2020). Thousands of Americans—including tourists, long-term residents, and an entire Semester at Sea ship of students and faculty—were stranded when commercial flights ceased. The U.S. mission worked with Ethiopian Airlines to operate chartered repatriation flights from Johannesburg and Cape Town (Semester at Sea 2020; U.S. Embassy Pretoria 2020). Globally, the State Department returned more than 100,000 U.S. citizens on 1,100 flights from 136 countries (U.S. Department of State 2020a).

Despite digital tools like the Smart Traveler Enrollment Program (STEP), the response looked strikingly familiar. Consular teams compiled paper manifests, verified travelers at the DHL Stadium in Cape Town, and collected signed Repatriation Loan paperwork—issued under the Department's Emergency Medical and Dietary Assistance (EMDA) authority—to cover seats on U.S. chartered evacuation flights. These loans enabled citizens to depart immediately, with ticket costs later billed to the traveler and reimbursed to the U.S. government (U.S. Department of State 2024a; 22 CFR § 71.10 [U.S. Code of Federal Regulations 2024b]).

The technology existed, but the systems did not. Databases could not share information, and every manifest was built by hand. AI tools might have cross-linked passport data and seating lists in minutes; instead, the Cape Town operation relied on improvisation and trust. It proved that digitization without interoperability changes appearance, not outcome.

The South Africa evacuations underscored a larger truth: technology alone does not modernize a system. Until crisis response tools connect data, decisions, and human judgment, even the most advanced platforms will continue to depend on handwritten lists and empathy in motion.

Across these three decades, the rhythm of emergencies changed faster than the systems designed to handle them. The challenge for consular officers and their teams now is not invention but integration—linking tools, data, and human judgment in real time.

Trust itself is at stake. If citizens feel their government's crisis messages are unreliable, intrusive, or discriminatory, they will turn to informal networks—social media rumors, private groups, or local intermediaries—that may prove less accurate and more dangerous. Transparency is therefore critical. Citizens should be told when AI systems are used, how their data is handled, and what avenues exist for appeal or correction. This openness reinforces the legitimacy of the mission and sustains public confidence in moments of fear.

For consular officers and staff, the balancing act is clear: act quickly, but act fairly. AI can compress hours into minutes, but without safeguards it can also compress rights into risks. Embedding privacy minimization, accessibility, transparency, and human oversight into every deployment ensures that crisis AI fulfills its purpose—to protect citizens, not to control them.

FIELD CHECKLIST: AI CRISIS TOOL STARTER PACK

Before any diplomatic mission adopts AI for crisis response, it must ensure that the essentials are in place. The goal is not to pursue cutting-edge tools for their own sake, but to guarantee that technology genuinely extends consular staff capacity without undermining trust. A well-prepared starter pack allows even the smallest sections to field-test AI responsibly.

The first element is scope definition. Diplomatic missions should articulate precisely what the system will and will not do—whether it is limited to multilingual alerts, whether it will cluster citizens by geography, or whether it will ingest social media feeds. This definition must also specify the privacy boundaries of the data used and the purpose limitation of the tool. Without this clarity, expectations can spiral beyond what the mission can credibly deliver.

The second is content readiness. Preapproved templates for emergency messages, translated into multiple languages and adapted for multiple channels (SMS, email, WhatsApp, voice calls, social media), should be loaded into the system before a crisis. Messages must be reviewed for tone, cultural appropriateness, and accuracy.

Officers must be able to push accurate, culturally appropriate messages instantly, without scrambling to draft in the heat of an emergency.

Third comes governance and safeguards. Each mission should identify a crisis AI lead, assign a data steward to enforce privacy rules, use locally employed staff to verify translations, and empower a duty officer to override automation at any time. Comprehensive audit logs must be activated from day one, capturing when alerts were sent, by whom, and with what sources, thereby ensuring full accountability.

Fourth is testing and red-teaming. Diplomatic missions should not wait for a flood or protest to discover flaws. Tabletop drills and adversarial exercises—such as simulating misinformation campaigns, spoofed identities, or mass nonresponse—expose weaknesses under controlled conditions. These exercises must specifically test the misinformation "claw back" process and build officer confidence before real lives depend on the system.

Metrics and review must be built in. Dashboards should track speed (time to first alert), reach (percent delivered across channels), equity (demographic distribution of acknowledgments), and trust (surveyed satisfaction post-crisis). These metrics should feed into after-action reviews and inform refinements, ensuring the system improves with each deployment.

This checklist does not require massive budgets. Even the most modest diplomatic missions can assemble the core pieces—defined scope, multilingual templates, governance roles, drills, and metrics—in a matter of weeks. With this starter pack, a consular section can launch responsibly, prove value quickly, and scale cautiously, all while keeping human judgment at the center of crisis response.

CLOSING REFLECTION

Crises strip consular work down to its essence: the duty to protect citizens when they are most exposed. In those moments, officers and their teams are judged not by abstract policy but by speed, clarity, and compassion. AI changes the rhythm of the work by making the next call clearer. In a crisis workflow, the system should distinguish confirmed safe citizens, unreachable citizens, conflicting location reports, medical or detention cases, and messages requiring immediate officer judgment. That sorting does not replace the officer who reassures a frightened family or negotiates safe passage; it helps the team identify where that human intervention is needed first.

The risks are not theoretical. Systems that overreach can erode privacy, exclude vulnerable groups, or miscommunicate in ways that undermine trust—risks that are amplified in a disaster. Civil society critiques correctly warn that technologies introduced during emergencies can outlast their purpose, turning into instruments of surveillance if guardrails are absent (Amnesty International 2024). Oversight bodies such as the U.S. Privacy and Civil Liberties Oversight Board remind us that speed must never come at the cost of transparency or fairness (PCLOB 2025). For consular officers and their staff, this means embedding human review, purpose limitation, and clear redress into every deployment, even under the pressure of disaster.

The promise of crisis AI is not found in complexity but in clarity. Picture a flood in Z City where multilingual alerts go out before dawn, where consular teams can see in minutes who is safe and who needs help, and where follow-up teams are already on the move. That is not a distant future—it is a glimpse of what well-governed AI can already do.

In the end, crisis work always comes back to people. Technology buys time and extends reach—and in consular crisis work, that Time Dividend is measured in the moments officers have to make the calls that matter, but it cannot console a frightened traveler or carry a stretcher through floodwater. Those acts remain human. The real partnership between AI and consular staff lies in freeing humans to do what only they can—exercise judgment, empathy, and care—so that even in the fog of disaster, citizens find not just information but trust.

Part III

Fraud, Forgery, and Identity Integrity

Consular work carries stakes that extend far beyond administrative efficiency. When fraudsters exploit document systems or impostors assume false identities to cross borders, the consequences touch national security and the integrity of international mobility itself. This section examines how AI strengthens consular capacity against these adversarial threats—and why governance matters most precisely where risks are greatest.

Fraud detection and identity integrity address threats that have grown more sophisticated as technology has advanced. Document mills now produce forgeries that look identical in isolation but reveal patterns when clustered across thousands of cases. Generative AI creates morphed photographs that can fool facial recognition systems. Impostors assume multiple identities across jurisdictions. The chapters in this section examine how AI surfaces these threats—through clustering algorithms, forensic analysis, biometric matching, and graph analytics—while confronting the arms race between detection and deception directly.

Throughout this section, governance receives sustained attention. The same tools that protect borders can harm legitimate applicants if poorly calibrated or opaquely deployed. Privacy protections, fairness audits, explainability requirements, and human-in-the-loop review are not bureaucratic hurdles but conditions of legitimacy. Civil society critiques and independent evaluations—from National Institute of

DOI: 10.1201/9781003634775-8

Standards and Technology's (NIST) demographic studies of biometric accuracy to Amnesty International's warnings about digital borders—inform every chapter.

By the end of this section, you will understand how AI can expose fraud rings and safeguard identity integrity—without becoming instruments of exclusion or surveillance.

6 Detecting Fraud and Forgery with AI

Just to dispel any fears that may exist, a human being is still responsible for every final decision … It is not possible for an AI system or an advanced analytics system to make a final determination on a person's admissibility or eligibility.

—Sean Fraser, former Minister of Immigration, Refugees and Citizenship, Canada (quoted in Raycraft 2023)

We're sprawling in the entire AI space. Actually, we can't keep up with the use cases that we're seeing.

—Mark James, former Director of Infrastructure and Support Services, U.S. Customs and Border Protection (quoted in Bracken 2024)

Algorithms are socially constructed, and our world is built on systemic racism and historical discrimination … These tools are going to replicate biases already inherent to the immigration system, not to mention create new ones based on very problematic assumptions about human behaviour.

—Petra Molnar, Associate Director of the Refugee Law Lab, York University (quoted in Ventura 2025)

Opening Vignette: The Seals Looked Real

At the consulate in the Republic of Z, the visa line moved briskly until a junior officer paused over a student's sponsorship letter. The seals looked official, the signature confident, and the formatting identical to hundreds of other letters the officer had reviewed that week. Nothing stood out on its own. The officer approved the visa, and the next, and the next. Only weeks later did the fraud prevention unit realize that dozens of nearly identical letters had been submitted, each fabricated by the same document mill and sold across the city. By then, the ring had slipped through.

The following year, the outcome was different. An AI-based clustering tool had been introduced to review digital submissions. Instead of looking at each sponsorship letter in isolation, the system compared seal impressions, signatures, and print artifacts across all incoming cases. Within minutes, it

DOI: 10.1201/9781003634775-9

flagged 37 applications that shared the same anomalies, highlighting them for officer review. When the fraud prevention team dug deeper, the pattern became unmistakable: one forged seal reused across dozens of letters, each doctored just enough to slip through.

The officer who had once felt overwhelmed by the sameness of cases now had a clearer view. Rather than relying on instinct alone, she entered interviews already aware of which applications warranted sharper questions. The AI had not made the decision—it had exposed the forgery. Human judgment remained the final arbiter, but judgment was now informed by evidence at scale.

This vignette is fictional, but its contours mirror real challenges in consular work. Fraud rings exploit volume, repetition, and the limits of human perception. AI shifts that balance, making it harder for deceptive patterns to hide in plain sight. In the Republic of Z, as elsewhere, the lesson is that the officer's instinct was never the problem—it simply could not see across thousands of files at once, and now it does not have to.

THE FRAUD LANDSCAPE: WHAT'S CHANGED, WHAT HASN'T

If Chapter 3 explored how AI helps confirm who applicants are, this chapter examines how it exposes who they are not.

Fraud in consular work is as old as the profession itself. Applicants have always forged bank statements, altered birth records, or rehearsed stories to fit perceived eligibility criteria. What has changed in recent years is not just the volume of attempts but the sophistication of the tools behind them. Generative AI, automated document design, and deep image manipulation now make it easy for small document mills to produce forgeries that, at first glance, rival genuine records.

Within this landscape, it helps to distinguish *forgery* from *fraud*. Forgery involves manipulating a document's content or appearance—altered seals, false stamps, or digitally fabricated records—while fraud encompasses broader acts of deception such as coached narratives, straw applicants, or organized misrepresentation. AI tools can assist with both: one by inspecting pixels, the other by mapping patterns.

The difference today is not only the scale of applications but the cognitive weight of adjudication itself. Thirty years ago, officers reviewed an applicant, a few paper documents, and perhaps a brief case note. Security checks—then performed manually on microfiche by locally employed staff and later verified by an officer—were slow, repetitive, and incomplete. Those analog systems kept attention centered on the interview but left critical intelligence fragmented.

The consequences could be profound. In 1990, Omar Abdel Rahman—later known as the "Blind Sheikh" and convicted for his role in the 1993 World Trade Center bombing—was issued a U.S. visa in Khartoum by an officer working under CIA cover. Although Abdel Rahman's name already appeared on a watchlist, the manual system failed to surface it during review, and the visa was issued (Roanoke

Times 1993). It was a case of successful fraud—an applicant concealing his true background—and a reminder that even skilled officers can be defeated by the limits of their tools.

In the years that followed, some high-fraud posts began experimenting with what officers informally called "no-paper interview days." On those days, consular managers instructed officers to adjudicate visas based solely on the interview and security checks—without reviewing supporting documents such as bank statements, employment letters, or birth certificates. The goal was to sharpen judgment and reduce dependence on papers of uncertain authenticity. Locally employed staff still prescreened submissions for completeness, but the officer's decision turned entirely on conversation, demeanor, and verified database results.

This approach reflected a broader institutional philosophy that took shape across the Bureau of Consular Affairs in the 1990s and 2000s: documents can lie, but people and data leave patterns. The Office of Fraud Prevention Programs (FPP) later codified that principle in its guidance and training, urging officers to rely on interviews, security vetting, and verified records rather than unverified paperwork. The FPP emphasized that forged civil and financial records remain pervasive worldwide and that officer discretion, supported by behavioral assessment and data analysis, provides the most reliable safeguard (U.S. Department of State 2019).

Although never formally quantified, anecdotal reporting from several high-fraud posts suggested that "no-paper" adjudications improved consistency and reduced vulnerability to document fraud. Officers often found the experience clarifying: freed from the clutter of counterfeit paperwork, they could focus on credibility, intent, and context. The practice also foreshadowed the philosophy behind today's AI systems, which seek to separate genuine signal from background noise—helping officers see patterns rather than pages.

Among professional identity forgers, the ultimate prize is an original, untampered blank passport. Such blanks are not themselves fraudulent—they are genuine documents awaiting personalization—but once stolen, they become the foundation for the most dangerous forgeries. A forged passport made from a stolen blank is authentic in every physical sense—paper, ink, and holograms—yet fraudulent in identity and intent. Intelligence and law enforcement reporting confirm that blank passport theft is not theoretical: over the past two decades, tens of thousands of blanks have been stolen from government stocks around the world, including in Europe, South America, and Africa (Interpol n.d.).

Belgium was among the countries affected, its losses viewed as a significant vulnerability to the Schengen system and a reminder that document security failures in one nation can ripple across many. Even diplomatic settings have not been immune. Veteran consular officers recall a European luncheon in the 1990s where a U.S. colleague circulated one of the short-lived green "Benjamin Franklin" passport blanks for others to examine. During the meal, the document quietly vanished—never recovered and never publicly resolved. Whether misplaced or deliberately taken, the incident underscored that even within trusted circles, document custody is paramount. Blank theft sits upstream of both forgery and fraud: a security breach that provides the substrate for counterfeit identities and false claims. Protecting these materials is therefore not peripheral to fraud prevention—it is its front line. And today, AI stands poised to help.

Modern AI-enabled border and identity systems can already detect the early signs of blank document misuse. By comparing issuance and use patterns across national databases, they can flag when a passport number never recorded as issued suddenly appears in circulation. Integrated with INTERPOL's Stolen and Lost Travel Documents (SLTD) database and ICAO's Public Key Directory (PKD), AI tools could provide near-real-time anomaly detection—surfacing compromised serials, mismatched chip signatures, or improbable travel histories long before manual systems would catch them (INTERPOL SLTD; ICAO PKD). In short, the same technology that exposes forged bank statements or deepfaked photos can also protect the physical foundations of identity itself.

The fundamentals, however, remain constant. Most fraudulent submissions still rely on human error, the constraints of time, and the reality that officers cannot scrutinize every pixel or every word in every file. A fraudulent diploma may be convincing in isolation but reveals its falsity when compared against dozens produced from the same template. A falsified ledger may appear credible until anomaly detection highlights round-number deposits or implausible transaction patterns. The challenge is compounded by modern workloads: unlike their predecessors, officers now navigate multiple digital systems, security platforms, and databases before each interview, leaving less time for contextual judgment.

AI alters that equation. Computer vision systems can detect irregularities invisible to the human eye—misaligned seals, inconsistent kerning, or suspicious compression artifacts. Natural language processing can identify stylistic fingerprints across supposedly independent sponsorship letters, suggesting a coached narrative. Anomaly detection models can flag financial statements with statistical irregularities unlikely to occur in authentic records. And graph analytics can map connections across applications—shared addresses, phone numbers, or email domains—that betray the presence of organized fraud rings (DocXPand Team 2024).

Civil society organizations have raised legitimate concerns about the risks of over-automation in this space. Amnesty International warns that poorly governed detection systems may unfairly penalize legitimate applicants whose documents deviate from expected norms because of cultural or economic context (Amnesty International 2024). This is why human-in-the-loop review, explainability, and redress mechanisms remain indispensable. The role of AI is to surface anomalies, not to assume guilt.

In short, the landscape of fraud has evolved, but so too have the tools available to consular officers. Where once they relied on instinct, rumor, and painstaking manual comparison, they now have access to systems capable of scanning thousands of files in seconds. Fraud detection is not a challenge unique to consular sections: it intersects with diplomatic security, border management, and intelligence functions across the full architecture of embassy operations, where AI is being applied with increasing sophistication (Kilburg 2025). The enduring challenge is the same: separating deception from authenticity while protecting fairness. AI strengthens that effort—but only when coupled with human judgment and ethical safeguards.

HIGH-YIELD AI USE CASES (AND WHAT GOOD LOOKS LIKE)

AI is valuable in fraud detection when it focuses on the repetitive vulnerabilities that fraudsters exploit—patterns too subtle or too numerous for officers to catch unaided. Its most effective uses are those that help consular teams see connections across cases, surface anomalies hidden in plain sight, and focus investigative energy where it matters most.

Document clustering and template reuse detection allows systems to identify repeated formats across large datasets. Fraud rings often recycle the same sponsorship letters, certificates, or templates, changing only names and dates. To one officer, each file may look plausible; across dozens, the repetition becomes clear. AI-driven clustering tools can group visually or structurally similar documents and flag them for review. This approach has been validated in benchmark datasets such as DocXPand-25k, which test document analysis algorithms at scale (Lerouge 2024). Properly implemented, clustering becomes a quiet back-end function—an extra set of eyes that exposes invisible patterns without altering officer discretion.

Computer vision analysis for document forensics builds on this by examining the physical features of digital images. Advanced processing can detect mismatched fonts, inconsistent letter spacing (*kerning*), seals printed at nonstandard resolutions, or layered compression artifacts that reveal tampering. The field of digital image forensics, pioneered by Hany Farid, provides a mature technical base for detecting such manipulations (Farid 2009). Pilot efforts such as the U.S. Department of Homeland Security's Document Verification Program (2023) and Canada's Immigration, Refugees and Citizenship Canada (IRCC) Advanced Analytics Initiative (2023) show how these methods can integrate into adjudication workflows while keeping human judgment at the center.

Logical consistency and contextual reasoning represent another frontier. Beyond pattern matching, AI can evaluate whether data make sense within known operational realities. In one recent South African case, a fraud ring created counterfeit U.S. consular seals to notarize real estate documents for property sales. The forged papers bore the name of the U.S. Consul General in Cape Town but listed the office location as "Pretoria"—a city where the U.S. has no consular section. Anyone familiar with local diplomatic operations would recognize the inconsistency immediately, as notarial services are performed only in Cape Town, Durban, and Johannesburg, and senior officers rarely perform them personally. An AI system cross-referencing officer roles and mission locations could have flagged the inconsistency instantly. Such reasoning mirrors what experienced officers do intuitively: compare claimed facts against institutional logic. By embedding that awareness into automated systems, AI can expose sophisticated frauds that rely on bureaucratic plausibility rather than obvious forgery.

Financial document anomaly detection applies similar logic to numbers. Fraudulent bank statements often display patterns that differ statistically from genuine ledgers—regular round-number deposits, identical transaction descriptors, or improbable balances. Machine learning models trained on verified exemplars can flag these anomalies, giving officers a reason to probe further without substituting for their judgment. Because access to formal banking systems varies widely, fairness parameters must ensure that applicants from cash-based economies are not penalized for legitimate irregularity.

Textual pattern analysis adds another dimension through natural language processing that detects coached narratives. Fraud networks frequently distribute prefabricated personal statements or letters of support. NLP tools can identify strikingly similar syntax or phrasing across unrelated submissions. The discovery of these linguistic fingerprints does not prove deception, but it alerts officers to probe deeper during interviews.

Network and ring discovery through graph analytics connects the dots across cases that appear unrelated. Many fraud schemes rely on coordinated deception—shared sponsors, phone numbers, or guarantors linking dozens of applications. Graph analytics models can map these relationships, revealing hidden brokers or document mills operating across missions. Several governments have piloted such tools: the U.S. Department of Homeland Security announced new AI-enabled pilots in 2024 to strengthen identity verification and data link analysis (U.S. Department of Homeland Security 2024), and ICAO's Traveler Identification Program (TRIP) promotes comparable network-based approaches among member states (ICAO n.d.). Visualizing these connections enables Fraud Prevention Units to identify and disrupt organized rings rather than treating each case in isolation.

What unites these applications is that none of them render verdicts. They act as investigative multipliers, surfacing weak signals that human officers can confirm, reject, or escalate. Good practice requires that every AI-generated alert include an explanation—*why* it was triggered—so officers remain accountable for final decisions. AI strengthens fraud detection not by replacing judgment but by amplifying it.

REFERENCE ARCHITECTURE (DROP-IN, NOT RIP-AND-REPLACE)

A persistent misconception about AI in fraud detection is that consular operations must rebuild their entire IT infrastructure before seeing any benefit. In practice, the most effective systems are modular. They layer onto existing workflows with minimal disruption, strengthening the tools officers already use rather than creating a parallel universe of adjudication.

The flow begins with ingestion—the point where records enter the digital pipeline. Across consular services, applicants already submit scanned or digital files for passport renewals, visa applications, or reports of birth abroad. AI systems can draw these directly into a preprocessing layer without requiring applicants or officers to change established submission procedures.

Next comes preprocessing and normalization. Optical character recognition (OCR) converts scanned text into machine-readable form; layout parsing records visual structure such as spacing, fonts, and headers; metadata extraction captures hidden attributes like creation software and timestamps.

Increasingly, provenance tagging attaches content credentials that indicate whether a file has been altered since capture. These methods mirror international standards developed by the Coalition for Content Provenance and Authenticity, or C2PA, and align with privacy and authenticity principles in the U.S. Department of

State's Department Privacy Program Plan 2023 (Coalition for Content Provenance and Authenticity 2025; U.S. Department of State 2023b).

The processed inputs feed a model ensemble—a family of algorithms tuned for distinct fraud signatures. A computer vision model inspects seals, logos, or background textures for tampering. A natural language model compares letters or affidavits for suspicious similarity. An anomaly detection model scores financial records, while a graph model links shared identifiers—addresses, sponsors, or guarantors—across cases. Each model produces signals, not verdicts.

Where historical records are retained—for example, prior visa or passport applications—AI can compare today's submission against the applicant's own history: face templates that remain stable over time, signatures that evolve gradually rather than abruptly, and biographic elements that should reconcile across filings. Biometric integration strengthens this process further. A case in London illustrated the point: a young British applicant appeared for a visa renewal, but the biometric system repeatedly rejected his fingerprints. The photographs matched, and he knew every detail of his prior interview, yet the data would not align. Eventually, he admitted that he and his identical twin brother had been sharing a single passport and visa to save money. They had not realized that even identical twins have distinct fingerprints—a reminder that biometric verification closes identity gaps that even perfect likeness cannot.

By contrast, notarial services operate within narrower boundaries. A consular officer does not determine whether an instrument's contents are true or lawful—only that the person appearing has been properly identified, that the act occurred in the officer's presence, and that a copy corresponds to the original presented. Fraud in this space therefore takes a different form: applicants may attempt to pass counterfeit or altered source documents across the window for certification, or present false statements under oath. AI support here would focus not on evaluating the truth of a declaration, but on verifying form and provenance—for example, confirming that the presented document matches known templates, that the individual signing appears in appointment or identity records, and that the act itself is logged and traceable. In this limited but critical way, automation can reinforce procedural integrity without crossing into substantive judgment.

All model outputs converge in a risk engine that fuses probabilities with reason codes. Instead of a blunt "high-risk" label, an officer might see: "shares 85% textual similarity with 12 prior submissions" or "signature deviates 40% from earlier visa applications." This transparency lets officers understand why a case was flagged and decide what to do next.

Probability scores and similarity flags are investigative prompts, not adjudicative recommendations—officers must be trained to treat them as the beginning of an inquiry, never as a substitute for independent judgment on the case.

Results appear in a human-in-the-loop console integrated into existing case management tools. Officers can open side-by-side comparisons, inspect cluster maps of related cases, and review the rationale behind each alert. Every override, escalation, or dismissal is logged, creating an audit trail that supports accountability, training, and continuous improvement.

The architecture also embeds governance and privacy controls. Data minimization limits what is stored; role-based access restricts who can view sensitive content; retention schedules tie data storage to clear investigative purposes. Drift monitoring triggers retraining when fraud tactics evolve, preventing models from hardening around outdated patterns.

The strength of this approach is its modularity. A small consular section might start with OCR and document clustering; a regional fraud prevention hub could add biometric matching, anomaly detection, and graph analytics. None of this requires replacing legacy systems. AI components drop in where they add measurable value and scale as consular operations build confidence, capacity, and trust.

But no matter how advanced the tools, their effectiveness depends on how they are governed—on clear rules for data use, transparent oversight, and the enduring presence of human judgment in every stage of the process.

Digital Frontlines: The Morphing Wars—How AI Criminals Are Rewriting the Rules of Identity Fraud

Face morphing has emerged as a significant operational threat, reshaping how governments approach identity verification. Criminals use AI algorithms to create facial images blending two individuals into a single portrait that can fool human and automated checks, effectively allowing two people to share one identity document.

Evidence from multiple European countries demonstrates the growing scale of morphing attempts. Slovenia's authorities have documented numerous cases since 2020 where two people successfully shared a single passport using AI-created morphed images (Ngan 2025; IEC 2025). Each detection represents a failure of traditional security measures and reveals how criminal organizations are industrializing identity fraud using machine learning tools.

In August 2025, the U.S. NIST issued unprecedented guidance on how government agencies should deploy AI-powered morph detection in real-world operations (Ngan and Grother 2025). The 84-page technical report details where to insert detection tools, how to triage algorithmic flags to human reviewers, when to divert suspicious applicants to supervised photo capture, and how to investigate borderline cases without revealing detection capabilities.

The criminal technique uses commercially available software to blend two facial images into a synthetic portrait maintaining enough similarity to both source faces to pass identity checks. When one person applies for a passport using the morphed image, the resulting document can potentially be used by either individual.

NIST's guidance emphasizes that single image detection—analyzing one photo for signs of manipulation—must be paired with "differential" detection comparing a fresh capture against stored portraits. The approach requires careful quality assurance, human oversight of algorithmic decisions, and investigative playbooks that don't reveal detection methods to the public (Ngan, Hanaoka, and Kuo 2025).

Standards organizations have rushed to address the threat. ICAO Document 9303, the international standard for machine-readable travel documents, now provides image quality baselines that morphing research references, while European research programs like iMARS and SOTAMD have created shared benchmarks for testing detection systems against evolving attack methods (ICAO 2025; Busch 2020; NTNU SOTAMD n.d.).

Operational challenges remain significant. Laboratory tests show impressive detection rates under controlled conditions, but accuracy drops when criminals use unfamiliar software, vary compression settings, or exploit differences between training data and real-world capture environments. The generalization gap means detection systems can only flag morphs they've been trained to recognize—creating a perpetual cat-and-mouse game.

As governments digitize more identity services—from visa applications to driver's license renewals—remote photo submission becomes increasingly common, creating new opportunities for morphing attacks. Government responses must balance deploying sophisticated detection systems while avoiding false positives that burden legitimate applicants, requiring clear communication strategies and human oversight mechanisms to prevent algorithmic bias.

OPERATIONAL WORKFLOWS (HOW IT RUNS AT POST)

For AI-driven fraud detection to deliver real value, it must integrate seamlessly into the established rhythm of consular operations. The most successful systems feel like natural extensions of existing tools, not new burdens. Officers and staff continue to adjudicate and assist as they always have—interviewing applicants, verifying identities, and applying judgment—while AI works quietly in the background, surfacing anomalies and connections that would otherwise remain hidden.

The process begins long before an applicant reaches the window. Fraud detection starts as soon as a visa, passport, or notarial appointment is scheduled or an online form is submitted. AI-enabled systems can scan for duplicate phone numbers, reused email addresses, suspiciously linked IP data, or recycled guarantor information—signals that a single network may be generating multiple applications. These early checks help ensure officers see the right information at the right time, without changing the applicant's experience.

During visa adjudications, AI serves as a silent advisor. When an officer opens a case, the system can flag unusual consistencies across supposedly unrelated applications, detect anomalies in supporting materials, or note potential connections to known fraud networks. A sponsorship letter that mirrors others word for word, or an address repeatedly linked to refused applicants, can be highlighted for deeper questioning. These insights remain advisory, ensuring that officer discretion and fairness govern every decision.

Fraud Prevention Units (FPUs) benefit from AI at the local, regional, and global levels. Instead of manually sampling files, FPUs can run analytic sweeps across months of application data, identifying cross-post trends or recurring brokers whose fingerprints appear across multiple systems. Visualization tools can reveal emerging hotspots of forged documents or identity reuse, helping posts coordinate with regional hubs and CA headquarters to disrupt networks rather than individual cases.

In passport and citizenship services, AI-assisted document forensics help detect anomalies in breeder documents—birth, marriage, or custody certificates—before they are accepted as the foundation for a U.S. passport or Consular Report of Birth Abroad. Optical and metadata analysis can reveal, for example, that a series of certificates were produced by the same printer or registration office within minutes of each other, even if submitted from different locations. Such insights allow officers to verify authenticity more efficiently and consistently, without depending solely on instinct.

In notarial services, the risks are narrower but no less significant. Consular officers are not responsible for verifying the truth of statements or the legality of an instrument—only for confirming the signer's identity and witnessing the act. Fraud here typically involves applicants presenting false source documents or fabricated powers of attorney for authentication. AI tools can assist by validating formats, verifying the officer's post location, and ensuring acts are recorded and traceable, reinforcing procedural integrity without encroaching on substantive judgment.

The guiding principle is graceful escalation. AI-generated flags should never automatically trigger refusals or denials. Instead, they function as investigative aids: an amber flag might prompt a peer review or secondary screening; a red flag might trigger consultation with the Fraud Prevention Manager or referral to the Regional Security Office. Every outcome is logged, creating an audit trail that supports both accountability and training for new staff.

By embedding AI into these operational workflows, consular operations move from reactive fraud detection—catching anomalies after issuance—to proactive prevention. The officer's and local staff's roles are not diminished; they are enhanced. Freed from repetitive tasks and supported by clearer data, consular teams can focus on what truly matters: interviewing, judgment, coordination, and the deeply human side of service delivery.

Yet the more seamlessly AI integrates into daily consular practice, the more essential it becomes to govern its use—through clear policies on privacy, transparency, and accountability that preserve both public trust and the officer's human authority.

DATA AND LABELING (FUEL FOR ACCURACY)

AI in fraud detection is only as good as the data that fuels it. Without carefully curated examples of both genuine and fraudulent documents, even the most advanced model will generate unreliable results. In consular operations, data stewardship is not an abstract technical function but a frontline responsibility—directly tied to the credibility of every visa, passport, or notarial act.

The first requirement is building a gold-standard dataset. FPUs already collect exemplars of known fraudulent submissions—cloned birth certificates, fabricated bank ledgers, falsified custody decrees, or digitally altered sponsorship letters. These can be catalogued with metadata describing how each case was detected, whether through officer judgment, host government verification, or forensic analysis. Equally essential is a parallel library of verified authentic documents. Without strong examples of what "good" looks like, algorithms risk overflagging legitimate applicants and eroding public confidence.

Effective labeling depends on structure and transparency. Each exemplar should be tagged not only as "fraudulent" or "genuine," but also with the specific feature that triggered concern—reused templates, metadata anomalies, inconsistent fonts, or coached narrative patterns. A consistent taxonomy ensures that models learn meaningful distinctions, and that officers reviewing AI-generated alerts can trace each flag back to a real-world pattern. This also supports explainability: when a model assigns a high-risk score, it must be able to show which attributes informed its conclusion rather than offering a black-box verdict.

Privacy protections are crucial throughout the process. Personally identifiable information should be masked or stripped wherever feasible. What matters for model training is the structure of a document—the layout of a certificate, the sequence of numbers in a ledger—not the personal details of an applicant. Data minimization and role-based access controls, already standard in most government privacy frameworks, should extend to AI training datasets as well. The U.S. Department of State's Department Privacy Program Plan 2023 offers one model of how such principles can be operationalized (U.S. Department of State 2023b).

Sustaining accuracy requires continuous labeling. Fraud tactics evolve, and static datasets quickly become obsolete. Quarterly reviews, red-teaming exercises using newly fabricated forgeries, and the inclusion of fresh exemplars help models keep pace with reality. Research by NIST on morph detection illustrates the risk: algorithms trained on one generation of document-tampering techniques can falter when confronted with newer attacks unless they are routinely retrained (Ngan and Grother 2025).

For officers and locally employed staff alike, the message is clear: data stewardship is operational work. It is as integral to fraud prevention as interviewing, verification, or field investigation. By systematically curating, labeling, and safeguarding examples of both genuine and deceptive submissions, consular operations ensure that AI serves as a trustworthy partner in adjudication rather than an unreliable distraction.

GOVERNANCE, ETHICS, AND DUE PROCESS

Fraud detection is among the most sensitive responsibilities in consular work. When a visa, passport, or citizenship case is flagged as potentially fraudulent, the consequences can be profound—delays, refusals, and sometimes a stigma that follows applicants across borders. AI introduces both opportunity and risk: it can reveal organized fraud networks invisible to human reviewers, yet it can also produce false positives that, if mishandled, erode fairness and trust. Governance and due process are therefore not optional; they are foundational.

The first safeguard is human-in-the-loop review. AI systems must never serve as the final arbiter of an applicant's honesty. Their purpose is to surface anomalies with transparent reason codes, not to render verdicts. Officers must retain full discretion to override, request clarification, or clear a case entirely. This principle aligns with the EU Artificial Intelligence Act, which designates migration and border control tools as "high risk" systems requiring continuous human oversight for consequential decisions (European Union 2024).

The second safeguard is explainability. Neither officers nor applicants can address an AI-generated flag if they cannot understand why it occurred. Risk engines must provide plain-language rationale—"this document shows repeated round-number deposits inconsistent with regional norms," or "this sponsorship letter shares 85% textual similarity with other submissions." Without such transparency, officers risk over-relying on opaque systems, and applicants lose meaningful avenues for correction or appeal.

Third, systems must be tested for fairness and equity. Research by the U.S. NIST has shown that biometric algorithms can perform unevenly across demographics, producing higher false match rates for certain groups (Grother, Ngan, and Hanaoka 2019). Fraud detection models face similar risks: applicants from cash-based economies may be flagged unfairly for lacking formal financial trails, while minority-language documents can be misclassified by models trained only on dominant languages. Regular audits and bias testing are essential to ensure that AI strengthens, rather than undermines, fairness.

Privacy protections are equally vital. Fraud detection often involves highly personal material—birth and marriage certificates, financial statements, or medical records. Systems must apply strict data minimization, retaining only what is necessary for adjudication and deleting information once its purpose is served. Privacy frameworks such as the U.S. Department of State's Department Privacy Program Plan 2023 and comparable national data protection regimes offer practical models for embedding these safeguards in AI deployments (U.S. Department of State 2023b).

Due process and redress must be built into every system. Applicants should have clear, accessible ways to clarify or challenge AI-generated findings—through supplemental documentation, interviews, or appeals. The U.K.'s experience with its visa-streaming algorithm—abandoned in 2020 after civil society groups documented discriminatory impacts—illustrates the risk of opaque automation (Cameron-Chileshe and Murgia 2020). By contrast, Canada's IRCC has strengthened public trust by publishing detailed transparency statements on its use of advanced analytics, explicitly confirming that officers always make the final decision and that automation is used only to support triage and workload management (Immigration, Refugees and Citizenship Canada 2024).

For consular professionals, governance is not a compliance formality—it is a matter of public trust. Fraud detection must protect the integrity of borders and documents while safeguarding the dignity of every applicant. AI can support that balance only when paired with the values that define consular work itself: fairness, transparency, and accountability. Embedding those values in daily practice requires proof that the systems actually work—measured not by their complexity or novelty, but by whether they make officers more effective, more accurate, and more fair.

MEASUREMENT: WHAT "BETTER" LOOKS LIKE

Fraud detection systems in consular work should not be judged by their novelty or technical sophistication, but by their results. The question is simple: do these tools make officers and staff more effective at protecting borders and documents while treating applicants fairly? To answer it, consular operations must measure performance consistently and transparently.

One critical measure is the detection rate—how many fraudulent cases are surfaced that would otherwise have slipped through. Weekly or monthly audits comparing flagged cases against confirmed fraud outcomes provide a baseline. Yet detection alone is not enough. An effective system must also minimize the false positive rate—the number of legitimate applications wrongly flagged as suspicious. A tool that identifies every fraud ring but overwhelms officers with innocent cases is not "better"; it is counterproductive.

Officer and staff efficiency is another key metric. If AI-generated flags reduce the time consular staff spend sifting through documents or verifying routine details, the system is delivering real value. Metrics such as average review time per case or total hours returned to officers per week can be captured through workflow logs. A well-calibrated system should increase throughput without compromising scrutiny, freeing staff to focus on interviews, case judgment, and coordination with host country partners.

Equity must be measured alongside efficiency. Demographic audits can reveal whether certain groups—by nationality, language, or socioeconomic status—are disproportionately flagged. As research by the U.S. NIST has shown in biometric testing, uneven performance across demographic groups is not hypothetical but measurable in practice (Grother, Ngan, and Hanaoka 2019). By monitoring outcomes disaggregated by demographic group, consular operations can identify and correct emerging bias, adjusting model thresholds or retraining data as needed.

Measurement must include usefulness as experienced by consular staff. Surveys and structured feedback loops allow employees to report whether reason codes are intelligible, whether clustering outputs are actionable, and whether the system integrates smoothly into workflows. An AI tool that produces technically accurate but incomprehensible outputs does not advance consular practice.

Better, in short, means sharper detection, fewer false alarms, regained staff time, equitable outcomes, and outputs that support—not confuse—human decision-makers. By committing to this balanced set of metrics, consular operations ensure that fraud detection AI enhances both security and fairness rather than privileging one at the expense of the other.

FAILURE MODES AND FIXES: A PLAYBOOK

No AI system introduced into consular operations will be flawless. Fraud prevention is a domain where adversaries adapt quickly and where false positives can harm legitimate applicants. Anticipating the most likely failure modes—and planning mitigations in advance—is essential to building systems that consular managers and staff can trust and that applicants can accept.

One common failure mode is over-automation. When a system is granted too much authority, consular staff may be tempted to treat red flags as verdicts rather than signals. This can result in legitimate applicants being unfairly delayed or refused. The fix is human-in-the-loop design: AI produces reason codes and similarity clusters, but an officer or supervisor must always decide the outcome. Training should reinforce that a "high risk" label is not a conclusion but a prompt for closer review.

Another failure mode is concept drift—the gradual decline in accuracy as fraud tactics evolve. A model trained on last year's forged diplomas may fail to recognize new digital watermarks or AI-generated forgeries. Drift can also arise when applicant demographics shift, introducing document formats the system has never seen. The fix is regular retraining and red-teaming. Quarterly reviews should inject new examples of both fraudulent and authentic documents, ensuring that the model adapts to emerging tactics rather than hardening around outdated ones.

A third vulnerability is adversarial manipulation. Fraudsters may deliberately craft documents to exploit weaknesses in detection systems—adding visual noise that confuses OCR or layering text to obscure anomalies. This is the AI arms race: as models improve, adversaries probe for blind spots. The fix lies in multi-signal forensics. Systems should combine metadata, image, and text analysis so that a forgery built to evade one layer is caught by another. Provenance tagging, such as standards from the Coalition for Content Provenance and Authenticity (C2PA 2025), provides an additional safeguard by embedding authenticity markers at the point of document creation.

Shadow IT presents a subtler failure mode. In the absence of approved tools, well-intentioned employees may experiment with consumer-grade AI platforms to analyze documents. This introduces security, privacy, and accuracy risks as sensitive applicant data can leak into ungoverned systems. The fix is twofold: provide staff with authorized, logged tools that meet operational needs, and foster a culture where innovation is encouraged but safely channeled within official frameworks.

Automation bias can creep into both technology and consular staff practices. When AI consistently flags certain patterns, staff may begin to defer uncritically—even when context suggests otherwise. Over time, this erodes the craft of adjudication itself. The fix is institutional: rotate staff, require supervisors to review both overrides and confirmations, and maintain dissent logs where staff record why they disagreed with the system. Such habits protect applicants while sharpening professional judgment.

A related failure mode is the loss of an equity lens. Automation bias does not affect all applicants equally, and even well-intentioned systems can amplify disparities already present in data or decision-making culture. If a model's training set reflects historic refusal rates for certain nationalities or document types, it may quietly encode those patterns into its recommendations. The fix is proactive bias testing—auditing outputs disaggregated by demographic group, language, or socioeconomic context—and ensuring diverse review teams examine edge cases. Equity must be built into both the system and the institution that governs it.

Graceful degradation is another essential safeguard: in low-bandwidth or outage-prone environments, AI systems may fail to load full visualizations or cluster maps, and officers need backup workflows—simplified alerts, static comparison views, or printed summaries—to ensure that fraud detection does not depend on a single digital point of failure.

By preparing for these failure modes, consular operations make AI a resilient partner rather than a brittle one. The goal is not to eliminate every mistake—that is impossible—but to ensure that when errors occur, they are caught, corrected, and learned from. In fraud detection, as in all consular work, success is measured not by perfection but by fairness, transparency, and continual improvement.

DRILLING DOWN INTO AI USE CASES

Fraud prevention has always been one of the most complex and high-stakes elements of consular work. Consular staff know that a single forged document can undermine the integrity of a visa system, but they also understand that overly aggressive screening can unfairly harm legitimate applicants. AI, used carefully, helps strike this balance. By surfacing hidden patterns and anomalies, AI provides staff with sharper investigative leads while leaving final decisions in human hands.

One of the clearest use cases arises during student visa adjudications, where sponsorship letters and financial documents are common targets for manipulation. In the Republic of Z, officers once faced floods of nearly identical bank ledgers that looked convincing in isolation. With AI anomaly detection, those ledgers can now be scored automatically, flagging suspiciously uniform deposits or repeated account structures. The officer receives a reason code explaining why the case deserves a closer look, enabling more targeted questions during the interview.

Another use case emerges in FPUs tasked with uncovering organized document mills. AI clustering tools can compare thousands of digital files and highlight groups that share suspicious similarities in formatting, metadata, or phrasing. Instead of working case by case, FPUs can identify networks, map connections between applicants, and escalate to host country authorities when broader criminal activity is suspected. This shifts the unit's role from reactive case clean-up to proactive disruption of fraud rings.

AI also proves valuable in passport issuance, particularly in verifying breeder documents such as birth or marriage certificates. Computer vision can analyze seals and signatures, while provenance-tagging standards such as those from the Coalition for Content Provenance and Authenticity (C2PA 2025) ensure that scanned documents carry a verifiable chain of custody. For staff, this reduces reliance on intuition alone and provides firmer grounds to escalate suspicious cases for secondary review.

A fourth use case operates at the management level. Dashboards powered by AI can reveal patterns across time—spikes in forged diplomas from a particular region, recurring anomalies tied to specific agents, or seasonal surges in coached narratives. This allows section chiefs to allocate fraud prevention resources strategically, brief headquarters with data-driven evidence, and design training for new staff based on real fraud signatures rather than abstract examples.

A fifth and often overlooked application is AI as an internal anticorruption audit layer. Because AI systems can analyze workflow data impartially, they can detect processing patterns that deviate from expected norms—serving as a quiet but powerful check against malfeasance or insider collusion. The U.S. Department of Justice, for example, prosecuted former Foreign Service Officer Michael T. Sestak, who was sentenced to 64 months in prison after admitting to accepting more than $3 million in bribes to approve fraudulent visas while assigned to Vietnam (U.S. Department of Justice 2015).

Comparable scandals have appeared elsewhere: in Kenya, six immigration officers and nine brokers were arrested for soliciting bribes to issue passports (Citizen Digital 2023); in India, a Ministry of Home Affairs official and three others were arrested in a visa bribery case that prompted a national inquiry (Deccan Herald 2018).

AI can flag such irregularities statistically rather than relying solely on whistle-blowers or audits. A model monitoring workflow data might identify an employee who consistently approves applications from the same broker, processes unusually high volumes after hours, or repeatedly overrides high-risk flags without justification. These patterns—approval clustering, biased overrides, or time irregularities—are statistically improbable to occur by chance. When detected early, they allow supervisors and oversight offices to intervene before systemic damage occurs.

Used this way, AI strengthens management and oversight only when alerts remain reviewable: the dashboard should identify the pattern, the comparison baseline, the cases affected, and the supervisor or oversight office responsible for follow-up. When implemented transparently, this record protects both the credibility of adjudications and the reputations of honest employees, ensuring that misconduct by a few does not erode the public trust earned by the many.

AI strengthens communication and accountability. Large language models, when linked to adjudication logs, can generate first drafts of fraud trend reports for headquarters, legislative offices, or host government counterparts. Consular staff refine these drafts with context and nuance, but the heavy lifting of sorting through data is automated. This ensures that fraud detection not only improves casework but also supports the broader diplomatic responsibility to report accurately, share lessons, and coordinate across agencies.

These scenarios make one point clear: AI in fraud detection is not about outsourcing judgment. It is about shifting the staff's workload from repetitive, detail-intensive scanning to investigative tasks that require discernment, empathy, and diplomacy. By giving consular teams stronger signals, clearer evidence, and better analytical tools, AI enhances their capacity to protect borders and documents while maintaining fairness and due process for applicants.

FIELD CHECKLIST: FRAUD DETECTION WITH AI

Before any consular section introduces AI into fraud detection, it must ensure the foundations are solid. Fraud prevention is too sensitive a domain for improvisation.

This checklist distills what every Consular Chief, Fraud Prevention Manager, and locally employed staff (LES) team should confirm before launch.

1. Define a clear scope and purpose
   Begin with one document type or workflow—bank statements, sponsorship letters, breeder documents, or integrity-monitoring dashboards. A narrow pilot builds confidence, creates measurable baselines, and prevents "AI drift" where enthusiasm outpaces control.
2. Integrate, don't reinvent
   Ensure AI tools drop into existing case management or fraud prevention systems. Use overlays or controlled access consoles that minimize disruption and protect data. Familiar interfaces foster trust and reduce training time.
3. Embed explainability and logging
   Every AI flag must display a clear reason code: metadata anomaly, duplicate phrasing, improbable deposit pattern. Automatic logging of staff actions—overrides, confirmations, escalations—creates transparency, supports audits, and generates authentic training data.
4. Protect privacy and limit retention
   Retain only the minimum data necessary. Mask personally identifiable information before any training use, and enforce deletion clocks with human confirmation before records are purged. Use Privacy Impact Assessments (as modeled on the Consular Consolidated Database) to ensure compliance and accountability (U.S. Department of State 2023b).
5. Audit regularly for bias and equity
   Bias can arise in both models and human practice. Schedule fairness audits—monthly or quarterly—to check whether certain nationalities, languages, or socioeconomic groups are flagged disproportionately. Retrain models or recalibrate thresholds when inequities appear.
6. Train and communicate across the team
   AI produces prompts, not verdicts. Table top simulations should let staff practice interpreting outputs, documenting dissent, and knowing when to escalate. Include LES as equal partners; their contextual expertise often spots what data cannot.
7. Monitor internal integrity and malfeasance risks
   Use AI as an impartial audit layer to flag unusual approval clustering, off-hours processing, or repeated overrides of high-risk alerts without justification. Such monitoring protects both applicants and honest staff.
8. Plan for continuous model stewardship
   Algorithms decay as fraud tactics evolve. Schedule regular updates, red-team tests with new forgeries, and document each model change with a note explaining what was retrained and why. Transparency sustains consular staff trust.
9. Predefine success metrics
   Establish how progress will be measured before launch—detection rates, false positive ratios, staff hours saved, demographic parity, user confidence. Review results weekly or monthly to decide whether to scale, refine, or retire a tool.

When all items are confirmed, the consular operation is ready to deploy AI responsibly. With clear scope, seamless integration, transparent reasoning, privacy and fairness safeguards, well-trained staff, integrity monitoring, active model stewardship, and evidence-based evaluation, AI becomes a trusted partner—enhancing precision without eroding humanity and reinforcing the public trust that underpins every visa, passport, and notarial act.

CLOSING REFLECTION

Fraud is the shadow that follows every consular service. It undermines the trust that visas and passports represent, diverts resources from legitimate applicants, and erodes public confidence in the integrity of borders. Yet fraud prevention has never been about eliminating risk entirely; it has always been about managing it responsibly—balancing vigilance with fairness. AI strengthens that balance when used wisely.

AI does not give consular staff supernatural powers of detection, nor does it absolve them of responsibility. What it offers is speed, scale, and focus. Systems that cluster near-duplicate documents, score suspicious ledgers, or flag metadata anomalies cannot decide who receives a visa or passport. But they can ensure that staff enter interviews and adjudications armed with sharper evidence. By shifting hours of repetitive review into seconds of machine analysis, AI returns time to consular teams' core tasks: exercising discretion, probing for credibility, and protecting the rights of legitimate travelers and citizens. That is the Time Dividend—and in fraud prevention, it is measured not just in hours saved but in the quality of scrutiny those hours make possible.

The risks, however, remain real. False positives can harm innocent applicants; over-automation can erode human judgment; bias can creep into systems trained on narrow datasets. The lesson from civil society critiques and past policy failures—such as the retirement of the U.K.'s visa-streaming algorithm after documented evidence of discrimination—is that technology without governance can undermine legitimacy as quickly as it promises to improve it (The Guardian 2020; Amnesty International 2024). Safeguards such as human-in-the-loop review, explainability, and redress are therefore not optional—they are the conditions of responsible use.

For consular staff, the test of fraud AI is what happens after the alert. A useful system records whether the flag was confirmed, cleared, escalated to the fraud prevention unit, or judged to reflect a local document practice rather than deception. False positives should be categorized, not forgotten, so the model learns the difference between a fraud signature and a harmless local variation.

In the end, AI protects not only borders and documents, but also the fairness and dignity at the heart of consular operations.

7 Identity Integrity and Biometric Analytics

Biometrics support operational missions across DHS to help determine whether an individual poses a threat, as well as whether to grant or deny benefits.

—Lisa MacDonald, Director, Identity Capabilities Management Division, Office of Biometric Identity Management, U.S. Department of Homeland Security (quoted in Lyons-Burt 2024)

Facial recognition technologies and other automatic biometric identification technologies should only be used when it is reasonably necessary for, and the risks to privacy are proportional to, the functions or activity.

—Carly Kind, Privacy Commissioner, Office of the Australian Information Commissioner (2024)

AI-generated slop is polluting our information ecosystem, and it's getting harder to tell what is real and what is not.

—Hany Farid, Professor, School of Information and Electrical Engineering & Computer Sciences, University of California, Berkeley (quoted in Wait 2025)

Opening Vignette: The Fingerprint That Flashed Twice

Late one evening in the Republic of Z, a junior consular officer ran a biometric query on a work visa applicant. On paper, the case looked routine: a clean application, neat paperwork, and supporting documents that raised no obvious concerns. But when the fingerprints were scanned, the system flashed a duplicate identity warning. A deeper search uncovered something startling: the same prints appeared in two other applications under different names—one filed in Z's own system a year earlier, another in a neighboring country. Further checks linked one alias to an active INTERPOL notice for suspected human trafficking.

The officer paused, aware of the stakes. A routine adjudication had suddenly become a matter of regional security and human vulnerability. Within minutes, the fraud prevention lead, a border liaison, and the designated privacy officer convened an emergency review. Together they placed a hold on the

DOI: 10.1201/9781003634775-10

case, confirmed the biometric match through independent checks, and alerted appropriate authorities. The result went beyond blocking a fraudulent visa: it disrupted a trafficking network and safeguarded a potential victim.

What made the difference was not sharper instinct or luck, but the presence of an AI-enabled biometric system capable of searching across vast datasets quickly and accurately. The machine surfaced the pattern; human officers interpreted it, weighed the implications, and decided how to act. The partnership was decisive.

Though fictional, this vignette mirrors real dilemmas faced daily by consular staff worldwide. Identity lies at the heart of consular affairs: the passport as proof of citizenship, the visa as authorization to cross borders, the biometric as evidence of continuity over time. Fraudsters exploit weaknesses in these systems—assuming multiple identities, forging breeder documents, or manipulating biometric templates. AI enhances integrity protection, but only when paired with transparency, fairness, and human oversight. In the Republic of Z, as elsewhere, the lesson endures: a duplicate fingerprint is sometimes not a paperwork problem but a person in danger—and catching it can matter far beyond the visa being decided.

WHY IDENTITY INTEGRITY MATTERS

Identity is the foundation of consular work. Every element of a national consular service's mission—whether adjudicating visas overseas, issuing passports to citizens at home, or assisting nationals in crisis abroad—depends on answering a deceptively simple question: is this person who they say they are? The U.S. Bureau of Consular Affairs processes tens of millions of these decisions each year, but the underlying challenge is universal.

When identity systems function well, they allow governments to facilitate legitimate travel, protect citizens in distress, and ensure border integrity. When they fail, the consequences extend far beyond any single diplomatic mission or consular office. Impostors can obtain fraudulent documents, human traffickers can move victims across borders, and legitimate applicants can suffer unjust delays or denials.

Passports are perhaps the most visible symbol of identity integrity. They are not merely travel documents but sovereign attestations of citizenship. If compromised, they threaten both national security and international trust. A fraudulently obtained passport can enable financial crimes, terrorism, or the evasion of justice. Visa systems carry comparable stakes: a single counterfeit identity can permit entry under false pretenses, undermining immigration controls and eroding public confidence. These threats are not only applicant-driven. Identity systems can also be compromised from within, when officials with legitimate access misuse their authority to issue documents improperly—a category of insider malfeasance that demands different safeguards than those used to detect external fraud.

For consular teams, the risks are not abstract. Staff routinely encounter cases where breeder documents—birth, marriage, or naturalization records—are falsified to establish eligibility for a passport or visa. Some identities evolve over time through aliases or altered biometrics meant to obscure a past record. As noted in Chapter 6, these tactics now include *morphing*—blending two facial images to create a synthetic identity that can defeat basic verification tools if proper safeguards are absent (Ngan and Grother 2025). Without strong countermeasures and AI-assisted detection, such methods can infiltrate even advanced identity infrastructures.

The stakes extend beyond fraud. Faulty or biased systems can harm legitimate applicants, disproportionately affecting vulnerable groups. The National Institute of Standards and Technology has documented demographic differentials in biometric accuracy, showing higher false match rates for certain age groups and skin tones (Grother, Ngan, and Hanaoka 2019). For consular professionals, integrity therefore means not only stopping impostors but ensuring fairness—so that citizens and applicants alike can rely on identity checks that are accurate and equitable.

Ultimately, identity integrity matters because it underpins trust: trust between governments, between citizens and their states, and between travelers and the global system of mobility. Consular officers, specialists, and support staff are custodians of that trust. AI can strengthen their ability to uphold it—but only if used with transparency, oversight, and a clear understanding that identity is more than data. The challenge of identity integrity extends well beyond consular sections: biometric verification, liveness detection, and AI-assisted identity checks are being deployed across the full range of border, immigration, and diplomatic security functions (Kilburg 2025), making the governance frameworks developed here relevant to a much wider audience. It is the foundation of belonging and the bedrock of public confidence in every passport and visa issued.

CORE CONCEPTS: PLAIN ENGLISH

For consular staff, the technical language around biometrics and AI can sometimes obscure more than it clarifies. Yet the concepts themselves are practical and learnable. Understanding them in plain terms helps adjudicators, fraud investigators, and local employees use these tools confidently—and explain them credibly to applicants or host government partners.

Modern biometric systems rely on modalities—the measurable physical or behavioral traits that help confirm identity. The most common are fingerprints, facial images, irises, and, increasingly, voice patterns. Other traits are emerging: gait, typing rhythm, and even signature dynamics—the speed and pressure of a handwritten signature—are now recognized as behavioral modalities (ISO/IEC 2382-37:2022). Signature analysis, long used in passport and notarial work, still provides valuable corroboration when digital captures fail.

Each modality carries trade-offs. Faces are easy to collect but change with age, weight, or surgery. Fingerprints are stable across decades yet can degrade with manual labor or certain skin conditions. Field studies and NIST briefings have documented high rejection rates among workers whose fingerprints are worn by repeated friction—farmers, mechanics, and cleaners who handle abrasive materials daily (NIST IR 8034 2014; World Bank 2019). Consular teams in agrarian regions have seen this firsthand: groups of applicants may need alternate identifiers when prints are unreadable.

No single modality is perfect. Multimodal systems—for example, combining face + fingerprint + iris—raise both accuracy and resilience. The trade-off is cost and complexity: each added modality demands new capture devices, secure storage, and added privacy safeguards.

Two core processes define biometric checks. Verification (one-to-one matching) compares a newly captured sample against the record already linked to that individual—for example, confirming that the person renewing a passport matches their prior record. Identification (1:N search) compares a new sample against an entire database to find any existing match, a process essential for uncovering duplicate or alias identities across visa or passport systems. These distinctions are codified in ISO/IEC 19795-1:2021 and NIST SP 500-305, which guide testing standards for biometric verification and identification.

A recurring challenge is proving that the biometric comes from a live person rather than a spoof. Liveness detection—formally known as presentation attack detection (PAD)—uses hardware and software checks such as blink patterns, pulse detection, or texture analysis to confirm vitality. ISO/IEC 30107-1 through -3 (2016–2023) set out global PAD benchmarks. As discussed in Chapter 6, even well-intentioned cultural or religious photo variations—such as fully covered faces—can complicate capture. Consular staff apply judgment and sensitivity while ensuring compliance with ICAO Doc 9303 (2015–2024) standards for unobstructed facial imagery.

Biometric accuracy also depends on input quality and threshold settings. Poor lighting, partial prints, or low-resolution cameras yield false rejections. Systems apply numerical confidence thresholds to decide what counts as a match, and there is no universal cutoff—acceptable thresholds vary by system design and risk tolerance (NIST SP 800-76-2 Rev. 1 2023). A high-volume border kiosk may accept a lower match score to keep traffic moving, while a passport-issuance environment demands near certainty. Consular teams and managers must understand these trade-offs: tightening thresholds reduces false accepts but increases false rejects, potentially inconveniencing legitimate travelers.

AI-enabled systems now generate not only match results but also reason codes and visual explanations—for instance, heat maps showing which facial features contributed most to a match. A simple *risk score* without a reason leaves adjudicators unable to defend or reconsider a result. Modern tools, including those evaluated through NIST's Face Recognition Technology Evaluation (National Institute of Standards and Technology 2025b), increasingly emphasize explainability so that adjudicators can apply judgment, document overrides, and ensure transparency during appeals.

Even the best algorithms produce outliers. Consular staff must know when to override a result, request secondary evidence, or escalate for review. AI can accelerate comparisons, but fairness and accountability still depend on human reasoning

SYSTEMS AND DATA ARCHITECTURE

Biometric systems may appear to work seamlessly—a finger pressed to a scanner, a face captured by a camera, a green checkmark flashing—but behind those simple interactions lies a complex architecture of capture, processing, comparison, and governance. For consular and immigration staff, understanding that flow of data helps demystify the technology and ensures it is used responsibly.

Every process begins with capture, the moment a biometric sample or photo is collected. Quality checks happen instantly: is the lighting correct, are both eyes visible, is the background uniform? Standards such as ICAO Doc 9303 define acceptable parameters for passport photos, but national variations persist—some countries prohibit smiling, others require both ears visible, and background colors range from white to light gray or blue depending on local regulations (ICAO 2015–2024; ISO/IEC 39794-5:2022). These seemingly minor differences illustrate a broader challenge: global interoperability depends on harmonizing how images are captured, stored, and interpreted.

Once a fingerprint or facial image is captured, the system does not store the raw photo or scan. Instead, it converts the biometric into a mathematical shorthand—a template—that captures the distinctive features of the face or fingerprint in a form that computers can compare quickly. Think of it as reducing a full portrait to a set of precise measurements: the distance between the eyes, the shape of the jawline, the pattern of ridges on a fingertip. The original image is not needed for future comparisons; the template is enough. These templates are encrypted and stored in secure government databases. In the U.S., that means the Consular Consolidated Database (CCD) for passport and visa records, and DHS's IDENT/HART (Homeland Advanced Recognition Technology) system—the current and next-generation biometric repositories managed by the Office of Biometric Identity Management—for border operations. Comparable systems exist abroad: the EU's EURODAC asylum database and the U.K.'s Home Office Biometrics (HOB) platform serve similar functions (European Union 2024c; U.K. Home Office 2024). Each of these databases allows governments to compare identities rapidly while maintaining strict controls over who can access the records.

What happens next depends on the question being asked. If an officer is processing a passport renewal, the system runs a one-to-one check: does this person's new template match the one already on file? That is verification—confirming that the person at the counter is the same person who was issued the original document. But if the question is broader—has this person ever appeared in our system under a different name?—the system runs a one-to-many search, comparing the new template against millions of records to uncover duplicates or aliases. Sometimes these searches extend beyond a single country's databases. A system might query INTERPOL's records or the EU's Entry/Exit System (EES) without copying all of that external data into its own servers—a method known as a federated query. The advantage is privacy: each agency keeps control of its own data, and only the match results are shared. The trade-off is that such cross-border queries demand strong agreements about who can search, what they can see, and how long results are retained (EDPS 2018).

Surrounding every stage are governance layers: access controls that limit who can view records, audit logs that record every search, and retention schedules that dictate how long data may be stored. In the U.S. passport system, internal audits automatically flag any employee who accesses a record without authorization—including those of public figures—and trigger a compliance review. In 2008, several contract staff were disciplined after viewing passport files of U.S. presidential candidates, an episode that underscored how tightly audit logs are monitored and how quickly breaches generate alerts (U.S. Department of State, Office of Inspector General 2008). Such oversight rules may feel intrusive, but they preserve public confidence by proving that even government employees are accountable for privacy and data protection.

Data results appear on adjudicator dashboards—interfaces that display confidence scores, highlight features that contributed to a match, and provide reason codes. These tools are increasingly common in large-scale border and immigration operations (U.S. Department of State 2023a; European Border and Coast Guard Agency. 2024). Dashboards help staff interpret machine output rather than simply accept or reject it, ensuring that human judgment remains central.

Around the world, identity verification has become more automated—and more visible. In the EU, facial recognition corridors now operate at major transport hubs, where cameras capture and compare live faces against travel records as passengers move through airport tunnels, part of the EU's EES and Smart Borders program (European Commission n.d.-c). In Russia, biometric databases have been repurposed for domestic monitoring; academic research notes that facial recognition systems have been used to identify men avoiding military conscription (Gofman and Villa 2023; Human Rights Watch 2022). These divergent cases show the dual nature of biometric infrastructure: it can streamline travel or extend surveillance, depending on how governance and oversight are applied.

Seen in its entirety, biometric architecture is not a black box but a sequence of transparent steps—capture, template, search, comparison, decision—each surrounded by governance controls. AI strengthens this structure by improving accuracy, speeding searches, and surfacing anomalies across databases. But the integrity of the system ultimately depends on staff who understand the flow, question the outputs, and apply judgment to protect both security and fairness.

CRITICAL USE CASES FOR BIOMETRIC AI AND IDENTITY INTEGRITY

AI becomes most valuable in identity management when it strengthens the everyday work of consular and immigration staff—detecting deception, protecting the vulnerable, and improving fairness. The following cases represent high-impact applications already shaping identity operations worldwide.

Duplicate identity detection remains one of the most consequential applications. Fraudsters often apply for documents under multiple names, sometimes across different missions or jurisdictions. AI-enhanced *identification (1:N) searches* scan millions of records to uncover these duplicates quickly. A fingerprint match that surfaces two visa applications under different identities can reveal either clerical error or deliberate deception. In earlier, manual eras, similar patterns were uncovered by comparing phone numbers, addresses, or handwriting across applications. Those small linkages once exposed extensive fraud rings—one reused contact number could connect dozens of suspicious files. Sometimes such overlaps proved legitimate (shared facilitators or family members), but other times they exposed traffickers or serial impostors. The principle endures: technology provides the signal; human adjudicators interpret its meaning.

Cross-system corroboration and federated queries extend this principle across databases. Modern systems connect consular, immigration, and law enforcement data through *federated search* rather than wholesale replication. A biometric template captured in one country can be checked against partner systems—such as INTERPOL or the EU's EES—without transferring all underlying data (European Data Protection Supervisor 2018; European Commission 2025c). AI helps reconcile discrepancies when personal details differ slightly between systems, highlighting records that merit review while respecting privacy boundaries.

DNA analysis has become a biometric of last resort in immigrant visa and citizenship cases, verifying claimed parent–child or sibling relationships when documents are missing or unreliable. In the U.S., both the Department of State and USCIS authorize voluntary DNA testing under strict chain-of-custody and consent procedures (U.S. Department of State n.d.-b; U.S. Citizenship and Immigration Services 2018). Oversight studies by the Government Accountability Office confirm that such testing has reduced fraud in complex family-based cases (U.S. Citizenship and Immigration Services 2018). Comparable procedures exist in the U.K., where Home Office policy allows voluntary DNA submissions in immigration and asylum matters, and in Canada, where DNA testing is used to confirm family links when documentary proof is insufficient (U.K. Government 2020; Government of Canada 2025). DNA evidence can decisively confirm family ties, reunite relatives separated by conflict or migration, and deter fraudulent claims. AI is beginning to assist in this domain as well—optimizing kinship probability calculations and detecting anomalies in sample collection.

Age progression and continuity of recognition address a quiet but persistent challenge: the passage of time. Citizens renewing passports or visas after decades may look little like their original photos. AI models trained on longitudinal datasets can predict natural aging patterns—skin elasticity, hair loss, facial structure—and still recognize the individual. Fingerprints and other stable modalities provide corroboration where facial recognition alone might fail. This capability saves time for applicants and staff while reducing false rejections that can unfairly burden older travelers.

Morphing, spoofing, and PAD guard against deliberate manipulation of biometrics. As noted in Chapter 6, *morphing*—the blending of two faces into a single synthetic identity—can defeat naïve verification systems. Advanced PAD techniques, defined in ISO/IEC 30107-1 through -3 (2016–2023), use texture analysis, blink or pulse detection, and micro-movement cues to verify that a live person, not a photo or mask, is present. AI continually retrains on new attack samples, helping staff spot anomalies that human eyes might miss.

Equity and edge cases remain central to mission credibility. Some applicants cannot provide standard biometrics: fingerprints worn down by years of agricultural work, facial scarring from injury, or disabilities that affect capture quality. NIST studies show measurable demographic differences in false match rates across age and skin-tone groups (Grother, Ngan, and Hanaoka 2019). AI can help reduce those disparities, but human discretion still ensures fairness. Consular teams may accept alternate identifiers, compare signatures, or rely on sworn statements when technology reaches its limits. Designing workflows that anticipate such exceptions prevents technology from becoming a barrier to service.

Adjudicator oversight and decision support tie these use cases together. AI provides probability scores, reason codes, and heat maps showing which features drove a match (National Institute of Standards and Technology 2025b). Yet no algorithm can grasp the contextual cues a human perceives—tone, confidence, or behavior. A real case from the Passport Section in London from 2003 illustrates the point. A gregarious American appeared for a routine passport renewal; the application seemed sound, and local staff recognized him from earlier visits. Something still felt off. Trusting that intuition, the adjudicator checked prior records through the then new PIERS system and discovered that the man was not the original passport holder but a skilled impostor using the same identity in multiple renewals. Further investigation confirmed serial fraud, and his documents were cancelled and flagged for interdiction. No algorithm raised that alert—human instinct did. AI may now perform many such pattern checks automatically, but the London case reminds us that judgment remains the final safeguard. The reverse can also be true: in a Chapter 6 case, identical twins shared a single passport and visa for years, evading every human check, until fingerprint matching exposed them—a reminder that judgment and biometrics each catch what the other misses.

Together, these use cases show why identity workflows need both automated matching and documented human review. AI can shorten repetitive checks and surface anomalies, but each contested match should leave a record of the evidence considered, the alternate identifiers reviewed, and the final human determination.

THE TOOLING LANDSCAPE

The biometric ecosystem available to consular teams today is diverse, spanning commercial platforms, open-source tools, and specialized government-built systems. AI has accelerated this landscape by improving accuracy, expanding the types of biometrics that can be compared, and introducing features that help officers understand and question results. For consular managers, understanding the broad contours of this tooling environment helps inform procurement, governance, and deployment choices.

At one end of the spectrum are large-scale matching engines known as Automated Biometric Identification Systems (ABIS). These are the workhorses of national identity programs—systems that can handle fingerprint, face, and iris recognition for both one-to-one verification and one-to-many identification searches across millions of records. Major vendors include IDEMIA, NEC, and Thales, and their platforms are deployed globally across U.S., EU, and African identity and border systems (U.S. Department of Homeland Security 2025). Modern ABIS platforms incorporate AI modules that can match faces even when the applicant has aged significantly, or compare across modalities—checking a fingerprint against an iris record, for instance. These systems are powerful but expensive and infrastructure-heavy, making them best suited for large consular operations or regional data hubs handling high case volumes.

A lighter-weight option is cloud-based biometric services. Providers such as Microsoft, Amazon, and Google offer pay-as-you-go recognition tools that can plug into existing case management systems without requiring local servers (Microsoft Ignite n.d.-b; Amazon Web Services n.d.). For a consular section that needs facial recognition capability but lacks the budget or infrastructure for a full ABIS platform, these services can fill the gap quickly. The trade-off is data sovereignty. When an applicant's biometric data passes through a third-party cloud, it may transit servers in countries with different privacy laws. Consular operations must ensure that any cloud-based tool complies with both host country regulations and U.S. or EU data protection obligations before sensitive information leaves the building.

At the other end of the spectrum are open-source biometric frameworks—tools like OpenCV, OpenBR, or SourceAFIS that provide flexible building blocks for smaller pilots or research projects. These are less polished than enterprise systems, but they allow consular teams with local technical capacity to experiment at low cost, customize models for regional conditions, and avoid being locked into a single vendor's ecosystem. Estonia's digital identity architecture illustrates what is possible: built on a transparent, citizen-centric model that combines state-issued digital IDs, encrypted authentication, and AI-assisted fraud monitoring, it demonstrates how even a small state can achieve interoperability and public trust simultaneously (Oxford Institute of Technology and Justice n.d.). Open-source approaches foster innovation, but they demand disciplined internal governance—someone must manage updates, run audits, and retrain models when performance slips.

One of the most valuable recent advances is not in matching accuracy but in explainability. Some newer facial recognition interfaces can show consular officers and their staff why the system reached its conclusion—displaying a confidence map or overlay that highlights which facial features contributed most to a match. Did the system rely heavily on the jawline? The spacing between the eyes? The shape of the ears? These visualization features, documented in academic and vendor research but not yet standard in U.S. consular tools (Ngan, Grother, and Hanaoka 2020), help adjudicators justify or challenge a result when responding to applicants, oversight bodies, or host government inquiries. As NIST's independent evaluations emphasize, accuracy alone is not enough—without explainability and demographic fairness testing, even a highly accurate system cannot be fully trusted (Grother, Ngan, and Hanaoka 2019).

Finally, there is a less visible but equally important part of the tooling conversation: keeping these systems healthy over time. Like any machine, an AI model degrades if it is not maintained. Fraud tactics evolve, applicant populations shift, and a system that performed well last year may quietly become less accurate this year—a problem known as model drift. Responsible operations build in routines to catch this early: regularly testing the system against fresh examples, logging its outputs so that patterns of declining accuracy can be spotted, and retraining the model when performance drops below acceptable thresholds. Large operations may invest in automated monitoring platforms that do this continuously. Smaller units can achieve the same goal with periodic manual checks—pulling a sample of recent cases, comparing the system's calls against officer judgments, and flagging discrepancies for review. Either way, the principle is the same: an AI tool is not a one-time purchase. It is a living system that requires ongoing care, and consular teams that neglect this maintenance will find their tools growing less reliable precisely when adversaries are growing more sophisticated.

The takeaway for consular teams is that the tooling landscape is not one-size-fits-all. Large operations may invest in enterprise ABIS systems integrated with national registries, while smaller units can experiment with cloud services or open-source frameworks. Around the world, national identity programs such as India's Aadhaar, the EU's EES and ETIAS, and the African Union's Digital Identity for Africa initiative all demonstrate the same principle: technology choices differ, but governance—transparency, accountability, and human judgment—remains the critical layer.

GOVERNANCE, EQUITY, AND OVERSIGHT

For consular managers and teams, the responsibility is not only to deploy new technology but to ensure it operates transparently, ethically, and accountably. AI in identity management magnifies both the power and the risk of administrative discretion. A false match can ground a traveler, delay a citizen's passport, or wrongly implicate an innocent person. A missed match can enable trafficking, fraud, or the creation of an untraceable identity. Effective governance requires systems that prevent both harms simultaneously—through sound design, strong oversight, and a culture of human accountability.

Governance frameworks now accompany most large-scale biometric deployments. In the U.S., privacy and civil liberties oversight is guided by the Privacy and Civil Liberties Oversight Board (PCLOB) and the E-Government Act of 2002, which require agencies to conduct Privacy Impact Assessments (PIAs) before deploying biometric systems (Privacy and Civil Liberties Oversight Board 2025; U.S. Department of State 2023b). Comparable mechanisms exist under the EU General Data Protection Regulation (GDPR) and the African Union Convention on Cyber Security and Personal Data Protection (European Union n.d.-c; African Union 2014). These frameworks ensure that consular and immigration operations are not only legally compliant but also socially legitimate.

Yet technical compliance alone cannot guarantee fairness. Amnesty International (2023) has warned that the expansion of biometric surveillance technologies, particularly remote facial recognition and large-scale biometric identification systems, can undermine fundamental rights by enabling disproportionate monitoring and discriminatory outcomes. Such critiques underscore the need for explicit purpose limitation, transparency in algorithmic design, and meaningful redress mechanisms. In consular practice, this means ensuring that applicants receive clear explanations when AI-supported tools contribute to assessments, while preserving accessible human review and appeal processes to prevent automated systems from becoming unchecked barriers to mobility.

Equity auditing is another essential pillar. NIST studies continue to show measurable demographic differentials in false match rates across skin tone, gender, and age (Grother, Ngan and Hanaoka 2019). Without corrective oversight, AI may replicate human bias at digital scale. Consular operations can mitigate this risk through diverse data sampling, regular model testing, and inclusion of under-represented populations in system training datasets. Partnering with national statistical offices or host country civil registries can improve demographic balance and accuracy.

Accountability must remain human. Even in high-volume adjudication environments, the adjudicator—not the algorithm—is responsible for the outcome. Consular staff must be trained not only to interpret system outputs but also to challenge them. The institutional culture should encourage a dissenting view when consular staff question an AI result or a management assumption, and those concerns should trigger review rather than reprisal. Embedding protected dissent into workflow—through secondary adjudications, appeal panels, or red-flag logging—turns skepticism into a quality control asset.

A real example illustrates the importance of this vigilance. In 2012, U.S. Embassy Dhaka reported that a single IP address was responsible for more than 634,000 entries in the Diversity Visa Program. Subsequent investigation by Bangladeshi authorities uncovered facilitator operations involving thousands of staged applications, fake education documents, and counterfeit marriage photos—patterns documented across multiple posts where unscrupulous "visa agents" prey on applicants lacking direct access to U.S. consular services (U.S. Government Accountability Office 2007). The discovery revealed not only large-scale document fraud but also the critical role of interagency coordination and post-level vigilance. Pattern detection—whether through data analytics, AI tools, or alert consular staff—remains central to exposing organized fraud networks. The Dhaka case exemplifies how transparency, data monitoring, and human accountability together protect the legitimacy of immigration systems.

Governance, equity, and oversight thus form the triad of ethical biometric deployment. Transparent policy, informed discretion, and institutional courage ensure that AI systems strengthen—not erode—the public trust that underpins every visa and passport issued.

Digital Frontlines: The Great Biometric Experiment—Inside America's Largest AI Surveillance Program

U.S. Customs and Border Protection's facial comparison system has processed more than 193 million travelers as of July 2022—the most recent comprehensive statistics available from the agency (CBP 2025a). The system represents one of the world's most ambitious deployments of computer vision AI in government operations, identifying more than 1,500 impostors while raising questions about privacy, accuracy, and algorithmic governance.

Performance data reveals significant variations across environments. At airports like Miami, where lighting is controlled and passenger galleries are built from airline manifests, facial recognition achieves its highest accuracy rates. Maritime environments function similarly well at cruise terminals under controlled conditions. But at land border crossings—particularly in vehicle lanes with variable angles, glare, and throughput pressures—deployment remains inconsistent and performance more sensitive to environmental factors (CBP 2025b).

The Government Accountability Office concluded in 2020 that CBP had not consistently provided clear information about facial recognition locations and that privacy signage was limited at many ports (GAO 2020). While CBP has since published clearer privacy guidance, oversight bodies continue monitoring whether field implementation matches policy promises.

Equity implications concern civil liberties advocates. Independent testing by the National Institute of Standards and Technology has documented measurable demographic differentials in facial recognition performance, with significant variations between algorithms and demographic groups (Grother, Ngan, and Hanaoka 2019; NIST 2022). These findings underscore why agencies need carefully calibrated thresholds, regular bias audits, and human escalation procedures when automated systems are uncertain.

CBP's published policy is straightforward: U.S. citizens may decline facial capture and receive manual document inspection by an officer, while permanent residents and most foreign nationals are expected to present for biometric processing where required by law (CBP 2025c). The practical experience varies significantly by location, with staff training and queue design determining whether refusal feels genuinely available without penalty.

The security benefits appear substantial. More than 1,500 impostors identified through facial comparison represents significant operational success—cases where people attempted to use documents that didn't match their actual identity and were caught by automated systems that human officers might have missed.

With over 193 million facial comparisons processed as of 2022, CBP has created one of the world's largest databases of biometric travel behavior—information generating detailed records not just of who crosses borders, but when, where, and with what frequency. Independent oversight continues examining both benefits and limitations of facial recognition deployment across different environments and use cases.

The technology's success has accelerated deployment timelines but intensified debates about appropriate boundaries of algorithmic surveillance, including questions about whether voluntary opt-outs for U.S. citizens will survive political pressure and what limits should exist on what governments can infer from citizens' faces.

GLOBAL IMPLEMENTATIONS AND LESSONS

The use of biometrics in identity systems is no longer experimental; it has become a global norm. Examining how governments and organizations have deployed AI-enabled biometrics offers practical lessons—both models to adapt and cautionary tales to avoid.

Across the EU, large-scale databases such as EURODAC and the now-operational EES illustrate how cross-border data sharing can enhance security while testing the limits of governance. EURODAC, originally designed for asylum management, now contains millions of fingerprint templates and underpins EU migration control. The EES collects biometric and biographic data from non-EU short-stay travelers, linking entries and exits across the Schengen area (European Commission 2025c). These systems demonstrate the power of scale for detecting impostors and overstays, but they also expose new privacy risks and the potential for *function creep* if access rules expand beyond their original purpose (EDPS 2024).

Singapore provides a contrasting success story. Its Immigration and Checkpoints Authority (ICA) has implemented full passport-less clearance at Changi Airport, using face and iris recognition to automate immigration control. The system's legitimacy rests on two foundations: adherence to ICAO biometric passport standards and rigorous local transparency requirements, including public reporting on false match rates and data retention periods (ICA 2024). Singapore's experience shows how multimodal biometrics can make travel seamless while maintaining accountability.

In Kenya and Nigeria, national ID programs have integrated biometrics with mobile and offline functionality, enabling authentication in rural or low-connectivity environments (World Bank Group 2023). These systems highlight the importance of designing for context: AI tools that can operate without constant internet access prevent exclusion of remote or vulnerable populations.

Estonia's digital identity framework offers a different model—an integrated ecosystem linking biometrics, encrypted e-IDs, and AI-assisted fraud monitoring within a single governance architecture. Each citizen holds a secure digital identity used for voting, banking, and health services, built on transparency and consent principles (Oxford Institute of Technology and Justice n.d.). For consular planners, Estonia demonstrates how small states can achieve interoperability and public trust simultaneously.

Australia provides one of the most mature examples of integrated identity management. Through its Document Verification Service (DVS) and related biometric systems, Australia links civil registries—births, deaths, and marriages—with passport and immigration databases in real time. The result is a "whole-of-life" identity model that prevents duplication and fraud without relying on a single central database (Government of Australia n.d.-b).

This framework is underpinned by the Intergovernmental Agreement on Identity Matching Services (IGA), which formalizes data-sharing arrangements between federal and state authorities while preserving jurisdictional control of core registries. Supported by strong privacy oversight from the Office of the Australian Information Commissioner (OAIC) and the new Australian government Digital ID System, the model demonstrates how federated governance and clear accountability can achieve national interoperability without centralization. For consular and identity programs worldwide, Australia illustrates that durable digital identity systems depend as much on institutional coordination and legal trust as on technological sophistication (Government of Australia n.d.-a).

India's Aadhaar program presents the opposite lesson: massive biometric reach coupled with contested privacy safeguards. Despite enrolling over a billion residents, Aadhaar faced legal challenges and official scrutiny for weak data protection and redress mechanisms (PRS Legislative Research 2018).

Global experience affirms that public legitimacy determines sustainability. Programs that succeed—such as Singapore's, Australia's, and Estonia's—combine transparency and convenience with strict accountability. Those that falter, including EU pilots for biometric "lie detectors" abandoned after ethical review (Sánchez-Monedero and Dencik 2019), reveal the hazards of deploying unproven or intrusive technologies.

Together, these examples confirm that biometric analytics are no longer theoretical—they are embedded in identity systems worldwide. The lesson for consular operations is to learn selectively: adapt best practices, avoid overreach, and remember that AI strengthens identity integrity only when paired with transparency, fairness, and local context.

OPERATING MODEL: PEOPLE, PROCESS, CONTROLS

Even the most advanced biometric systems will falter if they are not supported by clear operating models. For consular managers and teams, embedding AI-enabled biometrics into daily practice requires defined roles, consistent procedures, and robust internal controls. Technology provides the signal; people and processes ensure those signals are used responsibly.

The operating model begins with triaging alerts. Biometric systems typically return results as confidence scores, sometimes accompanied by visual or textual explanations. A practical approach—used in several immigration and identity programs—is the "stoplight" framework:

- Green cases are clear matches that proceed automatically.
- Amber cases require secondary human review.
- Red cases trigger immediate escalation and supervisory oversight.

Service-level agreements (SLAs) ensure that each category is acted upon within defined timeframes, preventing backlogs and maintaining consistency across adjudicators (National Institute of Standards and Technology 2023a).

Central to the model is the principle of human override and documentation. Adjudicators must be empowered to overrule system outputs when contextual factors suggest an alternative conclusion. A flagged passport renewal may involve legitimate changes in appearance due to age, medical treatment, or gender transition. Conversely, a low-confidence match that fails to trigger an alert might still raise concerns based on behavioral or documentary cues. Each override should be recorded in a structured log, providing both accountability and valuable feedback data for model retraining (ICAO n.d.).

Edge-case playbooks provide further guidance. Scenarios such as identical twins, trauma survivors with altered biometrics, or applicants with disabilities affecting capture quality require structured approaches that balance fairness with security. Written playbooks, similar to those issued through Canada's Operational Bulletins and Manuals, help ensure adjudicators follow consistent steps rather than improvising under pressure (Immigration, Refugees and Citizenship Canada 2024).

Transparent communication is another essential control. Applicants should be informed—in clear, nontechnical language—why additional checks are required and what steps they can take to resolve anomalies. Transparency prevents misunderstanding and reinforces procedural fairness. Staff who can explain that a biometric system has simply requested a "second look," rather than implying wrongdoing, sustain trust even in sensitive cases.

Building a responsible operating model requires a comprehensive five-pillar approach. First, triage processes should employ structured confidence score frameworks, such as stoplight models, to prioritize cases efficiently and consistently. Second, adjudicators must have the authority to override system outputs when contextual evidence indicates error, with documentation required for every override decision. Third, organizations should develop playbooks containing standardized responses for edge cases—including twins, medical changes, and technical anomalies—to ensure fair treatment across unusual circumstances. Fourth, clear communication is essential: review steps must be explained to applicants in accessible, nontechnical language to maintain trust and transparency throughout the process. Finally, oversight through regular audits and refresher trainings helps evaluate bias, accuracy, and procedural consistency, ensuring the system operates responsibly over time.

These oversight mechanisms tie the model together. Supervisors should conduct periodic audits of biometric adjudications, reviewing override logs, false match trends, and demographic patterns. Regular training can incorporate anonymized case studies to help staff understand both the capabilities and the limits of AI-enabled systems. In the U.K., biometric adjudication audits are formally mandated to evaluate system quality and fairness (U.K. Government 2025a). Embedding oversight into daily operations reinforces a culture of accountability that is as critical as the technology itself. When consistently applied, this operating model transforms AI biometrics from a technical layer into an operational asset, ensuring that systems enhance human judgment rather than replace it—protecting identity integrity while sustaining the fairness and transparency that define consular and immigration work.

FIELD CHECKLIST: BIOMETRIC AI READINESS

This field checklist offers a practical way for consular operations to translate strategy into daily management. It is not a rigid prescription but a framework adaptable to each context—large or small, visa or passport, regional or stand-alone. The aim is to align people, processes, and technology so that biometric tools enhance—not complicate—consular work.

Rather than imposing fixed timelines, many operations begin with a readiness assessment to identify which functions are AI-enabled, where human review is essential, and what data protection measures are already in place. ICAO and NIST both recommend phased evaluations before new technologies are deployed, emphasizing that early testing and calibration reduce long-term error rates (ICAO n.d.; National Institute of Standards and Technology 2023a).

A practical way to operationalize this is through five readiness domains, corresponding to the pillars of the operating model:

1. People: assess whether all staff—officers and locally employed colleagues alike—are trained in both the technology and the ethics of biometric adjudication.
2. Process: confirm that triage rules, overrides, and playbooks exist and are regularly reviewed.
3. Data: ensure that input sources are validated and that retention and privacy rules are documented.
4. Governance: verify that oversight bodies, redress mechanisms, and audit trails are functioning.
5. Communications: test whether staff can explain biometric procedures clearly to applicants.

Each domain can be scored qualitatively or quantitatively depending on local preference. Some operations use a traffic-light self-assessment to visualize strengths and gaps—green for established practices, amber for partial readiness, and red for areas needing reinforcement. The purpose is not compliance but awareness: recognizing that readiness evolves as systems and risks mature.

The resulting checklist becomes a living document, reviewed periodically as technology and policy advance. It can also inform broader engagement with partners—national data protection authorities, law enforcement, and other foreign ministries—ensuring that biometric deployments remain lawful, transparent, and trusted.

By merging procedural steps with adaptive governance, this checklist turns oversight from a one-time audit into a continuous learning process. In this way, AI-enabled biometrics become not only a security tool but a catalyst for better-managed, more accountable consular services.

METRICS AND KPIS

Effective measurement transforms a technical rollout into an accountable system. For consular operations, tracking the impact of AI-enabled biometrics is not simply about speed or volume; it is about balancing precision, fairness, and public trust.

Performance can be assessed first at the technical level, where biometric and AI systems must prove that they work as intended. Accuracy measures such as false match and false nonmatch rates, together with demographic testing, reveal how consistently the technology performs across gender, age, and skin-tone groups. These quantitative indicators, drawn from NIST's benchmark testing, show whether an algorithm meets acceptable thresholds not only for efficiency but also for equity.

At the operational level, AI should make the daily work of consular staff more effective, not more complicated. Many operations now monitor how automation changes workflow: the number of staff hours saved through automated deduplication, the speed with which backlogs are cleared, or the degree of consistency among different adjudicators reviewing similar cases. When tracked carefully, such measures demonstrate where technology truly improves productivity and where it may still create friction or confusion.

Yet the most meaningful outcomes are human-centered. A consular operation that saves time but loses public confidence cannot be called successful. Applicant satisfaction, clarity of communication, and the reliability of redress mechanisms are equally important indicators. Measuring how often errors are corrected by human review, or how quickly appeals are resolved, captures the ethical dimension of performance. These data tell us not just that the system functions, but that it functions *fairly*.

The strongest evaluation frameworks combine these perspectives into a continuous feedback loop. Technical indicators inform retraining of algorithms; operational findings refine procedures; and human-centered data guide communication and oversight. As both NIST's AI Risk Management Framework and the European Commission's Guidelines for Trustworthy AI emphasize, a responsible system must be assessed not only by what it achieves but by how it achieves it. For consular operations, this means that every metric ultimately serves one purpose: to ensure that the application of AI enhances judgment, fairness, and the integrity of identity itself.

Measurement closes the loop between vision and practice. Yet even the most refined metrics describe only where we are today. The next section looks forward—to how identity systems, governance models, and public expectations will continue to evolve in the years ahead.

FUTURE HORIZONS

Biometric systems are evolving rapidly, and AI is accelerating that transformation. For consular operations, the challenge is not simply to adopt new tools but to anticipate their implications—to ensure that governance, ethics, and public trust advance as quickly as technology itself.

One emerging horizon is privacy-preserving identity verification. Early-stage research in federated learning suggests it may become possible to compare biometric records across databases without centralizing sensitive data (Guo et al. 2024). Instead of building ever larger repositories that invite misuse, federated systems allow queries to run locally, sharing only the match results. For consular work, this approach could enable cross-border detection of duplicate identities while respecting privacy and national sovereignty.

Another frontier is multimodal fusion. Most systems today rely on face and fingerprint. Future ones may combine iris, gait, or behavioral markers such as voice or typing rhythm. AI excels at weighing these multiple modalities simultaneously, producing higher confidence scores and reducing demographic disparities. Yet every new trait captured raises new questions of governance: where should the line be drawn, and which aspects of personal identity must remain beyond the reach of automation?

AI will also become central to adversarial red-teaming. Just as fraudsters are using generative AI to create morphs, deepfakes, and synthetic fingerprints, agencies can use AI to stress-test their own systems. NIST's morph detection benchmarks already offer early models (Ngan and Grother 2025), but future fraud prevention will be a continuous contest of adaptation—one AI probing another. For consular staff, this means that fraud detection will evolve from static screening into an ongoing cycle of learning and defense.

Digital identity wallets and verifiable credentials offer a glimpse of a reimagined ecosystem. Standards such as the World Wide Web Consortium's Verifiable Credentials 2.0 envision a world where citizens carry cryptographically signed digital attestations that can be instantly verified across borders (W3C 2025a). Combined with AI-assisted validation, these tools could reduce reliance on vulnerable paper breeder documents. Yet they also raise questions of inclusion: how do people without smartphones, stable connectivity, or digital literacy participate in such systems without being excluded from mobility and services?

For consular affairs, the direction is clear: identity will be increasingly digital, multimodal, and contested by both innovators and adversaries. AI provides the analytical power to manage this complexity, but legitimacy will depend on whether privacy, fairness, and oversight are embedded into every layer of design and use. The technology may advance, but the responsibility remains human—to ensure that identity systems protect not only borders and data, but also the dignity of the people they are meant to serve.

As these technologies advance, the mission of consular work remains unchanged: to verify identity with fairness and to uphold trust across borders. The future may bring new algorithms, modalities, and credentials, but the foundation of legitimacy will still depend on people—those who interpret the data, apply the rules, and decide when technology serves justice rather than expedience.

CLOSING REFLECTION

Identity is the thread that runs through all of consular issues and programs. A passport is more than a travel document—it is a declaration of citizenship. A visa is more than a stamp—it is a sovereign decision about who may cross a nation's borders. Each rests on the assumption that identity can be verified with integrity, fairness, and confidence. AI enhances the ability of consular teams to protect that integrity, but it also magnifies the risks when governance fails.

AI-enabled biometrics offer speed, scale, and precision that human eyes alone cannot match. They can uncover duplicate identities spread across jurisdictions, expose morphing attacks designed to deceive, and confirm continuity of identity across decades. They return time to staff who would otherwise be consumed by manual checks and repetitive verification tasks—a Time Dividend that biometric AI delivers with every duplicate detected and every manual search compressed. Yet these gains are meaningful only when paired with fairness, transparency, and human oversight. A false positive that denies a legitimate applicant is not merely a technical error—it is a breach of trust.

Global experience underscores this tension. Estonia and Singapore demonstrate how well-governed biometric systems can deliver seamless service while reinforcing legitimacy. The EU's large-scale databases illustrate both the promise of integration and the dangers of overreach without strong privacy protections. Civil society critiques remind us that systems built for security can quickly become instruments of exclusion if left unchecked (Amnesty International 2024). Independent oversight—such as the U.S. Privacy and Civil Liberties Oversight Board's review of TSA face recognition—shows that governance frameworks can protect rights while allowing technology to serve its proper role (Privacy and Civil Liberties Oversight Board 2025).

For consular operations, the legitimacy of biometric analytics depends on a visible mismatch procedure. A low-confidence match should trigger second capture, review of alternate documents, supervisory consultation where needed, and a recorded explanation before any adverse action. The system may surface the signal, but the record must show how people interpreted it, what evidence they considered, and how the applicant could correct or contest an error.

As identity systems evolve toward richer modalities and digital credentials, consular work will remain anchored in trust. AI can strengthen that trust when governed responsibly, ensuring that borders are secure, documents are authentic, and citizens and applicants alike are treated with fairness and dignity. Done right, AI does more than protect identity—it protects the human bond between states and the people they serve.

Part IV

Operations and Deployment

The most sophisticated AI tools deliver no value if they cannot be integrated into the daily rhythm of consular operations. This section shifts from what AI can do to how you can actually deploy it—addressing the practical challenges of appointments, workflows, staffing, procurement, and governance that determine whether your pilots succeed or stall.

The operational inefficiencies of consular work are familiar to you. Your appointment calendars clog with no-shows that waste slots desperate applicants would fill in minutes. Your inboxes overflow with repetitive inquiries that bury urgent messages from citizens in distress. Your hours disappear into drafting routine correspondence, reconciling fees, or retyping data between systems. These burdens are not trivial—they erode morale, extend backlogs, and leave you with diminished time for the interviews, investigations, and human encounters that require your full attention.

Chapter 8 examines how AI can reclaim this lost capacity. Predictive models forecast no-shows and enable dynamic scheduling. Inbox triage systems separate routine questions from urgent cases. Drafting assistants produce first-pass summaries that you refine rather than create from scratch. Robotic process automation handles clerical tasks that add no judgment but consume enormous time. The goal throughout is not squeezing more productivity from you and your already stretched staff but protecting the space where fairness, empathy, and discretion can flourish.

Chapter 9 brings deployment down to the operational level—the individual embassies and consulates where consular work actually happens. AI need not arrive as a flagship enterprise project from headquarters—often the most impactful pilots begin

DOI: 10.1201/9781003634775-11

as scrappy experiments built by you and locally employed staff who see a need and act. This chapter provides a complete playbook: team models you can staff at any embassy or consulate, governance frameworks that channel innovation responsibly, guidance on choosing tools without regrets, and case studies illustrating patterns of success from diverse contexts.

By the end of this section, you will have practical tools for turning AI's potential into operational reality—starting small, measuring rigorously, and scaling only when results and governance align.

8 AI-Optimized Appointments and Internal Workflows

One of the things that we hear across government regularly is that technology ends up slowing people down instead of speeding them up, if it's not implemented right. That is not what anyone intends and that's not what we're investing for.

—Mina Hsiang, former administrator, U.S. Digital Service (quoted in Nihill 2024)

These questions highlight an important reality: improving government isn't only just about designing better policies or legislation—it's about ensuring they can be effectively implemented. As researchers, our job therefore isn't just to offer high-level policy ideas but to help operationalize those ideas in ways that work within real-world constraints.

—Elizabeth Linos, Associate Professor at the Harvard Kennedy School of Government (quoted in Center for Health Incentives and Behavioral Economics 2025)

There are really two ways to build capacity: having more of the right people doing the right things (including but not limited to leveraging technology like AI) and safely reducing the burdens we place on those people.

—Jennifer Pahlka, former U.S. Deputy Chief Technology Officer and Senior Fellow at the Niskanen Center (quoted in Pahlka 2024)

Opening Vignette: Three Hours Back in Z City

At the Republic of Z's busiest consular section, the morning line stretched around the block. Families arrived before dawn, students rehearsed answers in whispers, and business travelers tapped nervously at their phones. Inside, officers braced for another exhausting day. The appointment calendar was full, yet experience told them that nearly a third of scheduled applicants would never arrive. No-shows wasted slots, left others waiting weeks for an opening, and

DOI: 10.1201/9781003634775-12

drained morale from consular staff forced to spend precious hours juggling reschedules.

But today felt different. Overnight, an AI system had analyzed attendance histories, booking patterns, and seasonal data. By morning, the dashboard displayed predicted no-shows for each hour, along with recommended overbooking levels to compensate. Automated reminders, tailored to applicants' language and time zone, had gone out by SMS and email the night before. A live waitlist meant that when two applicants cancelled at the last minute, others were notified instantly and filled the spots within minutes.

By the end of the day, the no-show rate had dropped dramatically. Officers had each gained nearly three hours of usable time, which they devoted to complex interviews rather than idle waiting. Instead of frustration, there was a sense of momentum. Applicants noticed too—several remarked that the process seemed "fairer" and "less chaotic." The AI had not altered the standards of adjudication, but it had reshaped the conditions under which officers could apply them.

This fictional scene captures a reality many consular teams know well: the appointment is the atomic unit of service delivery. When appointments fail, everything downstream—processing, interviews, public trust—suffers. AI provides tools to optimize this system, transforming the daily grind of scheduling into an opportunity to reclaim time, reduce waste, and deliver fairer service.

WHY OPTIMIZATION MATTERS NOW

Consular work is built on appointments. Every service—visa interviews, passport renewals, notarial acts, or emergency assistance—depends on allocating consular team time in predictable units. When appointments fail, the consequences cascade. A missed slot means an empty chair in the waiting room, an applicant denied timely service, and an officer left with fragmented time that cannot be reclaimed. Multiply that across hundreds of daily appointments, and the result is systemic inefficiency that erodes both productivity and public trust.

The challenge has only grown sharper in recent years. Demand for passports and visas has surged in the aftermath of pandemic-era backlogs, creating queues that stretch for months in some diplomatic missions. In this environment, no-shows are more than a nuisance—they are a form of lost capacity that translates directly into longer wait times for others. A 2025 GAO report on U.S. passport operations emphasized that surges in demand cannot be met by staffing increases alone; efficiency gains are just as critical (GAO 2025). For consular officers and their teams, this reality means that optimization is not a luxury but a necessity.

AI provides new tools for addressing these challenges. Predictive models can forecast no-shows based on past attendance, booking channels, and applicant behavior. Tailored reminders can nudge attendance rates upward, as studies in healthcare have shown: one randomized trial found that making the cost of missed appointments explicit in text reminders significantly reduced no-shows (Hallsworth et al. 2015). Machine learning can also drive dynamic scheduling, adjusting overbooking levels hour by hour rather than relying on blunt averages.

The human toll of inefficiency is equally important. Consular teams know that wasted appointments and ballooning backlogs lead to rushed interviews, shorter time for judgment, and mounting stress. The irony is that inefficiency can undermine the very qualities—patience, empathy, discretion—that make consular officers and their teams effective. Optimization protects those qualities by returning time to where it matters most. As one U.S. pilot of AI-assisted scheduling showed, reducing wasted slots gave officers more space for complex cases, improving both morale and outcomes (Doubleday 2024a).

As the Z City example shows, optimization matters now because demand is rising, expectations are higher, and resources remain finite. The drive to reduce administrative friction through AI is not confined to consular sections: management officers, executive staff, and diplomatic mission support functions across embassy operations are grappling with the same pressures and exploring the same tools (Kilburg 2025), making the lessons of this chapter broadly applicable. By automating the predictable—forecasting no-shows, sending reminders, and reallocating cancellations—AI allows consular teams to focus on the exceptional: exercising judgment, assisting citizens in distress, and protecting the integrity of borders. Efficiency is not about cutting corners; it is about creating the conditions for fairness and humanity to flourish.

APPOINTMENT OPTIMIZATION: DESIGNS THAT ACTUALLY WORK

Appointments may seem like a logistical detail, but they are in fact one of the most consequential elements of consular practice. Every hour wasted on missed slots, double bookings, or poorly managed calendars is an hour not spent on substantive adjudication or emergency assistance (or staff training or any one of a dozen other tasks). AI offers tools to redesign appointment systems so they serve both applicants and consular operations more effectively.

Many consular sections are experimenting with scheduling reforms to tame appointment backlogs. Drawing from both public sector innovation and private sector scheduling practice, four design approaches are emerging as especially promising across different contexts. The Bureau of Consular Affairs has acknowledged that improving appointment systems and reducing technology bottlenecks are key modernization priorities (U.S. Department of State 2023a; Moodie n.d.).

The first design involves no-show forecasting. By analyzing signals such as prior attendance, booking channels, lead time between scheduling and appointment, and even seasonality, AI models can predict the likelihood of an applicant failing to appear. These predictions are not abstract. Studies in health services show that predictive models combined with tailored reminders reduce no-show rates significantly (Oikonomidi et al. 2022; Ulloa-Pérez et al. 2022). For consular operations, the same principles apply: an applicant who booked months in advance through a third-party agent may be more likely to skip than one who scheduled directly the week before. With these insights, consular operations can plan accordingly.

A second design is dynamic capacity management. Instead of setting static overbooking rates, AI allows consular operations to adjust in real time. If predictions suggest a 25% no-show rate for a morning block, the system can safely accept additional bookings. If afternoon attendance is expected to be stronger, it can tighten capacity to prevent bottlenecks. This kind of adaptive scheduling is already used in airline and hospital settings, where resources must be maximized without overwhelming staff (Zhou et al. 2023).

Smart waitlists provide another route to efficiency. When a cancellation occurs, an automated system can instantly notify qualified applicants and fill the empty slot within minutes. For consular officers and their teams, this means steadier throughput and fewer wasted hours. For applicants, it creates a sense of fairness—those waiting longest can move up quickly if they respond promptly. While digital tools can streamline scheduling, they must remain accessible to applicants with limited internet access or unreliable mobile coverage. The World Bank has cautioned that digital public services risk excluding low-connectivity users unless multiple channels—SMS, voice, and in-person options—are maintained (World Bank Group 2023).

AI can help detect and deter ghost bookings and intermediaries. In many parts of the world, unscrupulous agents book multiple appointments speculatively, holding slots they never intend to use. By analyzing booking patterns—time of reservation, frequency of cancellations, or repeated use of identical contact details—AI can flag suspicious activity. Dynamic reconfirmation requests, such as requiring applicants to reconfirm attendance within 48 hours, can prevent abuse without penalizing legitimate users.

What makes these designs effective is not complexity but alignment with real-world behavior. Applicants respond to timely reminders, calendars benefit from adaptive overbooking, waitlists reduce frustration, and fraudsters are discouraged by verification hurdles. AI provides the intelligence to manage each of these levers with precision. The result is not only greater efficiency but also a system that feels more predictable and fair to the public it serves.

INTERNAL WORKFLOW EFFICIENCY: GIVING CONSULAR STAFF THEIR DAY BACK

Appointments are only one side of the equation. Inside the consular section, consular staff also contend with a torrent of routine tasks that consume hours every week: sorting email inquiries, drafting repetitive responses, compiling case packets, reconciling fees, and attending meetings that generate more notes than action. These tasks are essential, but they often crowd out the higher-value work that requires judgment and empathy. AI offers tools to rebalance that equation by automating the predictable while keeping consular staff firmly in control.

One promising application is inbox triage and drafting assistance. Natural language processing systems can classify incoming messages by urgency, topic, and language. A distressed citizen reporting a lost passport can be flagged for immediate attention, while a routine question about photo requirements is routed to a standard reply. Large language models, when constrained to official content libraries, can draft responses complete with citations for officers or correspondence units to review and send. In early U.S. State Department pilots, tools like Northstar and FAM Search demonstrated how AI could cut hours off research and drafting by surfacing relevant guidance instantly (Doubleday 2024b).

Another tool is the officer copilot for writing and research. Drafting waiver summaries, refusal explanations, or congressional response letters consumes vast amounts of officer time. AI systems can generate first drafts that officers refine, allowing them to focus on nuance rather than formatting. Summarization models can also condense long email threads or media reports, helping officers get to the core of an issue without wading through pages of text. This is not automation of judgment but amplification of clarity.

Meetings, too, can be transformed by AI-enabled assistants. Transcription tools can capture discussions in real time, highlighting action items and deadlines. Instead of officers scribbling notes or revisiting recordings, they can leave meetings with a clear, structured summary ready for circulation. These tools free staff to participate more fully in discussions, ensuring that attention is on substance rather than clerical record-keeping.

Robotic process automation (RPA) can streamline back-office routines. Bots can reconcile fee payments against case records, send automated reminders for pending applications, or assemble case packets for officer review. Agencies across government have already documented the efficiency gains of RPA: the CIO Council reported significant time savings in federal agencies by automating repetitive digital tasks (CIO Council 2020). For consular operations, such gains can mean reclaiming staff hours that are better spent on interviews, fraud detection, or emergency services.

When taken together, these applications return something priceless: time. Time to probe a complex case more carefully, to reassure a citizen in distress, to mentor a new officer, or to strengthen relationships with host government counterparts. By offloading repetitive tasks, AI restores the human presence that defines diplomacy. In the end, workflow efficiency is not about doing more with less—it is about giving consular team members their day back.

A related frontier is reactive social media assistance. Many consular sections already monitor public channels to gauge sentiment and correct misinformation, but AI can make this process both faster and safer. Using natural language classifiers and open-source monitoring tools, a system can flag online posts that mention the consular section—such as questions about office hours, appointment wait times, or entry requirements—and automatically respond with an approved, factual link rather than free-text commentary. For example: "I see you're asking about U.S. visa appointment times in Nairobi—here's the official link for the latest schedule."

This approach does not generate new content or speculate; it simply connects users to curated, authoritative information from official sites. In doing so, it reduces staff workload, combats misinformation, and keeps public engagement responsive without compromising accuracy. The OECD's review of AI in government has emphasized that such tools should guide users toward trusted sources when deployed under transparent and accountable oversight (OECD 2024). Experts have likewise emphasized that AI in government must promote inclusion and trust by broadening—not narrowing—access to accurate information.

STAFFING AND SHIFT DESIGN

No matter how advanced scheduling or workflow tools become, the human capacity of a consular section remains finite. Officers and locally employed staff can only conduct so many interviews, process so many cases, or respond to so many crises in a day. The challenge for managers is to align staffing patterns with demand while protecting staff well-being. AI offers a way to support this balancing act, providing data-driven insights that can reshape how shifts are designed and resources allocated.

Predictive analytics can model demand patterns down to the hour. By analyzing historical data—appointment volumes, seasonal surges, or local holidays—AI can forecast when the waiting room will be busiest and when it will be quiet (Feng et al. 2024; IATA 2025). This enables managers to stagger shifts, ensuring that more officers are available during peak demand while still protecting blocks of uninterrupted time for complex adjudications or staff training. Research in healthcare has shown that adaptive scheduling, guided by predictive models, can reduce wait times while improving staff efficiency (Feng et al. 2024). In consular affairs, the same principles apply, with the added benefit of protecting officers and staff from burnout during seasonal workload surges.

AI can also inform cross-training and task allocation. By tracking workflow bottlenecks, dashboards may reveal that too much staff time is being consumed by photo rejections, fraud referrals, or passport intake. Managers can then assign or train staff to address these recurring chokepoints, creating flexibility in the team and distributing workload more evenly. For entry-level officers, this can provide valuable exposure to multiple aspects of consular work, while for locally employed staff it reinforces their critical role in sustaining operations and offers opportunities to develop new skills in AI-assisted workflows—from appointment analytics to inbox triage—that strengthen their professional value and career resilience.

Shift design has implications for morale and retention as well. Consular officers and staff often speak of feeling drained by the relentlessness of daily casework. If predictive scheduling can reduce wasted time and allow officers to leave on time more often, it improves job satisfaction and reduces attrition. AI tools that highlight predictable slow periods also create opportunities for deeper staff development, mentorship, and engagement with host government partners—tasks that often fall by the wayside during periods of overwhelming demand.

For section chiefs, staffing insights extend beyond the consular mission itself. Aggregated data across posts can inform headquarters about where surge staffing should be directed, whether through temporary duty assignments, expanded contractor support, or policy changes to alleviate pressure. Headquarters-based managers, in turn, can use these insights to advocate for resources with evidence rather than anecdotes, strengthening the case for sustainable staffing models. Past consular management reviews have shown that improved workflow design alone can eliminate major backlogs even without added staff (U.S. Department of State 2006).

AI cannot eliminate the stresses of consular work, but it can ensure that officers and staff are deployed intelligently, humanely, and fairly. By aligning shifts with actual demand, creating buffers for complex work, and reducing overtime pressures, AI-driven staffing models protect both the quality of adjudications and the well-being of those who carry them out.

Digital Frontlines: India's Facial Recognition Revolution—45 Million Journeys and Counting

DigiYatra, India's AI-powered passenger flow system, has become one of the world's largest deployments of facial recognition technology in civilian aviation. By mid-2025, the system was operating at 24 airports and had enrolled more than 52 million users (Press Information Bureau 2024, 2025).

Individual airport data demonstrates rapid adoption. Mumbai's Chhatrapati Shivaji Maharaj International Airport processed 6.3 million travelers through DigiYatra e-gates from April 2024 to August 2025, with monthly adoption rates climbing from 12% to 32% (Economic Times 2025). Kolkata extended the program in July 2025 to domestic transfer corridors, where roughly 28% of departing passengers were already using facial recognition for seamless connections between flights (Niyogi 2025).

The DigiYatra Foundation describes a system built on W3C standards for self-sovereign identity, using verifiable credentials and decentralized identifiers, with stated design goals that store biometric data on users' devices rather than in a central repository and share only the minimum information needed for each airport touchpoint (Ministry of Civil Aviation 2023).

The architecture has drawn attention from researchers examining trade-offs between convenience and privacy. Scholars analyzing the system have probed practical safeguards around consent mechanisms at crowded checkpoints and the degree to which India's Digital Personal Data Protection Act constrains secondary use of traveler data (Gyanchandani et al. 2025). Civil society organizations have raised additional concerns about non-consensual enrollment and about the DigiYatra Foundation's status as a private entity outside India's Right to Information Act, prompting calls for stronger transparency on data handling. The Financial Times has chronicled the system's rapid expansion alongside these ongoing surveillance concerns (Financial Times 2024).

System failures have also revealed vulnerabilities. During the global CrowdStrike incident affecting Microsoft Windows systems in July 2024, DigiYatra went offline at Delhi Airport alongside much of the airport's digital infrastructure, creating cascading queues (Sonali 2024). Trade and consumer reports have documented periods of app glitches, forced reinstallations, and kiosk fallbacks requiring manual processing (Gonzalez 2024)—experiences highlighting the critical importance of graceful degradation when AI systems encounter unexpected problems.

DigiYatra demonstrates that facial recognition can significantly compress queue times and improve traveler satisfaction when deployed at scale, but only when privacy guardrails, system resilience, and manual alternatives are built into the foundation. For appointment-heavy government services worldwide, the Indian experience offers a roadmap for pairing opt-in digital processing with visible, equal-dignity manual alternatives.

International observers are watching India's experiment closely as other countries consider similar deployments. The EU is developing its own smart border initiatives, while airports in North America and Asia are piloting comparable facial recognition systems. DigiYatra's success suggests that algorithmic identity verification is becoming the global standard for high-throughput travel environments.

GLOBAL ILLUSTRATIONS

The push to optimize appointments and internal workflows is not confined to any one country. Around the world, governments are experimenting with AI-driven scheduling, predictive analytics, and automation to reclaim staff time and improve fairness. For consular teams, these examples offer both practical models of what works and cautionary signals of where governance must keep pace.

Some of the initiatives cited in earlier chapters reappear here deliberately, underscoring that the same core tools—predictive analytics, automation, and human-in-the-loop design—are being adapted to new facets of consular work. In the U.S., the Department of State has piloted a suite of AI tools—StateChat for answering routine inquiries, Northstar for summarizing media and policy trends, and FAM Search for retrieving guidance quickly from the Foreign Affairs Manual. Together, these pilots have saved thousands of staff hours by reducing the friction of searching, drafting, and triaging repetitive work (Doubleday 2024b). While not yet applied universally to appointment optimization, they illustrate the value of embedding AI in the daily flow of consular operations rather than treating it as a standalone experiment.

Beyond the U.S., governments are adapting similar concepts to their own systems. Estonia's digital governance model integrates AI into multiple layers of public service, including scheduling, through the unified assistant Bürokratt (European Commission 2025a). Singapore's LifeSG platform (formerly Moments of Life) and Portugal's Simplex Program show how consistent, cross-agency appointment and workflow tools can streamline both citizen and staff experience (Govtech Singapore n.d.-b; European Commission n.d.-e). Canada's Immigration, Refugees and Citizenship Canada (IRCC) employs predictive analytics in its Global Case Management System to forecast visa workloads across missions (Immigration, Refugees and Citizenship Canada 2024). IRCC's 2026 AI Strategy reinforces this distinction, stating that tools may flag straightforward, low-risk files for expedited officer decision but should not refuse or recommend refusing applications.

Rwanda provides an especially relevant model for developing country contexts. Through its IremboGov digital platform, the government has consolidated more than 240 services from nearly 40 institutions—including passports, civil registrations, and driving tests—into a single online portal that uses workflow automation, SMS notifications, and tiered processing to manage demand at scale. Birth certificate processing has improved dramatically since 2020, with a substantial majority of applications now processed within an hour, and adoption has continued to expand across both urban and rural districts. By prioritizing accessible design and digital workflow over expensive infrastructure, Rwanda has expanded access to citizens across the country, demonstrating that efficiency and inclusion can advance together when digital systems are designed for accessibility from the start (Irembo n.d.).

While Rwanda's IremboGov platform shows what responsible digital innovation can achieve, experts have cautioned that similar tools can also be misused. Analyses across Africa note that rapid expansion of digital public infrastructure has at times outpaced the legal and ethical frameworks needed to protect privacy and free expression. Reports from Freedom House and the Press Council of South Africa warn that digital authoritarianism and AI-enabled surveillance are emerging risks in parts of the region (Freedom House n.d.; Retief 2024).

Ensuring transparency, accountability, and independent oversight is therefore essential if optimization gains are to build—not erode—public trust. Similar debates have surfaced in other regions as well—from concerns about algorithmic bias in Canada's immigration triage system to transparency challenges in the EU's digital identity pilots. These cases underline that governance gaps are not unique to any one country; they are a shared challenge of AI adoption in the public sector.

Even high-volume visa networks such as India's outsourcing partnerships are testing AI-supported appointment management, using predictive overbooking and smart waitlists to maximize throughput without overwhelming counters. These approaches are not free from controversy—overbooking can feel unfair to applicants if not clearly explained—but when implemented transparently, they reduce wasted capacity and shorten queues.

Smaller interventions matter too. In healthcare systems across the U.K. and Latin America, predictive SMS reminders have been shown to cut missed appointments dramatically (Hallsworth et al. 2015). Consular operations that adopt similar automated reminders—multilingual messages that make the cost of missing explicit—report measurable improvements in attendance without major infrastructure investment.

Collectively, these examples show that AI optimization does not require futuristic systems or enormous budgets. Modest pilots—predictive reminders, waitlist backfills, inbox triage—can deliver immediate gains. The constant across all successful programs is not the technology itself but the governance behind it: clear metrics, transparency to applicants, and human oversight. Without these, efficiency gains risk being undermined by perceptions of unfairness. With them, optimization becomes a way to deliver services that are faster, more predictable, and more humane.

HUMAN–AI COLLABORATION AND GUARDRAILS

The efficiency gains of AI in consular scheduling and workflows are real, but they must never come at the expense of fairness or consular team authority. Optimization is not about ceding control to machines—it is about collaboration. For this partnership to work, guardrails are essential.

Role clarity comes first. AI should predict and organize; consular teams must decide and communicate. A system might forecast a 25% no-show rate for a certain morning block, but the decision to add overbooking slots belongs to the section chief, who balances efficiency against applicant experience and staff workload. Likewise, an AI may cluster email inquiries by urgency, but the decision to escalate a case involving a distressed citizen remains with the human team.

Transparency is equally critical. Staff need to understand why a recommendation has been made—not merely what it is. A scheduling dashboard should display the variables influencing its forecast—seasonality, prior attendance, booking channel—so consular teams can judge credibility. Similarly, an inbox triage tool should show why one message is flagged urgent and another routine. Without explainability, human discretion can be displaced by blind reliance. Explainable systems are a foundation of trustworthy public sector AI (OECD 2024).

Human-in-the-loop oversight protects against automation bias. Predictive tools can err, especially when applicant behavior shifts unexpectedly—for example, during political unrest or natural disasters. Consular teams must retain override authority, and systems should log both the AI recommendation and the human decision. These logs become valuable not only for accountability but also for retraining the models—transforming human judgment into feedback that strengthens the system over time. Lifecycle oversight of this kind is a central recommendation of the U.S. AI Risk Management Framework (National Institute of Standards and Technology 2023a).

Fairness and inclusion require particular care. If optimization tools overbook too aggressively, they may disadvantage applicants who travel from remote areas or cannot wait for extended time slots. Predictive reminders may reach smartphone users easily but miss those with limited connectivity. AI must therefore be paired with inclusive design—voice call reminders for low-literacy applicants, multiple notification channels, and transparent communication about why scheduling changes are made. The OECD and World Bank have both warned that automation without inclusive access can deepen digital inequity (OECD 2024; World Bank Group 2023).

The U.S. Office of Management and Budget has emphasized that AI systems used in government must come with impact assessments, inventories, and clear safeguards for rights and accountability (Office of Management and Budget 2024). For consular missions, this means treating optimization not as a neutral technical fix but as a high-stakes public service intervention. Guardrails are not optional; they are the conditions that make AI adoption legitimate.

When these guardrails are in place, human–AI collaboration enhances rather than erodes consular operations. Consular teams regain time for judgment and empathy, while applicants experience processes that feel faster, fairer, and more predictable. The result is not simply efficiency—it is a recentering of human discretion in a system that too often pushes staff into rushing. AI protects time; consular teams protect trust.

RISKS, ETHICS, AND EQUITY

Efficiency gains are compelling, but they can mask risks if consular operations are not careful. Appointment optimization and workflow automation deal directly with access to government services, and missteps can disproportionately harm the very populations consular sections are meant to serve. For this reason, equity must be as central as efficiency in evaluating AI-driven systems.

One risk is fairness in access to appointments. If predictive models are calibrated poorly, they may overbook too aggressively or prioritize applicants with reliable internet connections, inadvertently disadvantaging those in rural areas or with fewer digital resources. A consular section that fills every cancelled slot within minutes via online waitlists may unintentionally reward applicants who refresh their browsers constantly, leaving behind those without the same connectivity. Ensuring fairness requires balancing efficiency with inclusivity—for example, by offering multiple channels for rescheduling: online, by phone, and in person (World Bank Group 2023; UNESCO n.d.).

FIELD OBSERVATION: ACCESS AND EQUITY IN PRACTICE.

Recently in South Africa, a consular-style government service center divided the public into two queues: one for those with smartphone appointments and another for those without. Those unable to book digitally—often because the system required a national ID number, reliable internet, or an expensive phone—were told to wait outside, seated on the ground without shelter or chairs, for as long as six hours. Inside, those with confirmed appointments moved through quickly, almost all from more affluent and predominantly white communities. Outside, frustration mounted among those excluded from the digital system; eventually, the waiting crowd began shouting at facilitators who explained that "the computer decides the order." The scene captured in real time how digital-first systems, when poorly designed, can replicate long-standing inequities under a modern veneer of efficiency.

Another risk involves transparency and trust. Applicants who experience unexplained reschedules or sudden appointment cancellations may perceive the system as arbitrary, even if predictions are technically accurate. In the U.K., controversy over opaque visa algorithms highlighted how lack of transparency can trigger public backlash and official review. A government investigation into bias in algorithmic decision-making found that poorly explained AI tools in visa processing and policing had eroded trust and required withdrawal (The Guardian 2020; U.K. Government, *Review into Bias in Algorithmic Decision-Making*).

AI can also reproduce systemic bias if left unchecked. Data used to train scheduling models may reflect existing inequities—such as higher no-show rates among low-income applicants who cannot afford repeated travel to far-away consular sections. If these patterns are treated as risk signals without context, the system risks penalizing vulnerable groups rather than addressing structural barriers. Fairness audits, similar to those recommended in biometric evaluations (Grother, Ngan, and Hanaoka 2019), are essential to detect and mitigate such effects.

Privacy must not be overlooked. Appointment systems capture sensitive data, including phone numbers, email addresses, and travel histories. If predictive models expand their scope without clear safeguards, "data creep" becomes a real danger. Privacy impact frameworks—such as those required for the U.S. State Department's Consular Consolidated Database, the EU's Data Protection Impact Assessments under GDPR, Canada's Algorithmic Impact Assessment model, and Australia's Privacy Impact Assessment guide—help ensure that personal data are collected and retained only for their stated purpose (U.S. Department of State, Bureau of Consular Affairs 2023b; European Union n.d.-a; Government of Canada n.d.; OAIC 2023).

Finally, there is the human dimension of staff trust. If consular teams believe that automation exists primarily to raise quotas rather than to protect their time, morale may erode. Messaging matters. Leaders must frame optimization as a way to give teams space for judgment, empathy, and complex cases—not as a tool for squeezing more interviews out of already overextended personnel.

The lesson is clear: optimization without equity and ethics is hollow. AI systems that accelerate scheduling or automate workflows can be valuable, but only when they reinforce fairness, transparency, and human discretion. Otherwise, they risk undermining the very legitimacy that makes consular services effective.

As consular operations continue experimenting with these systems, the next challenge is practical: how to anticipate failures before they harm the public. Just as aviation and medicine rely on checklists, consular AI requires a playbook—a concise guide to diagnosing, fixing, and learning from the most common failure modes before they cascade into full-blown crises.

TOOLING AND IMPLEMENTATION PLAYBOOK

For consular operations, the challenge is not imagining what AI could do but knowing where to begin. Appointment optimization and workflow automation lend themselves to small pilots that demonstrate value quickly while minimizing risk. A practical playbook helps consular teams translate ambition into action—moving step by step from baseline measurement to scaled, enterprise-level deployment.

Stage 1: Baseline Capture—and Diagnosing the Real Problem

Before introducing any AI tools, operations must measure current conditions. How many appointments are scheduled each week? What percentage are missed? How many hours do consular staff spend on email triage or manual reminders? Without this baseline, efficiency gains will be impossible to demonstrate. Even a simple spreadsheet or dashboard can provide the foundation for meaningful comparison.

Equally important is identifying the *real* constraint before investing in a technical fix. Too often, enthusiasm for automation leads to optimizing the wrong part of the process.

Field Observation: Diagnosing the Real Constraint

In one of the largest U.S. passport-issuing operations overseas in the early 2000s, severe delays were producing backlogs and public frustration. Managers conducted a time-and-motion study, attaching slips to each case file to record every step from intake to completion. When the data were compiled, the bottleneck proved unexpectedly simple: a single printing station for biometric passport pages could not keep pace with the rest of the process. The solution was modest but decisive—adding a second printer eliminated the delay almost overnight. As later OIG inspections of consular workloads in London and other high-volume operations confirmed, finding the true constraint often yields greater impact than introducing new technology to the wrong stage of the workflow (U.S. Department of State 2020).

The lesson: diagnose before you digitize. AI can now perform such diagnostics in real time, but the underlying discipline remains the same—understand your workflow before reinventing it.

Stage 2: Early Pilots in Assist Mode

Initial pilots should focus on low-risk, high-impact applications such as predictive reminders—sending SMS or WhatsApp messages that emphasize the cost of missed appointments. Evidence from behavioral science shows that such nudges can significantly reduce no-shows in healthcare and court systems (Hallsworth et al. 2015). In assist mode, AI models generate recommendations or draft messages, but consular staff retain full control over whether to send them. Pilots may also include natural language tools that translate inquiries, summarize correspondence, or retrieve policy references instantly. These lightweight pilots build confidence and digital literacy among staff without creating dependency.

Stage 3: Smart Integration

As confidence grows, operations can enable dynamic scheduling features that adjust overbooking levels based on predicted no-show rates. These tools should integrate into existing appointment systems rather than requiring staff to toggle between platforms. Similarly, inbox triage or copilot tools can connect directly to official email accounts, providing presorted queues and draft replies grounded in approved guidance. At a regional or enterprise level, integration may include centralized analytics dashboards that compare performance across operations, helping leadership allocate resources more equitably or detect early warning signs of backlogs.

Stage 4: Scaling with Guardrails

Once pilots demonstrate measurable success—lower no-show rates, faster response times, or staff hours regained—operations can expand to broader use. Scaling does not mean uniformity: each environment demands tailored calibration. Large metropolitan consular operations may benefit from high-capacity scheduling algorithms, while smaller or bandwidth-limited offices might rely on open-source or locally hosted systems. Guardrails must remain central. Staff must retain override authority, privacy protections must be documented, and fairness audits should accompany every expansion. At the enterprise level, standardized audit templates and shared privacy impact frameworks ensure that scalability does not outpace oversight (Office of Management and Budget 2024; National Institute of Standards and Technology 2023a; Government of Canada n.d.).

Stage 5: Continuous Learning and Adaptation

AI systems improve only when fed new data and human feedback. Weekly transcript reviews, monthly fairness checks, and quarterly retraining of models help keep systems aligned with reality. Reports to headquarters should include both metrics and narratives—how much time was saved, but also how that time was reinvested in complex interviews, fraud prevention, or citizen services.

At scale, continuous learning extends beyond any one consular section. Enterprise-wide implementation should include knowledge-sharing platforms where staff exchange lessons from pilots, identify unexpected risks, and crowdsource fixes. Collaboration with partner governments, outsourcing vendors, and private sector service providers can further refine design choices and enhance transparency. Some governments are experimenting with cross-agency AI boards or ethics councils to coordinate standards across departments—a model that consular services could emulate (OECD 2024; World Bank Group 2023).

Continuous learning also means widening participation. Consular operations can pilot additional tools beyond scheduling, including translation aids for multilingual communication, accessibility features for low-literacy applicants, and sentiment analysis to detect spikes in public confusion or frustration. Lightweight, open-source options can make these benefits accessible even to smaller operations with limited connectivity. Inclusion is not an afterthought; it is a design principle. The most successful enterprises treat AI as a collaborative ecosystem—iterative, transparent, and human-led.

By following this staged playbook, consular operations can introduce AI gradually, achieving tangible gains at each step. The lesson is that optimization does not require a grand leap; it requires measured progress, tested safeguards, and a steady commitment to ensuring that technology protects staff time while preserving fairness for applicants.

FROM TEMPLATES TO ENTERPRISE STANDARDS

While enterprise AI initiatives often start as small pilots, the most enduring progress comes from turning local innovations into shared standards. Across global consular operations, early adopters frequently create simple but powerful tools—message templates, triage taxonomies, or pilot checklists—that lower barriers for others. When these "small hacks" are captured and shared, they become the foundation for enterprise-wide learning.

Example: Framing Matters

Behavioral science research shows that the wording of reminders can influence attendance as much as timing. A message that simply says, "You have an appointment tomorrow" is less effective than one that makes the stakes explicit: "Missing this appointment delays your application and prevents others from being served" (Hallsworth et al. 2015). Consular operations adapting these templates to local languages and tone achieve both consistency and cultural fit.

Mechanisms like the Consular Management Assistance Teams (CMATs)—long used within the U.S. Bureau of Consular Affairs to share best practices across regions—illustrate how peer-to-peer learning can scale. By collecting successful templates, workflow guides, and metrics from individual operations, CMAT teams help convert field-tested innovations into global enterprise resources.

This same principle applies across governments: small, repeatable tools—shared checklists, fairness audit forms, multilingual templates—can evolve into enterprise standards that ensure each office begins innovation from a stronger baseline. The goal is not to standardize creativity but to democratize access to it.

Field Checklist: Appointments and Workflow Optimization

Piloting and leveraging AI in scheduling and workflow management requires more than enthusiasm or technical skill. Structured tools—checklists, worksheets, and templates—create the discipline that turns innovation into institutional memory. They ensure that what works in one office can be safely repeated in another, and that each pilot leaves a documented trail of accountability. Here are just some examples:

A readiness checklist helps determine whether conditions are truly right to begin. It asks whether baseline data such as no-show rates or inbox volumes have been collected, whether privacy and security reviews are complete, and whether escalation rules and ownership responsibilities are clearly defined. Addressing these questions before launch avoids the most common failure of AI pilots: adopting technology before understanding the operating environment. Oversight bodies from Washington to Ottawa and Brussels have emphasized that measurable baselines and clear accountability are essential precursors to responsible AI deployment (National Institute of Standards and Technology 2023a; Government of Canada n.d.; European Union 2024a).

Worksheets also record the variables driving predictive models—attendance history, booking channel, seasonality, or case type—so that teams understand what influences each output. When patterns shift, these records allow quick recalibration and prevent the quiet drift that can erode accuracy. A second set of worksheets tracks how inbox triage tools classify messages and whether human review aligns with algorithmic sorting. Logging discrepancies creates a feedback loop that steadily improves both accuracy and transparency (Office of Management and Budget 2024).

A guardrails checklist captures human oversight in practice, noting when flagged cases were reviewed, when overrides were applied, and how dissent was handled. These small procedural habits are the daily architecture of trust. They remind consular teams that automation bias is not defeated by policy alone but by steady, documented vigilance.

A Time Dividend worksheet captures the human return on efficiency: hours saved and how that time was reinvested—in longer interviews, additional citizen services cases, deeper fraud analysis, or mentoring. Recording those dividends reframes optimization as a means of strengthening fairness and human presence, not merely accelerating throughput.

Around the world, foreign ministries face the same challenge. Whether in Nairobi, Canberra, or Copenhagen, consular managers must prove that technology improves service without diminishing humanity. Checklists and worksheets are the connective tissue of that global accountability effort—bridging local pilots with international expectations of transparency, privacy, and fairness. They show that responsible innovation is not an abstract ideal but a repeatable practice: measured, documented, and human-led.

CLOSING REFLECTION

Appointments and internal workflows may seem like administrative details, but for consular teams they shape the rhythm of daily life. A missed slot, a flooded inbox, or an overbooked calendar is not just an inconvenience—it is lost time that could have been spent exercising judgment, assisting citizens in crisis, or mentoring colleagues. AI offers a way to reclaim that time, not by replacing staff, but by clearing away the inefficiencies that quietly drain energy, morale, and public trust.

The promise of optimization is visible in small victories: fewer empty chairs in waiting rooms, reminders that keep applicants on track, inboxes that surface the urgent from the routine, and dashboards that align staffing with demand. These are not headline-grabbing revolutions, but incremental improvements that compound into meaningful change. Each hour saved should be tracked against a reinvestment choice: deeper review of complex cases, faster response to urgent citizen messages, staff training, fraud analysis, or recovery time that reduces burnout.

The risks, however, are real. Over-automation can exclude applicants without reliable internet access. Poorly explained reschedules can erode confidence in fairness. Inbox classification errors can cause distress if urgent messages are missed. These vulnerabilities remind us that optimization must always be paired with governance—human oversight, fairness audits, transparency to applicants, and privacy safeguards. Without these, efficiency gains collapse into mistrust.

Ultimately, the lesson of this chapter echoes the larger themes of the book. AI succeeds in consular affairs not when it dazzles with novelty, but when it becomes quietly reliable—predicting no-shows, sorting emails, transcribing meetings, and reconciling fees. It is in the routine and the repetitive where the greatest dividends lie. By protecting staff time, AI allows the qualities that truly matter—judgment, empathy, and fairness—to rise to the surface.

Across the world, from passport agencies in the U.S., visa sections in Nairobi, and citizen services units in São Paulo, consular professionals face the same equation: finite time, rising demand, and the expectation of humanity in every interaction. When deployed wisely, AI gives consular operations not more work, but more room for the work that matters most.

Optimization, in the end, is a workload-governance project: if every saved hour simply becomes a higher quota, the Time Dividend has been spent before staff ever receive it.

9 Deploying AI at the Mission Level

Our goal with AI has always been to do what is necessary to decrease the time to experiment, reduce the organizational overheads so that ideas can be tested out quickly, and always have a next step available.

—Zach Whitman, Chief AI Officer and Chief Data Officer, U.S. General Services Administration (quoted in U.S. General Services Administration 2025a)

AI as a technology has a lot of potential to transform how services are being delivered within state governments, but it needs to be deployed in a human-centered way.

—Jenn Thom, Lead Data Scientist, Code for America (quoted in Fox-Sowell 2025)

Modernizing government technology is a marathon, not a sprint, and millions are counting on the next leg of the race to be even stronger.

—Clare Martorana, former U.S. Federal Chief Information Officer (quoted in The White House 2024)

Opening Vignette: A $1,000 Weekend Project in Z City

In the Republic of Z, the consular chief was frustrated. The consular inbox had become unmanageable—hundreds of repetitive questions arrived each week, burying urgent messages from citizens in distress. Consular officers and staff were spending hours each day typing the same responses about passport renewals, visa requirements, and fees. Morale was slipping as people felt their time drained away by work that added little value.

One weekend, a junior officer and a locally employed IT specialist decided to experiment. Using an open-source chatbot framework and the section's verified FAQs, they built a simple model in just a few days. The total cost was under USD 1,000. After a quick briefing to the Deputy Chief of Mission and a one-page review confirming that no sensitive applicant data would be stored,

DOI: 10.1201/9781003634775-13

they switched the bot on. By Monday, it could handle 50 of the most common inquiries in English and the dominant local language.

It was imperfect but transformative. Within a month, the chatbot had deflected nearly 40% of routine emails, freeing officers and staff to focus on fraud investigations and emergency cases. The system clearly identified itself as automated, offered an easy handoff to a human when needed, and logged all interactions for review. "We didn't need a million-dollar system," the consular chief said. "We needed something modest that actually worked."

The vignette is fictional, but its outline mirrors real pilots emerging across missions worldwide. AI rarely arrives from headquarters as a grand initiative. More often, it begins quietly in the field—as small, transparent, staff-led experiments built by consular professionals who see a need and act. When designed with care and governance, these modest projects can deliver real impact, build trust among colleagues, and create momentum for more ambitious innovation. The lesson from Z City, as from so many consular sections, is simple: AI doesn't have to be perfect to be useful—it just has to start.

WHY AI IS CLOSER THAN YOU THINK

For many consular professionals, AI can still feel distant—something for national agencies, research labs, or large border authorities, not for small consular sections juggling backlogs and staff shortages. Yet the reality is far closer. Modern AI tools are modular, low-code, and increasingly affordable. A single team member—or a small group with curiosity and a few free hours—can stand up a prototype that makes a measurable dent in workload.

This accessibility is both a strength and a risk. Consular operations no longer need to wait years for enterprise deployments from headquarters. They can test ideas locally, using secure, low-risk pilots that target immediate pain points such as inbox triage, document rejection, or appointment reminders. These so-called "Goldilocks problems," borrowing from Karlan and Gugerty's framework for "right-fit" design (Karlan and Gugerty 2018), can be a sweet spot for responsible innovation—projects big enough to matter but small enough to solve. Yet accessibility without oversight can create vulnerabilities: without clear boundaries, experiments risk becoming *shadow IT*, inadvertently handling sensitive data outside approved systems.

Research by the OECD Observatory of Public Sector Innovation and the World Bank shows that the most durable government modernization usually begins in the field rather than at headquarters, where experimentation and feedback are closest to service delivery. Their findings consistently point to field-level experimentation and decentralized learning as the most reliable predictors of sustained innovation in public institutions (OECD 2019; World Bank n.d.). This kind of grassroots experimentation mirrors patterns documented across diplomatic operations more broadly, where diplomatic teams at all levels are finding that modest, well-scoped AI pilots can deliver disproportionate impact without requiring enterprise-scale investment (Kilburg 2025). The same pattern is emerging across consular systems. Projects such as StateChat in the U.S., analytics pilots at Immigration, Refugees and Citizenship Canada (IRCC), and similar efforts in European foreign ministries demonstrate that small, well-governed interventions can have outsized impact on efficiency and morale.

Still, innovation operates within rules. Most foreign ministries and their equivalents—including the U.S. Department of State—require formal approval for any software that touches personal data. Successful teams respect those limits by testing tools in sandbox environments, using anonymized datasets, or collaborating with approved vendors. Local ingenuity need not violate central policy; framed as evidence-based prototyping rather than unauthorized development, it strengthens institutional trust.

For consular teams and managers, the reality is clear: AI is no longer futuristic, nor is it the sole domain of headquarters or contractors. It is a tool within reach, ready to be applied thoughtfully to the tasks that most erode professional time and morale. The challenge now is not access but design—to build pilots that protect privacy, ensure explainability, and keep human judgment firmly at the center. With those safeguards in place, AI becomes less a distant promise and more a practical colleague in daily consular life.

BUILDING THE RIGHT TEAM FOR RESPONSIBLE AI

Some assume that adopting AI requires armies of engineers or data scientists. In practice, most field-level pilots succeed with small, multidisciplinary teams made up of consular professionals who understand their own workflows best. Modern AI and automation tools are increasingly low-code and modular, allowing nontechnical users to test ideas safely and effectively (OECD 2024). The hardest part is rarely the technology itself—it is the leadership, trust, and coordination needed to deploy it responsibly.

One practical way to assemble a small pilot team is to organize the work around five core functions rather than five formal job titles. The framework below is an implementation model for mission-level AI pilots: it identifies the responsibilities that must be covered—operational ownership, technical configuration, data stewardship, communication, and senior-level support—while allowing each post to assign them according to local staffing and conditions. This functional approach aligns with broader lessons from consular management: 1CA's management model emphasizes defining challenges, setting goals, creating plans, measuring performance, and sharing practical solutions, while OIG reviews of consular programs underscore the need to evaluate whether internal initiatives create value and remain sustainable over time (U.S. Department of State OIG 2018, 2021).

At the heart of any pilot is a consular champion—the person who feels the friction of the current system most acutely. This could be a manager, officer, or locally employed staff member who spends hours each week handling repetitive inquiries, chasing documents, or untangling appointment backlogs. The champion defines the scope of the pilot and ensures it addresses a real problem rather than a theoretical one.

Supporting the champion is a technical lead—often a locally employed staff member with IT expertise or a team member familiar with low-code tools. This person configures the system, troubleshoots issues, and bridges vendor platforms with consular workflows. Their institutional knowledge and ability to translate operational needs into technical adjustments make them indispensable.

A data steward plays an equally vital role. They know what data exists, its quality, and how it can be used responsibly. The data steward enforces privacy protocols, ensures datasets are stripped of personal information where possible, and documents the system's data sources. Without this discipline, even a well-intentioned pilot can slip into compliance gaps that undermine credibility.

A communications liaison keeps both internal staff and external applicants informed. This person drafts clear disclaimers for automated tools, manages expectations, and ensures staff know when and how to escalate cases. Transparent communication reduces resistance and builds confidence that AI is a partner, not a replacement.

An idea ally serves as the bridge between innovation in the field and authorization at the next level up. This ally—often a Deputy Chief of Mission, section head, or headquarters contact—helps ensure that promising local ideas are visible, supported, and resourced appropriately. The ally's backing can provide modest funding, political cover if an experiment fails, and the institutional lift needed to bring a local solution into broader use. Without this role, many valuable pilots remain invisible or stall when staff rotate.

Together, these five roles—champion, technical lead, data steward, communications liaison, and idea ally—form a lean but resilient model for responsible experimentation. Each can be filled by people already in the section, requiring only modest additional effort. By distributing responsibility across these functions, field operations ensure that no single team member carries the burden of innovation alone. More importantly, they demonstrate that AI adoption is not the work of distant experts but of consular professionals improving their own tools—with leadership allies who help those ideas reach daylight.

GOVERNANCE AND GUARDRAILS THAT ENABLE PILOTS

Small pilots can deliver quick wins, but without governance they risk creating vulnerabilities in privacy, fairness, and accountability. The goal of governance in consular operations is not to stifle innovation but to channel it—ensuring that creative experiments remain aligned with legal obligations and professional standards.

The first principle is visible but light-touch leadership support. Pilots succeed when section chiefs, deputy chiefs of mission, or headquarters counterparts give explicit permission to experiment while setting clear boundaries. Consular teams should know they can test a new inbox triage tool or appointment reminder system, provided they log their work, restrict it to approved datasets, and pause if risks arise. This kind of top cover echoes the "idea ally" role described earlier: leadership that empowers experimentation while protecting both the staff and the institution. Innovation flourishes when leaders signal openness but insist on guardrails.

Second, every pilot must be designed with human-in-the-loop decision-making from the outset. AI may draft, cluster, or flag—but consular experts must decide.

A chatbot, for example, should never promise an outcome, only explain the process. A fraud detection pilot may surface anomalies, but it should never issue denials. Accountability must remain with people, and systems should make that distinction clear to both staff and applicants (OECD 2024).

A mini privacy pack provides another essential safeguard. Before any pilot launches, the team should complete a one-page privacy impact review specifying what data is used, how long it is retained, and who has access. Retention clocks and role-based permissions should be configured from the outset, not bolted on later. These steps mirror broader governance frameworks such as the U.S. Office of Management and Budget's guidance on federal AI governance, which requires inventories and impact assessments for any rights-affecting system (Office of Management and Budget 2024).

Pilots should borrow standards from established frameworks rather than inventing their own. The NIST AI Risk Management Framework provides practical tools for mapping, measuring, and mitigating risk (NIST 2023). The EU Artificial Intelligence Act classifies migration and border-related AI as "high risk," mandating transparency, explainability, and oversight (European Union 2024). Even at the operational level, these standards can guide daily practice—requiring reason codes, logging overrides, and ensuring that appeal paths exist.

When these guardrails are in place, consular teams can experiment confidently and leadership can support innovation with assurance. Governance does not slow pilots down; it makes them credible. Without it, AI becomes a liability. With it, AI becomes a trusted partner in consular work.

Digital Frontlines: Europe's AI Reckoning—The Law That Will Reshape Border Technology

The EU Artificial Intelligence Act officially entered into force in August 2024, setting in motion a legal framework that will fundamentally reshape how governments deploy AI systems in migration, asylum, and border control. AI systems banned under the Act faced restrictions starting February 2, 2025. General-purpose AI models fell under new obligations on August 2, 2025. But the real reckoning comes December 2, 2027, when "high-risk" AI systems—including virtually every algorithmic tool used in immigration and border management—must comply with unprecedented documentation, testing, and oversight requirements (European Commission 2025a).

Annex III(7) of Regulation (EU) 2024/1689 explicitly classifies AI systems used for "migration, asylum and border control management" as high-risk applications requiring the strictest regulatory scrutiny (European Union 2024b). The scope includes identity analytics algorithms that process visa applications, risk-scoring systems that screen travelers, biometric matching software that verifies documents, and automated triage tools that route cases.

High-risk AI providers and deployers must implement documented risk management systems, maintain technical documentation sufficient for regulators to understand and reproduce results, perform comprehensive record-keeping and logging, enable meaningful human oversight, meet strict accuracy and robustness benchmarks, undergo formal conformity assessments, and operate continuous monitoring systems that can trigger corrective action when problems emerge (European Union 2024a).

Agencies must produce model cards explaining how their AI systems work, data sheets documenting training information, bias testing results broken down by demographic groups, override logs tracking human intervention, and contractual language ensuring vendors deliver audit-ready documentation.

Existing systems aren't grandfathered out. While AI systems placed on the market before December 2027 are exempt unless significantly modified, large-scale government IT systems in justice and security domains have until December 31, 2030 to achieve compliance (European Commission 2025a).

The practical implications are forcing difficult conversations in government agencies worldwide. Pilots launched today must be designed to "graduate into" compliance, with governance frameworks built from the foundation. Procurement teams are working to understand what constitutes adequate vendor documentation, while legal departments grapple with liability questions when AI systems fail to meet regulatory standards.

For the AI industry, the regulation represents both opportunity and disruption. Companies that invest in compliance-ready systems and transparent documentation may gain competitive advantages in European markets and beyond, but organizations built on proprietary black-box algorithms face fundamental challenges around maintaining trade secrets while meeting transparency requirements.

Non-EU governments are studying whether to adopt similar frameworks, viewing EU compliance as a competitive advantage. Some are implementing voluntary standards that mirror EU requirements, betting that algorithmic accountability will become a global expectation.

THE DEPLOYMENT PLAYBOOK

For consular operations eager to experiment with AI, one of the most serious risks is not failure but overreach. A grand plan to overhaul an entire visa or passport process in one leap is almost certain to stumble. By contrast, narrow, well-scoped pilots that tackle a single "Goldilocks problem" can deliver meaningful results within a few weeks or months. A structured deployment playbook helps consular sections design these efforts so they remain practical, measurable, and replicable.

The first stage is problem definition. A pilot should target an issue that is significant enough to matter but contained enough to manage. Inbox overload, repeated applicant questions, or high photo rejection rates are all classic candidates. The team should define three success metrics upfront—such as reductions in inquiry volume, staff hours saved, or improved applicant satisfaction—so that progress can be measured honestly. The first rule of success is simple: do no harm. A pilot must never disadvantage, misinform, or create inequities for applicants.

Next comes standing up the pilot. The technical lead configures the tool—perhaps a chatbot trained on frequently asked questions or an email classifier using anonymized past inquiries. Escalation rules must be hardwired: if the system encounters an unfamiliar query, it automatically defers to a human. The consular champion recruits a small, trusted group of staff to test the pilot quietly, surfacing errors before any public use. Visible support from an idea ally—a Deputy Chief of Mission, section head, or headquarters contact—provides institutional cover and ensures lessons are shared beyond the local team.

The third stage is measurement and review. After a predetermined period—for example, 30 or 60 days—the team compares results against baseline metrics. Has inquiry volume actually fallen? Are consular staff reporting time savings? Are applicants receiving clearer responses? Equally important, are any errors understandable and easily corrected? Regular internal reviews maintain accountability and help refine the tool before broader use.

The final stage is scaling and handover. If at least two of the three success metrics are met, the pilot can be expanded to new use cases or larger audiences. Documentation becomes critical at this stage: standard operating procedures, maintenance schedules, and override protocols should be written down so that knowledge does not vanish with staff rotations. A designated owner should be named in advance for a set period—typically the first 90 days of operation—to ensure continuity and responsible stewardship.

Real-world examples show that this playbook works. In Southeast Asia, one post piloted waiver summarization with a small officer cohort, then scaled only after six weeks of measurable gains. In West Africa, a chatbot project cost under USD 1,000 but reduced inquiry volume by 40% once guardrails were in place. In Eastern Europe, a vendor bake-off used real, sanitized consular emails to compare accuracy and fairness before awarding a contract. Each case reflects the same principle: start small, measure hard, and scale only when results and governance align.

These examples are consistent with broader lessons from public sector innovation: pilots are most credible when they start with narrow use cases, use appropriate safeguards, define success metrics in advance, and are evaluated before they scale. Similar lessons have been reported by Canada's IRCC and the OECD, where government AI pilots using anonymized datasets and staged scaling have proven more sustainable than top-down deployments (IRCC 2023; OECD 2023; U.S. Department of State OIG 2018, 2021).

CHOOSING TOOLS AND VENDORS WITHOUT REGRETS

When consular managers decide to bring AI into daily operations, one of their most consequential choices is selecting the right tools and vendors. A well-chosen system can save consular teams many hours each week; a poor one can drain resources, create security vulnerabilities, and erode trust. The good news is that consular operations do not need to reinvent procurement standards. A few practical criteria can prevent the most common missteps.

One path is to rely on government-built tools, where available. Systems such as StateChat, Northstar, and FAM Search were developed within the U.S. Department of State to address recurring challenges like inquiry overload, media monitoring, and policy lookup (Doubleday 2024b). These tools are designed with privacy and oversight in mind and integrate directly into existing workflows. When headquarters solutions exist, they are usually the safest first option.

Another approach is to partner with established enterprise vendors. Large firms—such as CGI Federal with its Atlas360 platform—market integrated systems that promise to enhance visa or passport processing through AI overlays (CGI 2023). While these products offer scale and polish, consular operations should scrutinize claims carefully. Demonstrations may feature impressive dashboards without addressing consular law, privacy, or redress. Contracts should require explainability, verified performance on independent benchmarks, and clear exit clauses to prevent vendor lock-in.

Cloud platforms—including Amazon Web Services, Microsoft Azure, and Google Cloud—provide off-the-shelf AI services that can be piloted quickly at low cost. They offer translation engines, facial recognition APIs, and natural language processing modules that can plug into consular workflows. Yet convenience brings questions of data sovereignty: where is the applicant's data processed, and under which legal framework? For many governments, routing consular applicant data through foreign-owned cloud infrastructure is not merely a compliance question—it may be a legal impossibility or a direct violation of national data protection law. Consular managers must verify sovereignty requirements before piloting, not after, and must treat a prohibition as a firm constraint rather than a factor to be weighed against convenience.

Open-source frameworks like Rasa or Hugging Face offer flexibility and cost savings, especially for smaller pilots. Consular sections with technically capable staff can adapt these platforms to local needs while maintaining full control of data. The trade-off is responsibility: without vendor support, the team must manage updates, retraining, and troubleshooting. Open-source solutions are best suited for narrowly scoped pilots, not enterprise-wide deployments.

A proven best practice is the "bake-off": giving two or more tools the same sanitized, real consular inputs and comparing accuracy, explainability, and escalation quality. This approach grounds procurement decisions in evidence rather than marketing. It also reassures staff that a tool was chosen because it performed best in practice—not because it was easiest to buy or most heavily promoted.

In the end, choosing tools and vendors is less about technology than about governance. Consular operations that demand explainability, require fairness audits, and negotiate exit strategies will be well positioned to adopt AI responsibly and without regrets. Those that skip these safeguards risk not only wasted funds but also the erosion of the public trust on which the legitimacy of consular work rests.

The guidance above is written for consular professionals choosing tools, but it carries an equally important message for the private sector. If you are a technology provider, contractor, or consultant considering the consular market, understand that consular sections are not typical commercial clients. They operate within government procurement frameworks that prioritize data sovereignty, security, and accountability above convenience or cost. The AI tools they adopt must preserve human-in-the-loop design, explainability, and auditability—a product that functions as a black box will not pass muster, no matter how impressive its accuracy metrics.

Data ownership and privacy are nonnegotiable. The diplomatic mission retains control of all applicant and citizen data, full stop. Vendors who understand the operational reality of posts—limited IT staff, variable internet connectivity, multilingual environments, frequent staff rotations—and who design for those constraints rather than for ideal conditions will find a more receptive audience. Pilots are the entry point. Expect to prove value in a narrow, controlled test before any broader adoption is considered. And expect to be measured not only on efficiency but on fairness, transparency, and the degree to which your tools reinforce rather than undermine officer authority. The consular environment rewards partners who respect the mission's values, not just its pain points.

BUDGETING, PROCUREMENT, AND DATA READINESS

Even the best AI tool will falter without planning and preparation. Deploying AI in consular operations rarely requires vast budgets, but it does demand disciplined foresight. Too often, pilots fail not because the technology is ineffective but because costs were underestimated, contracts were vague, or data was unprepared. Consular managers and teams can avoid these pitfalls by approaching budgeting, procurement, and data readiness as inseparable pieces of the same puzzle.

Budgeting must account for the entire lifecycle of a tool, not just its initial build. A chatbot pilot may cost only a few hundred dollars to configure, but consular operations must plan for recurring expenses such as cloud hosting, translation memory upkeep, or system monitoring. Staff time—both U.S. and locally employed—spent on supervision, transcript review, and retraining must also be budgeted. Even micro-pilots require sustained attention. A realistic budget protects against the familiar failure of "one-off projects" that collapse when staff rotate or initial enthusiasm wanes (OECD 2024).

Procurement is where small sections can lock in safeguards—or leave themselves exposed. Even brief statements of work should specify requirements for privacy, explainability, and exit clauses. A strong contract might require that all AI-generated outputs display reason codes, that raw data remain on approved servers, and that vendors provide model documentation on request. Consular operations, with support from their parent ministries or headquarters, should also negotiate portability, ensuring that if they change vendors, content libraries and training data can move with them. Even modest contracts can model best practices for larger deployments (World Bank 2018).

Data readiness is perhaps the most overlooked factor. AI tools cannot function without structured, high-quality data. Before launching a pilot, consular teams should inventory what they already have: FAQs for chatbots, past appointment records for scheduling models, or anonymized emails for triage pilots. At least 150–300 labeled examples are typically needed for a model to produce reliable outputs (Oikonomidi et al. 2022). Equally important is removing personally identifiable information wherever it is not required. Poor data hygiene—outdated content, inconsistent labels, or unredacted details—will sabotage even the most promising pilot (NIST 2023).

Examples from practice underline the importance of preparation. In one West African consular section, a chatbot pilot succeeded because the team invested early in compiling and cleaning its FAQs, translating them into three languages, and verifying tone. In contrast, a European post's digital triage pilot faltered when messy datasets produced inconsistent outputs, eroding staff confidence before the system could prove its worth. These examples show that data quality and governance matter as much as technical capability.

By budgeting for the long term, procuring with safeguards, and preparing data responsibly, consular operations can maximize the odds that small pilots evolve into sustainable solutions. The goal is not just to save money or deploy tools quickly but to ensure that AI becomes a durable asset of consular practice—one that endures long after the original innovators have departed the section.

THE INSTITUTIONAL PREREQUISITES FOR AI ADOPTION

Policy guidance and pilot checklists can define the road map, but they remain paper exercises unless the institution behind them is ready. The most common reason AI pilots fail to scale is not the technology—it is the people, the data systems, and the contracts that surround it. Getting these three foundations right is what separates a one-off experiment from a lasting change.

The first foundation is people. Government agencies rarely win bidding wars for top data scientists, and they do not need to. What consular operations need are staff who can oversee AI tools intelligently—people trained not to build algorithms but to understand what goes into them and to question what comes out. That means creating roles focused on oversight: officers or locally employed staff who review model outputs for accuracy, monitor whether the system is drifting away from fair results, and flag problems before they compound. These are not exotic new positions; they are extensions of the supervisory review that consular managers have always performed, updated for a world where some of the work is done by machines. Without this internal expertise, the human-in-the-loop becomes a rubber stamp rather than a genuine check (OECD 2024).

The second foundation is data. AI tools are only as good as the information they draw from, and in many government settings that information lives in aging systems that were never designed to talk to each other. A visa database built in one decade may not connect easily to a passport system built in another. Records may be formatted inconsistently, duplicated across platforms, or missing key fields. A successful AI pilot must therefore be paired with practical investment in cleaning up and connecting the data it depends on—not a wholesale IT overhaul, but targeted work to ensure that the specific information the pilot needs is accurate, accessible, and structured (OECD 2024).

The third foundation is procurement. When a consular operation buys an AI tool from a vendor, it must retain the right to look under the hood. Contracts should explicitly grant the government full access to examine the model's training data, its performance history, and its inner workings. If a vendor claims that its system is proprietary and cannot be audited, that is a disqualifying condition, not a negotiating position. Systems used to make decisions affecting people's visas, passports, and identities must be open to government review without exception (U.K. Government n.d.-c).

When talent, data, and procurement are treated as strategic priorities rather than administrative afterthoughts, the institution builds the foundation it needs to sustain AI over the long term. A system that is not only ethical in principle but auditable and maintainable in practice is the clearest path to integration that lasts.

CHANGE MANAGEMENT AND STAFF TRUST

Introducing AI into consular operations is as much an organizational shift as a technical one. Staff across ranks—officers, specialists, and locally employed colleagues—carry the responsibility of safeguarding borders and serving citizens; their skepticism toward automation is both natural and necessary. Studies of digital transformation in government consistently show that trust and transparency are the strongest predictors of adoption success (OECD 2024; Fernandez and Rainey 2006). Without them, even promising pilots stall.

Change management begins with framing. Successful deployments, according to the U.S. State Department's OIG, have been those where leaders framed AI as a *time-saving partner* rather than a workforce reduction tool. When pilots were presented as freeing staff to focus on judgment and service quality, adoption increased; when framed purely as efficiency or cost reduction, resistance grew.

Inclusion is the second driver of trust. Research across OECD member states shows that projects with early involvement of frontline staff—including skeptics—achieve faster normalization and fewer ethical breaches (OECD 2024; World Bank 2018). Staff who test systems, identify false positives, or flag usability problems become advocates rather than opponents. By contrast, deployments that treat users as passive recipients of technology often face hidden resistance or quiet workarounds.

Training and procedural transparency reinforce that trust. Staff confidence rises when they can see both correct and incorrect system outputs and practice overriding them. According to NIST's AI Risk Management Framework (2023), "human-in-the-loop validation" and "explainable error logging" are essential for maintaining accountability in operational AI. This transparency—showing where the system might fail and how humans remain in charge—turns potential anxiety into confidence.

Visible short-term benefits accelerate acceptance. Pilots that start with the most universally disliked tasks—such as redundant data entry, photo rejections, or repetitive email drafting—build momentum. As one consular team member in a field pilot summarized: "Once the bot stopped me from retyping the same name 50 times a day, I stopped worrying about it replacing me."

Change management is not a single event but a continuing relationship between leadership, technology, and staff. Ongoing dialogue, visible feedback loops, and adaptive training all contribute to sustained trust (Fernandez and Rainey 2006). By embedding these principles, consular operations transform AI from a technical rollout into a shared professional evolution—one that strengthens morale, enhances accountability, and reinforces the enduring truth of consular work: judgment belongs to people, not machines.

HOW TO MEASURE AND SHOW VALUE

For any AI pilot to succeed in consular operations, leaders must be able to demonstrate its value. Without evidence, pilots risk being dismissed as novelties—or worse, as distractions from core consular responsibilities. Measurement provides the proof that tools are improving efficiency, quality, and fairness. Communicating that value, in turn, builds the legitimacy needed to sustain innovation through leadership rotations and staff changes.

Operational metrics provide the first layer of evidence. These include reductions in inquiry volume, faster response times, shorter appointment backlogs, or hours returned to staff. In one West African pilot, for instance, a simple chatbot cut routine email inquiries by roughly 40%, freeing time for fraud detection and citizen services. Quantifying such gains turns anecdotal enthusiasm into measurable performance (OECD 2024; World Bank 2018).

Quality metrics reinforce the story. AI outputs must be accurate, clear, and usable. Supervisory review of chatbot transcripts or email triage classifications can reveal whether a system genuinely helps or simply shifts errors downstream. A low rework rate and consistent "explainable output" scores—recommended in the NIST AI Risk Management Framework—are strong indicators of a well-scoped pilot (NIST 2023).

The human dimension is equally important. Staff feedback surveys and focus groups can track whether workloads feel lighter and morale has improved. Burnout proxies—such as overtime hours or leave use—can serve as indirect indicators. Applicants' perceptions also matter: shorter wait times, clearer instructions, and confidence that the process is fair. The OECD has emphasized that trust metrics carry as much weight as performance metrics when evaluating digital government services (OECD 2024).

Integrity metrics ensure that efficiency does not come at the cost of fairness. Pilots should track how often cases are escalated to humans, the rate of overrides, and the outcomes of appeals or redress. Systems that deflect routine work but mishandle complex cases undermine trust quickly. The U.S. Privacy and Civil Liberties Oversight Board has emphasized the importance of publishing not only success rates but also error and equity statistics to maintain accountability (PCLOB 2025).

Communicating results sustains momentum. A one-page "pilot scorecard" showing baseline metrics, results, staff feedback, and next steps helps leadership see progress at a glance. Sharing these outcomes with headquarters, regional bureaus, or host country counterparts demonstrates that innovation is grounded in evidence, not hype. As Fernandez and Rainey (2006) observed, evidence of small, credible wins is the most reliable catalyst for long-term organizational change.

By measuring and showing value in this way, consular operations can move beyond the question of whether AI works to the more constructive challenge of how to scale it while safeguarding fairness and human judgment. Evidence turns pilots into policy—anchoring AI not as an experiment, but as a trusted instrument of modern consular service.

CASE STUDIES AND PATTERNS

The value of operational-level AI becomes clearest when seen in practice. Around the world, small pilots have shown how modest interventions—sometimes built over a weekend, sometimes supported by vendors—can reshape consular workflows. These examples, drawn from patterns documented in Consular Systems and Technology modernization reviews and OECD case studies, reveal not just isolated successes but repeatable principles worth replicating (OECD 2024).

In Southeast Asia, a consular section piloted a waiver summarization tool after officers found themselves buried in case packets hundreds of pages long. By introducing an AI summarizer in "assist" mode, the team produced structured briefs highlighting key evidence, inconsistencies, and relevant policy citations. Within six weeks, supervisory review showed faster and more consistent adjudications. The pilot then expanded—carefully—to additional waiver categories. The pattern: start narrow, measure impact, and scale with safeguards.

In West Africa, another section faced crushing inquiry volume. Rather than wait for a headquarters solution, a locally employed IT specialist and a junior officer built an open-source chatbot trained on FAQs in English and the local language. The cost was under a thousand dollars; the payoff was substantial. Inquiry traffic dropped by roughly 40%, freeing time for fraud investigations and citizen services work. The pattern: local ingenuity and low-cost experimentation solving real pain points.

In Eastern Europe, a larger operation confronted a different challenge: selecting among competing vendors of AI-enhanced document analysis tools. Instead of relying on marketing claims, the section staged a vendor bake-off. Each company received a set of sanitized, real-world documents—both genuine and fraudulent—and was evaluated for accuracy, explainability, and escalation quality. The selected vendor prevailed not for polish, but for transparency and fairness. The pattern: evidence-based procurement through real-world testing.

Across these contexts, consistent lessons emerge. Successful pilots are scoped tightly, measured rigorously, and scaled only after proving their value. They depend on the insight of consular professionals closest to the problem, not on top-down directives. They build credibility through documentation, transparency, and demonstrable gains in time, quality, and fairness.

These examples reinforce the broader conclusion reached throughout this chapter: AI at the operational level succeeds when evidence, not enthusiasm, drives scale. Measured pilots that start small and grow cautiously create ripple effects that outlast individual innovators. The most enduring pattern is not technological but institutional—a culture where consular teams see AI as a disciplined instrument that protects judgment, not a disruption that replaces it.

COMMON PITFALLS AND ANTI-PATTERNS

If the preceding case studies show what good practice looks like, the anti-patterns reveal the traps that consular operations must avoid. Again and again, field pilots fall into the same predictable errors when experimenting with AI: over-automation, under-communication, tool sprawl, and the lure of big-bang projects. Each of these erodes trust and undermines the very efficiency gains AI promises.

Over-automation is the first and most damaging pitfall. When pilots give AI excessive authority—whether letting a chatbot answer sensitive legal questions or allowing a fraud-screening tool to block cases without human review—the results are predictable: errors, complaints, and loss of confidence. Research on *automation bias* confirms that people often defer uncritically to machine output, even when it conflicts with judgment (National Institute of Standards and Technology 2023a; OECD 2024). The remedy is straightforward but nonnegotiable: AI may assist, but people decide. Every system must embed human-in-the-loop oversight, clear escalation paths, and transparent audit trails.

A second pitfall is under-communication. Applicants and staff alike need to understand what has changed and why. A pilot that quietly modifies appointment scheduling or inbox triage without explanation risks confusion and resistance. Applicants may perceive the system as arbitrary; staff may distrust a process they cannot see. Transparency is the antidote. Clear disclaimers for applicants, regular staff updates, and open feedback channels ensure that pilots build legitimacy rather than suspicion (World Bank 2018).

Tool sprawl presents another familiar anti-pattern. When each team experiments independently, the result can be a patchwork of uncoordinated systems, each with separate logins, data flows, and vulnerabilities. The U.S. Department of State's OIG has warned that fragmented pilots increase maintenance costs and cyber risk while reducing scalability (World Bank 2018). Lightweight coordination—such as a consular technology working group or periodic portfolio reviews—helps align pilots with shared standards and encourages reuse rather than reinvention.

Many operations succumb to the big-bang temptation. Under pressure to modernize, leaders may announce sweeping transformation plans—"AI will overhaul visa processing in six months"—only to find expectations outpacing technical or policy readiness. Large-scale rollouts without iterative testing often fail dramatically. The U.K.'s visa-streaming algorithm, retired in 2020 after bias concerns, is a cautionary example: a high-profile project undone by lack of transparency and weak oversight (The Guardian 2020; OECD 2024; London Daily n.d.). The sustainable alternative is the incremental approach described throughout this chapter: start small, measure rigorously, and scale only when safeguards and value are proven.

These pitfalls are not unique to consular affairs; they recur across all sectors adopting AI. What makes them particularly damaging in the consular context is that they affect both service delivery and public trust. Applicants expect fairness and clarity. Consular professionals need tools that protect—not replace—their judgment. Avoiding these anti-patterns is less about technical sophistication than about discipline, humility, and institutional learning.

In the end, success is not defined by the absence of mistakes—that is impossible—but by keeping errors small, reversible, and instructive. By recognizing and steering clear of these common pitfalls, consular operations can make AI deployments not only effective but credible, ethical, and sustainable.

SUSTAINMENT: MAKE IT BETTER EVERY WEEK

Having avoided the common pitfalls, the next challenge for consular operations is sustaining progress. Launching an AI pilot is exciting; maintaining and improving it over time is often harder. Too many initiatives start strong, deliver early wins, and then fade as staff rotate, models drift, or attention shifts elsewhere. Sustainment means embedding AI tools into daily operations so that they improve incrementally—week after week—rather than being treated as short-lived experiments.

Feedback loops are the foundation of sustainment. Every interaction with a chatbot, every override of a triage classification, every missed appointment despite reminders—each is a data point. When logged and reviewed systematically, these data become raw material for retraining and refinement. The NIST AI Risk Management Framework identifies continuous monitoring as a core component of trustworthy AI (NIST 2023). A short weekly meeting where staff review transcripts or system logs can surface issues early and keep tools aligned with reality.

Role rotation is another critical safeguard. When only one staff member understands a system, it risks collapse as soon as that person departs. Consular sections should distribute technical and oversight responsibilities across multiple people to ensure continuity. As Fernandez and Rainey (2006) have shown, high staff turnover and uneven training undermine otherwise promising technology pilots. Shared ownership also builds trust: when several colleagues have hands-on experience, the tool feels less like a black box and more like a team asset.

Structured reviews keep pilots accountable. Weekly quick fixes address operational bugs, while quarterly reviews consider deeper issues such as bias audits, privacy compliance, or new use cases. Documentation—standard operating procedures, escalation protocols, and redress templates—must be written, not left to oral tradition. This institutional memory allows new staff to build on predecessors' work rather than start from scratch (Fernandez and Rainey 2006).

Leadership signaling reinforces sustainment. When section chiefs or deputy chiefs of mission regularly ask about metrics, lessons learned, and next steps, they send a clear message that AI tools are part of professional practice, not side projects. Conversely, when leaders stop asking, tools often stagnate. As the OECD notes, visible executive attention is one of the strongest predictors of successful digital maintenance in government (OECD 2024).

Above all, sustainment means treating AI not as a project but as infrastructure. Just as appointment systems or call trees require ongoing maintenance, so too must AI systems be nurtured. When consular operations commit to making tools slightly better every week, small refinements accumulate into lasting gains. The lesson is simple but enduring: a pilot's launch is only the beginning—its success depends on a culture of steady, evidence-based improvement.

CONNECT TO THE ENTERPRISE

Once local pilots prove their worth, the next challenge for consular operations is connecting them to the enterprise. Sustaining innovation requires not only continuous improvement in the field but also institutional pathways for sharing, scaling, and governing what works. Local tools achieve their greatest value when linked to broader consular systems, creating a network of learning rather than isolated experiments.

The first step is a marketplace mindset. Rather than reinventing the wheel, consular sections should contribute their proven tools—chatbot templates, waiver summarization prompts, appointment reminder scripts—into a shared repository managed at the bureau or enterprise level. Colleagues can then adapt and localize these resources while benefiting from peer review and cumulative refinement. This model mirrors Estonia's Bürokratt platform, which treats AI assistants as reusable public sector components shared across agencies (European Commission n.d.-b; OECD 2024). It demonstrates how interoperability and shared standards accelerate safe adoption without sacrificing local flexibility.

Integration with headquarters-built systems ensures continuity and governance. Platforms such as StateChat, Northstar, and FAM Search illustrate how centrally managed tools can provide common data safeguards, privacy controls, and explainability requirements (Doubleday 2024b). Field pilots that demonstrate measurable value should ultimately connect to these enterprise frameworks, preventing fragmentation and ensuring that successful ideas endure beyond staff rotations. The U.S. Department of State's OIG has repeatedly found that promising technology pilots fade when posts lack mechanisms to transition local tools into enterprise systems (U.S. Department of State 2021b).

Feedback loops to headquarters complete the cycle. When field consular operations document and share results—time saved, error rates, applicant satisfaction—they provide policymakers with evidence of what works in practice. These insights inform procurement, guide training priorities, and shape bureau-level AI policy. As the World Bank has noted, data from field experiments is among the most underutilized assets in public sector reform (World Bank 2018). Making it visible turns local success into institutional learning.

Connecting to the enterprise does not mean stifling creativity. On the contrary, it validates field innovation by giving it a pathway to scale. The most effective consular AI ecosystems operate as virtuous cycles: local ingenuity drives experimentation; enterprise governance ensures safety and consistency; and shared data enables faster, fairer, and more resilient service worldwide.

For consular teams, the lesson is clear. AI deployment need not remain a patchwork of isolated pilots. When connected to the enterprise, small wins compound into systemic improvement—strengthening not only efficiency but also institutional trust, fairness, and continuity across the global consular network.

The same logic extends beyond the diplomatic network. Healthcare systems managing patient triage, regulatory agencies processing license applications, and municipal governments handling permit backlogs all face structurally similar challenges: high volume, equity obligations, and the need to keep human judgment central. The patterns piloted in Z City are not parochial—they are portable. Any organization learning to deploy AI responsibly in service of people can draw directly from the playbook developed here.

FIELD CHECKLIST: MISSION AI PILOT READINESS

Before any consular operation launches an AI pilot, it must pause and ask a simple question: *are we truly ready?* Pilots that begin without preparation may waste staff effort, mishandle sensitive data, or erode public trust. A readiness checklist provides a disciplined framework to ensure that conditions for success are in place before a single line of code is written.

1. Define a precise use case.
   Start with a *Goldilocks problem*—an issue large enough to matter but small enough to solve. Typical examples include inbox overload, repetitive FAQs, or appointment no-shows. Each pilot should define three success metrics in advance, such as reduction in inquiry volume, hours returned to staff, or applicant satisfaction scores. This principle—specific scope plus measurable outcomes—is the cornerstone of effective field experimentation (OECD 2024; World Bank 2018).
2. Build the right team.
   A balanced team distributes both technical and ethical responsibility. Name a consular champion, a technical lead, a data steward, and a communications liaison before launch. These roles ensure continuity and governance even when staff rotate. The U.S. Department of State's OIG has reinforced this point, finding that successful technology pilots depend on clear ownership and redundancy of expertise to prevent collapse when personnel change (U.S. Department of State 2021b).
3. Embed human-in-the-loop safeguards.
   AI tools may assist, but human judgment must remain decisive. Escalation pathways—how an applicant reaches a person, how a flagged case is reviewed, how an override is logged, and who can pause the tool—must be documented before deployment. The NIST AI Risk Management Framework identifies human oversight as a core dimension of trustworthy AI, requiring that humans retain both the authority and the practical ability to override automated outcomes (NIST 2023).
4. Establish a verified baseline.
   Measure the status quo before introducing automation: inquiry volume, response times, error rates, and staff hours consumed. Without a baseline, efficiency claims are unprovable and unrepeatable. Baselines also provide the foundation for transparency and for learning what *did not* improve—a

requirement underscored in federal AI governance guidance (Office of Management and Budget 2024).

5. Complete a privacy and governance check.
   Every pilot handling applicant data must undergo a short privacy impact review detailing what data is used, how long it is retained, and who can access it. Logging should be enabled for every system output and staff override. These practices align with global standards for AI accountability (OECD 2024; European Union 2024a).
6. Test tools before launch.
   Whether government-built, vendor-provided, or open-source, tools should be tested with real but sanitized examples. A simple "bake-off" between options can expose weaknesses that glossy demos conceal. The best pilots use test data that reflects real operational diversity—different languages, document types, and applicant profiles—to avoid bias or false confidence.
7. Designate an owner for sustainment.
   Too many pilots collapse when their original sponsor rotates out. Name an owner responsible for at least the first 90 days of maintenance, staff training, and reporting. Ownership ensures accountability and signals that the pilot is part of professional operations, not a side project.

When these conditions are met—clear scope, defined roles, human oversight, verified baselines, privacy readiness, tested tools, and sustained ownership—a consular section can move forward with confidence. A pilot launched under this checklist is not just an experiment but a credible, auditable step toward lasting innovation in global consular service.

CLOSING REFLECTION

Having met the conditions for readiness, the next step is not to dream bigger but to deliver better. AI in consular operations is no longer a futuristic aspiration; it is already here—emerging through modest pilots built by consular professionals who understand their daily challenges best. A chatbot that answers repetitive inquiries, a scheduling tool that predicts no-shows, a triage system that sorts overflowing inboxes—these may seem small compared with enterprise platforms, yet for the staff who regain hours of their day, they are transformative.

The lesson of this chapter is that AI succeeds when it is practical, transparent, and governed. Oversight bodies such as the U.S. Department of State (2021b) and international frameworks like the OECD (2024) show that lasting progress rarely comes from sweeping reforms, but from disciplined iteration. Small pilots demonstrate that change takes hold through incremental steps that deliver measurable value and build trust over time. By starting narrow, measuring rigorously, and scaling cautiously, consular teams avoid the familiar traps of over-automation, tool sprawl, and under-communication.

Equally vital is the shutdown plan. A pilot should specify in advance who can pause it, what thresholds trigger review, and what happens if false positives rise, staff workload increases, one group is disproportionately burdened, or the vendor cannot explain a system change. Staff trust grows when they know adoption is reversible, auditable, and governed.

Consular professionals are custodians of both security and service. In that dual role, AI offers a way to strengthen both: securing workflows against overload and delivering services that are faster, clearer, and more humane. The most successful deployments are not the flashiest or the most invisible; they are the boringly reliable ones—systems as routine and dependable as the appointment calendar or the duty phone. When AI becomes part of the everyday fabric of consular work, it should also become inspectable: staff can see what it did, correct it when it is wrong, and explain its role without reaching for technical jargon.

The next chapter turns from process to purpose—from how to build responsibly to why it matters—to ensure that every technological gain strengthens the human heart of consular service.

Part V

People First

Throughout this book, you have examined specific applications of AI—in visa processing, passport services, crisis management, fraud detection, scheduling, and deployment. This section steps back to ask the deeper question: what kind of consular future do you want AI to create? Technology is not destiny. The choices you make about design, governance, and culture will determine whether AI strengthens or weakens the human mission of diplomatic service.

This closing section synthesizes lessons from preceding chapters into a human-centered framework. It begins with first principles, distinguishing tasks that must remain human from those suited for AI augmentation. Credibility assessment during visa interviews, the duty of care owed to citizens in crisis, and the empathy required to guide grieving families through tragedy are fundamentally human responsibilities. No algorithm can replicate the moral accountability that you bear when you decide who may cross a border or when you stand with citizens in their most vulnerable moments. AI excels at pattern recognition, translation, and repetitive processing—valuable precisely because they free you to do what only people can.

Ten design principles guide implementation, building on Chapter 1's five-principle foundation and extending it with operational guidance from the preceding chapters—covering everything from human-in-the-loop by default to graceful degradation when systems fail. Rather than diminishing your role, AI elevates distinctly human skills: credibility assessment, empathic communication, risk explanation, and the digital literacy to guide AI tools effectively.

This section also looks forward—to new career paths emerging for you as a consular professional, to culture change that makes AI "boringly reliable" rather than exotic, and to metrics that measure not just efficiency but time returned for human-centered

DOI: 10.1201/9781003634775-14

work. Practical tools including reusable workflow patterns, a leadership playbook, and a tear-out checklist translate principles into action.

The book closes where it began: AI succeeds in consular affairs not through technological dazzle but by protecting the time, presence, and judgment that you need to serve citizens with fairness and humanity.

10 A Human Future with AI at Our Side

The future is not preordained. We control the extent to which AI either expands human opportunity through augmentation or replaces humans through automation.

—Erik Brynjolfsson, Professor, Stanford Institute for Human-Centered AI (Brynjolfsson 2022)

When we see machine learning, let's make it collaborative learning. When we see user experience, let's make it about human experience.

—Audrey Tang, Minister of Digital Affairs, Taiwan (quoted in Contreras 2024)

It means recognizing AI is a tool. And tools don't have independent values—their values are human values. That means we need to be responsible developers as well as governors of this technology—which requires a framework.

—Fei-Fei Li, Sequoia Professor of Computer Science and Co-Director, Stanford Institute for Human-Centered AI (quoted in Li and Frueh 2024)

Opening Vignette: My Invisible Teammate in Z City

It was nearly six in the evening at the Republic of Z's largest consulate. For months, the consular team had been working late into the night, weighed down by backlogs, emergency inquiries, and a constant flow of case files. Tonight felt different. For the first time in weeks, an officer closed her laptop half an hour early. She had not cut corners or rushed through interviews. Instead, she had gained back time.

Earlier that day, AI systems had quietly shouldered part of the burden. A scheduling tool predicted which applicants were unlikely to appear, reshaping the day's appointments so fewer slots went to waste. A drafting assistant prepared first-pass waiver summaries and congressional replies, which the officer reviewed and edited in minutes rather than hours. An inbox triage system sorted routine inquiries from distressed citizens, ensuring that urgent

DOI: 10.1201/9781003634775-15

cases surfaced quickly. None of these tools made a single adjudication or decision. But together, they shifted the rhythm of the work.

As the officer packed up, she noticed a family in the waiting room who had arrived without an appointment. The father explained that their child had fallen seriously ill and needed immediate travel for medical treatment abroad. Because the officer was not drowning in backlogged emails or unfinished memos, she had the presence of mind—and the time—to listen fully, reassure the family, and coordinate an emergency passport issuance. Walking out into the evening air, she reflected that the AI tools had become like an invisible teammate: never replacing her judgment but creating the space for her to use it where it mattered most.

The vignette is fictional, but it captures a truth that resonates across all operations. AI is not about dazzling technology or dramatic transformation. Its success is measured in minutes regained, in attention restored, and in the human presence officers and consular staff can offer when freed from repetitive tasks. In the Republic of Z, as in consular sections worldwide, the promise of AI is not to replace officers and staff but to make them more present, more humane, and more effective.

FIRST PRINCIPLES: WHAT STAYS HUMAN, WHAT AI SHOULD DO

Any discussion of the future of AI in consular affairs must begin with a clear division of labor. The risk of overhyping AI is that it tempts organizations to let technology creep into spaces where human presence is indispensable. The risk of underusing it is that officers and staff remain trapped in repetitive tasks that machines could easily manage. First principles provide the compass: what consular work must remain human, and what AI can safely and usefully take on.

Certain responsibilities are nondelegable. Credibility judgments during visa interviews, the duty of care owed to citizens in crisis, and the empathy needed to guide a grieving family through a tragedy are fundamentally human tasks. No algorithm can replicate the moral accountability that officers and consular or immigration staff bear when they decide who may cross a border, or when they stand with citizens in their most vulnerable moments. These tasks involve not only law and policy but also trust, culture, and dignity—domains where human discretion is irreplaceable.

Other tasks are well suited for delegation to AI, provided governance is in place. Pattern recognition across thousands of visa applications, translation of FAQs into dozens of languages, automatic scheduling reminders, or the summarization of lengthy waiver files are all areas where AI provides clear value. These are tasks defined by volume and repetition, not by nuance or empathy. They consume staff time without engaging officer judgment, making them ideal candidates for automation under human review.

The dividing line between what stays human and what AI should do is not static. As tools evolve, new tasks may migrate from one side to the other. But the principle must remain constant: AI is there to create space for staff to do what only people can do—exercise judgment under uncertainty, extend empathy across cultures, and uphold the fairness and legitimacy that sustain public trust.

This principle is reflected in emerging governance frameworks. The EU Artificial Intelligence Act explicitly requires human oversight for "high risk" systems, including those used in migration and border management (European Union 2024a). U.S. federal guidance similarly emphasizes that AI may draft, flag, or summarize, but humans must decide (Office of Management and Budget 2024). For consular officers and teams, this means that the future of AI is not about replacement but about reinforcement: shifting the burden of repetition to machines while reserving responsibility for people. This means deliberately designing and redesigning roles of each member of the team, so each can take the lead on what it does best.

By beginning with these first principles, consular operations can approach every new pilot with clarity. They can ask: does this tool protect time without eroding judgment? Does it enhance fairness without compromising discretion? Does it provide good customer service? Is it responsible to the taxpayer and budget? If the answer is yes, then AI strengthens consular work. If not, it belongs firmly in the category of what must stay human.

TEN DESIGN PRINCIPLES FOR HUMAN-CENTERED CONSULAR AI

Designing AI for consular affairs is not just a technical exercise; it is a normative one. The way systems are built will shape how officers and consular teams more broadly interact with applicants, how fairness is perceived, and how trust is sustained. Chapter 1 introduced five principles for responsible adoption—human-in-the-loop, explainability, fairness, privacy, and security—as the book's governance foundation. The ten principles that follow build on and extend that foundation, translating the use cases of preceding chapters into operational guidance for design and deployment.

The first is human-in-the-loop by default. No AI system in consular affairs should be allowed to adjudicate or decide outcomes on its own. Human adjudicators must retain final authority, ensuring that accountability always rests with a human being.

Second, explainability over raw accuracy. An output that is 99% accurate but opaque is less useful than one that is 95% accurate and transparent. Officers and consular teams need to understand why a case was flagged, why an appointment was rescheduled, or why a biometric match was scored as low confidence. Transparency builds both staff trust and applicant legitimacy. It also aids in improvement of the systems.

Third, time-back as the primary KPI. The goal of AI is not novelty but the return of hours to consular staff for higher-value work. A chatbot that reduces routine inquiries or an auto-summarizer that saves hours on request packets for waivers of ineligibility should be judged by how much time it gives back—not by how flashy its interface is.

Fourth, accessibility first. Systems must be designed for multilingual contexts, low-connectivity environments, and applicants with disabilities. If an AI tool speeds processing for the majority but excludes minorities or vulnerable groups, it fails the test of fairness.

Fifth, graceful degradation. When AI fails—and it will—it must fail safely. That means seamless escalation to a human, transparent communication to the applicant, and continuity of service through backups. A missed SMS alert should default to a phone call; a failed biometric match should default to an interview.

Sixth, consent and clarity. Applicants and citizens deserve to know when AI is being used, what data it touches, and how long it will be retained. Opt-out mechanisms and clear privacy notices should be standard. Trust is built not by hiding automation but by declaring it openly.

Seventh, least data, shortest retention. AI systems should collect only the data necessary for their purpose and retain it no longer than required. Over-collection invites abuse; minimization protects both applicants and institutions.

Eighth, bias monitoring as routine. Just as consular staff check expiration dates on passports, consular operations and managers must regularly audit AI outputs for demographic disparities. NIST's studies of face recognition show why: systems can perform unevenly across age, gender, or skin tone if not monitored and retrained (Grother, Ngan, and Hanaoka 2019).

Ninth, small pilots, fast feedback. Consular operations should resist the temptation of sweeping deployments. Starting small, measuring quickly, and iterating builds team confidence and surfaces risks early.

Finally, vendor portability and content-centric design. Consular operations (whether at the field level or the enterprise level) should avoid lock-in by ensuring that knowledge bases, prompts, and training data remain under their control. If a vendor relationship ends, the consular operations should be able to take its content with it.

Together, these ten principles provide a blueprint for consular AI that is not only effective but legitimate. They align with broader frameworks like the EU Artificial Intelligence Act and the U.S. Office of Management and Budget's guidance on AI governance, while translating those standards into field-ready guidance. Most importantly, they reinforce the theme of this book: AI succeeds in consular affairs only when it serves people, protects trust, and amplifies the human qualities at the heart of diplomacy.

THE BENEFITS THAT ACTUALLY MATTER

It is tempting to measure AI's value in consular affairs purely by numbers: hours saved, inquiries deflected, documents flagged. These metrics matter, but they are not the whole story. The benefits that matter most are the ones that change how consular services feel—to the staff delivering them and to the people receiving them.

The first is consistency. Applicants often experience government services as unpredictable—one officer phrases instructions one way, another phrases them differently, and a third post interprets the same rule with subtle variations. AI tools grounded in a single, verified knowledge base deliver the same accurate answer regardless of who asks, which channel they use, or what time of day it is. When citizens discover they can rely on that consistency, trust follows.

The second is access. Multilingual chatbots, real-time translation, and voice-enabled alerts make it possible for applicants to receive services in their preferred language, at any hour, regardless of literacy level. For populations historically shut out by language barriers, this is not a convenience—it is the difference between being served and being ignored. UNHCR's WhatsApp-based bots for refugee populations have already demonstrated how AI can deliver clarity to those most in need (UNHCR 2022).

The third is resilience. AI does not tire, panic, or lose track under pressure. When passport demand surges or a crisis unfolds overnight, automated scheduling, triage, and alerting systems absorb the flood of routine tasks so that consular staff can focus on the cases that require human judgment. Operations that would otherwise be overwhelmed keep functioning—imperfectly, perhaps, but continuously.

The fourth is reclaimed time—and this may matter most of all. Consular staff consistently describe the frustration of being buried in repetitive work that leaves no room for the interactions that drew them to consular service in the first place. When AI handles inbox sorting, appointment reminders, or first-draft summarization, it gives consular teams back the hours they need to probe credibility in a complex interview, reassure a family in crisis, or coordinate with a host government. Those are the moments where diplomacy actually happens.

Together, these four benefits—consistency, access, resilience, and reclaimed time—reach beyond efficiency. They restore legitimacy and humanity to public service. Well-governed innovation is measured not by cases processed but by trust earned, access widened, and dignity protected.

THE RISKS—AND HOW TO DERISK THEM

Every promise of AI in consular affairs comes with a parallel risk. Efficiency can shade into exclusion if systems overlook vulnerable groups. Accuracy can be undermined by drift or adversarial manipulation. Even transparency can backfire if outputs appear authoritative but lack accountability. For consular staff, acknowledging these risks is not pessimism—it is professionalism. The measure of success is not whether mistakes occur, but whether they are anticipated, mitigated, and corrected quickly.

One risk is over-reliance and skill atrophy. If consular teams defer too often to AI, their ability to exercise judgment may weaken over time. A chatbot that drafts every reply or a biometric system that produces high-confidence matches can encourage complacency. The mitigation is deliberate: rotate tasks, require periodic manual reviews, and cultivate habits of dissent. Consular staff should be expected to document when they disagree with system outputs, ensuring that human judgment is sharpened, not dulled.

Another risk is false transparency. AI can produce outputs that appear precise—scores, reason codes, or summaries—while masking underlying uncertainties. A visa application flagged as "85% likely fraudulent" conveys an illusion of certainty if adjudicators do not understand how the score was generated. The safeguard is explainability. Systems must provide interpretable reasons, not just numbers, and officers must be trained to read them critically.

Erosion of discretion presents a subtler risk. If AI systems are integrated without clear boundaries, they may begin to shape outcomes in ways that leave little room for officer flexibility. Overbooking algorithms that maximize throughput, for instance, may pressure officers to rush interviews rather than take the time needed for careful adjudication. Guardrails such as explicit override authority and escalation protocols preserve discretion where it matters most.

Privacy is a constant concern. Data creep—where systems collect more information than necessary or retain it for longer than needed—undermines public trust. Oversight bodies like the Privacy and Civil Liberties Oversight Board have repeatedly stressed the importance of minimization and auto-deletion (PCLOB 2025). Consular operations must embed these practices in every pilot, ensuring that AI does not become a backdoor for surveillance.

Finally, algorithmic drift and vendor lock-in are operational risks. Models degrade over time unless retrained, and fraudsters adapt quickly to new detection tools. Without scheduled revalidation, systems that once seemed accurate may quietly fail. Similarly, if consular operations and consular leaders cannot transfer knowledge bases or content libraries between vendors, they risk being trapped in costly or insecure contracts. Mitigations include regular red-teaming, retraining schedules, and portability clauses written into procurement agreements.

Derisking AI does not mean eliminating uncertainty—it means embedding resilience. With human oversight, explainability, fairness audits, and privacy protections, missions can ensure that risks are caught early and corrected quickly. In consular work, where the stakes are identity, mobility, and trust, this resilience is the difference between AI as an asset and AI as a liability.

Digital Frontlines: The ETA Revolution—How Britain Normalized Algorithmic Travel Screening

Britain's Electronic Travel Authorization (ETA) system represents algorithmic governance at unprecedented scale. By spring 2025, the £16 system was processing millions of applications from visa-exempt nationals including Americans, Canadians, Australians, and—as of April 2025—European visitors, with most approvals arriving usually within a day despite official guidance to apply up to three working days in advance (GOV.UK 2025; Home Office 2025).

The system uses machine learning to analyze passenger data against watchlists, travel patterns, and risk indicators while creating operational infrastructure that enables real-time decision-making integrated with airline systems worldwide. Behind each instant approval lies sophisticated automated screening—algorithms trained to flag potential security risks while processing routine applications with minimal human intervention.

The compliance architecture reveals how thoroughly algorithmic systems have penetrated travel infrastructure. Airlines must verify ETA status at check-in under the Authority to Carry regime, with carriers facing penalties up to £50,000 if they transport passengers without proper digital authorization (U.K. Government 2025b). The Home Office has trained thousands of airline staff across Europe to check documents and immigration status, effectively making commercial agents the front-line enforcers of a state-controlled risk assessment system.

ETA refusals carry no right of appeal or administrative review, leaving applicants with limited options: reapply if circumstances change, or pursue a full visa application requiring biometrics and enhanced scrutiny (Home Office 2025; U.K. Government 2025b). The automated nature of most decisions triggers U.K. data protection rights allowing individuals to request human intervention, but Home Office guidance makes clear that caseworkers issue decisions based on available information without amending applications in progress.

Processing times measured in hours rather than days and integration with airline systems has largely eliminated check-in complications. Yet these efficiency gains come with transparency tradeoffs. The risk calculus operates in a black box that travelers cannot meaningfully contest. An ETA grants permission to travel but doesn't guarantee entry—a small percentage of approved travelers still face questioning at the border if their itinerary or history triggers additional screening.

ETA's normalization of pre-travel algorithmic screening has established a precedent that other regions are following. When the EU's ETIAS system launches in late 2026, both sides of the English Channel will require algorithmic permission for visa-exempt travel, potentially creating a new global standard where AI-mediated risk assessment becomes the default for international mobility.

The system's opacity raises questions about democratic accountability. Citizens can't see what data influences automated decisions, can't understand why similar applications receive different outcomes, and can't meaningfully appeal when algorithms render unfavorable judgments. For immigration lawyers and civil liberties organizations, ETA represents a shift toward algorithmic authority that operates beyond traditional legal safeguards—a system that works well for most travelers but whose very success makes it harder to challenge when it fails individuals or communities disproportionately affected by automated decision-making.

HUMAN SKILLS THAT BECOME MORE VALUABLE

As AI assumes more of the repetitive burden in consular affairs, the skills that remain in human hands become all the more critical. Rather than diminishing the officer and staff roles, AI heightens the value of distinctly human capacities—the abilities that cannot be automated because they rest on empathy, discretion, and judgment under uncertainty.

Foremost among these is credibility assessment. No matter how advanced natural language models become, they cannot (at least for now) replicate the human capacity to read hesitation in a voice, weigh cultural nuance in a story, or recognize when an applicant's demeanor suggests more than the words on a page. Consular interviews are as much about human interaction as about documents, and consular staff ability to gauge credibility grows more important as AI clears away background clutter.

Equally vital is empathic communication. When citizens abroad face arrests, accidents, or the sudden death of a loved one, they need consular team members who can listen, reassure, and guide them through bureaucratic steps with dignity. AI may send alerts or triage emails, but it cannot provide comfort. In fact, the more consular sections rely on automation for routine contact, the more meaningful those human moments of care become.

Another increasingly valuable skill is risk communication—explaining complex, uncertain situations in ways that are candid yet reassuring. A consular officer or staff member may have to tell applicants why an AI tool flagged their case for review, or explain to a citizen why crisis alerts contained errors. Doing so requires clarity, honesty, and cultural sensitivity. It is not enough to deliver information; officers must deliver it in a way that preserves trust.

Procedural fairness also becomes more visible in the AI era. Applicants must feel that their case was considered by a person, not dismissed by a machine. Consular teams who can explain how AI tools informed their work—and, more importantly, how human discretion shaped the final outcome—reinforce the legitimacy of the process. Fairness is not just about the decision itself but about the transparency and respect with which it is conveyed.

"Promptcraft" and digital literacy are emerging as new diplomatic skills. Consular team members will not need to code complex models, but they will need to know how to guide AI tools effectively: how to write prompts that yield accurate waiver summaries, how to test translations for tone, how to adjust thresholds to fit local context. Just as earlier generations of officers learned to navigate cable writing or data reporting, the next generation will be expected to wield AI fluently as part of their professional craft.

In this way, AI does not replace the human elements of consular affairs; it elevates them. By clearing away the noise, it throws into sharper relief the skills that define diplomacy at the consular window and in the field: judgment, empathy, clarity, and fairness. Far from being devalued, these human capacities will become the true measure of excellence in the AI era.

ROLES, TEAMS, AND CAREER PATHS IN THE AI ERA

The rise of AI in consular affairs will not eliminate jobs, but it will reshape them. As routine tasks are increasingly automated, the roles across consular teams play and the skills they cultivate will evolve. Far from narrowing careers, AI can broaden them—opening opportunities for consular professionals to lead in governance, innovation, and cross-disciplinary collaboration.

At the entry level, every officer and consular staff member will need to become an AI-aware practitioner. This does not mean coding or building models, but it does mean fluency in what AI can and cannot do. Consular staff will be expected to understand how chatbots generate answers, how biometric systems calculate confidence scores, and how predictive models forecast no-shows. This baseline literacy ensures that officers can use tools responsibly while maintaining authority over final decisions.

New specialized roles are also emerging. Consular operations will need data and knowledge stewards, staff who maintain content libraries, manage labeling processes, and ensure that knowledge bases are updated when policies change. These roles may often be filled by locally employed staff with institutional memory, making them central to sustaining continuity across officer rotations.

For locally employed staff, this represents not a threat but an evolution: AI creates roles that formalize and elevate the institutional knowledge they have always provided informally, anchoring their contribution in the diplomatic mission's operational architecture rather than leaving it unrecognized.

At the mid-career level, officers may step into operations leadership roles where AI oversight becomes part of their managerial portfolio. A consular chief might oversee not only visa lines and citizen services but also dashboards tracking the performance of fraud detection tools, inbox triage systems, or biometric verification platforms. These roles require balancing efficiency with ethics, ensuring that fairness audits, privacy reviews, and officer feedback loops are embedded in daily operations.

For senior officers and headquarters-based staff, AI opens paths into policy and governance leadership. Bureau directors and deputy assistant secretaries will be asked to shape enterprise-wide standards for transparency, procurement, and oversight. Their career paths may include leading task forces on responsible AI, representing the department in international negotiations on digital identity, or coordinating with civil society on rights-based safeguards. These roles extend consular leadership beyond service delivery to the very architecture of how diplomacy adapts to emerging technologies.

Even outside consular affairs, AI literacy will increasingly complement the skills expected of senior leaders. As AI reshapes economic diplomacy, public diplomacy, and security cooperation, consular officers with proven experience in deploying AI responsibly will bring valuable perspective to senior management roles. Their ability to connect technology to human outcomes will be an asset across the interagency and on the global stage—alongside the regional expertise, judgment, and leadership experience that have always defined the foreign service's best.

Career paths in the AI era, then, are not diminished but enriched. By taking visible ownership of AI-enabled workflows, consular staff can redefine themselves not only as adjudicators and service providers but also as stewards of trust in an age where technology and diplomacy converge.

WHAT TO MEASURE WHEN YOU SAY "HUMAN-CENTERED"

Declaring that AI in consular affairs should be "human-centered" is easy. Proving it requires measurement. Without metrics, the term risks becoming a slogan rather than a standard. For consular officers, consular teams, and leaders, the question is not only whether AI works but whether it works in ways that preserve fairness, restore time, and reinforce trust.

Time-back—the hours returned to staff when AI deflects inquiries, drafts responses, or optimizes appointment calendars—is the most intuitive measure. Consular operations should not only count time saved but also track how it is reinvested: longer interviews, more citizen services cases handled, staff training and development, or deeper fraud investigations. When hours regained translate into more human presence, the metric becomes a measure of dignity as much as efficiency.

Quality is the necessary companion to speed. Error rates, appeal reversals, and rework percentages show whether AI tools improve accuracy or create hidden costs. A system that speeds up processing but doubles the number of cases requiring supervisory correction is not human-centered; it is shifting burdens rather than reducing them.

Access ensures that efficiency gains are shared equitably. AI should expand services to those historically disadvantaged by language, literacy, or connectivity barriers. Metrics here include inquiries answered in preferred languages, alerts delivered through multiple channels, and accessibility features used by applicants with disabilities. Equity dashboards—showing demographic breakdowns of false matches, flagged cases, or processing times—help ensure that efficiency gains are distributed fairly.

Resilience rounds out the operational picture. Human-centered AI should help missions perform under pressure, not collapse during surges. Metrics include surge response times, alert delivery rates during crises, and the proportion of backlog reduced after high-demand periods. Resilience is measured not only by speed but by continuity of fairness when systems are stressed.

The final measure—well-being and trust—turns the lens inward. Staff surveys can capture whether officers and staff feel less burned out and more supported. Applicant satisfaction scores, complaint resolution times, and transparency about redress outcomes demonstrate whether publics see the system as fair. Oversight bodies like the Privacy and Civil Liberties Oversight Board have emphasized that publishing such indicators, even when imperfect, strengthens legitimacy (PCLOB 2025).

When measured this way, "human-centered" stops being aspirational and becomes auditable. Time-back, quality, access, resilience, and well-being form a scorecard a section chief can review: what changed, who benefited, who was burdened, and whether staff time was actually returned.

REUSABLE PATTERNS

Across the pilots and case studies described in this book, certain patterns repeat themselves. They are simple workflows that have proven effective in different contexts, regardless of the specific tool or vendor. By recognizing these patterns, consular teams can replicate success without reinventing the wheel, adapting them to local needs while keeping human oversight intact.

One is the triage-then-decide pattern. AI is used to cluster or prioritize cases—grouping visa renewals, highlighting anomalies in financial documents, or flagging potential duplicate identities. The system presents options, but human adjudicators decide which cases to pursue further. This pattern ensures that scale and speed serve human discretion, not replace it.

Another is the draft-then-edit pattern. AI prepares a first draft of a waiver summary, refusal explanation, or crisis alert. Consular staff then edit for accuracy, tone, and cultural appropriateness. This saves time without ceding authority. Early experiments with large language models in drafting showed that even imperfect drafts cut officer workload dramatically while still leaving space for professional judgment (Doubleday 2024b).

A third is the detect-then-investigate pattern. AI surfaces signals—suspiciously similar sponsorship letters, anomalous ledger entries, or biometric mismatches. Officers then investigate, interviewing applicants, consulting colleagues, or escalating to fraud prevention units. This pattern reframes AI not as an adjudicator but as a sensor, extending the consular team's reach into patterns too diffuse for the human eye.

Finally, there is the alert-then-assure pattern, common in crisis management. AI systems generate rapid multilingual alerts, while officers focus on confirming receipt, managing exceptions, and providing reassurance. In the Republic of Z flood vignette, this division of labor allowed AI to handle thousands of alerts while officers concentrated on those who did not respond. The machine provided speed; the human provided care.

These patterns—triage-then-decide, draft-then-edit, detect-then-investigate, and alert-then-assure—are reusable across domains. They create a common language for missions experimenting with different pilots, making it easier to share lessons across posts. Most importantly, they anchor AI firmly as a partner: fast, tireless, and scalable, but always serving human judgment, empathy, and accountability.

CULTURE CHANGE: MAKING AI "BORING"

Perhaps the greatest challenge of AI in consular affairs is not technical but cultural. New technologies often arrive with hype, anxiety, or skepticism. Consular staff members may worry about fairness, applicants fear automation, and managers struggle to separate real value from vendor promises. For AI to succeed, it must move past novelty and become what one senior officer once called "boringly reliable"—a tool so well integrated into consular practice that it feels no more exotic than the appointment system or the duty phone.

This culture shift begins with narrative framing. When leaders present AI as a way to replace staff, resistance grows. When they show exactly which task changes, which review remains, and how staff can override the tool, acceptance follows. The strongest message is not that AI replaces people, but that it removes avoidable drudgery while preserving the expertise, relationships, and judgment that make consular work possible.

Quick wins accelerate this shift. Consular operations that start by automating universally disliked tasks—drafting routine emails, chasing down missing photos, or reconciling fee records—demonstrate immediate value. Consular staff who see their workload lighten are more inclined to trust the next round of pilots. Change management literature emphasizes that visible, early successes build momentum far more effectively than abstract strategies (Kotter n.d.).

Transparency about limitations also builds credibility. Consular staff are more likely to respect leaders who acknowledge when a pilot fails or when an AI tool cannot deliver. By admitting weaknesses, consular operations avoid the trap of false promises that erode trust. Pilots should be evaluated openly, with lessons—positive and negative—shared across posts.

Institutionalizing learning makes AI part of the culture. Regular "AI office hours" where staff can raise questions, dissent logs where officers record disagreements with system outputs, and shared repositories of prompts or templates all contribute to normalization. Over time, AI becomes less of an experiment and more of a routine colleague—quietly present, occasionally fallible, but consistently helpful.

Culture change takes time, but the end goal is not excitement—it is reliability. When AI becomes boring, it becomes trusted. And when it is trusted, it can deliver on its promise: freeing officers from drudgery so they can exercise judgment, empathy, and discretion in the moments that matter most.

30–60–90 DAY LEADERSHIP PLAYBOOK

For consular leaders, the question is not just whether to adopt AI but how to introduce it in ways that build confidence and legitimacy. A structured 30–60–90 day playbook provides a suggested roadmap for turning interest into action, ensuring that early steps are measured, transparent, and sustainable.

Days 1–30: Listen and baseline. The first month should focus on understanding the pain points of the section. Leaders can hold listening sessions with their teams, asking what tasks consume the most time and what frustrations undermine morale. At the same time, they should capture baseline metrics such as: inquiry volumes, average appointment wait times, officer overtime hours, or error rates in photo submissions. These baselines anchor future claims of efficiency in real evidence.

Days 31–60: Pilot narrow, measure hard. The second month is the time for a carefully scoped experiment. This might be a chatbot seeded with FAQs, a waiver summarizer in assist mode, or a no-show reminder system. The pilot should be narrow enough to manage but important enough to matter. Safeguards—privacy reviews, human-in-the-loop oversight, clear escalation paths—must be in place from the start. Leaders should insist on weekly reviews of metrics and transcripts, treating the pilot as a learning exercise rather than a final solution.

Days 61–90: Expand cautiously, embed governance. In the third month, leaders evaluate whether the pilot has met at least two of its three success metrics. If so, it can be expanded to additional use cases or a larger applicant pool. At this stage, fairness audits, bias dashboards, and public-facing transparency notices should be introduced. Applicants deserve to know when AI is being used and how they can reach a human officer. Leaders should also assign clear ownership for sustainment, ensuring that the tool does not vanish when its initial champion rotates.

The playbook is not meant to be rigid but illustrative. Its purpose is to show that AI adoption can be deliberate rather than chaotic, cautious rather than reckless. By moving in disciplined phases—listen, pilot, expand—leaders protect officer trust, preserve applicant fairness, and demonstrate to headquarters that missions can innovate responsibly.

In this way, the 30–60–90 day playbook transforms AI from an abstract aspiration into a concrete managerial practice. It empowers leaders to introduce technology in ways that feel safe, measured, and aligned with the mission of consular work: protecting borders while serving people with fairness and empathy.

SIDEBARS AND FIELD NOTES

Sometimes the most enduring lessons about technology are not found in formal policy documents but in the everyday practices that officers share with each other—those small hacks, warnings, and reminders that shape culture as much as systems. Capturing these as sidebars and field notes makes them available across posts, offering quick guidance in the middle of busy days.

One recurring lesson is about the words that build trust. Applicants are far more likely to accept AI-assisted processes when consular staff use language that emphasizes support rather than substitution. Saying, "This tool helps us get you an answer faster," reassures; saying, "The system decided this," undermines legitimacy. Framing matters, not just in public diplomacy but at the consular window itself.

Another field note concerns when to turn AI off. Certain cases demand full human attention, with no mediation from automation. Grief cases, asylum claims, or complex identity disputes may be best if not funneled through automated triage or chatbots. Officers and consular staff must retain the discretion to shut down automation and step in directly, signaling to applicants that their situation is being treated with the dignity it deserves.

A third sidebar highlights myths versus realities. One enduring myth is that AI replaces people; the reality is that AI replaces busywork. Another myth is that AI always introduces bias; the reality is that bias already exists in human systems, and AI can either worsen or mitigate it depending on governance. Consular teams that internalize these distinctions can better explain them to applicants, host governments, and skeptical colleagues.

Field experience shows the importance of keeping equity visible. Dashboards and reports often emphasize efficiency metrics—cases processed, hours saved—but rarely highlight who benefits and who risks exclusion. A fairness audit that shows alert delivery rates across different languages, or biometric false match rates across demographics, reminds staff that equity is not incidental but central to legitimacy.

These sidebars and field notes function like marginalia in a well-used manual. They may not be as formal as statutes or checklists, but they guide behavior in the real moments when officers must act quickly. By carrying these reminders forward, missions make sure that AI remains a tool in service of human judgment, never a substitute for it.

FIELD CHECKLIST: HUMAN-CENTERED AI IN ONE PAGE

The best safeguard for responsible AI is simplicity: a concise checklist that missions can use to evaluate whether their systems are truly serving people. This one-page framework distills the lessons of pilots, governance standards, and oversight reviews into practical steps that officers can apply anywhere in the world.

1. Declare use openly.
   State clearly where AI is used and how applicants can reach a human when needed.
2. Guarantee human review.
   No rights-affecting decision—visa, passport, or emergency—should rest solely on AI.
3. Measure "time-back."
   Record hours returned and how they're reinvested in empathy-driven work.
4. Run fairness and quality dashboards.
   Track error and bias metrics; share findings internally and with oversight bodies.
5. Enforce privacy and retention rules.
   Collect only necessary data and flag records for deletion when retention limits are reached, with an authorized officer confirming before purging.
6. Design graceful escalation.
   Ensure applicants can reach a human in two steps and staff can override at any time.
7. Keep skills sharp.
   Rotate teams through manual reviews; log and learn from disagreements with AI.
8. Build vendor exit plans.
   Retain ownership of content and datasets; include portability clauses in contracts.
9. Engage the public.
   Publish short, multilingual notices explaining where AI is used and how redress works.
10. Deliver one quick win every quarter.

Start small, prove value, and expand. Momentum builds through visible results.

This checklist does not replace policy guidance or regulatory frameworks, but it translates them into daily practice. By following these ten points, missions can ensure that their use of AI remains squarely human-centered: reliable at the routine, respectful in the exceptional, and always accountable to the people it serves.

CROSS-CHAPTER BRIDGES

The themes of this final chapter do not stand alone; they weave together the lessons of the entire book. Each consular service—visas, passports, overseas citizen services, fraud prevention, crisis management—offers a distinct vantage point, yet the underlying principles of human-centered AI remain constant.

By tracing these bridges across chapters, consular teams, local staff, and policymakers can see how small pilots fit into a larger architecture of trust and accountability.

From visa adjudication in Chapter 2, we learned that AI can triage, summarize, and flag, but only humans can weigh credibility. The principle of "triage-then-decide" echoes here in Chapter 10 as a reusable pattern, showing that across domains AI narrows the haystack while people still find the needle.

From passport operations in Chapter 3, we saw how biometric systems enforce global standards yet must be governed carefully to avoid exclusion. The same fairness concerns apply to every AI tool described here. Whether in photo compliance, facial recognition matching, or appointment scheduling, equity and transparency are not incidental but foundational.

From multilingual and accessibility pilots in Chapter 4, we saw how AI extends reach across languages, time zones, and connectivity barriers. In this chapter, that becomes part of the broader promise of access: technology can widen fairness only when paired with clarity and human escalation pathways.

From crisis management in Chapter 5, we saw how AI compresses minutes into seconds—sending alerts and triaging messages before staff even arrive at post. Here, that same capability defines resilience: AI sustains operations during surges, while legitimacy still rests on consular professionals who provide assurance, empathy, and accountability.

From fraud detection and identity integrity in Chapters 6 and 7, we explored the tension between accuracy and fairness. Bias audits, privacy protections, and redress procedures are as vital in detecting forged documents as they are in inbox triage or scheduling optimization. Chapter 10 reaffirms that these safeguards—anchored in frameworks like the EU Artificial Intelligence Act, NIST standards, and PCLOB oversight—are the guardrails that make innovation legitimate.

From operational optimization and pilot deployment in Chapters 8 and 9, we learned that success depends on disciplined steps: define the problem, measure results, start small, scale cautiously, and build governance into every stage. The idea of "time-back as legitimacy" runs through them all, culminating here as the test of whether AI truly strengthens the human side of diplomacy.

These bridges remind us that consular work is an ecosystem. The purpose remains constant; what changes is the workflow: systems narrow the queue, surface the exception, and document the handoff, while people preserve fairness, explain decisions, and remain accountable to those they serve.

IF YOU ONLY DID ONE THING THIS YEAR ...

The sheer variety of AI applications described in this book can feel overwhelming. If a consular operation could do only one thing this year, where should it start? The answer is the Time Dividend. Choose the one task that consumes the most consular team hours without requiring the most officer judgment—an FAQ chatbot, a waiver summarizer in assist mode, or a predictive no-show reminder—and automate just enough to reclaim that time.

This approach generates a quick win that staff can feel: lighter inboxes, fewer wasted appointments, concise briefs in place of 200-page documents. Visible relief builds trust for further innovation. More importantly, it demonstrates the core purpose of AI in diplomacy: not replacing staff, but protecting their time so they can do what only people can—exercise judgment, extend empathy, and safeguard fairness. Start there, and everything else builds more sustainably.

CLOSING REFLECTION

Consular officers and staff have always worked at the intersection of law, service, and humanity. They adjudicate visas that shape lives, issue passports that confirm citizenship, and guide citizens through crises abroad. Each of these responsibilities depends on trust: trust in the integrity of documents, trust in the fairness of decisions, and trust in the humanity of the officer across the counter. AI, when used wisely, can strengthen that trust. When used carelessly, it can erode it.

Throughout this book, we have seen how AI can help consular operations reclaim time, surface hidden patterns, extend access across languages, and sustain resilience in crises. These are not speculative scenarios but grounded use cases, already piloted in missions and governments worldwide. The promise of AI lies in making scarce professional attention more deliberate: handling repetitive work, surfacing exceptions, and leaving a record that shows where human judgment entered the process.

We have also seen the risks. Over-automation can strip away fairness, false transparency can mislead, and data creep can endanger privacy. Civil society critiques remind us that technologies introduced for security can slip into surveillance if guardrails are absent (Amnesty International 2024). Oversight bodies insist that speed must never come at the expense of rights (Privacy and Civil Liberties Oversight Board 2025). These warnings are not obstacles to innovation but conditions for its legitimacy.

The path forward is clear, but it must be designed into workflows rather than declared as a principle. Humans decide only when they can see the evidence, challenge the output, document disagreement, and stop the system when it no longer serves the public.

Consular affairs has always been about people—the officer across the counter, the applicant whose life turns on a decision, the citizen abroad who needs someone to answer when everything goes wrong. AI does not change that fundamental truth. It changes only the conditions under which consular teams can honor it—clearing away the repetitive, the administrative, and the routine so that judgment, empathy, and fairness have room to breathe. The future this book has tried to map is not one of gleaming technology or frictionless automation. It is one where a consular professional, somewhere in the world, closes her laptop on time because an invisible teammate handled what machines do well—and walks back into the waiting room ready to give full attention to what only people can do. That is the promise. That is the measure. And that is worth building toward.

The consular window is not the only place where this promise matters. Everywhere that humans use AI to make consequential decisions—in emergency rooms and courtrooms, in refugee processing centers and social services offices, in immigration tribunals and crisis hotlines—the same disciplines apply. Start narrow. Measure rigorously. Keep humans in the loop. Audit for fairness. Earn trust before scaling. The specific context changes; the stakes change; the languages, forms, and bureaucracies change. But the core challenge does not: how do you deploy powerful tools responsibly in places defined by urgency, volume, vulnerability, and trust? Consular affairs offers one answer—not the only answer, but a deeply human-tested one, forged in the daily reality of professionals around the world who must be simultaneously efficient and fair, fast and careful, systematic and humane. If the ideas and practices developed here travel beyond the consular window—into hospitals, courts, aid organizations, and public agencies of every kind—then this book will have done more than its title promised.

The book closes where it began: AI is not an end in itself. It is a means of amplifying the human heart of consular affairs. Done right, it will make services faster, borders more secure, and officers more effective. But its greatest achievement will be quieter: giving consular teams the time and clarity to be more present, more empathetic, and more humane. In that sense, the future of consular AI is not about technology—it is about people.

Epilogue

The Choice We Practice

This book opened with an epigraph that made three observations. We are one species on one planet, but we have spent much of our history sorting ourselves into groups and keeping others out. Yet we have also shown, in our finest moments, that the virtue of common humanity is as real as the instinct toward tribe. And now we are building AI that will carry our values forward far beyond our own lifetimes. What we encode is what will endure. The epigraph called this the choice of our generation: not whether to build AI systems, but what to teach them about who we are and who we intend to become.

You have now read an entire book about how to refine the very machinery that epigraph called into question. This tension is not accidental, and it will not resolve. It is the permanent condition of this work, long after the specific technologies in these pages have been replaced by ones we cannot yet imagine.

The work of borders is not optional. In a world of vast inequality, competing interests, and uneven rule of law, borders provide the structure that makes governance, protection, and social trust possible. The work done at every consular window, immigration counter, and border crossing in the world is not a necessary evil. It is necessary, full stop.

But if our ambition extends no further than maintaining these divisions forever, we have failed the test of our own intelligence. The purpose of borders is to provide order while humanity grows. They are a means, not an end. John Lennon and Yoko Ono's "Imagine" gave popular voice to a vision of peace beyond borders, tribal divisions, and organized violence. That vision was dismissed by many as naive. The naivety lies not in the aspiration. It lies in believing we can build the most powerful intelligence in the history of our planet and never ask it to help us reach for our highest ideals.

This is why the systems we design matter far beyond their immediate function. The tools built in any generation should not be designed merely to optimize the status quo. They should be designed to evolve. If we are thoughtful, we can build systems with the flexibility to become more inclusive over time, to gradually expand access, reduce arbitrary exclusion, and adapt as humanity matures. The instruments of tribalism were not built in a day. They will not be transcended in a day. If they are transcended at all, it will be the work of centuries. But the architecture we put in place now will either make that long evolution possible or lock us into the divisions of the present.

AI can be a partner in this journey, but only if we ask it to be. It can surface unfair outcomes and help us correct them. It can make services accessible across every language and culture. And it can free the people who serve at the front lines from repetitive work, restoring the time and presence to treat each person before them with the care that dignity requires. Throughout this book we have called that restored

DOI: 10.1201/9781003634775-16

capacity the Time Dividend. But time itself is neutral. An hour returned can reinforce division just as easily as it can practice dignity. The real dividend we are seeking is not time. It is values. A values dividend, in which every hour reclaimed, every system designed, every interaction conducted moves us closer to the kind of species we are capable of becoming. Not a species confined to sorting itself on one small planet, but one building the wisdom, unity, and moral imagination worthy of a future among the stars.

What does this look like in daily practice? Every time you override an automated recommendation because fairness requires it, you affirm that wisdom cannot be automated. Every time you treat the person before you with dignity, even when the answer must be no, you demonstrate the kind of governance that earns trust. Every time you refuse to let a machine make a consequential decision about a human life without human review, you hold the line that separates responsible governance from automated control. These choices do not require heroism. They require attentiveness. And taken together, across millions of interactions, across generations, they are evidence of what kind of species we are choosing to be.

We come full circle now. If a superior intelligence looks at humanity and finds only tribes refining the tools of exclusion, it will see no reason to serve us. But if it finds a species that maintains necessary order while working to outgrow it, that builds powerful tools and insists on governing them with conscience, it will find something else: a partner worth joining. Not a perfect species, but one reaching. And a species reaching for its better nature, with the most powerful tools ever created in its hands, is not merely fit to govern a planet. It is fit to reach beyond it.

The future is not written by algorithms. It is shaped by those who choose, in each interaction, to uphold the values that make this work worth doing: fairness, transparency, compassion, and the conviction that every person who stands before you is a member of your own species, deserving of dignity not because of what passport they carry, but because of what they are.

This book was dedicated to consular professionals everywhere, who carry the judgment that cannot be automated and the humanity that must never be surrendered. That dedication is also a charge. The judgment is yours. The humanity is yours. What you build with these tools is the message you leave for every generation that follows, and for every intelligence yet to come.

Let that message say we pointed our most powerful tools not toward perfecting our divisions, but toward outgrowing them.

Practice accordingly.

Appendix 1: 100 AI Use Cases for Consular Affairs

This appendix presents one hundred illustrative examples of how AI can support consular operations. Each entry describes a specific capability and provides a brief example to make it concrete. The use cases are grouped into ten conceptual clusters, organized not by chapter but by what the AI is actually doing and why a practitioner would reach for it. The potential AI use cases described in the chapters of this book are truly unlimited, but we distill one hundred cases here for easy reference and discussion.

A few orienting points for all readers. First, AI in consular affairs is always a support tool: officers retain full authority over every decision. Second, every use case here reflects a human-in-the-loop philosophy—AI surfaces information, drafts content, or flags anomalies, but humans act. Third, every entry is an expression of the Time Dividend—the idea, developed throughout this book, that AI's true value lies in the hours it returns to staff for judgment, empathy, and discretion. Fourth, cross-reference notes in each cluster point to the chapters where these topics are treated in depth. Finally, these are illustrative examples, not operational directives; any deployment must be subject to appropriate legal, privacy, and ethical review.

A disclaimer appears at the end of this appendix.

IDENTITY VERIFICATION AND BIOMETRICS

Note: These use cases address the foundational consular question: confirming who someone is. AI in this cluster supports staff in verifying biometric continuity, detecting manipulated images, and flagging identity anomalies—always subject to human review and determination. See Chapters 3 and 7 for full treatment.

1 **AI-enabled passport photo compliance checks**
Automatically screens submitted photos against International Civil Aviation Organization (ICAO) standards before they enter the processing workflow.

Example: Applicants receive instant prompts to adjust lighting or background before visiting the consulate, reducing repeat visits and counter rejections.

2. **Liveness and antispoof detection for passport photos**
Identifies whether a submitted image was captured from a live person rather than a printed photograph, screen capture, or digitally altered file.

Example: An applicant uploading a digitally altered photo is prompted to take a brief live selfie, preventing fraudulent images from reaching adjudicators.

3. **Age progression continuity matching**
   Compares current passport photos with older records on file while accounting for natural aging, improving the reliability of renewal verification.

Example: A 20-year passport renewal is matched confidently despite significant changes in the applicant's appearance, preventing unnecessary secondary review.

4. **AI-enhanced fingerprint matching for identity continuity**
   Improves matching quality when fingerprints have degraded due to age or manual labor, reducing the rate of inconclusive results.

Example: A manual worker with worn fingerprints is still reliably matched through AI-assisted comparison, avoiding unnecessary delays and preserving the applicant's dignity.

5. **Multimodal biometric fusion (face and fingerprint)**
   Combines multiple biometric identifiers to improve the overall accuracy of identity verification.

Example: A low-confidence facial match is confirmed by fingerprint comparison, allowing officers to clear a renewal that would otherwise have required lengthy secondary review.

6. **AI-based morph detection in facial images**
   Identifies artificially blended or manipulated passport images designed to allow two individuals to use the same document.

Example: A passport renewal photo that subtly combines features of two faces is flagged for officer review, helping prevent fraudulent identity creation.

7. **AI quality checks for biometric capture**
   Alerts consular staff when camera conditions, lighting, or fingerprint scanner quality are insufficient for reliable biometric enrollment.

Example: The system warns that a photo captured under poor lighting is unlikely to support reliable future matching, prompting a retake before the applicant leaves the window.

8. **Cross-database duplicate identity checks**
   Compares an applicant's identity information across authorized national, regional, or international databases to surface potential duplicates.

Example: An applicant who appears under two slightly different names in separate authorized systems is flagged, prompting officers to clarify identity before proceeding.

9. **AI-assisted impostor recognition at intake**
   Flags cases in which the person presenting at the consular window does not appear to match the registered identity on the application.

Example: During passport pickup, a staff member receives an alert that the presenting individual does not match the applicant's photograph, preventing potential identity fraud.

10. **AI detection of inconsistencies between biographic and biometric records**
    Highlights mismatches between an applicant's stated personal history and their biometric records on file.

Example: An applicant claims to be applying for a passport for the first time, yet the biometric system shows a prior identity record, prompting officers to investigate before proceeding.

11. **Cross-border identity reconciliation support**
    Helps verify identity continuity for applicants who have lived or traveled in multiple jurisdictions by comparing records across authorized identity repositories.

Example: A visa applicant with residency history in three countries is cross-matched against authorized records, helping officers confirm a consistent identity record.

12. **AI-based name transliteration consistency checks**
    Verifies that name transliterations are consistent across passports, visas, and civil documents to prevent future misidentification.

Example: A transliteration mismatch between a passport and a civil registry extract is flagged, prompting officers to confirm identity before issuance.

DOCUMENT AUTHENTICITY AND FRAUD DETECTION

Note: These use cases help officers detect deception in submitted materials—from forged documents and fabricated financials to coached narratives and broker networks. AI surfaces patterns that exceed human capacity to spot in high-volume environments; officers investigate and decide. See Chapters 6 and 7 for full treatment.

13. **AI-assisted fraud clustering for sponsorship letters**
    Identifies repeated or template-based sponsorship documents submitted across multiple unrelated applications.

Example: Officers notice that a week's worth of student applicants share nearly identical invitation letters, prompting a fraud inquiry that stops a document mill early.

14. AI detection of forged financial statements
Flags suspicious patterns in submitted bank records, such as round-number deposits, improbable balances, or repeated ledger formats across multiple applicants.

Example: Bank records from a group of applicants in different locations show the same transaction pattern, helping officers escalate the cases to fraud review.

15. Metadata anomaly detection in document uploads
Examines the embedded data in PDF and image files to identify suspicious edits, batch fabrication, or inconsistencies between document content and file history.

Example: Uploaded files from several applicants share identical creation timestamps, alerting staff to potential third-party document fabrication.

16. AI-assisted coached narrative detection
Identifies patterned language in interview responses or written statements suggesting that applicants may have received scripted answers.

Example: Officers notice that several unrelated tourism applicants use the same unusual phrasing to describe their travel plans, helping them focus their interviews accordingly.

17. AI scoring for document authenticity probability
Assesses the likelihood that a submitted document follows expected structural norms for its type and country of origin.

Example: A birth certificate appears visually unremarkable but is flagged for an unusual seal placement, prompting officers to seek verification from local civil registry authorities.

18. AI-assisted breeder document verification
Analyzes birth certificates, marriage certificates, and other civil documents for authenticity indicators such as font consistency, seal placement, and formatting norms.

Example: A birth certificate with unusual font spacing is flagged for officer review, helping staff decide whether to seek verification from local civil registry authorities.

19. AI detection of repeated guarantor or reference details
Surfaces cases in which unrelated applicants share the same guarantor names, phone numbers, or reference contacts—a common indicator of broker networks.

Example: Ten nominally unrelated visa applicants all list the same guarantor phone number, prompting officers to investigate a potential intermediary operation.

20 AI-assisted fraud tip categorization

Organizes public fraud tips received by email or through online reporting channels into structured categories for investigator review.

Example: Instead of sifting through vague messages, fraud prevention unit (FPU) investigators receive grouped tips organized by type—employment fraud, identity fraud, document mills—enabling faster prioritization.

21. AI early-warning dashboard for fraud surges

Alerts staff when unusual fraud patterns appear suddenly across a volume of cases, allowing early intervention before the problem widens.

Example: A spike in counterfeit marriage certificates triggers a regional fraud alert, enabling officers to act before additional fraudulent cases are processed.

22. AI-assisted review of civil registry discrepancies

Compares consular records with host country civil registries, where authorized, to identify formatting or sequence inconsistencies that may indicate document problems.

Example: A marriage certificate submitted in support of a visa application is flagged because its registry number sequence deviates from local norms, prompting officers to seek verification.

CASE TRIAGE AND FILE MANAGEMENT

Note: These use cases help officers focus on what matters most. AI in this cluster sorts, summarizes, assembles, and prioritizes—compressing the preparation work that consumes officer time before a single interview or adjudication takes place. This is where the Time Dividend is most directly realized. See Chapters 2, 3, and 8.

23. AI triage for visa renewals

Sorts returning applicants into routine, complex, or elevated review lanes based on application history and compliance records.

Example: Officers begin the day with a structured list that distinguishes low-risk renewals from cases requiring closer attention, allowing them to allocate their time more effectively.

24. AI-assisted long-file summarization

Condenses large visa submissions—such as business plans, financial records, or waiver packets—into concise summaries that highlight key facts and potential gaps.

Example: A 200-page investment visa file is distilled into a one-page brief that surfaces key issues and required evidence, saving officers several hours per case.

25. AI support for identifying incomplete applications
Flags missing attachments, inconsistent form answers, or contradictory statements before an applicant's interview date.

Example: Before an interview, an officer sees that AI detected a missing employment letter, giving staff time to request it in advance rather than turning the applicant away at the window.

26. Passport application completeness checks
Automatically identifies missing or inconsistent fields before a passport application is accepted for intake.

Example: Applicants are alerted to missing parental consent forms or expired supporting documents, reducing resubmissions at the counter.

27. Passport identity consistency scoring
Flags discrepancies between biographic data on a new passport application and information already on file from prior issuances.

Example: An officer is alerted when a subtle discrepancy in birthdate formatting differs from previous records, prompting a straightforward clarification before adjudication.

28. Risk indicator surfacing for visa cases
Highlights patterns in an application that may warrant officer attention—without rendering a recommendation or decision of any kind.

Example: An officer sees a case note prompting them to clarify employment history gaps, helping focus the interview without prejudging the outcome.

29. AI-supported prioritization of identity anomalies
Ranks flagged identity issues for officer review based on potential seriousness, helping staff focus on high-priority cases first.

Example: A daily dashboard surfaces three cases with possible duplicate fingerprints as urgent, while minor name spelling variations are grouped separately for routine review.

30. AI-assisted case-file packet assembly
Automatically organizes supporting documents into a standard format for officer review, reducing manual sorting before adjudication.

Example: Officers receive neatly organized digital case packets rather than unsorted document uploads, improving consistency and reducing preparation time.

31. Duplicate passport identity detection
Searches national databases for potential duplicate identities or records linked to the same individual.

Example: An applicant who previously attempted to obtain a passport under a slight name variation is flagged automatically, allowing officers to resolve the identity question early in the process.

32. **Passport fraud pattern detection**
    Identifies repeated anomalies across multiple recent passport applications that may indicate coordinated fraud.

Example: Several applications from different districts arrive with nearly identical supporting affidavits, prompting a targeted fraud review across the cluster of cases.

33. **AI-supported fraud incident reporting**
    Assembles fraud indicators, case histories, and supporting evidence into a structured report format ready for headquarters review.

Example: After uncovering a document mill, staff produce a polished investigative report in minutes rather than hours, preserving time for follow-up action.

APPLICANT COMMUNICATION AND MULTILINGUAL ACCESS

Note: These use cases extend the mission's reach to applicants—across languages, literacy levels, and time zones. AI in this cluster handles the informational volume that would otherwise consume staff hours, ensuring consistent, accessible, and accurate guidance at scale. See Chapter 4.

34. **Multilingual consular chatbot for routine inquiries**
    Provides accurate, round-the-clock answers to common applicant questions in multiple languages, reducing demand on consular staff for routine guidance.

Example: Applicants who previously emailed questions such as "How do I book an appointment?" now receive instant, consistent answers without staff involvement.

35. **AI-assisted policy explanation in plain language**
    Translates complex visa eligibility rules, fee schedules, or document requirements into clear, jargon-free explanations accessible to general audiences.

Example: Confusing visa eligibility criteria are converted into simple, plain-language explanations that applicants can understand without misinterpretation.

36. **AI-supported document preparation guidance**
    Validates that uploaded documents meet required formats and notifies applicants of deficiencies before their appointment.

Example: The system alerts an applicant that their academic certificate requires translation or notarization, reducing last-minute refusals at the window.

37. AI-enabled voice guidance for low-literacy applicants
Provides phone-based spoken guidance for applicants who have difficulty reading or navigating online content.

Example: Applicants with limited literacy receive verbal instructions about required documents, reducing mistakes at the window and improving equity of access.

38. AI translation assistance for public announcements
Drafts and translates consular notices, fee changes, and procedural updates into local and minority languages for broad accessibility.

Example: When appointment procedures are updated, translated announcements are available immediately across multiple languages, ensuring applicants receive timely and accurate information.

39. AI-supported social media inquiry response
Identifies consular questions posted on social media platforms and responds with links to verified official guidance.

Example: When community members ask about passport procedures on local platforms, the system responds automatically with the correct official consular webpage, reducing misinformation.

40. AI-supported responses to public inquiries during visa application
Provides multilingual, accurate answers to common applicant questions through automated online channels, reducing inbox volume for consular staff.

Example: Applicants who previously sent staff emails asking how to upload a document now receive instant automated guidance, freeing officers for higher-complexity work.

41. AI-supported website content consistency checks
Detects outdated, contradictory, or mismatched information across consular web pages and flags it for staff review.

Example: The system alerts staff when one page reflects an updated fee schedule while another still shows the old amount, preventing applicant confusion.

42. AI translation support for in-person citizen services cases
Provides real-time interpretation assistance when a citizen presents at the consular window in a language not spoken by available staff.

Example: A distressed visitor reporting a theft in a minority language receives immediate assistance, reducing misunderstanding and improving service quality.

APPOINTMENT AND SCHEDULING SYSTEMS

Note: These use cases address one of the most visible pain points in consular operations: making every appointment slot count. AI in this cluster predicts no-shows, fills cancellations, deters abuse, and matches case complexity to available capacity. See Chapter 8.

43. **AI prediction of appointment no-shows**
    Forecasts which scheduled applicants are unlikely to attend based on historical patterns, allowing staff to plan the day accordingly.

Example: Morning dashboards alert managers to predicted attendance gaps, enabling on-the-fly adjustments so interview windows are not wasted.

44. **AI-powered dynamic appointment management**
    Adjusts daily scheduling—including modest overbooking and waitlist backfill—based on predicted attendance patterns to maximize available officer capacity.

Example: The system adds a small number of standby applicants to compensate for predicted no-shows, filling interview windows without overwhelming staff.

45. **Smart waitlist auto-fill**
    Automatically offers newly opened appointment slots to qualified applicants on the waitlist when cancellations occur.

Example: When two afternoon applicants cancel, waitlisted individuals receive immediate notifications and fill the slots within minutes, maintaining a full and productive schedule.

46. **AI-driven appointment reminder messages**
    Sends personalized pre-appointment reminders that specify required documents and arrival times, reducing preparation failures.

Example: No-show and rejection rates decline after applicants receive reminders specifying exactly what to bring and when to arrive.

47. **Automated appointment reminders for visa interviews**
    Sends targeted reminders to applicants before their scheduled interviews, including guidance on required documents.

Example: No-show rates decline after applicants receive reminders specifying which financial records they need to bring and when to arrive.

48. **Real-time appointment rescheduling assistance**
    Automatically offers newly opened appointment slots to qualified applicants on waiting lists when cancellations occur.

Example: A family waiting several weeks for a visa appointment is notified immediately when a next-day slot becomes available, improving both fairness and applicant satisfaction.

49. **AI detection of appointment system abuse**
    Identifies patterns of mass booking or resale by intermediaries who exploit the appointment system at the expense of genuine applicants.

Example: Dozens of appointments booked from identical IP addresses trigger a safeguard review, protecting fair access to appointment slots for all applicants.

50. **AI detection of incomplete applications at scheduling**
    Identifies missing documents before an applicant selects an appointment slot, prompting them to complete their file first.

Example: Applicants attempting to book an interview without required uploads are redirected to complete their submissions, reducing same-day refusals at the window.

51. **AI-based time-of-day scheduling optimization**
    Recommends optimal interview times for different case types based on observed processing throughput and officer performance patterns.

Example: Complex family reunification cases are shifted to quieter periods of the day, improving interview quality and reducing downstream backlogs.

52. **Visa appointment distribution optimization**
    Balances daily appointment loads across available officer capacity to prevent surges and idle windows.

Example: Rather than alternating between overloaded days and empty ones, appointments are distributed evenly, reducing staff burnout and increasing overall throughput.

CRISIS MANAGEMENT AND EMERGENCY RESPONSE

Note: These use cases address the conditions under which consular work becomes most consequential—and most difficult. AI in this cluster compresses the time between a crisis event and a coordinated response, helping officers reach the right people with the right information before conditions worsen. Human judgment and human contact remain essential throughout. See Chapter 5.

53. **AI-generated multilingual crisis alerts**
    Drafts and translates emergency messages into the key languages spoken by citizens in an affected area, ready for officer review before distribution.

Example: When a cyclone strikes overnight, the duty officer finds pregenerated evacuation guidance already available in five languages, requiring only a quick review before sending.

54. **AI-assisted citizen geolocation clustering**
    Groups registered citizens in an affected area based on last known locations or reported check-ins, helping officers identify who may need urgent contact.

Example: During a flood affecting multiple districts, the system clusters citizens by proximity to rising water levels, allowing officers to prioritize outreach to those in highest-risk areas.

55. **AI-supported risk-of-harm scoring during emergencies**
    Estimates which citizens may be at elevated risk during an active crisis based on location data, vulnerability indicators, and nonresponse patterns.

Example: During civil unrest, citizens in high-risk zones who have not responded to check-in messages are flagged for priority follow-up by consular staff.

56. **AI filtering of crisis inbox surges**
    Sorts large volumes of incoming emergency messages into categories—such as safe, trapped, missing, or urgent medical need—so staff can triage immediately.

Example: Instead of scrolling through hundreds of unorganized messages, the duty officer sees a structured summary: 23 urgent cases, 48 needing follow-up, and over a hundred informational.

57. **Automated rumor and misinformation detection**
    Identifies false reports circulating online that could confuse or endanger citizens during an emergency.

Example: The system detects a viral social media post falsely claiming that the consulate is distributing emergency supplies at a location it does not control, prompting staff to issue a rapid correction.

58. **Crisis logistics optimization**
    Recommends evacuation routes, assembly points, or transport allocation based on real-time conditions and available resources.

Example: After a landslide blocks the primary road to an airport, the system suggests an alternate evacuation corridor that successfully routes most citizens to safety.

59. **AI-driven emergency call handling support**
    Transcribes incoming calls, identifies the nature of each need—medical, legal, or safety—and routes cases to the appropriate officer.

Example: Late-night calls from distressed citizens are automatically summarized and categorized, helping the duty officer respond quickly even under heavy call volume.

60. Predictive disruption modeling
Forecasts how a developing crisis may evolve—including road closures, infrastructure failures, or access restrictions—to support advance planning.

Example: Before protests escalate, the system alerts staff that key intersections are likely to become impassable within hours, informing evacuation planning before conditions worsen.

61. AI-supported missing citizen tracking
Cross-references family inquiries, citizen registries, and last known contact information to help identify individuals who remain unaccounted for.

Example: After an earthquake, the system consolidates reports from multiple families and highlights names requiring immediate outreach, reducing the time officers spend manually cross-checking records.

62. AI-generated after-action reporting
Compiles communication logs, alert timelines, and citizen outcome data into a structured draft report after a crisis concludes.

Example: Following a flood response, the system produces a draft after-action summary in minutes, allowing staff to focus on lessons learned rather than manual data collation.

CITIZEN SERVICES AND WELFARE

Note: These use cases support the mission's duty to its own nationals abroad—in routine moments and urgent ones alike. AI in this cluster extends responsiveness, improves routing, and ensures that citizens in distress reach a human officer faster. The human contact must always be available; AI creates the conditions for it. See Chapter 5 and related sections.

63. AI triage for citizen services inbox inquiries
Sorts incoming messages into categories—such as lost travel documents, arrests, deaths, medical emergencies, or routine service requests—to help staff prioritize responses.

Example: An urgent hospitalization message is surfaced immediately rather than remaining buried under routine notarial questions, allowing staff to respond faster during inbox surges.

64. AI drafting for emergency travel document instructions
Generates clear, multilingual instructions explaining the steps and documents required for emergency travel document replacement.

Example: A citizen needing urgent travel receives customized plain-language guidance within minutes, reducing confusion during a high-stress situation.

65. Biometric-supported emergency passport issuance
Accelerates identity verification during urgent or crisis situations by cross-referencing stored biometrics when an applicant has lost all travel documents.

Example: A traveler who lost all documents at an overseas airport is quickly verified through stored biometric records, allowing consular staff to issue an emergency travel document within minutes.

66. AI scheduling for urgent citizen services cases
Automatically prioritizes appointment availability for citizens facing documented medical, legal, or family emergencies.

Example: A family needing immediate travel for a medical emergency is offered the next available appointment slot without staff having to manually reorganize the calendar.

67. AI-assisted welfare-and-whereabouts checks
Sends automated check-in messages to citizens in affected areas during a crisis and flags nonresponses for follow-up.

Example: After a major storm, citizens in affected neighborhoods receive an automated welfare message; those who do not respond are moved to a high-priority outreach list for direct staff follow-up.

68. AI-enhanced routing for citizen services phone calls
Identifies keywords and caller intent to route emergency calls directly to the appropriate officer, bypassing generic phone menus.

Example: A late-night caller mentioning "police" or "hospital" is forwarded immediately to the duty officer rather than navigating an automated phone menu.

69. AI guidance for citizens seeking notarial or civil services
Provides clear pre-appointment instructions for common citizen services such as notarial acts, civil registrations, or document certifications.

Example: Citizens arrive at their appointments better prepared after receiving automated guidance explaining required documents and applicable fees, reducing delays at the window.

70. AI pattern detection for citizen safety trends
Analyzes citizen services case data over time to identify rising patterns—such as common scams, theft hotspots, or safety incidents—that may warrant a public advisory.

Example: Staff detect an uptick in street robbery reports concentrated in one district and issue a timely security alert, helping prevent further incidents.

71. **Automated reminders for document pickup**
    Notifies citizens when replacement travel documents or civil certificates are ready for collection.

Example: Fewer documents remain unclaimed because citizens receive personalized pickup reminders, allowing the section to manage document storage and workflow more efficiently.

INTERNAL WORKFLOWS AND OPERATIONAL EFFICIENCY

Note: These use cases target the administrative overhead that consumes officer and locally employed staff (LES) time without requiring their expertise. AI in this cluster automates the clerical, streamlines the repetitive, and frees staff for work that demands human judgment. See Chapter 8.

72. **Interview question generation support**
    Suggests tailored interview prompts based on an applicant's file history and patterns in similar cases—while the officer retains full discretion over what to ask and how to proceed.

Example: For a student applicant with limited financial documentation, the system suggests clarifying questions that help the officer focus the interview efficiently.

73. **AI-assisted workload balancing across officers**
    Distributes complex and routine cases across available staff to ensure equitable workloads and maintain adjudication quality.

Example: The system detects that one officer is receiving a disproportionate share of complex cases and redistributes the workload to prevent fatigue and maintain consistency.

74. **AI-assisted queue flow monitoring**
    Analyzes foot traffic and processing speed in real time to help supervisors adjust window staffing before bottlenecks develop.

Example: When biometric capture slows unexpectedly, supervisors receive an alert and can temporarily redeploy staff to prevent a queue from backing up.

75. **Internal meeting transcription and summarization**
    Produces concise, searchable summaries of section meetings, capturing action items and decisions for easy reference.

Example: Staff spend less time on note-taking and can quickly review an automatically generated summary of action items after the weekly operations meeting.

76. **AI drafting of internal standard operating procedure (SOP) updates**
    Generates first drafts of procedure revisions when regulations or host country requirements change, reducing the administrative burden on section leadership.

Example: When host country civil documentation rules are revised, the system produces an updated SOP draft that staff review and finalize, rather than starting from a blank page.

77. **Automated fee reconciliation using robotic process automation (RPA)**
    Matches payment records with case files automatically, reducing manual data entry and the errors that accompany it.

Example: Staff spend significantly less time reconciling fees, and payment errors drop as repetitive manual matching is replaced by automated verification.

78. **AI tracking of pending workload and bottlenecks**
    Identifies which queues, case types, or service lines are accumulating delays, helping supervisors intervene before backlogs compound.

Example: A dashboard reveals that notarial services are generating disproportionate delays due to incomplete submissions, prompting targeted corrective action.

79. **AI-enhanced training needs assessment**
    Analyzes processing patterns to identify where staff may benefit from refresher training or updated policy guidance.

Example: Officers who consistently escalate similar document types are identified as a group, helping the section design targeted training rather than one-size-fits-all sessions.

80. **Automatic policy change detection**
    Monitors official sources to alert staff when new host country regulations, documentation requirements, or fee changes are published.

Example: Staff receive immediate notice when the host government updates its civil document requirements, allowing consular guidance to be revised the same day.

MISSION LEADERSHIP AND STRATEGIC OVERSIGHT

Note: These use cases give section chiefs, deputy chiefs of mission, and headquarters staff the visibility to manage proactively rather than reactively. AI in this cluster aggregates, forecasts, and synthesizes—translating operational data into the strategic picture that leadership needs. See Chapter 9.

81. AI-generated consular management dashboards
Summarizes appointment volumes, processing times, service-line performance, and emerging bottlenecks in a single visual interface for section leadership.

Example: A section chief begins the week with a dashboard highlighting which service lines are under pressure, enabling smarter staffing decisions before queues develop.

82. AI-supported performance trend analysis
Identifies patterns in case processing or interview throughput that may indicate training needs, procedural drift, or emerging workload pressures.

Example: A spike in rework for a particular case type is detected early, allowing supervisors to provide coaching before delays compound across the section.

83. AI drafting for consular reporting
Generates first-pass summaries of high-level operational trends and statistics for monthly or quarterly reporting, reducing manual data compilation.

Example: Instead of assembling data by hand, staff receive a draft narrative highlighting operational trends that they can refine with contextual knowledge before submission.

84. AI-based forecasting for seasonal workload surges
Predicts upcoming spikes in visa, passport, or notarial workloads based on historical patterns and known calendar events.

Example: Knowing a surge is likely six weeks ahead, the mission arranges additional staffing support before backlogs develop.

85. AI monitoring of public sentiment around consular services
Analyzes publicly available comments and feedback for emerging patterns of frustration or confusion about consular services.

Example: Rising complaints about appointment availability are flagged for management review, prompting updated public guidance before trust in the section erodes.

86. AI-supported budget planning for consular sections
Generates workload-based resource projections that can support staffing and budget requests.

Example: A section chief uses AI-generated demand projections to build a data-supported case for an additional LES position ahead of anticipated workload growth.

87. AI-assisted duty roster and shift planning
Optimizes duty schedules based on historical inquiry volumes, known surge periods, and staff availability.

Example: Rather than relying on intuition alone, managers adjust the duty roster to align coverage with predictable evening surges in citizen inquiries.

88. AI-supported extraction of suspicious patterns across posts
Aggregates fraud indicators across multiple missions to help identify cross-border fraud schemes that no single post could see in isolation.

Example: Staff learn that three neighboring missions have each encountered similar counterfeit diplomas, enabling a coordinated regional investigation.

GOVERNANCE, ETHICS, AND ACCOUNTABILITY

Note: These use cases ensure that AI in consular affairs remains trustworthy, equitable, and accountable. They reflect the book's four governance pillars—transparency, explainability, fairness and equity, and privacy—and are as operationally necessary as any other cluster. AI that is not governed is AI that cannot be trusted. See Chapters 1 and 10.

89. AI-supported fairness audits
Examines processing outcomes for demographic disparities across visa, passport, or citizen services case types to identify and address inequities.

Example: An alert shows that processing times for applicants in one language group are trending longer than average, prompting a review of whether guidance materials or staffing patterns may be contributing.

90. AI-supported consistency monitoring
Flags where staff workflows or processing behaviors are deviating from established standard operating procedures, supporting consistent and equitable service delivery.

Example: The system detects inconsistent approaches to identity verification across the section and prompts a refresher briefing to restore alignment.

91. AI-supported transparency notices for applicants
Drafts clear, plain-language explanations of how and where AI tools assist consular processes, suitable for publication on consular websites.

Example: Updated website text informs applicants that automation supports efficiency but that consular officers make all decisions—reinforcing public trust in the process.

92. Redress case triage using AI
Groups applicant complaints and appeals by urgency and complexity, helping management prioritize responses to those with the most immediate needs.

Example: A sudden rise in complaints about appointment system access is detected and escalated to section leadership for immediate review.

93. AI-assisted logging of human–AI disagreement
Records instances in which officers override an AI suggestion, along with the officer's reasoning, creating an audit trail that supports system improvement and accountability.

Example: An officer disagrees with an AI fraud flag and notes the reason; these logs are later reviewed to refine the system's parameters and reduce false positives.

94. Graceful failure monitoring for AI tools
Detects when automated systems encounter errors or edge cases they cannot handle reliably, and routes those tasks back to human staff.

Example: When a chatbot repeatedly fails to recognize a particular type of inquiry, it automatically escalates the conversation to the consular inbox rather than generating an unhelpful or inaccurate response.

95. AI-supported privacy impact assessments
Helps consular staff draft and update privacy impact assessments (PIAs) when new tools or workflows are introduced, ensuring data use is documented and justified.

Example: When a new scheduling tool is deployed, staff receive a PIA draft outlining data flows, retention periods, and access controls—reducing administrative burden while meeting governance requirements.

96. AI-guided ethical risk scoring for pilot programs
Evaluates proposed AI pilots for fairness, privacy, and operational risk before deployment, surfacing potential concerns for leadership review.

Example: Before a new triage tool is activated, an ethical risk assessment highlights a potential data retention issue, prompting a design adjustment that avoids the problem before launch.

97. Responsible AI checklist automation
Ensures that all new AI deployments meet minimum governance standards before going live, covering human oversight, data minimization, and escalation pathways.

Example: Before activating a new inbox triage tool, staff complete a structured checklist confirming that human review is built in, data use is proportionate, and a clear escalation path exists.

98. AI generation of human-centered design recommendations
Analyzes applicant error patterns and service delivery data to suggest improvements that make consular services more accessible, equitable, and easy to use.

Example: The system recommends simplifying appointment-booking instructions after identifying a recurring pattern of applicant errors, improving both equity and throughput.

99. AI-assisted equity monitoring across service channels
Tracks whether AI-supported services are reaching all applicant groups equitably, including those with limited digital access, language barriers, or disabilities.

Example: A review of chatbot usage data shows that applicants in one language group have significantly lower engagement rates, prompting staff to assess whether guidance is adequately accessible in that language.

100. AI support for officer well-being and workload sustainability
Monitors aggregate indicators of officer workload and flags patterns—such as sustained overtime or concentrated complexity—that may indicate unsustainable conditions.

Example: The system alerts a section chief that one team has been handling a disproportionate share of high-complexity cases for several weeks, informing a staffing conversation before burnout takes hold.

DISCLAIMER

The AI use cases in this appendix are illustrative examples only. They are not legal advice, operational directives, or authorization to deploy any specific technology. Any organization considering AI in consular work must conduct its own legal, ethical, and technical reviews; comply with all applicable laws and human rights obligations; implement robust privacy and fairness safeguards; and maintain full human oversight of all consequential decisions. The authors and publisher accept no responsibility for how these examples are interpreted or applied in practice.

Appendix 2: Glossary of AI Terms for Consular Affairs

A

Adaptive AI
AI that keeps learning from new data and officer feedback, updating its behavior over time instead of staying fixed at deployment.
Example: A no-show prediction model continuously recalibrates based on season, local holidays, and agent behavior, improving appointment overbooking at a busy consulate.

Algorithm
A step-by-step set of rules a computer follows to transform inputs (like DS-160 data or passport photos) into outputs (like risk scores or quality checks).
Example: An algorithm ranks visa applications into "green/amber/red" lanes based on past overstay patterns and document anomalies, so officers know where to focus interviews.

Artificial Intelligence
Computer systems that perform tasks which normally require human intelligence—such as pattern recognition, translation, summarization, or anomaly detection.
Example: AI spots a cluster of near-identical sponsorship letters across student visa cases in Z City, triggering a fraud review that a single officer would never have seen alone.

B

Bias Mitigation
Techniques to detect and reduce unfair differences in AI performance across groups (e.g., by gender, age, skin tone, nationality).
Example: A mission runs periodic audits on its face-matching system after NIST studies show demographic performance gaps in face recognition, then adjusts thresholds and workflows to protect fairness.

Big Data
Very large, complex datasets that can't be analyzed reliably with manual methods or simple spreadsheets.
Example: A central consular data platform aggregates millions of visa, passport, biometric, and crisis registration records to detect global fraud trends and surge patterns.

Blockchain in Borders and Identity
A tamper-resistant ledger that can store hashes or credentials for travel or civil documents so later checks can confirm they haven't been altered.
Example: A pilot uses blockchain anchors for digital birth certificates submitted in passport applications; passport systems verify that the hash on the ledger matches the applicant's certificate before issuance.

C

Chatbots (Conversational Agents)
AI systems that interact with users via text or voice to answer questions or complete simple tasks.
Example: A consular chatbot answers 24/7 questions about passport renewals, machine-readable visa (MRV) fee payment, and visa wait times in multiple languages, escalating ACS emergencies to the duty officer.

Collaborative AI (Human–AI Teaming)
Systems explicitly designed to support, not replace, human decision-makers.
Example: A dashboard clusters suspicious visa cases and proposes talking points, but the consular officer decides which questions to ask and whether to issue or refuse.

Computer Vision (CV)
AI techniques that interpret images and video.
Example: A photo-checking tool uses computer vision to validate passport photos against ICAO Doc 9303 rules for head size, background, and lighting before the file ever reaches an officer.

Content Provenance (C2PA/Content Credentials)
Standards for tagging digital content with secure metadata showing when, how, and by whom it was created or edited.
Example: A passport agency tests C2PA-style credentials on applicant-submitted digital documents so AI tools can quickly see whether the scan is original or has been manipulated in editing software.

D

Data Sovereignty
The principle that data is subject to the laws and governance structures of the country where it is collected or stored.
Example: A mission must ensure that cloud-hosted AI tools processing visa biometrics keep data in approved jurisdictions and comply with local and home country privacy rules.

Deep Learning
AI models with many layers (neural networks) that learn complex patterns from large datasets.

Example: A deep learning model improves face-matching between current live captures and decades-old passport photos to support continuity of identity checks.

Digital Diplomacy (in Consular Context)
Use of digital platforms—including AI—to deliver consular services, communicate in crises, and manage public expectations.
Example: During floods in Z, AI-translated crisis posts on social media explain evacuation points and passport replacement options, while officers handle complex ACS cases.

E

Ethical AI
AI that is designed, deployed, and governed to respect human rights, fairness, and transparency.
Example: A consular section commits to never letting an AI system refuse a visa or passport without human review, and regularly audits biometric tools for demographic bias.

Enterprise AI (Consular Enterprise)
AI services deployed across an entire foreign affairs network, integrated with core systems like the CCD, appointment platforms, and ACS tools.
Example: A department-wide "consular copilot" can summarize visa waivers, search policy (FAM equivalent), and draft congressional responses for officers in posts worldwide.

EU Artificial Intelligence Act
The EU's 2024 law that regulates AI, with strict rules for "high risk" uses—including migration, asylum, and border control AI systems.
Example: A Schengen state consular post must document human oversight, data quality, and risk management for AI used in visa triage because it falls under the Act's high-risk category.

Explainable AI (XAI)
AI systems that provide human-readable reasons for their outputs instead of just scores.
Example: A fraud detection tool explains that it flagged a student visa case because the bank statement shows repeated round-number deposits and cloned formatting from other applications, helping the officer decide what to ask in interview.

F

Facial Recognition
AI that analyzes facial images to verify or identify a person.

Example: At a passport counter, facial recognition compares the live image with the chip photo from the previous passport and with watchlist entries, with officers reviewing all low-confidence or ambiguous matches.

Federated Learning/Federated Queries (Consular Sense)
A way to train or query models across multiple databases without moving all raw data into one place.
Example: A "federated" identity check queries a consular database, a border control system, and an INTERPOL index for a fingerprint hit, but each system keeps its own data under its own laws.

Forecasting with AI
Using AI to predict future volumes, risks, or needs based on historical data.
Example: A regional bureau uses AI to forecast where visa demand will spike after a new travel policy and pre-positions surge staff and appointment capacity accordingly.

G

Generative AI
AI models (like large language and image models) that create new content—text, images, or video—based on patterns in training data.
Example: Officers use a tightly governed generative model to draft first-pass refusal explanations or ACS outreach emails, always reviewing and editing before sending.

Governance in AI (Consular Governance)
Policies, oversight structures, and processes that control how AI is procured, tested, used, and audited in consular operations.
Example: A mission-level AI committee approves pilots, ensures privacy and fairness reviews, and logs every AI system that touches visa or passport data.

H

Human-in-the-Loop (HITL)
Designing AI systems so that people remain responsible for all rights-affecting decisions.
Example: An AI risk score can suggest extra scrutiny, but only an officer can refuse a visa or deny a passport—and the system forces a human click-through and note for any adverse decision.

Hybrid Intelligence
Combining human judgment with AI's speed and pattern recognition.
Example: AI clusters suspicious visa cases; a fraud prevention officer reviews the clusters against local knowledge and decides which to investigate and which to clear.

Hyper-automation
Coordinated use of AI, RPA, and workflow tools to automate many small steps in a process.
Example: A visa section links AI triage, auto-generated applicant emails, and RPA data entry so routine renewals move with minimal manual handling, while complex cases are held for officers.

I

ICAO Doc 9303 (Machine-Readable Travel Documents)
The international standard that defines how machine-readable passports, visas, and other travel documents must be formatted and secured so they work reliably worldwide.
Example: AI-based passport photo and chip validation tools are built directly against ICAO Doc 9303 so that documents produced in Z are readable and trustworthy at foreign borders.

Identity Graph
A map of all the data linked to a person's identity—visas, passports, biometrics, travel histories, and breeder documents—across systems.
Example: When a passport renewal raises questions, an identity graph view helps an officer see prior visa refusals, fingerprints, and ACS records in one place, without automatically drawing conclusions.

Inference (AI Inference)
The phase where a trained AI model is used to make predictions or classifications on new, incoming data.
Example: Once a fraud model is trained, each new sponsorship letter is run through it at "inference time" to assign a risk score for the officer's review.

Innovation Sandbox
A controlled environment for testing AI tools on realistic but carefully governed consular data.
Example: A mission runs a weekend pilot of a chatbot on deidentified email histories before connecting it to live inboxes.

Internet of Things (IoT) in Missions
Network-connected devices (cameras, sensors, kiosks) that feed data into consular or security systems.
Example: Smart cameras at a consular gate log crowd levels and feed into an AI tool that helps predict safe appointment volumes on high-risk days.

L

Large Language Models (LLMs)
AI models trained on massive text corpora that can summarize, translate, answer questions, and draft text.
Example: An LLM constrained with retrieval augmented generation drafts a summary of a complex inadmissibility waiver, with inline citations to the file and policy for the officer to check.

Legal AI (for Consular Use)
AI tools that assist with searching, summarizing, and drafting legal or policy-heavy texts.
Example: A legal-aware model searches the FAM-equivalent manual and produces a short, cited explanation of the legal basis for a 214(b) refusal to include in a front-office briefing.

Liveness Detection/Presentation Attack Detection (PAD)
Techniques used to confirm that a biometric sample (face, fingerprint, iris) comes from a real, live person and not from a mask, photo, or synthetic image. ISO/IEC 30107 defines the global PAD framework and test methods.
Example: A kiosk refuses a passport photo if the system detects that a user is presenting a printed image instead of their live face, and flags the attempt for a fraud note in the case.

Localization in AI
Adapting AI systems to local languages, legal frameworks, and cultural norms.
Example: The same appointment reminder AI uses different languages, date formats, and behavioral "nudges" in West Africa than it does in East Asia.

M

Machine Learning (ML)
A family of AI techniques where models learn patterns from historical data instead of being explicitly rule-coded.
Example: An ML model learns which combinations of booking channel, lead time, and applicant type predict appointment no-shows and suggests dynamic overbooking levels.

Machine-Readable Travel Document (MRTD)
A passport, visa, or other travel document that follows ICAO Doc 9303 so it can be read by optical or chip readers worldwide.
Example: An AI-assisted document checker validates that a MRV from Z conforms to Doc 9303 Part 7, reducing manual inspection at borders.

Model Training
The process of teaching an AI model by exposing it to labeled examples until it can generalize to new cases.
Example: A fraud model is trained on past confirmed fraud and clean cases so it can learn what "sponsorship letter templates" typical fraud rings use.

Multimodal AI/Multimodal Biometrics
AI systems that combine different data types—such as text + images, or face + fingerprints—for better accuracy.
Example: A passport renewal system fuses face and fingerprint matches so that an applicant who looks very different after 20 years can still be verified confidently.

N

Narrow AI (Weak AI)
AI designed for a specific task rather than "general intelligence."
Example: A passport photo compliance checker that does only one thing—approve or reject photos against ICAO rules—is narrow AI.

Natural Language Processing (NLP)
AI that understands and generates human language.
Example: NLP classifies incoming emails as "routine info," "urgent ACS," or "fraud tip" so officers see the most critical messages first.

Neural Machine Translation (NMT)
Modern AI translation based on neural networks, generally more fluent and accurate than older rule-based systems.
Example: NMT produces first-pass translations of ACS crisis alerts into minority languages, which LES staff then review before sending.

P

Predictive Analytics
Using statistical and ML methods to anticipate future events or volumes.
Example: A regional dashboard predicts visa demand for the next six months and suggests where to send TDY (temporary duty) officers to avoid backlogs.

Preprocessing (Data Preprocessing)
Cleaning and structuring raw data so AI can use it reliably.
Example: Before training a model, a consular section removes PII from historical emails and standardizes fields like date formats and case numbers.

Presentation Attack Detection
See *Liveness Detection* above—industry term for detecting attempts to fool biometrics with fake or altered samples, standardized in ISO/IEC 30107.

Privacy-Preserving AI
Methods that let AI extract insights from data while minimizing exposure of personal details (e.g., anonymization, federated learning, secure computation).
Example: Duplicate identity checks are run with privacy-preserving methods so partner countries can detect cross-border fraud without exchanging raw biometric images.

R

Reinforcement Learning
A way of training AI by rewarding good decisions and penalizing bad ones over many simulations.
Example: A research project simulates appointment-booking strategies, rewarding models that minimize no-shows and wait times, before any changes are tried in a live consular calendar.

Retrieval Augmented Generation (RAG)
A pattern where an LLM retrieves relevant documents from an approved knowledge base and then drafts an answer using only that material.
Example: A consular drafting assistant uses RAG to answer an officer's question about a complex 221(g) scenario by pulling only from official policy, with citations, instead of "making up" an answer.

Risk Management in AI
Identifying, assessing, and mitigating risks (bias, drift, privacy, security) associated with AI systems.
Example: A mission documents model drift checks, fairness audits, and incident response plans for its fraud detection AI, in line with the NIST AI Risk Management Framework.

Robustness in AI
An AI system's ability to keep working even when inputs are noisy, incomplete, or slightly unusual.
Example: A face matcher remains accurate when photos are taken under different lighting conditions or applicants age significantly, without suddenly spiking false rejections for certain groups.

S

Scalability in AI
The ability of AI systems to handle more data, more users, or more missions without a full redesign.

Example: A chatbot piloted at one embassy scales to 50 posts by reusing the same core model and content library, with only local FAQs and languages added.

Sentiment Analysis
AI that estimates emotional tone in text.
Example: A regional public diplomacy team uses sentiment analysis on social media posts about visa backlogs to help consular leadership understand public frustration and refine messaging.

Swarm Intelligence (in Crisis and Logistics)
Optimization techniques inspired by group behavior in nature, applied to routing and resource allocation.
Example: A crisis logistics tool uses swarm-like algorithms to adjust evacuation bus routes as roads close and fuel becomes scarce.

T

Text Mining
Using AI to extract useful patterns from large collections of text.
Example: A fraud unit text-mines thousands of case notes to find common phrases in coached student visa narratives.

Transfer Learning
Reusing an AI model trained on one task and fine-tuning it for a related consular task.
Example: A generic document forgery model is fine-tuned on local marriage certificates and birth records to improve breeder document checks in passport work.

Transparency in AI
Making AI systems, their purposes, limitations, and impacts understandable to officers, applicants, and oversight bodies.
Example: A mission publishes a short public explainer stating that AI is used to sort routine visa renewals but that officers still make all final decisions.

V

Virtual Envoy/Virtual Consular Assistant
A hypothetical or early-stage AI agent that handles routine interactions with the public, always with escalation routes to human staff.
Example: A "virtual consular assistant" handles first contact for ACS inquiries, answering FAQs and gathering key facts before passing cases to the duty officer.

Virtual Reality (VR) for Training and Outreach
Immersive digital environments used for training staff or informing the public.
Example: New officers train in a VR simulation of a high-volume visa line during a crisis to practice interviewing and crowd management under stress.

Voice Recognition
AI that converts speech into text or verifies identity from voice patterns.
Example: A call center tool transcribes emergency ACS calls in real time, tagging key details (location, names, case numbers) for the duty officer.

W

Weak AI (Narrow AI)
See *Narrow AI* above—systems built for one well-defined task.

Weighted Models
Models that assign different importance ("weights") to various inputs to produce a final score.
Example: A risk model weighs prior overstay more heavily than social media signals when suggesting which visa cases belong in the red lane.

Workflow Automation
Using AI and RPA to move data and tasks between systems without manual retyping.
Example: Once a visa is issued, an automated workflow updates the consular case system, triggers fee reconciliation, and sends a notification to the applicant.

Z

Zero-Day Threat Detection
AI-driven identification of previously unknown cyber vulnerabilities or attacks.
Example: An embassy's security operations center uses AI to flag unusual access patterns into consular systems that may indicate a new exploit targeting the CCD or biometric store.

Zero-Shot Learning
AI's ability to handle new tasks or categories it wasn't explicitly trained on, by generalizing from related knowledge.
Example: A consular chatbot that has never seen questions about a sudden new travel ban can still give a decent first answer by drawing on related policy documents and then flagging the exchange for officer review and content updates.

Zero-Trust Security
A security model where no user or device is trusted by default; every access request is verified.
Example: Even officers must pass multi-factor checks and device health checks before opening AI dashboards that contain passport or visa data.

Bibliography

Abdekhoda, Mohammadhiwa, and Afsaneh Dehnad. 2025. "Strategies to Combat Infodemics in Public Health." *Eastern Mediterranean Health Journal* 31 (5): 340–49. https://doi.org/10.26719/2025.31.5.340.

ABTA. 2025. "ABTA Offers Clarity for Travellers between the UK and Europe as New Requirement Comes In." ABTA. www.abta.com/news/abta-offers-clarity-travellers-between-uk-and-europe-new-requirement-comes.

ACI Europe. 2019. *The Entry-Exit System (EES) — A Guide for European Airports*. https://www.aci-europe.org/downloads/publications/THE%20ENTRY-EXIT%20SYSTEM%20-%20A%20GUIDE%20FOR%20EUROPEAN%20AIRPORTS.pdf.

African Union. 2014. *Convention on Cyber Security and Personal Data Protection (Malabo Convention)*. Adopted June 27, 2014. https://ccdcoe.org/uploads/2018/11/AU-270614-CSConvention.pdf.

AI Security Institute (UK). 2025. "Inspect: A Framework for LLM Evaluations." AI Security Institute. https://inspect.aisi.org.uk/.

Alder, Madison. 2024a. "Federal Government Discloses More Than 1,700 AI Use Cases." FedScoop, December 18, 2024. https://fedscoop.com/federal-government-discloses-more-than-1700-ai-use-cases/.

Alder, Madison. 2024b. "From Translation to Email Drafting, State Department Turns to AI to Assist Workforce." FedScoop, December 2024. https://fedscoop.com/state-department-ai-chatbot-email-drafting-northstar-famsearch/.

Alder, Madison. 2025. "Mobile App, Cable Queries among Planned Expansions of State Department's AI Chatbot." FedScoop, March 28, 2025. https://fedscoop.com/state-departments-ai-chatbot-mobile-app-cable-queries/.

Alms, Natalie. 2025. "Trump Administration Hopes AI Can Mitigate Staffing Losses, Federal CIO Says." Nextgov, August 18, 2025. www.nextgov.com/artificial-intelligence/2025/08/trump-administration-hopes-ai-can-mitigate-staffing-losses-federal-cio-says/407514/.

Amazon Web Services. n.d. "Image Recognition Software, ML Image & Video Analysis." Amazon Web Services, Inc. Accessed March 2, 2026. https://aws.amazon.com/rekognition/.

Amnesty International. 2024. *The Digital Border: Migration, Technology, and Inequality*. London: Amnesty International. www.amnestyusa.org/wp-content/uploads/2024/06/The-Digital-Border-Migration-Technology-and-Inequality.pdf.

Arora, Shivam. 2023. *Privacy-Preserving Financial Anomaly Detection via Federated Learning and MPC*. arXiv. https://arxiv.org/abs/2310.04546.

Association for Diplomatic Studies & Training. 2020. "9/11 Terror Attacks: A Consular Officer's Perspective on Visas and Government Intelligence." Association for Diplomatic Studies & Training, July. https://adst.org/2020/07/9-11-terror-attacks-a-consular-officers-perspective-on-visas-and-government-intelligence/.

Austin, Tasha, and Sean Davis. 2023. "Bolstering American Statecraft with Artificial Intelligence Technologies." Federal News Network, May. https://federalnewsnetwork.com/commentary/2023/05/bolstering-american-statecraft-with-artificial-intelligence-technologies/.

Australia. Department of Home Affairs. 2024. "Digital Assistant Tool." https://immi.homeaffairs.gov.au/help-support/tools/digital-assistant.

Bailey, Joanna. 2025. "Scammers Target UK Travellers amid EU Entry Confusion." Euronews, March 4. www.euronews.com/travel/2025/10/09/etias-scams-eu-travel-eta-launch-confusion.

Barker, Elaine. 2020. *Recommendation for Key Management: Part 1 – General.* NIST SP 800-57pt1r5.Gaithersburg, MD National Institute of Standards and Technology. https://doi.org/10.6028/NIST.SP.800-57pt1r5.

BCD Travel. 2024. *Will the UK's Changing ETA Rules Affect Business Travelers?.* www.bcdtravel.com/blog/will-the-uks-changing-eta-rules-affect-business-travelers/.

Beduschi, Ana, and Marie Mcauliffe. 2020. *World Migration Report 2022: Chapter 11 – Artificial Intelligence, Migration and Mobility: Implications for Policy and Practice.* May 21, 2020. https://publications.iom.int/books/world-migration-report-2022-chapter-11.

Bernard, Zoë. 2017. "'Artificial Intelligence Is Not Our Friend:' Hillary Clinton Is Worried about the Future of Technology." Business Insider. Accessed March 2, 2026. www.businessinsider.com/hillary-clinton-is-worried-about-ai-social-media-and-the-future-of-tech-2017-11.

Bioenable. n.d. "US Facial Recognition: Urgent Need for Laws and NIST Advice to Shield Civil." Accessed March 2, 2026. www.bioenabletech.com/news/us-facial-recognition-urgent-need-for-laws-and-nist-advice-to-shield-civil.

Biometric Update. 2024. *DigiYatra App Users Face Glitches, Data Privacy Concerns.* www.biometricupdate.com/202404/digi-yatra-app-users-face-glitches-data-privacy-concerns.

Bjola, Corneliu. 2019. "Diplomacy in the Age of Artificial Intelligence." Elcano Royal Institute, October 14. www.realinstitutoelcano.org/en/analyses/diplomacy-in-the-age-of-artificial-intelligence/.

Bjola, Corneliu. 2022. *Artificial Intelligence and Diplomatic Crisis Management: Addressing the "Fog of War" Problem.* Oxford Digital Diplomacy Research Group. www.qeh.ox.ac.uk/sites/default/files/2023-08/DigDiploROxWP6.pdf.

Blaser, Virginia. 2022. *The Manager's Workbook: Six Worksheets for Performance Evaluation and the Annual Cycle.* Independently Published.

Blaser, Virginia, and Don Kilburg. 2025. "How Artificial Intelligence Can Modernize Consular Services." *The Diplomatic Diary*, May 18, 2025. https://diplomaticacademy.us/2025/05/18/artificial-intelligence-consular-services/.

Blinken, Antony J. 2024. "Remarks at a UN Security Council Meeting on Artificial Intelligence." W.State.Gov. https://2021-2025.state.gov/secretary-antony-j-blinken-at-a-un-security-council-meeting-on-ai/.

Bracken, Matt. 2024. "For Customs and Border Protection, AI Has Been a 'Game-Changer.'" FedScoop, October 17, 2024. https://fedscoop.com/customs-border-protection-ai-tools/.

Brynjolfsson, Erik. 2022. "The Turing Trap: The Promise & Peril of Human-Like Artificial Intelligence." *Dædalus* 151 (2): 272–287. https://doi.org/10.1162/DAED_a_01915.

Buch, Amanda M., David M. Eagleman, and Logan Grosenick. 2022. "Engineering Diplomacy: How AI and Human Augmentation Could Remake the Art of Foreign Relations." *Science & Diplomacy*, February 25, 2022. https://doi.org/10.1126/scidip.ade6798.

Burt, Charles Lyons. 2024. "Biometrics at DHS 'Continuing to Grow,' Per Top Official." Government Technology. *GovCon Wire*, November 2024. www.govconwire.com/articles/biometrics-dhs-lisa-macdonald-homeland-security-summit.

Burt, Chris. 2019. "DHS to Store Tens of Thousands of Refugee Biometric Records from UNHCR | Biometric Update." August. www.biometricupdate.com/201908/dhs-to-store-tens-of-thousands-of-refugee-biometric-records-from-unhcr.

Busch, Christoph. 2020. *Face Morphing Attacks: What Needs to Be Done.* https://christoph-busch.de/files/Busch-iMARS-Frontex-2019.pdf.

Carahsoft. n.d. "Guidance_M-24-10_Advancing_Governance_Innovation_and_Risk_Management_for_Agency_Use_of_Artificial_Intelligence.Pdf." Accessed March 2, 2026. https://static.carahsoft.com/concrete/files/5817/1326/3848/Guidance_M-24-10_Advancing_Governance_Innovation_and_Risk_Management_for_Agency_Use_of_Artificial_Intelligence.pdf.

Center for Health Incentives and Behavioral Economics (CHIBE). 2025. "How to Apply Behavioral Insights at an Organization-Level: Tips from Dr. Elizabeth Linos." https://chibe.upenn.edu/blog/how-to-apply-behavioral-insights-at-an-organization-level-tips-from-dr-elizabeth-linos/.

CentroStudiEuropeo. 2025. *Artificial Intelligence: Redefining Diplomacy in the Digital Age – Hermes – Centro Studi Europeo*. July 16, 2025. www.hermescse.eu/en/artificial-intelligence-redefining-diplomacy-in-the-digital-age/.

CGI. 2023. "Corporate Announcement: CGI to Integrate AI into Visa Processing Support at U.S. Embassies and Consulates across Asia Pacific." www.cgi.com/en/cgi-integrate-ai-into-visa-processing-support-u-s-embassies-consulates-across-asia-pacific.

Chandler, Caitlin. 2025. "Inside the Black Box of Predictive Travel Surveillance." *Wired*, January 13, 2025. www.wired.com/story/inside-the-black-box-of-predictive-travel-surveillance/.

Chen, Stephen. 2018. "Artificial Intelligence, Immune to Fear or Favour, Is Helping to Make China's Foreign Policy." *South China Morning Post*, July 30, 2018. www.scmp.com/news/china/society/article/2157223/artificial-intelligence-immune-fear-or-favour-helping-make.

Citizen Digital. 2023. "Six Immigration Staff, 9 Brokers Arrested for Soliciting Bribes to Issue Passports at Nyayo House." Citizen Digital, October 5. www.citizen.digital/news/six-immigration-staff-9-brokers-arrested-for-soliciting-bribes-to-issue-passports-at-nyayo-house-n328808.

Clark, Caitlin. 2025. "How AI Tools Are Transforming Disaster Response, Preparedness." Texas A&M Stories, October 1, 2025. https://stories.tamu.edu/news/2025/10/01/how-ai-tools-are-transforming-disaster-response-preparedness/.

Coalition for Content Provenance and Authenticity. n.d. "C2PA | Providing Origins of Media Content." Coalition for Content Provenance and Authenticity (C2PA). Accessed October 20, 2025. https://c2pa.org/.

Coalition for Content Provenance and Authenticity (C2PA). 2025. "C2PA Specifications." https://c2pa.org/specifications/specifications/2.2/index.html.

Collins, Elodie. 2024. "CGI Federal Wins New Visa Processing Support Task Orders From State Department." *GovCon Wire*, October 23, 2024. www.govconwire.com/2024/10/cgi-federal-state-department-contract-award/.

Content Authenticity Initiative. 2025. "How It Works: Content Credentials." September 28. https://contentauthenticity.org/how-it-works.

Contreras, Cesareo. 2024. "How Can We Use AI to Build More Democratic Societies? The Key Lies in Transparency, Taiwan's Digital Affairs Minister Says." Northeastern Global News, April 5, 2024. https://news.northeastern.edu/2024/04/05/ai-democracy-governance/.

Corrigan, Jack. 2019. "DHS Is Collecting Biometrics on Thousands of Refugees Who Will Never Enter the U.S." Nextgov, August 2019. www.nextgov.com/emerging-tech/2019/08/dhs-collecting-biometrics-thousands-refugees-who-will-never-enter-us/159310/.

Council on Foreign Relations. 2020. "China's Digital Aid: The Risks and Rewards." www.cfr.org/china-digital-silk-road/.

Council on Foreign Relations. n.d. "The Next Chapter for Artificial Intelligence." Accessed March 2, 2026. www.cfr.org/event/next-chapter-artificial-intelligence.

CPD Immigration News. 2025. *Airline Staff Trained to Block UK-Bound Passengers Without Visas – CPD Immigration UK*. June 21, 2025. https://cpdimmigration.com/airline-staff-trained-to-block-uk-bound-passengers-without-visas/.

Deccan Herald. 2018. "MHA Official, 3 Others Arrested for 'bribe-for-Visa' Case; Orders Inquiry." *Deccan Herald*. Accessed March 2, 2026. www.deccanherald.com/india/mha-official-3-others-arrested-bribe-visa-case-orders-inquiry-671056.html.

Deloitte. n.d. "The State of AI in the Enterprise – 2026 AI Report | Deloitte US." Accessed March 2, 2026. www.deloitte.com/us/en/what-we-do/capabilities/applied-artificial-intelligence/content/state-of-ai-in-the-enterprise.html.

Department of Homeland Security. 2024. "Department of Homeland Security Unveils Artificial Intelligence Roadmap, Announces Pilot Projects to Maximize Benefits of Technology, Advance Homeland Security Mission | Homeland Security." March 18, 2024. www.dhs.gov/archive/news/2024/03/18/department-homeland-security-unveils-artificial-intelligence-roadmap-announces.

Department of Homeland Security. 2025. *CBP Faces Limitations Detecting and Preventing Aliens' Use of Fraud and Deception to Gain Admission into the United States*. OIG-25-40. Washington, DC. www.oig.dhs.gov/sites/default/files/assets/2025-09/OIG-25-40-Sep25.pdf.

DiploFoundation. n.d. *AI Diplomacy: Geo-Politics, Topics and Tools in 2025 | Diplo*. Accessed October 3, 2025. www.diplomacy.edu/topics/ai-and-diplomacy/.

Doubleday, Justin. 2024a. "State's AI Chatbot Journey Started with Collaboration." Nextgov, September 2024. www.nextgov.com/artificial-intelligence/2024/09/states-ai-chatbot-journey-started-collaboration/399933/.

Doubleday, Justin. 2024b. "With New AI Tools Available, State Department Encourages Experimentation." Federal News Network, June 28, 2024. https://federalnewsnetwork.com/artificial-intelligence/2024/06/with-new-ai-tools-available-state-department-encourages-experimentation/.

Economic Times (Travel). 2025. *Mumbai Airport Sees a Surge in Self-Service Adoption with 6.3 Million DigiYatra Users*. https://travel.economictimes.indiatimes.com/news/technology/mumbai-airport-sees-a-surge-inself-service-adoption-with-63-million-digiyatra-users/124138562.

EDPS (European Data Protection Supervisor). 2024. *Artificial Intelligence Act*. www.edps.europa.eu/artificial-intelligence/artificial-intelligence-act_en.

Eggeling, Kristin Anabel, and Rebecca Adler-Nissen. 2024. "Diplomatic Negotiations in the Digital Context: Key Issues, Emerging Trends, and Procedural Changes." In *The Oxford Handbook of Digital Diplomacy*, edited by Corneliu Bjola and Ilan Manor. Oxford University Press. https://doi.org/10.1093/oxfordhb/9780192859198.013.6.

Eggers, William D., David Schatsky, and Peter Viechnicki. 2017. *AI-Augmented Government: Using Cognitive Technologies to Redesign Public Sector Work*. Deloitte University Press. www2.deloitte.com/us/en/insights/focus/cognitive-technologies/artificial-intelligence-government.html.

Engstrom, David Freeman, Daniel E. Ho, Catherine M. Sharkey, and Mariano-Florentino Cuéllar. 2020. *Government by Algorithm: Artificial Intelligence in Federal Administrative Agencies*. Administrative Conference of the United States. https://law.stanford.edu/wp-content/uploads/2020/02/ACUS-AI-Report.pdf.

European Border and Coast Guard Agency. 2024. *Annual Risk Analysis 2024*. Warsaw: Frontex. https://www.frontex.europa.eu/publications/risk-analysis-for-2024-2025-URioQg.

European Commission. n.d.-a. "AI Act Service Desk – Timeline for the Implementation of the EU AI Act." Accessed March 2, 2026. https://ai-act-service-desk.ec.europa.eu/en/ai-act/timeline/timeline-implementation-eu-ai-act.

European Commission. n.d.-b. "Digital Public Services Based on Open Source: Case Study on Bürokratt | Interoperable Europe Portal." Accessed March 2, 2026. https://interoperable-europe.ec.europa.eu/collection/open-source-observatory-osor/document/digital-public-services-based-open-source-case-study-burokratt.

European Commission. n.d.-c. "Entry-Exit System – Migration and Home Affairs – European Commission." Accessed March 2, 2026. https://home-affairs.ec.europa.eu/policies/schengen/smart-borders/entry-exit-system_en.

European Commission. n.d.-d. "Ethics Guidelines for Trustworthy AI | Shaping Europe's Digital Future." Accessed March 2, 2026. https://digital-strategy.ec.europa.eu/en/library/ethics-guidelines-trustworthy-ai.

European Commission. n.d.-e. "Portugal AI Strategy Report – AI Watch – European Commission." Accessed March 2, 2026. https://ai-watch.ec.europa.eu/countries/portugal/portugal-ai-strategy-report_en.

European Commission. 2016a. *Proposal for a Regulation of the European Parliament and of the Council Establishing an Entry/Exit System (EES) to Register Entry and Exit Data and Refusal of Entry Data of Third-Country Nationals Crossing the External Borders of the Member States and Determining the Conditions for Access to the EES for Law Enforcement Purposes.* COM (2016) 194. Brussels: European Commission. https://eur-lex.europa.eu/legal-content/EN/TXT/?uri=CELEX%3A52016PC0194.

European Commission. 2020. *Entry/Exit System (EES) — Migration and Home Affairs.* https://home-affairs.ec.europa.eu/policies/schengen/smartborders/entry-exit-system_en.

European Commission. 2025a. "Bürokratt – A Single Chatbot for Estonia." January 27. https://interoperable-europe.ec.europa.eu/collection/public-sector-tech-watch/burokratt-single-chatbot-estonia.

European Commission. 2025b. "EES — Travel to Europe." September 28. https://travel-europe.europa.eu/en/ees.

European Commission. 2025d. "ETIAS — Travel to Europe." September 28. https://travel-europe.europa.eu/en/etias.

European Commission. 2025e. *Report Abuse — ETIAS, Travel to Europe.* 2025. https://travel-europe.europa.eu/en/etias/your-rights/report-abuse.

European Commission, Directorate-General for Migration and Home Affairs. 2016b. *Intelligent Portable Border Control System (iBorderCtrl).* https://doi.org/10.3030/700626.

European Data Protection Board (EDPB). 2023. *Guidelines 05/2022 on the Use of Facial Recognition in Law Enforcement (Final v2.0).* Brussels. www.edpb.europa.eu/system/files/2023-05/edpb_guidelines_202304_frtlawenforcement_v2_en.pdf.

European Data Protection Supervisor (EDPS). 2018. *Opinion 4/2018 on Interoperability of EU Large-Scale Information Systems.* Brussels. www.edps.europa.eu/sites/default/files/publication/2018-04-16_interoperability_opinion_en.pdf.

European Migration Network (EMN) and Organisation for Economic Co-operation and Development (OECD). 2022. *The Use of Digitalisation and AI in Migration Management.* Brussels. www.oecd.org/content/dam/oecd/en/topics/policy-issues/migration/EMN-OECD-INFORM-FEB-2022-The-use-of-Digitalisation-and-AI-in-Migration-Management.pdf.

European Union. n.d.-a. "Art. 35 GDPR – Data Protection Impact Assessment." *General Data Protection Regulation (GDPR).* Accessed October 22, 2025. https://gdpr-info.eu/art-35-gdpr/.

European Union. n.d.-b. "Eu-e-Lisa-Smart-Borders-Pilot-Interim-Report." Accessed March 2, 2026. www.statewatch.org/media/documents/news/2015/sep/eu-e-lisa-smart-borders-pilot-interim-report.pdf.

European Union. n.d.-c. "General Data Protection Regulation (GDPR) Compliance Guidelines." GDPR.Eu. Accessed March 2, 2026. https://gdpr.eu/.

European Union. 2016. *Directive (EU) 2016/681 (PNR)*. https://eur-lex.europa.eu/eli/dir/2016/681/oj/eng.

European Union. 2017. *Regulation (EU) 2017/2226 of the European Parliament and of the Council of 30 November 2017 Establishing an Entry/Exit System (EES) to Register Entry and Exit Data and Refusal of Entry Data of Third-Country Nationals Crossing the External Borders of the Member States*. Official Journal of the European Union L 327: 20–82. https://eur-lex.europa.eu/eli/reg/2017/2226/oj.

European Union. 2018. *Regulation (EU) 2018/1240 (ETIAS)*. https://eur-lex.europa.eu/eli/reg/2018/1240/oj.

European Union. 2024a. *Regulation (EU) 2024/1689 Laying Down Harmonised Rules on Artificial Intelligence (Artificial Intelligence Act)*. Official Journal of the European Union. https://eur-lex.europa.eu/eli/reg/2024/1689/oj/eng.

European Union. 2024b. "Annex III: High-Risk AI Systems Referred to in Article 6(2)." Artificial Intelligence Act, European Union, June 13. https://artificialintelligenceact.eu/annex/3/.

European Union. 2024c. *Regulation (EU) 2024/1358 of the European Parliament and of the Council of 14 May 2024 on the Establishment of Eurodac for the Comparison of Biometric Data*. Official Journal of the European Union. https://eur-lex.europa.eu/legal-content/EN/TXT/?uri=OJ:L_202401358.

European Union. 2025. *Regulation (EU) 2025/12 (Advance Passenger Info)*. https://eur-lex.europa.eu/eli/reg/2025/12/oj/eng.

Farid, Hany. 2009. *Digital Image Forensics*. Hanover, MA: A K Peters. https://farid.berkeley.edu/downloads/tutorials/digitalimageforensics.pdf.

Farid, Hany. 2016. *Photo Forensics*. MIT Press.

Federal Register. 2025. "Visas: Enhancing Vetting and Combatting Fraud in the Diversity Immigrant Visa Program." Federal Register, August 5. www.federalregister.gov/documents/2025/08/05/2025-14784/visas-enhancing-vetting-and-combatting-fraud-in-the-diversity-immigrant-visa-program.

Fella, Stefano. 2025. *The EU Entry/Exit System and EU Travel Authorisation System*. October 13, 2025. https://commonslibrary.parliament.uk/the-eu-entry-exit-system-and-eu-travel-authorisation-system/.

Feng, Han, Yiwu Jia, Siya Zhoe, and Hongyi Chen. 2024. "An Adaptive Decision Support System for Outpatient Appointment Scheduling." *Scientific Reports* 14 (2024). https://doi.org/10.1038/s41598-024-77873-x.

Fernandez, Sergio, and Hal G. Rainey. 2006. "Managing Successful Organizational Change in the Public Sector." *Public Administration Review* 66 (2): 168–176. https://doi.org/10.1111/j.1540-6210.2006.00570.x.

FIDO Alliance. 2024a. *Displace Password + OTP Authentication with Passkeys*. https://fidoalliance.org/white-paper-displace-password-otp-authentication-with-passkeys/.

FIDO Alliance. 2024b. *Replacing Password-Only Authentication with Passkeys in the Enterprise*. https://fidoalliance.org/white-paper-replacing-password-only-authentication-with-passkeys-in-the-enterprise/.

FIDO Alliance. 2025. *Passkeys: The Journey to Prevent Phishing Attacks*. https://fidoalliance.org/white-paper-passkeys-the-journey-to-prevent-phishing-attacks/.

Financial Times. 2024. *India Expands Airport Facial Recognition amid Surveillance Fears.* 2024. www.ft.com/content/f1ba12ac-fe1d-4a51-b2e7-077f392115a7.

Financial Times. 2025. *EU Fingerprint Scanners Will Not Cause Delays, Eurotunnel Boss Says.* 2025. www.ft.com/content/635eae4f-0051-45e2-a388-1ce5bce2257b.

Fingold, J. n.d. "Basics of the Microsoft Bot Framework – Bot Service." Accessed March 2, 2026. https://learn.microsoft.com/en-us/azure/bot-service/bot-builder-basics?view=azure-bot-service-4.0.

Foxglove. 2020. "Home Office Says It Will Abandon Its Racist Visa Algorithm – after We Sued Them." August 4. www.foxglove.org.uk/2020/08/04/home-office-says-it-will-abandon-its-racist-visa-algorithm-after-we-sued-them/.

Fox-Sowell, Sophia. 2025. "For Most States, AI Adoption Is Still in Early Stages, Code for America Report Shows." StateScoop, July 8, 2025. https://statescoop.com/state-ai-adoption-code-for-america-report/.

Franke, Ulrike. 2021. *Artificial Intelligence Diplomacy | Artificial Intelligence Governance as a New External Policy Tool.* PE 662.926. Brussels: European Parliament.

Freedom House. n.d. "Rwanda: Freedom on the Net 2024 Country Report." Freedom House. Accessed March 2, 2026. https://freedomhouse.org/country/rwanda/freedom-net/2024.

French, Mallory. n.d. *Department of State Enterprise AI Strategy.* www.state.gov/wp-content/uploads/2023/11/Department-of-State-Enterprise-Artificial-Intelligence-Strategy.pdf.

Frontex. n.d.-a. "About ETIAS." Accessed March 2, 2026. www.frontex.europa.eu/what-we-do/etias-ees/about-etias/.

Frontex. n.d.-b. "Annual-Risk-Analysis-2024–2025." Accessed March 2, 2026. https://prd.frontex.europa.eu/wp-content/uploads/annual-risk-analysis-2024-2025.pdf.

Frontex. 2024. *Beware of Risks Posed by Unofficial ETIAS Websites.* www.frontex.europa.eu/media-centre/news/news-release/beware-of-risks-posed-byunofficial-etias-websites-eNZniu.

"FSOs and FSNs Recall Sept. 11." 2001. *The Foreign Service Journal* 78, no. 11 (November): 20–25. https://afsa.org/sites/default/files/fsj-2001-11-november_0.pdf.

Future of Life Institute. n.d. *EU Artificial Intelligence Act | Up-to-Date Developments and Analyses of the EU AI Act.* Accessed October 13, 2025. https://artificialintelligenceact.eu/.

GAO (U.S. Government Accountability Office). 2020. *Facial Recognition: CBP and TSA Are Taking Steps to Implement Programs, but CBP Should Improve Its Efforts to Limit Privacy Risks.* www.gao.gov/products/gao-20-568.

Gofman, Mikhail I., and Maria Villa. 2023. "Identity and War: The Role of Biometrics in the Russia-Ukraine Crisis." *International Journal on Engineering, Science and Technology* 5 (1): 89–111. https://doi.org/10.46328/ijonest.143.

Goldwasser, Shafi, Silvio Micali, and Charles Rackoff. 1985. "The Knowledge Complexity of Interactive Proof-Systems." *Proceedings of the Seventeenth Annual ACM Symposium on Theory of Computing* (New York, NY, USA), STOC '85, December 1, 1985, 291–304. https://doi.org/10.1145/22145.22178.

Gonzalez, Bianca. 2024. "Digi Yatra App Users Face Glitches, Data Privacy Concerns | Biometric Update." April 2. www.biometricupdate.com/202404/digi-yatra-app-users-face-glitches-data-privacy-concerns.

Google. 2023. "So Long Passwords, Thanks for All the Phish." *Google Security Blog*, May 3, 2023. https://security.googleblog.com/2023/05/so-long-passwords-thanks-for-all-phish.html.

Google. n.d. "Dialogflow." Google Cloud. Accessed March 2, 2026. https://cloud.google.com/dialogflow/docs.

Gosier, Chris. n.d. "How Should AI Be Used in Immigration? Cautiously, Experts Say." Accessed March 2, 2026. https://now.fordham.edu/university-news/how-should-ai-be-used-in-immigration-cautiously-experts-say/.

Government of Australia. n.d.-a. "Digital ID | Digital ID System." Accessed March 2, 2026. www.digitalidsystem.gov.au/.

Government of Australia. n.d.-b. "Digital Transformation Agency Annual Report 2023-24." Accessed March 2, 2026. www.transparency.gov.au/publications/finance/digital-transformation-agency/digital-transformation-agency-annual-report-2023-24.

Government of Canada. 2025. "How Canada Uses DNA Tests As Part of Family Immigration and Citizenship Processing." September 9. https://immigration.ca/how-canada-uses-dna-tests-as-part-of-family-immigration-and-citizenship-processing/.

Government of Canada. n.d. *Directive on Automated Decision-Making*. Ottawa: Treasury Board of Canada Secretariat. Accessed March 2, 2026. https://www.tbs-sct.canada.ca/pol/doc-eng.aspx?id=32592.

Government of New Zealand. n.d. "Standards New Zealand." Accessed March 2, 2026. www.standards.govt.nz/shop/isoiec-18013-52021.

Government of the United Kingdom. 2025. *AI Safety Institute (Now AI Security Institute)*. www.gov.uk/government/organisations/ai-safety-institute.

Govtech Singapore. n.d.-a. "Health Appointment System." Government Technology Agency of Singapore (GovTech Singapore). Accessed March 2, 2026. www.tech.gov.sg/products-and-services/for-citizens/health/health-appointment-system/.

Govtech Singapore. n.d.-b. "Moments of Life Is Now LifeSG – The Story so Far." Government Technology Agency of Singapore (GovTech Singapore). Accessed March 2, 2026. www.tech.gov.sg/technews/moments-of-life-is-now-lifesg-story-so-far/.

GOV.UK. 2025. "Get an Electronic Travel Authorisation (ETA) to Visit the UK." www.gov.uk/eta.

Grother, Patrick. 2019. *FRVT Part 3: Demographic Effects*. NIST IR 8280. https://doi.org/10.6028/NIST.IR.8280.

Grother, Patrick. 2022. *FRVT Part 8: Summarizing Demographic Differentials*. NISTIR 8429. https://pages.nist.gov/frvt/reports/demographics/nistir_8429.pdf.

Grother, Patrick, and Mei Ngan. 2019. *Face Recognition Vendor Test (FRVT) Part 3: Demographic Effects*. NISTIR 8280. https://nvlpubs.nist.gov/nistpubs/ir/2019/nist.ir.8280.pdf.

Grother, Patrick, Mei Ngan, and Kayee Hanaoka. 2019. *Face Recognition Vendor Test (FRVT) Part 2: Identification*. NIST IR 8271. Gaithersburg, MD: National Institute of Standards and Technology. https://doi.org/10.6028/NIST.IR.8271.

Gugerty, Mary Kay, Dean Karlan, Mary Kay Gugerty, and Dean Karlan. 2018. *The Goldilocks Challenge: Right-Fit Evidence for the Social Sector*. Oxford, New York: Oxford University Press.

Guo, Jiajie, Hao Mu, Xian Liu, Heng Ren, and Chong Han. 2024. "Federated Learning for Biometric Recognition: A Survey." *Artificial Intelligence Review* 57 (8): 208. https://doi.org/10.1007/s10462-024-10847-7.

Gyanchandani, Vandana, Jayanti Dhingra, Kavya Agrawal, Laasya Sarojini, and Sanya Singh. 2025. "Balancing Convenience and Data Privacy in the Digi Yatra App." *Journal of Data Protection & Privacy* 7 (4): 383–405. https://doi.org/10.69554/IPOK9437.

Hallsworth, Michael, Dan Berry, Michael Sanders, Anna Sallis, Dominic King, Ivo Vlaev, and Ara Darzi. 2015. "Stating Appointment Costs in SMS Reminders Reduces Missed Hospital Appointments: Findings from Two Randomised Controlled Trials." *PloS One* 10 (9): e0137306. https://doi.org/10.1371/journal.pone.0137306.

Halper, Mark. 2025. *How Software Bugs Led to 'One of the Greatest Miscarriages of Justice' in British History – Communications of the ACM*. January 8, 2025. https://cacm.acm.org/news/how-software-bugs-led-to-one-of-the-greatest-miscarriages-of-justice-in-british-history/.

Hamidouche, Karim. 2021. "Artificial Intelligence: A New Tool for Diplomats." In *Artificial Intelligence and Digital Diplomacy: Challenges and Opportunities*, edited by Fatima Roumate, 25–32. Cham: Springer International Publishing. https://doi.org/10.1007/978-3-030-68647-5_2.

Hamieh, Bassel. n.d. "The Meaning of Red and Green in User Interfaces for the Color Deficient." Accessed March 2, 2026. https://pdxscholar.library.pdx.edu/honorstheses/924/.

Harvard University, dir. 2015. The Role of Dignity in the Development of Trust and Ethically Healthy Organizations. *Donna Hicks*. 17:05. www.youtube.com/watch?v=E3VaeSYrLvg.

Haseley, Alex, Chandan Karnik, Brian Kamoie, Ipshita Sinha, Joe Mariani, and Alison Muckle Egizi. 2023. *Leveraging AI in Emergency Management and Crisis Response*. Deloitte. www2.deloitte.com/us/en/insights/industry/public-sector/automation-and-generative-ai-in-government/leveraging-ai-in-emergency-management-and-crisis-response.html.

Hickling, Adam. n.d. "The Impact of Electronic Travel Authorisation on Airlines: Compliance and Communication." Fragomen – Immigration Attorneys, Solicitors, and Consultants Worldwide – The Impact of Electronic Travel Authorisation on Airlines: Compliance and Communication. Accessed March 2, 2026. www.fragomen.com/insights/the-impact-of-electronic-travel-authorisation-on-airlines-compliance-and-communication.html.

Hogarth, Robin M., and Emre Soyer. 2014. "Using Simulated Experience to Make Sense of Big Data." *MIT Sloan Management Review*, December 16, 2014. https://sloanreview.mit.edu/article/using-simulated-experience-to-make-sense-of-big-data/.

Hollister, Sean. 2024. *US Online Passport Renewal Is Now Fully Open for Business*. www.theverge.com/2024/9/19/24249413/us-onlinepassport-renewal-website.

Home Office. 2020. *UK Home Office Visa Application Streaming Algorithm: Algorithmic Transparency Recording Standard – Alpha Phase: Documentation and Review*. Surrey: Identity Theft & Fraud Solutions.

Home Office. 2025. "Electronic Travel Authorisation (ETA) Factsheet." Home Office in the Media, April. https://homeofficemedia.blog.gov.uk/electronic-travel-authorisation-eta-factsheet-april-2025/.

Höne, Katharina E., Lee Hibbard, Marília Maciel, Katarina Anđelković, Nataša Perućica, and Virdžinija Saveska. 2019. *Mapping the Challenges and Opportunities of Artificial Intelligence for the Conduct of Diplomacy*. Geneva: DiploFoundation. www.diplomacy.edu/resource/mapping-the-challenges-and-opportunities-of-artificial-intelligence-for-the-conduct-of-diplomacy/.

Honley, Steven Alan. 2005. "After the Tsunami: Assisting Americans in Distress." *The Foreign Service Journal* 82 (4): 23–27. https://afsa.org/after-tsunami-assisting-americans-distress.

Hubard, Steven. n.d. "Invisible Gatekeepers: DHS' Growing Use of AI in Immigration Decisions." American Immigration Council. Accessed September 30, 2025. www.americanimmigrationcouncil.org/blog/invisible-gatekeepers-dhs-growing-use-of-ai-in-immigration-decisions/.

Human Rights Watch. 2022. "Russia Uses Facial Recognition to Hunt Down Draft Evaders." October 26. www.hrw.org/news/2022/10/26/russia-uses-facial-recognition-hunt-down-draft-evaders.

IATA. n.d. "Courses & Diplomas." Accessed March 2, 2026. www.iata.org/en/training/courses/digital-identity-fundamentals/apc020veen01/en/.

IBM Center. n.d. "AI and Government Communications | IBM Center for The Business of Government." Accessed March 2, 2026. www.businessofgovernment.org/blog/ai-and-government-communications.

ICAO (International Civil Aviation Organization). n.d. "TRIP-and-Year-of-Facilitation." Accessed March 2, 2026. www.icao.int/sites/default/files/Security/FAL/TRIP-and-Year-of-Facilitation.pdf.

IEC (International Electrotechnical Commission). 2025. *Combatting Morphing in ID Fraud.* www.iec.ch/blog/combatting-morphing-id-fraud.

Immigration & Checkpoints Authority (ICA), Singapore. 2024. *Passport-Less Clearance Fully Rolled-Out at Changi Airport.* www.ica.gov.sg/news-and-publications/newsroom/media-release/passport-less-clearance-fully-rolled-out-at-changi-airport.

Immigration, Refugees and Citizenship Canada. 2022. "Advanced Data Analytics to Help IRCC Officers Sort and Process Temporary Resident Visa Applications." https://www.canada.ca/en/immigration-refugees-citizenship/news/notices/analytics-help-process-trv-applications.html.

Immigration, Refugees and Citizenship Canada. 2024. "Advanced Analytics and Automation for Processing Applications." November 18. www.canada.ca/en/immigration-refugees-citizenship/corporate/transparency/digital-transparency-advanced-data-analytics/processing-applications.html.

Immigration, Refugees and Citizenship Canada. 2025. "Immigration, Refugees and Citizenship Canada's 2025–26 Departmental Plan." June 17. www.canada.ca/en/immigration-refugees-citizenship/corporate/publications-manuals/departmental-plans/2025-26-departmental-plan/departmental-plan-2025-2026-full.html.

International Air Transport Association (IATA). 2025. *Fact Sheet: One ID.* www.iata.org/en/iata-repository/pressroom/fact-sheets/fact-sheet-one-id/.

International Civil Aviation Organization (ICAO). n.d. "ICAO Public Key Directory (PKD)." Montreal: ICAO. Accessed March 2, 2026. www.icao.int/icao-pkd.

International Civil Aviation Organization (ICAO). 2015. *Doc 9303: Machine Readable Travel Documents, 8th Ed., Parts 1–12.* Montreal: ICAO. www.icao.int/publications/doc-series/doc-9303.

International Civil Aviation Organization (ICAO). 2020. *ICAO PKD Regulations.* Montreal: International Civil Aviation Organization. www.icao.int/sites/default/files/2025-06/ICAO-PKD-Regulations_Version_July2020.pdf.

International Civil Aviation Organization (ICAO). 2022. *Digital Travel Credentials (DTC) — Physical Component and Protocols (DTC-PC), Version 1.1.* Montreal: ICAO. www2023.icao.int/Security/FAL/TRIP/PublishingImages/Pages/Publications/ICAO%20TR%20-%20Digital%20Travel%20Credentials%20PC.pdf.

International Civil Aviation Organization (ICAO). 2025. "Doc 9303, Machine Readable Travel Documents (Series Overview)." September 28. www.icao.int/publications/doc-series/doc-9303.

International Organization for Migration. n.d. "Ch11-Key-Findings_Final." Accessed March 2, 2026. https://worldmigrationreport.iom.int/sites/g/files/tmzbdl1691/files/documents/Ch11-key-findings_final.pdf.

International Organization for Migration. 2024. *World Migration Report 2024.* Geneva: IOM. https://worldmigrationreport.iom.int/.

International Organization for Standardization. n.d.-a. "ISO 9001:2015." ISO. Accessed March 2, 2026. www.iso.org/standard/62085.html.

International Organization for Standardization. n.d.-b. "ISO 9182-3:2023." ISO. Accessed March 2, 2026. www.iso.org/standard/83522.html.

International Organization for Standardization. n.d.-c. "ISO/IEC 19794-4:2011." ISO. Accessed March 2, 2026. www.iso.org/standard/50866.html.

International Organization for Standardization. n.d.-d. "ISO/IEC 19794-14:2013." ISO. Accessed March 2, 2026. www.iso.org/standard/50872.html.

International Organization for Standardization (ISO) and International Electrotechnical Commission (IEC). 2019. *ISO/IEC 39794-5:2019 — Information Technology — Extensible Biometric Data Interchange Formats — Part 5: Face Image Data*. Edition 1. Geneva: ISO/IEC. www.iso.org/standard/72156.html.

International Organization for Standardization (ISO) and International Electrotechnical Commission (IEC). 2022. *ISO/IEC 2382-37:2022 — Information Technology — Vocabulary — Part 37: Biometrics*. Edition 3. Geneva: ISO/IEC. www.iso.org/standard/73514.html.

International Organization for Standardization (ISO) and International Electrotechnical Commission (IEC). 2023a. *ISO/IEC 30107-3:2023 — Information Technology—Biometric Presentation Attack Detection—Part 3: Testing and Reporting*. Geneva: ISO/IEC. www.iso.org/standard/79520.html.

International Organization for Standardization (ISO) and International Electrotechnical Commission (IEC). 2023b. *ISO/IEC 42001:2023 — Information Technology—Artificial Intelligence—Management System*. Geneva: ISO/IEC. www.iso.org/standard/42001.

International Organization for Standardization and International Electrotechnical Commission (IEC). 2023c. *ISO/IEC 23894:2023 — Information Technology—Artificial Intelligence—Guidance on Risk Management*. Geneva: ISO/IEC. www.iso.org/standard/77304.html.

Interpol. n.d. "Stolen and Lost Travel Documents Database." Accessed March 2, 2026. www.interpol.int/en/How-we-work/Border-management/SLTD-database-travel-and-identity-documents.

IQ, Federal Budget. n.d. "OMB Imposes Comprehensive AI Use, Procurement, and Risk Management Requirements." Federal Budget IQ. Accessed March 2, 2026. https://federalbudgetiq.com/insights/omb-imposes-comprehensive-ai-use-procurement-and-risk-management-requirements/.

IRCC. 2025. *Peer Review for Advanced Analytics Triage of Overseas TRV Applications*. https://open.canada.ca/data/en/dataset/6cba99b1-ea2c-4f8a-b954-3843ecd3a7f0.

Irembo. n.d. "Irembo." Accessed March 2, 2026. https://irembo.com/case-studies/.

ITPro. 2025. *NCA Confirms Arrest after Airport Cyber Disruption*. www.itpro.com/security/cyber-attacks/nca-confirms-arrest-after-airport-cyber-disruption.

Johnson, Bridget. n.d. "No More 'Big Bang' for IT Modernization as DHS Strategy Emphasizes Building Smaller, Data Agility, Smart AI – HSToday." DHS. www.Hstoday.Us/. Accessed March 2, 2026. www.hstoday.us/featured/no-more-big-bang-for-it-modernization-as-dhs-strategy-emphasizes-building-smaller-data-agility-smart-ai/.

Johnson, Bridget. 2023. "CIO Hysen Named First DHS Chief AI Officer as New Policies Released on AI Acquisition and Facial Recognition Technology." *Homeland Security Today*, September 14, 2023. www.hstoday.us/featured/cio-hysen-named-first-dhs-chief-ai-officer-as-new-policies-released-on-ai-acquisition-and-facial-recognition-technology/.

Karas, Sergio, and Reeva Goel. n.d. "Artificial Intelligence and Canada's Immigration System." Accessed March 2, 2026. www.ibanet.org/artificial-intelligence-in-immigration.

Kilburg, Don. 2025. *AI Use Cases for Diplomats: Applying Artificial Intelligence to Diplomacy*. 1st ed. Boca Raton, FL: Chapman and Hall/CRC. https://doi.org/10.1201/9781003612308

Kimery, Anthony. n.d. "CBP Biometric Exit Blurs Lines between Convenience and Surveillance." Biometric Update. Accessed March 2, 2026. www.biometricupdate.com/202509/cbp-biometric-exit-blurs-lines-between-convenience-and-surveillance.

Kind, Carly. 2024. "Biometrics Institute Asia-Pacific Conference 2024." Office of the Australian Information Commissioner, Government of Australia. www.oaic.gov.au/news/speeches/biometrics-institute-asia-pacific-conference-2024.

Kotter, John. n.d. "The 8-Step Process for Leading Change." Accessed March 2, 2026. www.kotterinc.com/methodology/8-steps/.

Lacy, Gharun. 2024. "Artificial Intelligence May Augment Diplomatic Data Security." *FedTech Magazine*, October 10, 2024. https://fedtechmagazine.com/article/2024/10/artificial-intelligence-may-augment-diplomatic-data-security.

Lanius, Candice, Ryan Weber, and William I. MacKenzie. 2021. "Use of Bot and Content Flags to Limit the Spread of Misinformation among Social Networks: A Behavior and Attitude Survey." *Social Network Analysis and Mining* 11 (1): 32. https://doi.org/10.1007/s13278-021-00739-x.

Lerouge, Julien, Guillaume Betmont, Thomas Bres, Evgeny Stepankevich, and Alexis Bergès. 2024. "DocXPand-25k: A Large and Diverse Benchmark Dataset for Identity Documents Analysis." arXiv:2407.20662. Preprint, arXiv, July 30. https://doi.org/10.48550/arXiv.2407.20662.

Letzing, John. 2024. "Microsoft's CEO, Satya Nadella, on AI and Limiting 'Unintended Consequences.'" World Economic Forum, January 17. www.weforum.org/stories/2024/01/microsoft-ceo-ai-technology-consequences/.

Li, Fei-Fei. 2018. *Mission and Vision: Human-Centered AI.* Vision Statement. Stanford, CA: Stanford Institute for Human-Centered Artificial Intelligence (HAI).

Li, Fei-Fei, and Sara Frueh. 2024. "'AI Is a Tool, and Its Values Are Human Values.'" *Issues in Science and Technology*, (3) (2024). https://doi.org/10.58875/LBZG7966.

London Daily. n.d. "UK Home Office Drops 'Racist' Algorithm for Visa Applicants after Migrants' Rights Campaigners Launch Legal Challenge." *London Daily*. Accessed March 2, 2026. https://londondaily.com/uk-home-office-drops-racist-algorithm-for-visa-applicants-after-migrants-rights-campaigners-launch-legal-challenge.

Luck, Shaina. n.d. "Immigration Lawyers Concerned IRCC's Use of Processing Technology Leading to Unfair Visa Refusals | CBC News." Accessed March 2, 2026. www.cbc.ca/news/canada/nova-scotia/immigration-canada-ircc-technology-1.7632130.

Lyons-Burt, Charles. 2024. "Biometrics at DHS 'Continuing to Grow,' Per Top Official." *GovCon Wire*, November 11, 2024. www.govconwire.com/2024/11/biometrics-dhs-lisa-macdonald-homeland-security-summit/.

Madan, Monique O. 2024. "The Future of Border Patrol: AI Is Always Watching." Government Executive, March 22, 2024. www.govexec.com/technology/2024/03/future-border-patrol-ai-always-watching/395167/

MandG World. 2022. "Improve IRCC Efficiency Using Data for Visa Processing." MandG World, February 2022. www.mandgworld.com/blog/advanced-data-analytics-to-help-ircc-officers-sort-and-process-temporary-resident-visa-applications/.

Meissner, Christian A., and John C. Brigham. 2001. "Thirty Years of Investigating the Own-Race Bias in Memory for Faces: A Meta-Analytic Review." *Psychology, Public Policy, and Law* 7 (1): 3–35. https://doi.org/10.1037/1076-8971.7.1.3.

Microsoft Ignite. n.d.-a. "Introduction to Azure AI Search – Azure AI Search." Accessed March 2, 2026. https://learn.microsoft.com/en-us/azure/search/search-what-is-azure-search.

Microsoft Ignite. n.d.-b. "What Is the Azure AI Face Service? – Azure AI Services." Accessed March 2, 2026. https://learn.microsoft.com/en-us/azure/ai-services/computer-vision/overview-identity.

Miller, Harry. 2023. "Immigration Minister Says AI Isn't Making Final Immigration Decisions." *Canada News Media*, May 2023. https://canadanewsmedia.ca/immigration-minister-says-ai-isnt-making-final-immigration-decisions-cbc-ca/.

Ministry of Civil Aviation (India). 2023. *Digi Yatra Policy (DIGI YATRA): Digi Yatra Biometric Boarding System (DY-BBS)*. New Delhi: Government of India, Ministry of Civil Aviation. https://www.civilaviation.gov.in/sites/default/files/2023-07/Digi%20Yatra%20Policy%20%28DIGI%20YATRA%29.pdf.

Moodie, Alison. n.d. "U.S. Consulates Struggle with Tech and User Experience." Accessed March 2, 2026. www.boundless.com/blog/consular-affairs-tech-report.

Mostafaei, Hamidreza, Shirin Kordnoori, Mohammadmohsen Ostadrahimi, and Saeed Seyed Agha Banihashemi. 2025. "Applications of Artificial Intelligence in Global Diplomacy: A Review of Research and Practical Models." *Sustainable Futures* 9 (June): 100486. https://doi.org/10.1016/j.sftr.2025.100486.

Nalbandian, Lucia. 2021. "Using Machine-Learning to Triage Canada's Temporary Resident Visa Applications." *Working Papers*, no. 2021/9 (July 2021).

National Archives. 2020. "UK to End Controversial Visa Screening Algorithm." *Politico*, August 4, 2020. www.politico.eu/article/uk-to-end-controversial-visa-screening-algorithm-rights-group-says/.

National Archives. 2021. "Shutting Down the Sky: The Federal Aviation Administration on 9/11." September 10, 2021. https://text-message.blogs.archives.gov/2021/09/10/shutting-down-the-sky-the-federal-aviation-administration-on-9-11/.

National Institute of Standards and Technology. 2023. *Artificial Intelligence Risk Management Framework (AI RMF 1.0)*. NIST AI.AI.100-1. National Institute of Standards and Technology. www.nist.gov/publications/artificial-intelligence-risk-management-framework-ai-rmf-10.

National Institute of Standards and Technology (NIST). 2021. *NIST Evaluates Face Recognition Software's Accuracy for Flight Boarding*. www.nist.gov/news-events/news/2021/07/nist-evaluates-face-recognition-softwares-accuracy-flight-boarding.

National Institute of Standards and Technology (NIST). 2023a. *Artificial Intelligence Risk Management Framework (AI RMF 1.0)*. Gaithersburg, MD: National Institute of Standards and Technology.

National Institute of Standards and Technology (NIST). 2023b. "Artificial Intelligence Safety Institute Consortium (AISIC)." National Institute of Standards and Technology.

National Institute of Standards and Technology (NIST). 2024a. *Artificial Intelligence Risk Management Framework: Generative AI Profile*. NIST AI 600-1. https://doi.org/10.6028/NIST.AI.600-1.

National Institute of Standards and Technology (NIST). 2024b. *U.S. AI Safety Institute (AISI)—Guidelines*. www.nist.gov/aisi/guidelines.

National Institute of Standards and Technology (NIST). 2025a. *"Center for AI Standards and Innovation (CAISI)."* www.nist.gov/caisi.

National Institute of Standards and Technology (NIST). 2025b. *Face Recognition Technology Evaluation (FRTE) 1:1 Verification (Ongoing)*. https://pages.nist.gov/frvt/html/frvt11.html.

National Research Council. 2010. *Biometric Recognition: Challenges and Opportunities*. Washington, DC: National Academies Press. https://doi.org/10.17226/12720.

NATO. 2024. "Summary of NATO's Revised Artificial Intelligence (AI) Strategy." NATO. Accessed March 2, 2026. www.nato.int/cps/en/natohq/official_texts_227237.htm.

NCSC (UK National Cyber Security Centre). 2025. *Phishing: Spot and Report Scam Emails, Texts, Websites and Calls*. www.ncsc.gov.uk/collection/phishing-scams.

NEC. n.d. "Biometric Authentication: Products & Solutions | NEC." Accessed March 2, 2026. www.nec.com/en/global/solutions/biometrics/.

Ngan, Mei, and Patrick Grother. 2025. *Face Analysis Technology Evaluation (FATE) MORPH Part 4B: Considerations for Implementing Morph Detection in Operations.* NIST Interagency Report 8584. Gaithersburg, MD: National Institute of Standards and Technology. https://doi.org/10.6028/NIST.IR.8584.

Ngan, Mei, Patrick Grother, and Kayee Hanaoka. 2020. *Ongoing Face Recognition Vendor Test (FRVT) Part 6A: Face Recognition Accuracy with Masks Using Pre-COVID-19 Algorithms.* NIST IR 8311. Gaithersburg, MD: National Institute of Standards and Technology. https://doi.org/10.6028/NIST.IR.8311.

Ngan, Mei, Patrick Grother, and Kayee Hanaoka. 2022. *Morph Detection Algorithms.* NISTIR 8430. https://nvlpubs.nist.gov/nistpubs/ir/2022/NIST.IR.8430.pdf.

Ngan, Mei, Kayee K. Hanaoka, and Jamie Kuo. 2025. *Face Analysis Technology Evaluation (FATE) Part 4B: Considerations for Implementing Morph Detection in Operations (NISTIR 8584).* https://pages.nist.gov/frvt/reports/morph/fate_morph_4B_NISTIR_8584.pdf.

Nihill, Caroline. 2024. "USDS Impact Report Showcases 'a Year of Launching Things.'" FedScoop, May 9, 2024. https://fedscoop.com/usds-impact-report-showcases-a-year-of-launching-things/.

NIST (National Institute of Standards and Technology). 2022. *Demographic Effects in Face Recognition—FRVT.* https://pages.nist.gov/frvt/html/frvt_demographics.html.

Niyogi, Subhro. 2025. "Kol Airport Flags Off DigiYatra for Transit Flyers." *Times of India*, July 17, 2025. https://timesofindia.indiatimes.com/city/kolkata/kol-airport-flags-off-digiyatra-for-transitflyers/articleshow/122668289.cms.

Nozulela, Mthobisi. 2025. "Experts Urge Responsible Use of AI to Drive Inclusion and Growth in Public Sector." IOL. https://iol.co.za/business/jobs/2025-07-01-experts-urge-responsible-use-of-ai-to-drive-inclusion-and-growth-in-public-sector/.

NTNU SOTAMD. n.d. "State of the Art of Morphing Detection (SOTAMD)." Accessed October 1. 2025. *State of the Art of Morphing Detection (SOTAMD).* www.ntnu.edu/iik/sotamd.

Ntsele, Gugu. n.d. "NIST Releases New Guidelines for Detecting Face Morphing Attacks." Accessed March 2, 2026. www.paubox.com/blog/nist-releases-new-guidelines-for-detecting-face-morphing-attacks.

OAIC. 2023. "Privacy Impact Assessments." OAIC, June 23. www.oaic.gov.au/privacy/privacy-guidance-for-organisations-and-government-agencies/privacy-impact-assessments.

OASIS. 2010. *Common Alerting Protocol (CAP) v1.2.* https://docs.oasis-open.org/emergency/cap/v1.2/CAP-v1.2-os.html.

O'Carroll, Lisa. 2025. "Biometric Checks to Visit EU Could Take Nine Months to Fully Enforce." *The Guardian*, September 25. https://www.theguardian.com/travel/2025/sep/25/biometric-checks-to-visit-eu-to-get-phased-rollout-from-october.

OCHA Centre for Humanitarian Data. 2025. *Data Responsibility Guidelines.* United Nations Office for the Coordination of Humanitarian Affairs. https://data.humdata.org/dataset/2048a947-5714-4220-905b-e662cbcd14c8/resource/8bc5b848-8ece-4f1f-a78b-18dd972bb21a/download/data-responsibility-guidelines-2025.pdf.

OECD. n.d.-a. "How Artificial Intelligence Is Accelerating the Digital Government Journey: Governing with Artificial Intelligence | OECD." Accessed March 2, 2026. www.oecd.org/en/publications/governing-with-artificial-intelligence_795de142-en/full-report/how-artificial-intelligence-is-accelerating-the-digital-government-journey_d9552dc7.html.

OECD. n.d.-b. "OECD Framework for the Classification of AI Systems: A Tool for Effective AI Policies." Accessed March 2, 2026. https://oecd.ai/en/classification.

OECD. n.d.-c. "Public Sector Artificial Intelligence Observatory." Accessed March 2, 2026. https://oecd.ai/en/dashboards/policy-initiatives/public-sector-artificial-intelligence-observatory-4061.

OECD. 2019. "Embracing Innovation in Government: Global Trends 2019." Observatory of Public Sector Innovation, February 2019. https://oecd-opsi.org/publications/global-trends-2019/.

OECD. 2024. *Governing with Artificial Intelligence: Are Governments Ready?* OECD Artificial Intelligence Papers No. 20. Vol. 20. OECD Artificial Intelligence Papers. https://doi.org/10.1787/26324bc2-en.

Office of Management and Budget. 2024. *Advancing Governance, Innovation, and Risk Management for Agency Use of Artificial Intelligence.* M-24-10. Washington, DC: Executive Office of the President. www.whitehouse.gov/wp-content/uploads/2024/03/M-24-10-Advancing-Governance-Innovation-and-Risk-Management-for-Agency-Use-of-Artificial-Intelligence.pdf.

Office of Management and Budget. 2025. *Memorandum for the Heads of Executive Departments and Agencies: Accelerating Federal Use of AI through Innovation, Governance, and Public Trust.* M-25–21. Washington, DC: Office of Management and Budget, Executive Office of the President.

Oikonomidi, Theodora, Gill Norman, Laura McGarrigle, Jonathan Stokes, Sabine N. van der Veer, and Dawn Dowding. 2023. "Predictive Model-Based Interventions to Reduce Outpatient No-Shows: A Rapid Systematic Review." *Journal of the American Medical Informatics Association* 30 (3): 559–569. https://doi.org/10.1093/jamia/ocac242.

Oladipo, Doyinsola. 2024. "Americans Will Be Able to Renew Their Passports Online Starting on Wednesday | Reuters." September. www.reuters.com/world/us/americans-will-be-able-renew-their-passports-online-starting-wednesday-2024-09-17/.

Organization for Security and Co-operation in Europe (OSCE). 2016. *ICAO Public Key Directory (PKD) in the OSCE Region.* Vienna: OSCE TNTD. www.osce.org/files/f/documents/1/1/275156.pdf.

Oxford Institute of Technology and Justice. n.d. "Estonia | AI for Crime Prevention." Accessed March 2, 2026. www.techandjustice.bsg.ox.ac.uk/research/estonia.

Pahlka, Jennifer. 2024. "Testimony: Jennifer Pahlka on Harnessing AI to Improve Government Services and Customer Experience." Niskanen Center, January 10, 2024. www.niskanencenter.org/testimony-jennifer-pahlka-on-harnessing-ai-to-improve-government-services-and-customer-experience/.

Pandev Law. n.d. "E2 Visa Processing Time | E2 Visa Renewal Timeline | Pandev Law." Accessed March 2, 2026. www.pandevlaw.com/blog/e2-visa-processing-time/.

Parikh, Amit, Kanal Gupta, Alan Wilson, Karrie Fields, Nora Cosgrove, and John Kostis. 2010. "The Effectiveness of Outpatient Appointment Reminder Systems." *The American Journal of Medicine* 123 (6): 542–48.

Pokhriyal, Neeti, and Till Koebe. 2023. "AI-Assisted Diplomatic Decision-Making during Crises—Challenges and Opportunities." *Frontiers in Big Data* 6 (May). https://doi.org/10.3389/fdata.2023.1183313.

Press Information Bureau (Government of India). 2024. *Digi Yatra Facility Launched at 9 More Airports; Total Number of DigiYatra-Enabled Airports Increases to 24.* www.pib.gov.in/PressReleasePage.aspx?PRID=2052596.

Press Information Bureau (Government of India). 2025. *Transforming India's Transport Infrastructure (2014–2025).* www.pib.gov.in/PressNoteDetails.aspx?ModuleId=3&NoteId=154624.

Press Trust of India. 2024. "CBI Arrests 2 IRS Officers, 5 Others in SEEPZ Mumbai Corruption Case." Republic World, December 18. www.republicworld.com/india/cbi-arrests-2-irs-officers-5-others-in-seepz-mumbai-corruption-case.

PreventionWeb. 2017. *Scaling up Haze Gazer: An Analysis and Visualization Tool for Haze Crisis Management.* January 26, 2017. www.preventionweb.net/news/scaling-haze-gazer-analysis-and-visualization-tool-haze-crisis-management.

Privacy and Civil Liberties Oversight Board (PCLOB). 2025. *Use of Facial Recognition Technology by the Transportation Security Administration.* Washington, DC: Privacy and Civil Liberties Oversight Board.https://documents.pclob.gov/prod/Documents/OversightReport/90964138-44eb-483d-990e-057ce4c31db7/Use%20of%20FRT%20by%20TSA%2C%20PCLOB%20Report%20%285-12-25%29%2C%20Completed%20508%2C%20May%2019%2C%202025.pdf.

Prosci. n.d. "AI Adoption: Driving Change with a People-First Approach." Accessed March 2, 2026. www.prosci.com/blog/ai-adoption.

PRS Legislative Research. n.d. "Committee Reports." Accessed March 2, 2026. https://prsindia.org/policy/report-summaries/free-and-fair-digital-economy.

Quaintance, Zack. 2024. "'AI Is Going to Cause the Next Digital Divide.'" GovTech, February 16. www.govtech.com/network/ai-is-going-to-cause-the-next-digital-divide.

RASA. n.d. "Welcome to the Rasa Docs | Rasa Documentation." Accessed March 2, 2026. https://rasa.com/docs/.

Raycraft, Richard. 2023. "Immigration Minister Says AI Isn't Making Final Immigration Decisions." *CBC News*, May 26, 2023. www.cbc.ca/news/politics/immigration-minister-new-tech-ai-1.6856479.

Resnik, Philip, and Noah A. Smith. 2003. "The Web as a Parallel Corpus." *Computational Linguistics* 29 (3): 349–380. https://doi.org/10.1162/089120103322711578.

Resolve Team. 2025. "8 Statistics Pointing to Increased Fraud Detection via Machine Learning." August. https://resolvepay.com/blog/statistics-pointing-increased-fraud-detection-via-machine-learning.

Retief, Johan. 2024. "Digital Authoritarianism a Growing Concern, Says State of Internet Freedom in Africa Report." The Press Council of South Africa, October 2024. https://presscouncil.org.za/2024/10/04/state-of-internet-freedom-in-africa-report-unveils-promises-and-challenges/.

Reuters. 2025a. "Britain Imposes New Travel Permit Requirement on Europeans." *Daily Maverick*, April 2. www.dailymaverick.co.za/article/2025-04-02-britain-imposes-new-travel-permit-requirement-on-europeans/.

Reuters. 2025b. "Collins Aerospace Working on Restoring Software for Airlines Hit by Cyberattack." Aerospace & Defense. *Reuters*, September 24, 2025. www.reuters.com/business/aerospace-defense/collins-aerospace-working-restoring-software-airlines-hit-by-cyber-attack-2025-09-24/.

Reuters. 2025c. *Gradual Rollout of Digital EU Border System Will Avoid UK Disruption, Says Eurotunnel.* September 23, 2025. www.reuters.com/world/uk/gradual-rollout-digital-eu-border-system-will-avoid-uk-disruption-says-2025-09-23/.

Rodríguez-Espíndola, Oscar, Hossein Ahmadi, Diego Gastélum-Chavira, Omar Ahumada-Valenzuela, Soumyadeb Chowdhury, Prasanta Kumar Dey, and Pavel Albores. 2023. "Humanitarian Logistics Optimization Models: An Investigation of Decision-Maker Involvement and Directions to Promote Implementation." *Socio-Economic Planning Sciences* 89 (October): 101669. https://doi.org/10.1016/j.seps.2023.101669.

Rosen Jacobson, Barbara, Katharina E. Höne, and Jovan Kurbalija. 2018. *Data Diplomacy: Updating Diplomacy to the Big Data Era.* Geneva: DiploFoundation. www.diplomacy.edu/wp-content/uploads/2019/07/Data_Diplomacy_Report_2018.pdf.

Royal Netherlands Marechaussee. 2025. "Privacy: Entry/Exit System (EES)." Royal Netherlands Marechaussee, July 14. https://english.marechaussee.nl/privacy/entry-exit-system.

Ryan, Mary A. 2001. "Statement of Mary A. Ryan Before the Judiciary Committee Subcommittee on Immigration Concerning Effective Immigration Controls to Deter Terrorism." October 17. https://avalon.law.yale.edu/sept11/ryan_001.asp.

Ryan, Mary A. 2003. "9/11 Terror Attacks: A Consular Officer's Perspective on Visas and Government Intelligence." Oral history interview. Association for Diplomatic Studies and Training (ADST). https://adst.org/2020/07/9-11-terror-attacks-a-consular-officers-perspective-on-visas-and-government-intelligence/.

Saffir, Leonard. 1993. *Power Public Relations: How to Get PR to Work for You.* New York: McGraw-Hill.

Saffir, Leonard, and John Tarrant. 2000. *Power Public Relations: How to Master the New PR.* 2nd ed. Lincolnwood, Ill: NTC Business Books.

Sánchez-Monedero, Javier, and Lina Dencik. 2019. *The Politics of Deceptive Borders: 'Biomarkers of Deceit' and the Case of iBorderCtrl.* https://arxiv.org/abs/1911.09156.

Sanders, Mark S., and Ernest J. McCormick. 1993. *Human Factors in Engineering and Design.* 7th ed. New York: McGraw-Hill.

Semester at Sea. 2020. "Spring 2020 Voyage Timeline Regarding COVID-19 Outbreak." www.semesteratsea.org/spring-2020-voyage-timeline-regarding-covid-19-outbreak/

Scheel, Stephan. 2019. *Autonomy of Migration? Appropriating Mobility within Biometric Border Regimes.* London: Routledge.

Shimohata, Mitsuo, Eiichiro Sumita, and Yuji Matsumoto. 2003. "Retrieving Meaning-Equivalent Sentences for Example-Based Rough Translation." *Proceedings of the HLT-NAACL 2003 Workshop on Building and Using Parallel Texts: Data Driven Machine Translation and Beyond*, 50–56. https://aclanthology.org/W03-0311/.

Siebold, Sabine, and Christoph Steitz. 2025. "European Airports Struggle to Fix Check-in Glitch after Cyberattack." Aerospace & Defense. *Reuters*, September 22, 2025. www.reuters.com/business/aerospace-defense/european-airports-race-fix-check-in-glitch-after-hacking-disruption-2025-09-21/.

Simon, Yara. n.d. "Why Is Pollo Campero Better in Central America? An Investigation." Accessed March 2, 2026. https://remezcla.com/lists/culture/pollo-campero-better-in-central-america/.

Sonali. 2024. "Delhi Airport Continues to Faces Disruption, Chaos: DigiYatra down, Long Queues Intact at IndiGo Counters after Microsoft Outage – BusinessToday." *Business Today*, July 20. www.businesstoday.in/industry/aviation/story/delhi-airport-continues-to-face-disruption-chaos-digiyatra-down-long-queues-intact-at-indigo-counters-after-microsoft-outage-437900-2024-07-20.

South African Government. 2020. "President Cyril Ramaphosa: Measures to Combat Coronavirus COVID-19 Epidemic." March 15, 2020. www.gov.za/news/speeches/president-cyril-ramaphosa-measures-combat-coronavirus-covid-19-epidemic-15-mar-2020

Stanzel, Volker, and Daniel Voelsen. 2022. *Diplomacy and Artificial Intelligence: Reflections on Practical Assistance for Diplomatic Negotiations*. Berlin: Stiftung Wissenschaft und Politik (SWP). www.swp-berlin.org/publications/products/research_papers/2022RP01_Diplomacy_and_AI.pdf.

Sumsub. n.d. "2024 Identity Theft & Fraud Statistics." Sumsub. Accessed March 2, 2026. https://sumsub.com/fraud-report-2024/.

Tang, Audrey. 2024. "Rebooting Democracy in the Age of AI." Northeastern University, April 5. https://news.northeastern.edu/2024/04/05/ai-democracy-governance/.

Tapia, Juan E., Daniel Shulz, and Christoph Busch. 2025. *Single-Morphing Attack Detection Using Few-Shot Learning.* www.sciencedirect.com/science/article/pii/S0925231225007052.

Tazzioli, Martina. 2019. *The Making of Migration: The Biopolitics of Mobility at Europe's Borders.* London: SAGE.

The Guardian. 2020. *Home Office to Scrap 'Racist Algorithm.'* August 4, 2020. www.theguardian.com/uk-news/2020/aug/04/home-office-to-scrap-racist-algorithm-for-uk-visa-applicants.

The Guardian. 2024. *Ukraine Unveils AI-Generated Foreign Ministry Spokesperson.* May 3, 2024. www.theguardian.com/technology/article/2024/may/03/ukraine-ai-foreign-ministry-spokesperson.

The Roanoke Times. 1993. "CIA Official's Error Let Muslim Cleric Enter U.S., State Department Finds." Accessed March 2, 2026. https://scholar.lib.vt.edu/VA-news/ROA-Times/issues/1993/rt9307/930713/07130100.htm.

The Royal United Services Institute for Defence and Security Studies. 2007. "The Threat Posed by the Trade in Stolen Passports." RUSI. November 26. www.rusi.org/publication/threat-posed-trade-stolen-passports.

The Times (London). 2025. *EES Launches on October 12 — Here's What It Means for Your Holiday.* September 26, 2025. www.thetimes.co.uk/article/ees-launches-on-october-12-heres-what-it-means-for-your-holiday-6r6mf9ql7.

The Verge. 2025. *UK Arrests Man in Airport Ransomware Attack That Caused Delays across Europe.* www.theverge.com/news/784786/uk-nca-europe-airportcyberattack-ransomware-arrest.

The White House. 2024. "Driving Digital Transformation Across Government for Lasting Impact | OMB." The White House, December 12. https://bidenwhitehouse.archives.gov/omb/briefing-room/2024/12/12/driving-digital-transformation-across-government-for-lasting-impact/.

The White House. 2025. "White House Unveils America's AI Action Plan." July 23, 2025. Accessed April 11, 2026. www.whitehouse.gov/releases/2025/07/white-house-unveils-americas-ai-action-plan/.

The World Bank. n.d. "Improving Public Sector Performance: Through Innovation and Inter-Agency Coordination." Text/HTML. World Bank. Accessed March 2, 2026. www.worldbank.org/en/topic/governance/publication/global-report-on-public-sector-performance.

Times of India Tech Desk. n.d. "How VFS Global Will Use AI to Improve Visa Processing – Times of India." Accessed March 2, 2026. https://timesofindia.indiatimes.com/technology/tech-news/how-vfs-global-will-use-ai-to-improve-visa-processing/articleshow/109701144.cms.

U.K. Department for Science, Innovation and Technology. 2023. *Introducing the AI Safety Institute (Overview).* https://assets.publishing.service.gov.uk/media/65438d159e05fd0014be7bd9/introducing-ai-safety-institute-web-accessible.pdf.

U.K. Government. n.d.-a. "Biometric Enrolment: Policy Guidance (Accessible)." GOV.UK. Accessed March 2, 2026. www.gov.uk/government/publications/biometric-information/biometric-information-enrolment-accessible.

U.K. Government. n.d.-b. "Consular and Crisis Strategy 2022." GOV.UK. Accessed March 2, 2026. www.gov.uk/government/publications/consular-and-crisis-strategy-2022/consular-and-crisis-strategy-2022.

U.K. Government. n.d.-a. "Content Design: Planning, Writing and Managing Content." GOV.UK. Accessed March 2, 2026. www.gov.uk/guidance/content-design.

U.K. Government. n.d.-b. *Review into Bias in Algorithmic Decision-Making*. Centre for Data Ethics and Innovation. https://assets.publishing.service.gov.uk/media/60142096d3bf7f70ba377b20/Review_into_bias_in_algorithmic_decision-making.pdf.

U.K. Government. n.d.-c. "Guidelines for AI Procurement (Print Version).Pdf." Accessed March 2, 2026. https://assets.publishing.service.gov.uk/media/60b356228fa8f5489723d170/Guidelines_for_AI_procurement.pdf.

U.K. Government. 2020. *DNA Policy Guidance*. Home Office. https://assets.publishing.service.gov.uk/government/uploads/system/uploads/attachment_data/file/873640/dna-v4.0ext1.pdf.

U.K. Government. 2024. *Accounting Officer Assessment: Home Office Biometrics (HOB) Programme*. London: Home Office, December 6, 2024. www.gov.uk/government/publications/home-office-major-programmes-accounting-officer-assessments/6-december-2024-accounting-officer-assessment-home-office-biometrics-hob-programme.

U.K. Government. 2025a. "Biometric Information: Caseworker Guidance." GOV.UK, October 2. www.gov.uk/government/publications/biometric-information.

U.K. Government. 2025b. "Electronic Travel Authorisation: Caseworker Guidance (Accessible)." https://assets.publishing.service.gov.uk/media/67c5928b68a61757838d21a2/Electronic%2BTravel%2BAuthorisation%2BGuidance.pdf.

Ulloa-Pérez, Ernesto, Paula R. Blasi, Emily O. Westbrook, Paula Lozano, Katie F. Coleman, and R. Yates Coley. 2022. "Pragmatic Randomized Study of Targeted Text Message Reminders to Reduce Missed Clinic Visits." *The Permanente Journal* 26 (1): 64–72. https://doi.org/10.7812/TPP/21.078.

UN Global Pulse / UNHCR. 2018. *Project Jetson: Using AI to Model Displacement in Somalia*. www.unglobalpulse.org/project/using-artificial-intelligence-to-model-displacement-in-somalia/.

UNESCO. n.d. "Bridging the Digital Divides | UNESCO." Accessed March 2, 2026. www.unesco.org/en/articles/bridging-digital-divides.

UNHCR. 2018. *Strategy on Digital Identity and Inclusion*. Geneva. www.unhcr.org/blogs/wp-content/uploads/sites/48/2018/03/2018-02-Digital-Identity_02.pdf.

UNHCR. 2022. *Biometrics for Refugees and Asylum-Seekers*. https://help.unhcr.org/jordan/wp-content/uploads/sites/46/2022/04/Biometrics-EN_Final_April2022.pdf.

United Nations. n.d. "Security Council Debates Use of Artificial Intelligence in Conflicts, Hears Calls for UN Framework to Avoid Fragmented Governance | UN Meetings Coverage and Press Releases." Accessed March 2, 2026. https://press.un.org/en/2024/sc15946.doc.htm.

U.S. Citizenship and Immigration Services. 2018. *DNA Evidence of Sibling Relationships*. PM-602-0161. U.S. Citizenship and Immigration Services. www.uscis.gov/sites/default/files/document/memos/2018-04-17-PM-DNA-Evidence-of-Sibling-Relationships.pdf.

U.S. Code of Federal Regulations. 2024. "22 CFR § 71.10 — Loans to Destitute Nationals." *Code of Federal Regulations*, Title 22 (Foreign Relations), Part 71 (Issuance of Passports). www.ecfr.gov/current/title-22/chapter-I/subchapter-F/part-71/section-71.10

U.S. Commission on Civil Rights. 2024. "U.S. Commission on Civil Rights Releases Report: The Civil Rights Implications of the Federal Use of Facial Recognition Technology." (Press release), September 19, 2024. www.usccr.gov/news/2024/us-commission-civil-rights-releases-report-civil-rights-implications-federal-use-facial.

U.S. Congress. Senate Select Committee on Intelligence. 2023. "Open Hearing: Advancing Intelligence in the Era of Artificial Intelligence: Addressing the National Security Implications of AI." S.Hrg. 118-118. September 19, 2023. Accessed April 11, 2026. www.congress.gov/event/118th-congress/senate-event/LC72459/text.

U.S. Customs and Border Protection. 2025. "Collection of Biometric Data from Aliens upon Entry to and Departure from the United States." Final rule with request for comments. Federal Register No. 2025-19655, October 27, 2025. www.regulations.gov/document/USCBP-2025-0033-0001.

U.S. Customs and Border Protection. 2025a. "Biometrics: Environments." U.S. Customs and Border Protection. www.cbp.gov/travel/biometrics/environments.

U.S. Customs and Border Protection. 2025b. "Biometrics: Privacy Policy." U.S. Customs and Border Protection. www.cbp.gov/travel/biometrics/privacy-policy.

U.S. Customs and Border Protection (CBP). 2022. *Statement for the Record on Assessing CBP's Use of Facial Recognition Technology*. www.cbp.gov/about/congressional-resources/testimony/statement-record-assessing-cbps-use-facial-recognition-technology.

U.S. Customs and Border Protection (CBP). 2025a. "Biometrics — Enhanced Passenger Processing." www.cbp.gov/travel/biometrics/enhanced-passenger-processing.

U.S. Customs and Border Protection (CBP). 2025b. "Biometrics — Land Border Ports of Entry." www.cbp.gov/travel/biometrics/environments/land-border-ports-of-entry.

U.S. Customs and Border Protection (CBP). 2025c. "Simplified Arrival Expansion." www.cbp.gov/newsroom/national-media-release/cbp-completes-simplified-arrival-expansion-all-us-airports.

U.S. Department of Homeland Security. n.d.-a. "DHS Enterprise – AI Use Cases | Homeland Security." Accessed March 2, 2026. www.dhs.gov/ai/use-case-inventory/dhs-enterprise.

U.S. Department of Homeland Security. n.d.-b. "FACT SHEET: DHS Deploys Pilot Programs, Expands Efforts to Leverage AI to Secure Nation's Critical Infrastructure | Homeland Security." Accessed March 2, 2026. www.dhs.gov/archive/news/2024/07/26/fact-sheet-dhs-deploys-pilot-programs-expands-efforts-leverage-ai-secure-nations.

U.S. Department of Homeland Security. n.d.-c. "Office of Biometric Identity Management | Homeland Security." Accessed March 2, 2026. www.dhs.gov/obim.

U.S. Department of Homeland Security. n.d.-d. "The 9/11 Terrorist Attack and Overseas Travel to the United States: Initial Impacts and Longer-Run Recovery." www.Dhs.Gov. Accessed March 2, 2026. www.dhs.gov/xlibrary/assets/statistics/publications/ois_ni_911_wp.pdf.

U.S. Department of Homeland Security. n.d.-e. "United States Citizenship and Immigration Services – AI Use Cases | Homeland Security." Accessed March 2, 2026. www.dhs.gov/ai/use-case-inventory/uscis.

U.S. Department of Homeland Security. 2024. "Traveler Entity Resolution, Use Case ID: DHS-80." DHS Simplified AI Use Case Inventory, U.S. Customs and Border Protection.. www.dhs.gov/ai/use-case-inventory/cbp.

U.S. Department of Homeland Security. 2025. "Collection of Biometric Data from Aliens upon Entry to and Departure from the United States." Federal Register 90, no. 207 (October 27). www.federalregister.gov/documents/2025/10/27/2025-19655/collection-ofbiometric-data-from-aliens-upon-entry-to-and-departure-from-the-united-states.

U.S. Department of Homeland Security (DHS). 2025. *2024 Update on DHS's Use of Face Recognition & Face Capture Technologies*. www.dhs.gov/archive/news/2025/01/16/2024-update-dhss-use-face-recognition-face-capture-technologies.

U.S. Department of Homeland Security (DHS) and Customs and Border Protection (CBP). 2023. *Privacy Impact Assessment—Advance Collection for Undocumented Individuals*. Washington, DC. www.dhs.gov/sites/default/files/2023-01/privacy-pia-cbp076-advance-collection-for-undocumented-individuals-jan2023_0.pdf.

U.S. Department of Homeland Security (DHS), Office of Biometric Identity Management. 2024. *Privacy Impact Assessment Update for the Homeland Advanced Recognition*

Technology System (HART) (DHS/OBIM/PIA-004[a]). www.dhs.gov/sites/default/files/2024-08/24_0826_priv_pia-obim-004a-HART-update.pdf.

U.S. Department of Homeland Security (DHS), Office of Biometric Identity Management (OBIM). 2020. *Privacy Impact Assessment for the Homeland Advanced Recognition Technology System (HART) — Increment 1. DHS/OBIM/PIA-004.* www.dhs.gov/sites/default/files/publications/privacy-pia-obim004-hartincrement1-february2020_0.pdf.

U.S. Department of Homeland Security (DHS), Office of Biometric Identity Management (OBIM). 2024. *Homeland Advanced Recognition Technology (HART) — Update.* www.dhs.gov/publication/dhsobimpia-004-homeland-advanced-recognition-technology-system-hart-increment-1.

U.S. Department of Homeland Security (DHS) and Transportation Security Administration (TSA). 2022. *PIA-046: Travel Document Checker Automation Using Facial Recognition.* www.dhs.gov/publication/dhstsapia-046-travel-document-checker-automation-using-facial-recognition.

U.S. Department of Homeland Security (DHS) and UNHCR. 2019. *PIA — UNHCR Data Sharing (PIA-081).* www.dhs.gov/sites/default/files/publications/privacy-pia-uscis081-unhcr-august2019.pdf.

U.S. Department of Justice. n.d. "Office of Public Affairs | Former U.S. Consulate Official Sentenced to 64 Months in Prison for Receiving Over $3 Million in Bribes in Exchange for Visas." Accessed March 2, 2026. www.justice.gov/archives/opa/pr/former-us-consulate-official-sentenced-64-months-prison-receiving-over-3-million-bribes.

U.S. Department of State. n.d.-a. "8 FAM 402.1 Passport Photographs." Accessed March 2, 2026. https://fam.state.gov/fam/08fam/08fam040201.html.

U.S. Department of State. n.d.-b. "9 FAM 601.11." Accessed March 2, 2026. https://fam.state.gov/fam/09fam/09fam060111.html.

U.S. Department of State. n.d.-c. "Department of State 2025 AI Inventory – United States Department of State." Accessed March 2, 2026. www.state.gov/department-of-state-2025-ai-inventory.

U.S. Department of State. n.d.-d. "Department of State Washington File: Transcript: Albright Speech at AAAS Meeting." Accessed March 2, 2026. https://usinfo.org/wf-archive/2000/000222/epf206.htm.

U.S. Department of State. n.d.-e. "Department-Privacy-Program-Plan-2023." Accessed March 2, 2026. https://2021-2025.state.gov/wp-content/uploads/2023/11/Department-Privacy-Program-Plan-2023.pdf.

U.S. Department of State. n.d.-f. "DS-7675." Accessed March 2, 2026. https://eforms.state.gov/Forms/ds7675.PDF.

U.S. Department of State. n.d.-g. "Emergency Financial Assistance | Travel.State.Gov." Accessed March 2, 2026. https://travel.state.gov/en/international-travel/help-abroad/financial.html.

U.S. Department of State. n.d.-h. "E-Visas – Treaty Trader (E1) and Treaty Investor (E2) Visas – U.S. Embassy in Paraguay." Accessed March 2, 2026. https://py.usembassy.gov/e-visas-treaty-trader-e1-and-treaty-investor-e2-visas/.

U.S. Department of State. n.d.-i. "Form Finder." Accessed March 2, 2026. https://eforms.state.gov/.

U.S. Department of State. n.d.-j. "Functional Bureau Strategy – Bureau of Consular Affairs." Accessed March 2, 2026. www.state.gov/wp-content/uploads/2023/12/FBS_CA_03NOV2023_PUBLIC.pdf.

U.S. Department of State. n.d.-k. "Inspection of Embassy Bogota, Colombia | Office of Inspector General." Accessed March 2, 2026. www.stateoig.gov/report/isp-i-19-14.

U.S. Department of State. n.d.-l. "Inspection of the Bureau of Consular Affairs' Office of Fraud Prevention Programs." Accessed March 2, 2026. www.stateoig.gov/uploads/report/report_pdf_file/isp-i-18-42_1.pdf.

U.S. Department of State. n.d.-m. "Inspection of the Bureau of Consular Affairs, Office of 1CA: Leadership, Management, and Innovation | Office of Inspector General." Accessed March 2, 2026. www.stateoig.gov/report/isp-i-21-28.

U.S. Department of State. n.d.-n. "Online-Passport-Renewal-OPR-PIA." Accessed March 2, 2026. https://2021-2025.state.gov/wp-content/uploads/2021/04/Online-Passport-Renewal-OPR-PIA.pdf.

U.S. Department of State. n.d.-o. "Passport-Records-Imaging-System-Management-PRISM-PIA." Accessed March 2, 2026. www.state.gov/wp-content/uploads/2020/12/Passport-Records-Imaging-System-Management-PRISM-PIA.pdf.

U.S. Department of State. n.d.-p. "Report of Inspection – Embassy San Salvador." Accessed March 2, 2026. www.stateoig.gov/uploads/report/report_pdf_file/isp-i-06-31a_1.pdf.

U.S. Department of State. n.d.-q. "Security Clearance FAQs – United States Department of State." Accessed March 2, 2026. www.state.gov/security-clearance-faqs/.

U.S. Department of State. n.d.-r. "STEP." Accessed March 2, 2026. https://mytravel.state.gov/s/step.

U.S. Department of State. 2013. "Review of the Process for Establishing Language Designated Positions." www.State.Gov, April. www.stateoig.gov/uploads/report/report_pdf_file/isp-i-13-24_1.pdf.

U.S. Department of State. 2015. *Privacy Impact Assessment: Passport Records Imaging System Management (PRISM)*. www.state.gov/wp-content/uploads/2020/12/Passport-Records-Imaging-System-Management-PRISM-PIA.pdf.

U.S. Department of State. 2020a. "Department of State Coronavirus Repatriation Statistics." https://2017-2021.state.gov/coronavirus/repatriation/

U.S. Department of State. 2021a. *Enterprise Data Strategy 2021: Empowering Data Informed Policy*. Washington, DC. www.state.gov/wp-content/uploads/2021/09/Reference-EDS-Accessible.pdf.

U.S. Department of State. 2021b. *Review of the Bureau of Consular Affairs' ConsularOne Modernization Program — Significant Deployment Delays Continue*. ISP-I-22-03. Washington, DC: Office of Inspector General. https://www.stateoig.gov/uploads/report/report_pdf_file/isp-i-22-03_7.pdf.

U.S. Department of State. 2022. "Artificial Intelligence." June 16. www.state.gov/artificial-intelligence/.

U.S. Department of State. 2023. *Enterprise Artificial Intelligence Strategy FY 2024–2025: Empowering Diplomacy through Responsible AI*. Washington, DC. www.state.gov/wp-content/uploads/2023/11/Department-of-State-Enterprise-Artificial-Intelligence-Strategy.pdf.

U.S. Department of State. 2024a. "AI in Action: Risk Management and Innovation Help Shape the Future of Diplomacy." *State Magazine*, December 2024. https://statemag.state.gov/2024/12/1224feat03/.

U.S. Department of State. 2024b. *Department of State AI Inventory 2024*. https://2021-2025.state.gov/department-of-state-ai-inventory-2024/.

U.S. Department of State. 2024c. "Uploading a Digital Photo." https://travel.state.gov/content/travel/en/passports/how-apply/online-renewal-photo.html.

U.S. Department of State. 2025a. "Applying as a Person with a Disability." Travel.State.Gov. https://travel.state.gov/content/travel/en/passports/how-apply/disability.html.

U.S. Department of State. 2025b. "Renew My Passport Online." Travel.State.Gov. https://travel.state.gov/content/travel/en/passports/have-passport/renew-online.html.

U.S. Department of State. 2025c. "Renew or Replace a Passport." U.S. Department of State. https://travel.state.gov/content/travel/en/passports/have-passport.html.

U.S. Department of State. 2025d. "U.S. Passport Photos." U.S. Department of State. https://travel.state.gov/content/travel/en/passports/how-apply/photos.html.

U.S. Department of State, Bureau of Consular Affairs. 2023b. *Consular Consolidated Database (CCD) — Privacy Impact Assessment*. www.state.gov/wp-content/uploads/2023/05/Consular-Consolidated-Database-CCD-PIA.pdf.

U.S. Department of State, Bureau of Consular Affairs. 2024. *Report of the Visa Office 2023*. Washington, DC. https://travel.state.gov/content/travel/en/legal/visa-law0/visa-statistics/annual-reports/report-of-the-visa-office-2023.html.

U.S. Department of State, Office of Inspector General. 2019. *Inspection of Embassy Bogota, Colombia*. ISP-I-19-14. April 2019. www.stateoig.gov/report/isp-i-19-14.

U.S. Embassy Pretoria. 2020. "Health Alert: Update on Ethiopian Airlines and Qatar Airways Repatriation Flights." May 18, 2020. https://za.usembassy.gov/health%E2%80%AFalert%E2%80%AFupdate-on-ethiopian-airlines-and-qatar-airways-repatriation-flights-u-s-embassy-pretoria-south-africa

U.S. General Services Administration. 2025a. "Artificial Intelligence Delivers Real Results through GSA." *GSA Blog*, January 10, 2025. www.gsa.gov/blog/2025/01/10/artificial-intelligence-delivers-real-results-through-gsa.

U.S. General Services Administration. 2025b. "Plain Language Guide Series." Digital.gov, September 2025. https://digital.gov/guides/plain-language.

U.S. Government. n.d. "Cultural, Social, and Legal Considerations – Biometric Recognition – NCBI Bookshelf." Accessed March 2, 2026. www.ncbi.nlm.nih.gov/books/NBK219893/.

U.S. Government. 2025. "Artificial Intelligence – Digital.Gov." March 26. https://digital.gov/topics/artificial-intelligence.

U.S. Government Accountability Office (GAO). n.d. "GAO-07-1154T State Department: Staffing and Foreign Language Shortfalls Persist Despite Initiatives to Address Gaps." Accessed March 2, 2026. www.gao.gov/assets/gao-07-1154t.pdf.

U.S. Government Accountability Office (GAO). 2007. *Border Security: Fraud Risks Complicate State's Ability to Manage Diversity Visa Program*. GAO-07-1174. https://www.gao.gov/products/gao-07-1174.

U.S. Government Accountability Office (GAO). 2008. *Visa Waiver Program: Actions Are Needed to Improve Management of the Expansion Process, and to Assess and Mitigate Program Risks*. GAO-08-967. www.gao.gov/assets/a280868.html.

U.S. Government Accountability Office (GAO). 2022. *Consular Affairs: Revenue Trends and Management of Consular Fees (GAO-22-104424)*. www.gao.gov/assets/gao-22-104424.pdf.

U.S. Government Accountability Office (GAO). 2023. *Biometric Identity System: DHS Needs to Address Shortcomings in Its Cost Estimate for HART (GAO-23-105959)*. www.gao.gov/products/gao-23-105959.

U.S. Government Accountability Office (GAO). 2025. *State Department Should Identify Milestones and Resource Needs to Improve Passport Processing Times (GAO-25-107164)*. https://files.gao.gov/reports/GAO-25-107164/index.html.

U.S. National Commission on Terrorist Attacks. 2004. *Staff Statement No. 1: Entry of the 9/11 Hijackers into the United States*. January 26. https://govinfo.library.unt.edu/911/staff_statements/staff_statement_1.pdf.

U.S. National Institute of Standards and Technology. 2025. "NIST Guidelines Can Help Organizations Detect Face Photo Morphs, Deter Identity Fraud." NIST, August 18, 2025. www.nist.gov/news-events/news/2025/08/nist-guidelines-can-help-organizations-detect-face-photo-morphs-deter.

U.S. Office of Personnel Management. n.d. "General Schedule." U.S. Office of Personnel Management. Accessed March 2, 2026. www.opm.gov/policy-data-oversight/pay-leave/pay-systems/general-schedule/.

USDA Food and Nutrition Service. 2023. *Analysis of Robotic Process Automation in Supplemental Nutrition Programs*. Washington, DC. https://fns-prod.azureedge.us/sites/default/files/resource-files/snap-bots-rpa-final-report.pdf.

Valdivia, Ana, Júlia Corbera-Serrajòrdia, and Aneta Swianiewicz. 2021. *There Is an Elephant in the Room: Towards a Critique on the Use of Fairness in Biometrics*. https://arxiv.org/abs/2112.11193.

Van Buren, Edward, William D. Eggers, Tasha Austin, Joe Mariani, and Pankaj Kishnani. 2021. *Scaling AI in Government*. Deloitte Insights. www2.deloitte.com/us/en/insights/industry/public-sector/government-ai-survey.html.

Veerubhotla, B. 2025. "(PDF) Spatial Data Integration for Disaster/Emergency Management: An Indian Experience." *ResearchGate*, ahead of print, August 10, 2025. https://doi.org/10.1007/s41324-017-0087-5.

Ventura, Tiago. 2025. "Amnesty: AI Surveillance Risks 'Supercharging' US Deportations." *ComputerWeekly.com*, September 15, 2025. www.computerweekly.com/news/366631297/Amnesty-AI-surveillance-risks-supercharging-US-deportations.

VFS Global. n.d. "VFS Global | Insight." Accessed March 2, 2026. www.vfsglobal.com/en/individuals/insights/pioneering-ethical-ai-in-visa-and-consular-services-the-vfs-global-story.html.

VFS Global. 2023. *ViVA—AI Voice/Chat Assistance for Visa Services*. www.vfsglobal.com/en/individuals/insights/how-ai-voice-technology-can-revolutionise-travel.html.

VFS Global. 2025. *VFS Global Launches AI-Powered Chatbot for UK Visa Customers in 141 Countries*. www.vfsglobal.com/en/PDF/media-releases/2025/FinalMR_190225_UKVI-Chatbot-Press-Release-(UK-Approved).pdf.

Vota, Wayan. 2024. "How State Department Uses AI Strategically in Modern Diplomacy." *ICTworks*, August 23, 2024. www.ictworks.org/state-department-uses-ai-strategically/.

Wait, Liana. 2025. "Hany Farid to Receive McGuire Prize for Societal Impact." *Dartmouth News*, November 24, 2025. https://home.dartmouth.edu/news/2025/11/hany-farid-receive-mcguire-prize-societal-impact.

Warrell, Helen. n.d. "Home Office Drops 'Biased' Visa Algorithm." *The Financial Times*. Accessed March 2, 2026. www.ft.com/content/a02c6c42-95b1-419c-a798-0418011d2018.

Watson, Craig I., Gregory P. Fiumara, Elham Tabassi, Wayne J. Salamon, and Patricia A. Flanagan. 2014. *Fingerprint Vendor Technology Evaluation*. NIST IR 8034. Gaithersburg, MD: National Institute of Standards and Technology. https://doi.org/10.6028/NIST.IR.8034.

Watts, Tim. n.d. "Supporting Australians in Crisis Overseas." Government of Australia. Accessed March 2, 2026. https://ministers.dfat.gov.au/minister/tim-watts/speech/supporting-australians-crisis-overseas.

Wilson, Jamie, and Nick Hopkins. 2001. "Warning That Flight Chaos May Continue for Weeks." UK News. *The Guardian*, September 14, 2001. www.theguardian.com/uk/2001/sep/14/september11.usa2.

World Bank. n.d. "Open Knowledge Repository." Accessed March 2, 2026. https://openknowledge.worldbank.org/entities/publication/7617f89d-2276-413d-b0a7-e31e7527d6af.

World Bank. 2018. "Improving Public Sector Performance: Through Innovation and Inter-Agency Coordination." Washington, DC: World Bank. www.worldbank.org/en/topic/governance/publication/global-report-on-public-sector-performance.

World Bank. 2019. *ID4D Practitioner's Guide: Version 1.0.* Washington, DC: World Bank. https://documents1.worldbank.org/curated/en/248371559325561562/pdf/ID4D-Practitioner-s-Guide.pdf.

World Bank Group. 2023. *Putting People at the Center of Digital Public Infrastructure (DPI): Annual Report 2023.* Washington, DC: World Bank.

World Wide Web Consortium (W3C). 2025a. *Verifiable Credentials Data Model 2.0.* www.w3.org/TR/vc-data-model-2.0/.

World Wide Web Consortium (W3C). 2025b. *Web Authentication: An API for Accessing Public Key Credentials (Level 3).* www.w3.org/TR/webauthn-3/.

Wycliffe Global Alliance. n.d. *Global Scripture Access.* Accessed October 13, 2025. https://wycliffe.net/global-scripture-access/.

Yale Law School. n.d. "The Avalon Project: Statement of Mary A. Ryan Before the Judiciary Committee Subcommittee on Immigration Concerning Effective Immigration Controls to Deter Terrorism; October 17, 2001." Yale Law School. Accessed March 2, 2026. https://avalon.law.yale.edu/sept11/ryan_001.asp.

Yang, Yiran, Frederik Zuiderveen Borgesius, Pascal Beckers, and Evelien Brouwer. 2024. *Automated Decision-Making and Artificial Intelligence at European Borders and Their Risks for Human Rights.* https://arxiv.org/abs/2410.17278.

Young, Shalanda D. n.d. *M-24-10 Memorandum for The Heads of Executive Departments and Agencies.* www.whitehouse.gov/wp-content/uploads/2024/03/M-24-10-Advancing-Governance-Innovation-and-Risk-Management-for-Agency-Use-of-Artificial-Intelligence.pdf.

Zeleny, Jeff, and Brian Knowlton. 2008. "Passport Files of 3 Candidates Were Breached." *The New York Times*, March 22. www.nytimes.com/2008/03/22/us/politics/22passport.html.

Zeng, Li, Peisong Shen, Xiaojie Zhu, Xue Tian, and Chi Chen. 2025. "A Review of Privacy-Preserving Biometric Identification and Authentication Protocols." *Computers & Security* 150 (March): 104309. https://doi.org/10.1016/j.cose.2024.104309.

Zhou, Yuan, Amith Viswanatha, Ammar Abdul Motaleb, Prabin Lamichhane, Kay Yut Chen, Richard Young, Ayse P. Gurses, and Yan Xiao. 2023. "A Predictive Decision Analytics Approach for Primary Care Operations Management: A Case Study of Double-Booking Strategy Design and Evaluation." *Computers & Industrial Engineering* 177: 109069. www.sciencedirect.com/science/article/abs/pii/S0360835223000931.

Authors' Note on Independence and Compliance

This book, *AI Use Cases for Consular Affairs: Smarter Passports, Visas, and Border Security*, was authored in a personal capacity and is not affiliated with, nor does it represent the views of, the U.S. Department of State or the U.S. government. The content was prepared in full compliance with all relevant legal, ethical, and regulatory requirements for current and former federal employees. In accordance with 11 FAM 614.5 and 5 C.F.R. § 2635, the authors are permitted to receive compensation for this work as it does not relate to official duties past or present or in substantial part. The authors did not receive any government funding, grants, or contractual support for this book. Any financial proceeds from its publication are entirely personal and unrelated to any government employment, duties, or obligations.

As former U.S. government officials, the authors draw upon their professional experience to provide context and analysis. That experience informs the perspectives presented in this work; however, the book does not describe internal government systems, operational procedures, or nonpublic government practices. Discussions of workflows, decision environments, and administrative processes are presented at a conceptual and analytical level for educational purposes and should not be interpreted as descriptions of specific internal systems or operational procedures. Illustrative anecdotes and field observations derived from professional experience are presented as anonymized, representative composites rather than accounts of specific identifiable individuals, posts, cases, or internal deliberations. Any discussion of technological capabilities, security processes, or decision support tools does not disclose operational techniques, system configurations, vulnerabilities, safeguards, or implementation details used by any government or private organization, and does not negate any firsthand professional experience the authors may have acquired through public service roles.

The authors' prior roles in consular affairs inform the analytical framework of this book; however, none of the AI applications, use cases, or technological initiatives discussed were matters in which the authors had exclusive or nonpublic involvement during their government service. The analysis also reflects the authors' professional experience, including firsthand exposure, field testing, operational support, implementation perspectives, and policy or leadership responsibilities relevant to government technology modernization, while avoiding reliance on privileged, confidential, proprietary, or classified information. The book is based on general AI principles, publicly available information, and forward-looking analyses, with no direct reference to current or anticipated government programs or operations beyond what the department has already shared publicly. AI is a rapidly evolving field, and its applications in diplomacy are subject to ongoing technological, ethical, and policy developments. The content of this book reflects the state of knowledge and public discourse at the time of writing and may not fully align with future advancements, regulations, or interpretations.

The authors have taken all necessary steps to ensure there is no conflict of interest in the publication of this book, consistent with applicable post-employment restrictions governing former federal officials, including 18 U.S.C. § 207. No nonpublic, classified, or privileged information obtained through the authors' prior government service has been used in this manuscript. The book is based on publicly available information, academic research, generally accepted industry standards, and professional knowledge lawfully acquired through the authors' government service and related experience. The authors have taken all reasonable steps to ensure that no copyrighted material has been used without appropriate permissions or attributions, and that all references, quotations, and ideas are properly cited to respect intellectual property rights and avoid inadvertent plagiarism. Care has been taken to ensure that the synthesis or aggregation of publicly available information does not reconstruct, infer, or reveal internal government systems, classified insights, or nonpublic operational frameworks.

This book, authored by former U.S. government employees, is intended for informational and academic purposes only. Readers from other jurisdictions should be aware that legal, ethical, and diplomatic considerations regarding AI may vary by country and are subject to different regulatory and policy frameworks. The authors' prior affiliation with the U.S. Department of State is noted solely for biographical purposes and in compliance with 5 C.F.R. §§ 2635.702-705. The mention of the authors' prior titles as U.S. diplomats or U.S. foreign service officers does not imply any official endorsement of their views or content expressed in this book.

The fictional vignettes and composite scenarios in this book are designed to illustrate real operational dynamics and are not intended to represent or identify any specific post, individual, or government program. Illustrative anecdotes, field observations, case studies, and scenarios discussed in this book are either historically documented in publicly available sources, hypothetical, or drawn from the authors' combined professional experience and presented as anonymized composites for educational purposes.

No individual, post, case, applicant, employee, agency, or event is identified or identifiable. Unnecessary identifying details—including names, locations, dates, titles, unusual circumstances, or distinctive combinations of facts—have been removed, generalized, or altered where appropriate to preserve anonymity while retaining analytical and storytelling value. Any resemblance between these illustrative examples and actual persons, posts, policies, or events—past or present—is coincidental and unintentional. The analyses are representative, forward-looking, and intended to illuminate broader operational, technological, leadership, or policy themes rather than describe specific government matters.

While the authors have made every effort to ensure the accuracy of the content, no responsibility is assumed for how the information may be interpreted or applied. The authors and publisher disclaim any liability for damages, direct or indirect, resulting from the use or application of this book's content. Readers assume full responsibility for any actions taken based on the information provided, and they are encouraged to consult subject matter experts before making decisions influenced by the material herein.

The overall AI use cases in diplomacy project was submitted for prepublication review by the Bureau of Global Public Affairs (GPA) and approved on October 1, 2024, in accordance with 11 FAM 614.5 and the prepublication review requirements outlined in 11 FAM 600. The authors have adhered to all applicable guidelines, including those outlined in 5 C.F.R. § 2635, and have taken care to avoid any misuse of prior official position or appearance of endorsement consistent with 5 C.F.R. §§ 2635.702–705. This work was completed using personal time and resources, without any use of government facilities or resources.

Descriptions of potential applications of AI or digital systems in government contexts are analytical and exploratory in nature and should not be interpreted as operational guidance, legal advice, procurement specifications, security recommendations, or government policy directives. Readers should not rely on this work as a substitute for official government guidance, operational manuals, legal counsel, or regulatory directives.

Index

D

G

H

T

U

V

For Product Safety Concerns and Information please contact our EU representative GPSR@taylorandfrancis.com
Taylor & Francis Verlag GmbH, Kaufingerstraße 24, 80331 München, Germany

www.ingramcontent.com/pod-product-compliance
Lightning Source LLC
LaVergne TN
LVHW021353100926
847619LV00019B/166
9781041063018